Island at the End of the World

Island at the End of the World

The Turbulent History of Easter Island

STEVEN ROGER FISCHER

REAKTION BOOKS

Dedicated to all the people of Easter Island

Published by Reaktion Books Ltd
79 Farringdon Road
London EC1M 3JU, UK

www.reaktionbooks.co.uk

First published 2005
Copyright © Steven Roger Fischer 2005

Printed and bound in Great Britain
by Cromwell Press, Trowbridge, Wiltshire

British Library Cataloguing in Publication Data
Fischer, Steven R.
    Island at the end of the world: the turbulent history of Easter Island
    1. Easter island – History
    I. Title
    996.1'8
    ISBN 1 86189 245 4

Contents

Introduction   7

one
The Polynesian Frontier   13

two
White Men and Birdmen   45

three
Pirates and Priests   86

four
Rancho Isla de Pascua   135

five
Museum Island   199

References   265
Bibliography   285
Acknowledgements   293
Photographic Acknowledgements   294
Index   295

Introduction

The South Pacific's loneliest terminus was Earth's infant. Erupting from the sea only half a million years ago, soon it was courting a volcanic neighbour that had appeared some 20 kilometres to the south-west.[1] Whereupon, less than 400,000 years ago, the young island pair witnessed the birth of a third land mass to the north, but this, however, soon outgrew both volcanic antecedents. Around 130,000 years ago, this colossus then afforded one last, spectacular performance – which no human eye yet beheld.[2]

The three volcanoes – later to be called Pōike, Rano Kau and Terevaka – had by then formed a nearly 170-square-kilometre triangle of sides measuring 16, 18 and 22 kilometres.[3] But this was only the small tip of an Olympus that rose almost 3,000 metres from the ocean floor. The perfect island that the trio now comprised – at latitude 27°s and longitude 109°w – topped the western fringe of what would be known as the 'Easter Seamount Chain'. One of the island's closest neighbours – Pitcairn of *The Bounty* fame – lay 2,112 kilometres to the north-west. The Galápagos were 3,474 kilometres to the north-east. And 3,680 kilometres to the east was South America.

Fifteen *motu* or islets huddled up to 1.5 kilometres offshore, in random distribution. There was never a fringing coral reef here: the island's young geologic age, rate of erosion, southerly latitude, water temperature and climate had prevented the formation of one.[4] Always a unique isolate in the Pacific, the island occupied a subtropical environmental zone with marked seasons. Capricious events included drought.

Over æons, the sea, the wind and even bird transport introduced a number of floral species: trees, grasses, sedges (grasslike plants), reeds, shrubs and others, mainly from South-East Asia via western Polynesia.[5] (Only a small contribution came from South America.) The small tree *Sophora toromiro* grew abundantly. Shrubs like *Cæsalpinia bonduc* and *Lycium carolinianum* similarly flourished. Already 30,000 years ago the *nga'ahu* reed (the *totora* or *Scirpus riparius*) was dominating the fresh-water swamps of each of the three volcanoes. By then, the island had become heavily forested. It would remain so, even during the Last Glacial Maximum, when a drier climate heralded an increase of grasses.[6] Eventually dominating the island's flora was a species of palm closely related to the Chilean wine palm, the *Jubæa chilensis*, at up to 20 metres in height one of the world's largest palm trees.[7] (The island's *Jubæa sp.* may, in fact, have been the same species.) Perhaps as many as 16 million of these palms, with a common height of 10 metres and diameter of at least 0.5 metres, luxuriated the island. The magnificent palm survives on the island today – albeit only in the island's pollen record, in buried bole traces, in small rat-nibbled coconut remains (found in caves and at archæological sites) and in recent replantings.[8]

Marine species probably arrived as 'widely dispersed propagules carried by ocean currents, floating debris, or even by swimming, as in the case of some fishes'.[9] Because there was never a reef and the local seawater maintained only poor nutrient levels (sustaining fewer of those plants required by animal life), the island's marine life was always sparse. The southern latitude also deprived the island of the warmer temperatures and intense solar radiation that made the systems of tropical islands so productive. Out of the island's 164 fish species known today, 107 are shore fishes, a quarter of these unique. (In the Indo-Pacific region, only the Hawaiian Islands have a higher percentage of endemic fish species.) Carnivorous eventually far outnumbered herbivorous species. In the island's north-east, turtles deposited their eggs on a pair of sandy beaches. Numerous species of dolphins, seals and whales ranged the triangular island's three coasts.

The island's extreme isolation also inhibited the arrival of terrestrial fauna: very few land species ever arrived, and nearly all of them were insects.[10] Two mollusks are probably endemic, and the only indigenous vertebrate species to have landed before humans were two types of skink (a kind of lizard). There were no terrestrial mammals.

Seabirds, however, nested on the island and offshore *motu* in immense numbers. In fact, it was one of Earth's greatest aviaries, with as many as 25 different species of albatrosses, terns, petrels, shearwaters, boobies, herons, frigates, noddies (tropical terns) and others.[11] Half a dozen land birds also called the island home, including parrots, pigeons, doves and barn owls. The still unnamed island could well have been called Bird Island – and this for tens of thousands of years.

Pollen analyses have shown that over the past 38,000 years, if not considerably longer, in response to climatic oscillations the island avoided such extreme floral fluctuations as to lead to species extinction.[12] The higher regions hosted mainly grasses, sedges and occasional shrubs. Palms, small trees, shrubs and ferns grew abundantly everywhere else. The moist climate that this vegetation invited guaranteed several perennial streams; large quantities of fresh water also accumulated in the three crater swamps. Throughout the Holocene – that is, the past 10,000 years – climate and vegetation appear to have remained stable.

But then, a little over 1,000 years ago – or three minutes before midnight on the 24-hour clock of this remote island's geological history – forest and scrub were being destroyed, soon to be replaced in scattered environments by grasses, sedges and weeds. Burning then denuded and scoured entire landscapes, whereupon soil erosion took place on an unprecedented scale. Several endemic species disappeared. The subsequent decline of forest, and the general depredation of local flora and soil in the palæobotanic and recent geological record, had to be the result of only one thing.[13]

Humans had arrived.

The celebrated Swiss anthropologist Alfred Métraux had lamented of this island in 1940: 'I know of few places in the Pacific where so little remains of the ancient culture'.[14] By the twenty-first century, Easter Island can offer perhaps the region's best-understood story. This achievement is due in no small way to the selfless dedication of scores of international scholars and scientists, each inspired by the greater epic of this magical mote lost in the vastness of the south-eastern Pacific. What they have accomplished enables an informed history of Easter Island for the first time, a work long overdue: a general history of Easter Island's protracted human saga, informed by the most recent developments in historiography, archæology, palæobotany, historical linguistics, genetics, physical anthropology, geography, sociology, ethnography and a host of other disciplines.

Foremost it is the Easter Islanders' own story, from their first voyaging canoes to their present struggle for political autonomy.

Please note the following conventions in writing the Rapanui (Easter Island) language.[15]

Vowels. Each vowel is pronounced as in Spanish or Italian. Thus

a is *ah*
e is *eh*
i is *ee*
o is *oh* (American) / *aw* (British)
u is *oo*

What appear to be diphthongs are actually separately pronounced syllables:

ae is *ah-eh* (Rapanui *pa'e* 'foundation stones' is *pah-eh*, not English 'pie')
ai is *ah-ee* (Rapanui *tai* 'ocean' is *tah-ee*, pronounced quickly)
ao is *ah-oh* or *ah-aw*
au is *ah-oo*
ei is *eh-ee* (close to the vowel in Standard English 'day')
oe is *oh-eh* or *aw-eh*
ou is *oh-oo* or *aw-oo*

Consonants. All Rapanui consonants, except two, closely resemble English equivalents. The *ng*, however, as in Rapanui *rangi* 'sky', is like the *ng* in English 'sing' but highly nasalized, with the back of the tongue pressed high against the palate. The glottal stop (here written '), as in the personal name *Nga'ara*, Rapanui's *'ariki mau* or paramount chief in the 1850s, is the same sound heard in English 'oh-oh'. The macron, as in the geographical name *Pōike*, marks all long vowels.

This book follows the current convention, found in most publications, of writing Easter Island's Polynesian name in Chilean fashion as *Rapa Nui*, its people and language in pan-Polynesian fashion as *Rapanui*.[16]

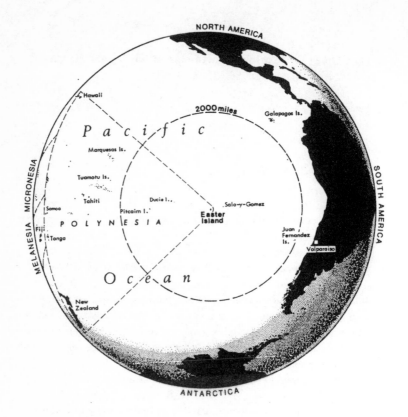

Map 1: Easter Island and the Pacific Ocean.

one

The Polynesian Frontier

Island elders in the first half of the twentieth century were insistent: Makemake was the Primeval Being. 'He took a gourd, made a hole and fucked.'[1] But it was not good. 'He took a stone, made a hole and fucked.' Again it was not good. 'So he formed a mound of soil, made a hole and fucked: [there resulted] a human to occupy the land.'

Providing a unique, if exasperatingly blunt, prospect of its earliest human story, Easter Island's indigenous myth, legend and 'history' are mostly inventions. Contrary to the West's monochronic concept of time – which is linear and one-way – until only very recently 'Polynesian time' was an eternal present. That is, past and future were always to be adjusted to the here and now. This was done for a variety of reasons, but chiefly to validate 'hereditary' land claims.[2] Like all Polynesians, Easter Islanders have always told several different creation or settlement stories – some of them supplemental, most frustratingly contradictory. (Conspicuously missing is the name 'Hawaiki', that mythical homeland of most Polynesians.)

'Rapa Nui used to be a large continent', Mateo Veriveri, for one, would recount to family and foreigners in the 1930s. 'The man Uoke raised it with a pole, then sank it. That's how the island became so small.'[3] The myth might well be of ancient provenance. A genealogy from Hiva 'Oa in the Marquesas Islands names a certain 'Voke' as mythical father of the important islands of Vavau, Hawaiki, Fiji, Tongatapu and others.[4]

Easter Island's most important tradition, however, involves a founding figure first named in the 1880s as Hotu Matu'a, a name (not the tradition itself) perhaps introduced by Mangarevan catechists in the 1860s.[5] The story is a final synthesis of various streams of original island traditions 'narrated when there were hardly any listeners left'.[6] The 'Hotu Matu'a Cycle', as it came to be known in the twentieth century, was of supreme importance to all Easter Islanders, especially in the late nineteenth century when aggressive foreign intrusion forced a reinvigoration of the island's communal identity. 'At the same time, this theme provided a background for the ideology of the island king who had lost his political powers.[7]

The story is rich in ethnic and natural detail.[8] On the island of Marae Renga (or Marae Toe Hau) there lived Haumaka, who, in a dream, saw a far-off country. When he awoke he told six scouts to search for it. The six left, discovered Easter Island, reconnoitred, judged it was perfect for settlement and so planted yams (for later settlers to harvest). Whereupon they returned to tell their chief, 'Hotu Matu'a'. Having just lost three battles to a neighbouring chief, Hotu Matu'a wished to flee with his people. So he had two canoes built, captained one himself and let Tu'u ko Iho captain the other. At the moment of their arrival at Easter Island, Hotu Matu'a's heir Tu'u mā Heke was born. Tu'u ko Iho, to whom a daughter was simultaneously born, came and bit off the heir's navel cord; then he did the same for his daughter. After which ... *he tomo te tangata, he rotu, he noho* ('The people landed, they gathered, they stayed').[9]

'After a short stay in 'Anakena [on the north-eastern coast] to rest', or so island elders told the Roman Catholic missionary Father Hippolyte Roussel in the 1860s, 'the new settlers walked all over the island, and some established themselves at one place and others at another. Everyone proceeded immediately to plant the products brought from abroad. Hotu, who was the king, resigned soon after in favour of his son, Tu'u mā Heke.'[10]

Already, however, when the six scouts had initially been reconnoitring Easter Island they had met a lone settler – Ngā Tavake 'a Te Rona. And this settler had told them there had been yet another, Te Ohiro 'a Te Runu, who had already died. Later, Ngā Tavake witnessed the arrival of Hotu Matu'a's royal canoe.

These two figures – Ngā Tavake 'a Te Rona and Te Ohiro 'a Te Runu – probably recall historical names that once had been prominent in early settlement tradition. Their true significance, however, remains obscure. Ngā Tavake happens to be a village in the main Rikitea region of the island of Mangareva; it is also the name of the mountain between the two main peaks there, as well as that of the general region north-west of Rikitea.[11] And Hanga Ohiro (Hanga 'o Hiro) is the name of the 'Anakena Bay area of Easter Island, traditional landing point of the 'immigrant queen' Ava Rei Pua. Perhaps not the names of individuals, but those of two discrete groups are preserved in these two earliest proper names from Easter Island.[12]

Sadly, the oral testimony – because of the island's severe depopulation and cultural contamination in the latter nineteenth century – is too unreliable to serve even as a basis for historical conjecture. Similar Easter Island traditions reflect an idealized and half-legendary account, certainly not that 'objective historical reality' familiar to Westerners.[13] If truth is to be found in the island's early history, then it lies instead in the stones and bones of archæology, tongues of linguistics, grains of palynology, DNA of genetics and other material evidence serving an array of modern disciplines – that is, those drawing knowledge from hard data and their systematic analysis and interpretation.

And their story confirms, in each and every detail, that Easter Island was the ultimate Polynesian frontier.

ORIGINS

Easter Island's one-and-only settlers were not South Americans.[14] In the last quarter of the twentieth century this long-contentious issue was resolved once and for all by the cumulative scientific evidence that confirmed Easter Island's exclusively Polynesian patrimony. Early Easter Islanders did not experience any subsequent major intrusion either, as historical linguistics makes clear.[15] Until the relatively recent European trespass, only one single, unbroken, Oceanic lineage occupied Easter Island. Their origin lay in southern China.

Around 6,000 BC, once rising seas had attained maximum levels and global mean temperatures had effected a major climate change, a distinct cultural complex – one that scholars are beginning to identify only now[16] – singled out a diverse, but interrelated, southern Asian population that was settled along China's southern coast. About 2,000 years later, members of this complex left the Asian mainland to settle on Taiwan, where, over centuries, their language(s) developed into Proto-Austronesian.[17] Expansion then followed: south to the Philippines, west and south-west to Vietnam and Cambodia, the Malay Peninsula, Borneo, Sumatra and Java. Other Austronesians sailed directly south of the Philippines to colonize Sulawesi, Timor, southern Halmahera and Western Papua (Western New Guinea).

By about 2,000 BC the same people were settling the islands of New Britain and New Ireland in the Bismarcks, east of Papua New Guinea, generally keeping apart from the indigenous Papuans there, an altogether different people. In this region the newcomers then proceeded to elaborate a new and distinctive culture – Lapita – as they also struck out beyond Near Oceania to colonize the islands of Remote Oceania. They were greatly aided in this endeavour by their invention of large double-hulled voyaging canoes, capable of transporting immense loads over vast distances. In time, Lapita came to identify the Austronesians' entire cultural complex in the Pacific Islands. Colonization of Remote Oceania was an Austronesian initiative.

The first branches of Lapita tentatively advanced throughout Island Melanesia around 1,300 BC, then continued on to settle on Fiji about a century later. (Tonga and Samoa soon followed.) Fiji was the cradle of Eastern Lapita Culture. For perhaps 1,000 years, under mutual stimulation and competition, a new island people developed there an Archaic Polynesian Culture that was unique in the world, one inspired and enriched by local environmental resources. Ocean voyaging continued, but only within the Fiji–Tonga–Samoa crescent and with such distant neighbours as Tokelau, Niue, Rotuma, East Futuna, East 'Uvea and other islands, which, in turn, were beginning to develop distinct societies of their own.

There are many competing theories about remote island settlement – 'accidental' drift, fanning out (with great human loss), blind flight and others. But most scholars now agree that the initial discovery of an island was customarily accomplished by well-equipped scouts, on two-way exploratory journeys.[18] These scouts would have set out with a given amount of food, sailing close to the wind; if no land had been found by the time half the food was consumed, then the scouts returned to their home island easily, sailing downwind. If land was found, then the scouts returned to report its location and suitability for settlement. Settlers then repeated the voyage, after having completed careful preparations involving a complex arrangement of safeguards initiated by the entire community. Once settlement occurred, communication with the founding community was maintained. The new island was no isolate, but an addition to the voyaging network.

Islands were thus deliberately navigated to, using a range of navigational skills that made use of stars, ocean swells, changes in water temperature, cloud movements, the paths of both diurnal and ranging birds, collections of driftwood and seaweed, flashing 'blue streaks' of phosphorescence that glow up to 140 kilometres offshore, even the distinctive smell of vegetation and perilous reefs. The settlers' canoes contained all the necessary foodstuffs and plantings, domesticated animals (pigs, dogs, poultry), sacred stones and images of deified ancestors, and many other items. Each carried up to 30 or more settlers, many of whom were *tufunga* (canoe and house builders, toolmakers, expert carvers, priests, orators and so on), and a large complement of women of child-bearing age. In other words, each settling canoe held a complete Polynesian society.[19]

Perhaps prompted by unusual climatic conditions and a particular social situation, Samoans at last crossed 3,000 kilometres of open ocean to colonize the Marquesas Islands in East Polynesia about AD 300. (Some scholars see the West Polynesian thrust occurring through the Society Islands instead.) Here the founding population prospered and grew.

About AD 500 their descendants apparently left to colonize the eastern Tuamotus, the Gambiers (Mangareva), Pitcairn and Henderson, 'island-hopping' their way ever further to the south and east, testing the periphery of the Pacific. It was a process that might have taken as long as two centuries, during which time the voyagers were turning into a distinct South-East Polynesian people. At the same time, and for several centuries thereafter, other Marquesan departees and their descendants were colonizing the Society Islands, Hawai'i, the Australs, the Cooks and many others, including, in the end, New Zealand and the Chathams. It was the widest migration of one ethnicity in Earth's human history.

There were conceivably many reasons for East Polynesia's continued colonization. Historians often cite such clichés as drought, warfare, over-population, resource depletion, status competition and the like. These, however, seem insufficient to explain the pioneering of so vast a region, and over so many centuries. Perhaps the most contributory factor was simply that exploring and colonizing had become an essential part of the Pacific Islanders' cultural heritage (just as science and technology were to be in the West). Undisputed is the fact that it was the East Polynesians who surpassed humankind's collective navigational achievements, by several degrees of magnitude.

Easter Island was, of course, their climax, the geographical terminus of the Austronesians' 3,000 years of eastward expansion. (Until the nineteenth century it would remain Earth's most isolated inhabited island.) And South-East Polynesians probably 'island-hopped' to it from a prominent neighbour – Mangareva.[20]

Only in recent years has the cumulative weight of evidence urged archæologists to accept that Mangareva itself might have been settled before AD 800.[21] A date for the initial occupation of the neighbouring smaller island of Henderson – already well on the way towards Easter Island – as early as AD 700 now seems possible. Perhaps Mangareva was even settled some time in the sixth century AD, resulting in Easter Island's settlement and coloniza-tion shortly thereafter. An initial and wider human impact on the environ-ment of Easter Island, as chiefly the pollen record witnesses, can perhaps be dated to between the sixth and eighth centuries AD.[22] The earliest reliable radiocarbon date for Easter Island – from *ahu* Tahai's first construction phase, on the island's west coast, close to today's single community of Hanga Roa – is accepted to be AD 690 ± 130.[23] (It is possible that this *ahu* or monu-mental platform was constructed after being occupied for a couple of cen-turies; but it could also be the immediate continuation of the home island's *ahu* size and style.)

Although in several artefactual categories one might acknowledge a number of parallels between Mangareva and Easter Island,[24] there is never-theless a lack of sufficiently early Mangarevan deposits and significant arte-factual material that might prove any definite connection to Easter Island's settlement. Of course, it has long been appreciated that anthropometrical and skeletal evidence identifies Mangarevans to be the Easter Islanders' clos-est relations.[25] A recent linguistic study has also identified Mangareva to be the possible key to a hitherto unrecognized sub-family of languages – South-

East Polynesian to which Easter Island also belongs.[26] For the present, it is perhaps the cumulative evidence that most strongly argues for the Easter Islanders being South-East Polynesians, but with immediate origins in the greater Mangarevan–Pitcairn–Henderson interaction sphere.[27]

Much as the nineteenth-century traditions relate, 'Mangarevan' scouts, then, sailing safely close to the wind, would first have found and reconnoitred Easter Island, then assessed its suitability for settlement. Whereupon the island's position was noted by the rising stars, to enable the subsequent settlers – should settlement be chosen – to find it again. Contrary to earlier estimates of two to three months, the voyage to the Pacific's most isolated island might in fact have taken just under three weeks, if undertaken from Mangareva. (In 1999, for example, the traditional Hawaiian sailing canoe *Hōkūle'a* sailed from Mangareva to Easter Island in just seventeen and a half days, aided by fortuitous northerlies that allowed it to reach across the wind, the most favourable angle for such voyaging canoes.)[28] Undoubtedly the first humans to set foot on the island, these Mangarevan scouts would have met dense forest, perhaps even rainforest.[29] To them, Easter Island would have appeared to be a 'garden paradise', ideal for settlement. And this is just what they would have told their chief on their return to Mangareva.

Settlement was eventually chosen, but the true reason for it, with all respect to nineteenth-century accounts, will never be known. In all likelihood, neither a Hotu Matu'a nor a Tu'u ko Iho ('Tu'u the Sublime', recalling the ancient Polynesian war god) led the prehistoric settlers. But whoever he (never a she) was, he would have been a strong, dictatorial leader of royal lineage. Since extant traditions reflect the belief that the historical Easter Islanders at least thought of themselves as one stock, perhaps this leader in fact headed a single lineage.[30] His would have been an *ivi* or 'smaller kin group', voyaging in perhaps two canoes of equal numbers of approximately 35–40 men and women.

On board were tools and animals (probably pigs, dogs, poultry), drinking water in plugged canes and, for immediate consumption, preserved fish, fruits, vegetables and coconuts periodically cooked in a sandbox over continuously tended embers.[31] Also on board was the small Polynesian rat, the *Rattus concolor*, possibly as an emergency food source. (It proved to be a calamitous inclusion.) Of vital importance, of course, was the cargo of plantings needed to sustain the fledgling colony.[32]

Taro (*Colocasia antiquorum*) soon came to be Easter Island's staple crop, cultivated in terraces in well-watered ravines, such as east of central Vaitea or 'White Water'. (Once the island began losing its perennial streams, however, taro's importance declined before the *kumara* or sweet potato imported from South America.) Eighteen varietal names for taro were collected on

1   The Polynesian discovery of Easter Island.

the island in 1934, several being of recent introduction.[33] Another major food crop was the *'uhi* or yam (*Dioscorea alata*), of which no fewer than 41 varietal names were collected on the island at the beginning of the twentieth century.[34] Equally important was *toa* or sugar cane (*Saccharum officinarum*). *Maika* or banana (*Musa sapientum*), of which there were also several varieties, was often later grown, like the paper mulberry, in special sheltered *manavai* or stone enclosures to protect it from wind and sea salt. The *mahute* or paper-mulberry (*Broussonetia papyrifera*) was cultivated for the manufacture of tapa cloth for clothing. Ti (*Cordyline fruticosa*) was used for spears and for wrapping food to be cooked in earth ovens. The *pua* or turmeric (*Curcuma longa*) provided a condiment, daub for body and limbs, and yellow dye. (Possibly the turmeric, too, like the sweet potato and bottle gourd, was acquired on a voyage to South America.)

Also aboard was cargo that would not survive: the tropical coconut palm (if this was even brought, mainly for its fruit), the breadfruit tree and various fruit trees.[35] Of the imported animals, only the South-East Asian chickens were to outlive the centuries.

Most importantly, the settlers brought their cultural baggage along: their language, dress, oral literature, customs, beliefs, social structure, art and – most crucial of all – ancestors (see below). In short, everything that identified them as being south-east Polynesians.

19

The new arrivals appear to have first settled the island's south-west (where the population is concentrated today). Until their plantings produced a harvest, they relied on birds, eggs, fish and shellfish for sustenance. Bird meat and fresh eggs would have been abundant. At least 1,200 years ago the Islanders began clearing forest inside the south-west's Rano Kau caldera.[36] As the centuries passed, they continued to burn vegetation and clear forest over the entire island without regard to the consequences, ravishing the resources – a commonplace of Polynesian colonization. Not only bird life, but also sea life was adversely affected. Excavations at 'Anakena ('Gannet Cave') on the north-eastern coast unearthed more than 6,000 identifiable bones, of which 2,583 were porpoise.[37] (The indigenous name for 'porpoise' disappeared centuries ago, as none was left locally.) At first, Islanders remained few. But when numbers increased exponentially, the flora and fauna crashed. Even then, it took nearly a millennium to ruin Easter Island.

Kinship groups ramified. Already within a century or two the new Easter Islanders, slowly developing their own unique culture, began establishing individual *ivi* on the north-eastern coast as well. Some villages started at the head of bays, where canoes could land after fishing: Hanga Roa ('Long Bay') itself, today's solitary community, was among such founding establishments.[38] Others – like the north-western Te Peu ('The Force'), Vai Mata ('Communal Water') and Puna Marengo ('Bald Spring') – arose on high sea cliffs. All such larger villages were never far from fresh water. For centuries, one of the island's most reliable wells guaranteed the eminence of the north-eastern Vaitara Kai 'Ua ('Winter West Wind Eating Rain') as a leading community.[39]

Contrary to earlier belief, Easter Islanders did not suffer a mind-numbing isolation after the initial settlement. 'Rather, the level of [their] interaction, both to the west, and perhaps on occasion to the east, was simply less repetitive or continuous than elsewhere in eastern Polynesia.'[40] A voyage from Mangareva could take less than three weeks. Archæological sourcing studies have demonstrated that, for their part, both the Mangarevan and Pitcairn groups were in continuous interaction with one another, at least from about AD 1000 to well into the sixteenth century.[41] By the thirteenth century, Mangareva even appears to have been linked to the basalt source on 'Ei'a'o in the north-west Marquesas and may also have enjoyed indirect contact with the Society Islands.[42]

Therefore, once arrived at Easter Island, the colonists probably maintained, at least initially, regular and intimate links with their home village(s). Perhaps for as long as two or three centuries – that is, until the Easter Island population was large enough to survive independently – they probably relied on home for trade, disaster relief and even the genetic pool. Once independent survival was guaranteed, contact would then have become more infrequent. All the same, it appears that relations long remained strong with Mangareva. 'Four hundred years after their settlement, the two cultural assemblages [from Mangareva and Easter Island] have not yet diverged very much.'[43]

For such interaction, the Easter Islanders would, of course, have had a name for their new island, to distinguish it from the others. But this original Polynesian name disappeared forever when the voyaging sphere later collapsed. For all Easter Islanders, their island was then simply *kāinga* or 'territory'.

SOCIAL ORGANIZATION

From their home island the colonists brought with them that fundamental trinity of Polynesian rank and status: *'ariki* ('nobles'), *tuhunga* ('experts', from **tufunga*) and *'urumanu* ('commoners'). Only one *'ariki mau* or 'paramount chief' ever held sway at any given time on Easter Island, and this until the end of the nineteenth century. Closest in lineage to the *'ariki mau* were the *'ariki paka* or 'nobles' (later comprising everyone in the dominant Miru 'clan'). Specialists, from holy priests to master canoe builders, comprised the *tuhunga*. Nearly everyone else was then *'urumanu* – those responsible for food, clothing and general construction.

The demarcation between *'ariki* and *'urumanu* initially began as one of gradation, but later became categorical: that is, it identified and maintained two genealogical ranks.[44] By the 1700s the rankless *matato'a* or 'professional warriors' had come to comprise a transitional rank between the two (what on other Polynesian islands was called *rangatira*).

Most highly developed of all was the concept of aristocracy.[45] Kin group leaders had the power of life or death. Status was inherent through lineage, with social eminence being invested in the *atariki* – the first-born son of an *atariki* – back through the generations to some mythical founder-ancestor. Since he was a direct descendant of the home island's paramount chief, Easter Island's first *'ariki mau* held this right by virtue of primogeniture. All subsequent *'ariki mau* would then trace their lineage directly back to him. Only one kin group – later identified as the Miru – ever established *'ariki* titles on Easter Island. Leaders of other groups were simply *tangata hōnui* ('persons of authority').

As a result, all of society was the demesne of the *'ariki mau*, literally the 'true *'ariki*'. He was the one individual

with the most aristocratic pedigree and the most exalted social position on the island. His person was overflowing with mana and his sacredness caused him to be feared and respected. His function in society was to insure through his very being the abundance of crops and the fertility of the ground and to exercise his influence on animal life. Certain religious activities were derived from his sacredness and he held supervisory control over various practices connected with religion.[46]

In the first few centuries of colonization the 'ariki mau would certainly have been considered a living deity, wielding absolute power. Over time he lost all secular power, although he retained most supernatural power, together with specific personal privileges. Even in the final century of traditional life on the island, the functions of the 'ariki mau 'had a strong bearing upon the magico-economic structure of the island culture'.[47] He remained inviolate, sacred. Only two special servants could enter his house: the tu'ura for daily provisions, and the haka'apa'apa for attendance. At least towards the end of the tradition, the 'ariki mau would always wear a yellow-stained tapa cloak and feather hats. From his neck would be hanging, front and back, six wooden balls (tahonga) and six wooden pectorals (rei miro). Only when his atariki or first-born son married did the 'ariki mau hand over his power. Unsurprisingly, the 'ariki mau customarily delayed this marriage until his atariki was well on in years.

Following the 'ariki in rank were the tumu ivi 'atua (literally, 'divine lineage stock'), the tuhunga who fulfilled the functions of 'priest'. The actual mediary of the deified ancestors, however, was always each successive 'ariki mau himself, who was the island's highest priest: he was, in fact, a 'priest-chief'.[48] The tumu ivi 'atua were shamans, officiaries at rituals and special attendants to the 'ariki mau in any sacred capacity. Feared and respected by all Islanders, they would have been held in the highest regard.

Otherwise, tuhunga were experts in all the arts and trades. (In the 1880s, returnees from Tahiti replaced the Old Rapanui word tuhunga with mā'ori.) These could be master carvers, canoe builders, orators, construction and transport engineers – in short, any expert served by pupils, apprentices or jobmen. Some formed a privileged 'class', their profession, much like that of European contemporaries, passed along from father to son.

The 'urumanu or 'commoners' stood on the lowest rung of ancient Easter Island society. These were labourers, fishermen and tenant farmers, those who made up the majority of the island's population. They supplied the food, provided the clothing and performed all construction and menial tasks under the supervision of 'ariki and tuhunga. In times of war, 'urumanu could become kio or conquered enemies, who temporarily worked their victor's land as slaves (see chapter Two). Land rights were maintained during such episodes by upholding traditional economic stratification in order to prevent complete social chaos.

The original settlement comprised an *ivi* of approximately 70 to 80 descendants of a common (Mangarevan?) ancestor. Later members of this group ranged further with their *mahingo* or 'extended family' to establish new settlements. Over time, larger groupings made up an *ure* or 'local segmentary descent group or lineage'. Once kinship lines became too ramified to observe proper status requirements, these in turn made up a *mata* or 'large kinship group'. This was neither a 'tribe' nor a 'clan', for the first is a social grouping and the second is an exclusive kin grouping (which actually applied to the whole island). Rather, the *mata* was a social grouping with a kin core. In the first few centuries of settlement, Easter Island's *mata* would have represented the principal land-holding groups.[49]

By at least the fifteenth century, however, the island's *mahingo*, those extended families living together in one hut and possessing land in common, were each identifying themselves as members of a larger *ure* which claimed three or more local *ahu* or monumental platforms. About 100 such *ure* (and more than 300 *ahu*) were then located in scattered settlements about the island, mostly along the coast. Each formed part of approximately ten greater *mata* claiming either a specific or general territory and led by a *tangata hōnui*. And two *hānau* or 'confederations of *mata*' had since emerged: the Tu'u and the 'Otu 'Iti (from the 1880s called Hotu 'Iti). Both described a loose 'nation' of territorial organizations, based primarily on lineage.

The western and northern Tu'u held the all-important *mata* of the royal Miru, then the Hāmea, Marama, Hau Moana, Ra'ā, Ngā Ure and Ngā Timo. The eastern 'Otu 'Iti was made up of the *mata* of the Tūpa 'Otu (later called Tūpahotu), Ure 'o Hei (Hiti Uira) and the Koro 'o Rongo. (Further minor *mata* are sometimes also mentioned.) Some *mata* lay wholly within the territory of another: the Hāmea and Ra'ā, for example, lay within Miru territory. The three *mata* of the eastern 'Otu 'Iti, on the other hand, had apparently no distinct districts of their own, 'but were mixed and scattered between the north coast and the south coast, east of [']Anakena and Akahanga'.[50]

Each *mata* claimed a common ancestor, its defining criterion. Later, this ancestor was generally acknowledged to be a son or grandson of the island's mythical 'settler'. Over subsequent centuries such plastic 'genealogies' were used, and abused, to enhance and manipulate territorial claims (which explains the many contradictions in Easter Island's earliest informant data). In turn, each *mata* comprised genealogical sub-groupings of *ure*. The royal Miru, for one, held the *ure* of the Honga (Ongo), Te Kena, Mata Iva, Rau Vai, Kao, Toko te Rangi, Ma'ari, Ko Era, Hāhai, Mātapu, Moa Tahu, Kai Hūharu, Te Niu and the Tu'u ko Iho.

As the Miru's senior line, the Honga lived at the royal seat at 'Anakena; the Te Kena, their nearest relations, occupied neighbouring Ovahe to the east. Endogamy – marrying within one's immediate descent group – was

2 The reconstructed Tahai complex, with Hanga Roa's shoreline in the distance.

endemic with this most royal *ure* of the Miru: Honga men were allowed to marry only women of the Te Kena or Kao *ure*. Modern osteological studies have confirmed genetic isolation on prehistoric Easter Island as a result of such concentrated inbreeding.[51]

Claiming direct *atariki* descent from the leader of the original settlers, the Miru *mata* was always the island's primary descent group. By the historical period its royal centre lay at 'Anakena on the north-eastern coast. The west coast, however, certainly held its earliest 'capital': perhaps first Tahai (see illus. 2), later Te Peu. As the *mata* grew, so the Miru's domain expanded, eventually to dominate the entire western and northern Tu'u 'nation'. Although by the fifteenth century its absolute secular power had waned, the Miru *mata* still maintained control over all supernatural authority on the island, something that obtained well into the 1800s.

MATERIAL CULTURE AND PRODUCTION

Easter Islanders lived in a thatched hut, rock overhang or cave, with associated *'umu* or 'earth oven', stone 'chicken' house(s) and, later, stone garden enclosures to protect plantings.[52] Most settlements lay along the coast, but better inland soil and the desire to protect plantings from wind and salt spray encouraged the Easter Islanders early on to settle on slopes and rocky heights as well. Several settlements would group to form a village complex, its huts up to 200 metres distant from a ceremonial site with *ahu* and perhaps one or more standing *mo'ai* or 'anthropomorphic statue'. Closer to the *ahu* and its holy courtyard, some 50 to 100 metres inland, were long elliptical thatched houses – with stone kerbing and often fronting patios of smooth fitted boulders – for high-ranking individuals such as local family leaders and special *tuhunga* like the *tumu ivi 'atua*. Entrances of nearly all the dwellings faced the *ahu* and the sea.[53]

Most huts, very low affairs of only one metre in height, had a single crawl hole as entrance. Up to dozens of people would sleep inside. In the early twentieth century elderly informants recalled how they used to eat their evening meal inside the family hut, later sleeping parallel to the length of the hut, which was shaped like an upturned boat, their head towards the crawl hole. The old people slept in the centre, the young at either end. Reed mats, stone pillows and occasional carvings comprised the only appointments. These were sleeping shelters, not houses. All waking life was spent outdoors (except in inclement weather).

There is also a local tradition of stone houses, corbelled with a keystone on the top, as can still be seen at the south-west ceremonial centre of 'Orongo on the cusp of Rano Kau. In 1770 González noted that 'priests' – doubtless *tumu ivi 'atua* – lived in little stone houses near the *mo'ai* or 'statues', whereas elders and other leaders, the *tangata hōnui*, lived in the long elliptical huts.[54]

Everywhere lay the *'umu pa'e*. These were the stone-lined earth ovens, today the island's most ubiquitous archæological inheritance. They number in their hundreds, if not thousands, throughout the island. Already in 1722 the Dutch noted how the Easter Islanders were preparing chicken 'in holes in the ground in which they had stones that were heated glowing hot by burning bushes'.[55] Most *'umu pa'e* lay on the seaward side of a hut. Domestic *'umu*, fashioned without stones, were simple earthen pits, many used in the same spot for centuries, it appears.

Because of the dense forest that generated generous precipitation, early Islanders enjoyed fresh water from several perennial streams, such as the one that flowed down the eastern flank of the main mountain Terevaka and into the sea at 'Anakena. Fresh water was also to be had from the three crater swamps, Rano Aroi, Rano Kau and Rano Raraku (*rano* means 'crater lake'). Pools collected frequently in the island's many lava tubes. Even in later, drier centuries, intermittent streams – such as Ava 'o Kiri ('Kiri's Channel'), just inland from Ovahe on the north-east coast – could provide a welcome relief.

The earliest settlers lived off seabirds and land birds in their millions. This superabundant store of protein, including unlimited eggs, would have taken centuries to exhaust. Most nesting then occurred on the several off-shore islets, whereupon these were plundered too. Small shellfish were gathered and eaten raw or boiled; crayfish and crabs were caught, always a delicacy. A small number of turtles and seals supplemented the local diet.

Fishing was always of supreme importance on Easter Island. Since the island lacked a lagoon, net fishing remained insignificant. Instead, the Islanders mostly practised angling, spearing and hand fishing close to shore, for smaller fish and eel. Open-sea fishing for larger fish occurred less often, but supplied surpluses that could be traded for inland crops. Nearly 400 fish-hook motifs, 93 per cent of them from the north-eastern coast, have been identified in Easter Island's rock art. All display the type of hook of stone or human bone used for open-sea fishing, particularly of tuna.[56]

This type of fishing was 'largely a monopoly of the occupants of the western and northern areas, particularly the high-ranking Miru clan'.[57] It also reflects the better fishing grounds, the *hakanononga*, to leeward, controlled by the island's dominant descent group (a characteristic feature of most pre-contact Polynesian societies). It was the Miru alone who effected fishing's *tapu* ('sacred bans') and *rāhui* ('temporary restrictions'), giving Miru preferred access to both *tapu* and restricted species.

For deepwater fishing, large seagoing canoes were required. The construction of a canoe was always a major communal undertaking. Immense logs, probably of *Alphitonia zizyphoides*, a hard resistant wood excellent for canoe-making (as in Tahiti and in Marquesan Fatuiva), were taken from forests on Terevaka (lit. 'Sail Canoe'). This mountain's semi-hard *Elæocarpus rarotongensis* would have furnished canoe paddles (as it did in Rarotonga and the Australs).[58]

At the same time that the western and north-eastern Miru *mata* were specializing in fishing – by the fifteenth century, at the latest – the southern and eastern descent groups, above all the *mata* of the 'Otu 'Iti, were specializing in intensive agriculture. This included terraced cultivation of taro, the island's original staple food crop, within well-watered ravines. Other intensive cultivation (yams, sugar cane, banana) took place inside the well-protected craters of Rano Kau and Rano Raraku. 'This brought about institutionalized exchange mechanisms between these areas as well as between coastal and inland zones.'[59] Other *ure* and *mata* enjoyed access to crucial resources: not only special timbers, but also volcanic tuff, basalt, obsidian, red scoria, paper mulberry, red ochre, reeds and other desirables that, being highly localized, were eminently tradable.

Early European visitors to the island remarked how the Easter Islanders divided their arable land into square fields with furrows. The Dutch remarked during their exceedingly brief visit in 1722 that what little they saw looked quite bountiful, and indeed it must truly have been so before the island's environmental depredation. By the end of the eighteenth century, as the French explorer La Pérouse observed, perhaps only one-tenth of the island was being cultivated; on the other hand, the cultivated fields were being weeded, watered and even fertilized (with the ash of burned stalks).

Regular lines of bananas were also to be seen. In 1804 the Russian Lisjanskij, for example, remarked that 'every house was planted around with sugar cane and bananas'.[60]

Property distribution occurred at three types of special feasts – each of them loud and colourful displays, proof of descent-group wealth and power. The most commonly distributed item was foodstuffs, especially chickens. It was not the 'ariki mau who assumed the most frequent role of economic redistribution on Easter Island, but the leaders of the ure themselves, those subdivisions of the ten major mata. As paramount 'chief', the 'ariki mau received his ritual tithe of a tuna catch only then to distribute this among the 'important old men'[61] – the tangata hōnui or leaders of the greater mata – for further redistribution among the many ure.

BELIEF SYSTEM AND ART

No Pacific Islanders before the arrival of Europeans or Americans practised any form of worship. Whereas Melanesian and Micronesian 'devotion' was placatory, to be manipulated by ritual, Polynesians entreated and bargained with ancestral deities.[62] Two fundamental concepts defined Polynesian socio-religious life: mana and tapu.

Only high-ranking individuals possessed mana – that is, socio-spiritual power – which ultimately derived from ancestors, but also became evident through an individual's remarkable deeds and successful undertakings. The concept of mana maintained Polynesia's hierarchy of authority. It also channelled community efforts towards stratified remuneration, combining the secular and divine (a Western dichotomy).

To maintain uncontaminated mana and ensure continued success, very early Polynesian society devised a ritual restrictive complex or tapu. Varying in its implications from island to island, the tapu affected use of land, crops, buildings, precincts and the sanctity of individuals, but also behaviour, speech, diet, sexual practices, beliefs and attitudes. Tapu was more than a mere rule. The tapu set aside and elevated from the common domain some sacred function, station, its holder and his or her person, tools, prerogatives and possessions. It could obtain for generations. The tapu complex embraced a way of thinking, a philosophy of life. It was a rigorously enforced social code against which the position and actions of each member of the island community were daily defined. There is no true equivalent to tapu in the English language.[63]

Polynesian mana and tapu were inextricably linked to the veneration of ancestral deities. All Polynesians, and thus all Easter Islanders, believed every deity to be ancestral.[64] Those the Easter Islanders brought with them from Mangareva were seemingly revered, without change, for more than 1,000 years. (Only upon contact with non-Polynesians, in the eighteenth century, did this apparently change; see chapter Two.) Deified ancestors were, in fact, the settlers' most important baggage, since from them emanated the *mana* that ensured survival.

The 'religion' of ancient Easter Island was political, in that supernatural belief was yet another expression of the ruling class's hold on the commoners. It was promoted above all to maintain and legitimize those in authority.[65] At times the East Polynesian deities, in particular, might perhaps have resembled the ancient Greek pantheon in being departmental entities who sometimes appeared to mix with mortals and exert specific influences on nature and human activity. Unlike the Greek gods, however, these were deified human ancestors who stood not remotely, but in 'traceable' lineages to the living. They were not 'gods'. The word 'god' is actually misleading for all of prehistoric Polynesia, since it suggests Western analogies that do not obtain.

Similar to the earliest European religions before Christianity, ancient Polynesian belief focused not on righteousness, morality and goodness, but on success, strength and influence. The deified ancestors were not ideals, but tools to be used to benefit oneself and one's descent group, and to guard from storm, drought and attack. Religion offered no scheme for personal 'salvation' or proper social behaviour – it offered protection, power and wealth. Those who sacrificed to the ancestors, received from them in return. Ancient Polynesian 'religion' was thus no different from the rest of society, as nothing particularly distinguished it. 'Religion' was merely the supernatural extension of the descent group's lineage.[66]

Two classes of ancestral deities obtained for all ancient East Polynesians, including Easter Islanders: the major mythical, who were the old inherited deities; and the lesser legendary, being more recent local innovations. Ruling the 'pantheon' of Easter Island was Tangaroa the 'sea god', patron of winds, ocean and fish. He was to survive only in legend – in the place name Ma'unga ('Mount') Tangaroa, by Hanga Roa in the west – and in the Old Rapanui name for October: Tangaroa 'Uri ('Dark Tangaroa'). As late as the nineteenth century, Tangaroa was named as the head of one genealogy of 'ariki mau. Tāne, patron of forests and their bounty, is missing entirely in Easter Island legend (Easter Islanders had lost their forests centuries before), but survived in the nineteenth century in the Old Rapanui name for the 27th night of the moon, Rongo Tāne. Rongo, patron of cultivations, is mentioned after Tangaroa in an 'ariki genealogy and his name once identified both the 26th and the 27th nights of the moon. Tu'u, patron of warfare, evidently played a major role in ancient Easter Island society: his name survives in that of the island's dominant moiety, the Tu'u *hānau* (of which the Miru are the chief *mata*); in the place name Ma'unga Tu'u, near Ma'unga Tangaroa; and in the name Tu'u ko Iho ('Tu'u the Sublime'), mythical 'co-founder' of the island, who, in legend, also brought the statues and 'caused them to walk'. He appears in most *'ariki* genealogies as well. The ancient Polynesian deity Hiro was invoked on Easter Island for rain, and Hina was the female 'moon' deity.

Among the many lesser ancestral deities were Tiki te Hatu ('Tiki the Lord'), Hiva Karā Rere, Tive, Tare and the numerous *'atua* (a deified ancestor in general) and *akuaku* who freely ranged the island at night.

These latter were ghosts, spirits of the recently departed. Many lingered for years, it was believed, guarding the territory of their lineage from trespassers. The *'atua* or *akuaku* were family deities, who, as a rule, were known only to their living relatives or descendants and were confined to their respective *kāinga* or 'territory'. 'As long as all members of the kin group lived and behaved according to custom, the *'atua* or *akuaku* were believed to be well disposed, helpful and protective towards them and their property, but mischievous or even hostile and aggressive towards all strangers'.[67] (Today, belief in the *akuaku* persists.) 'Potentially, the number of [Easter Island] numina equals that of the [Easter Island] people's departed ancestors, on Easter Island and beyond. To know them all is neither possible nor useful.'[68]

The art of the Easter Islanders was the visible and tangible expression of their belief system, the natural and supernatural witnessed and touched. All Polynesian art was an impersonal expression upholding the sacredness of the ruling authority. In this, it was 'political art'. Religion, art, politics – all occupied the same space in the pre-contact Polynesian psyche, yet spared the West's compartmentalization and personalization.[69]

The settlers of Easter Island would have brought from Mangareva the art of carving human figures out of wood, a craft at which they came to excel. The carving of wooden ancestral statues is a common activity among East Polynesians. (Larger figures of stone also graced sacred sites in the Marquesas and Australs; forms that developed in later centuries on Easter Island reflect both the ancient heritage and the influences of the active voyaging spheres, which disseminated new sculptural styles.) To all pre-contact Polynesians, wood was a sacred substance. To the Easter Islanders, 'objects of wood that were used to solicit the supernatural might appear to be instruments of personal survival'; their value increased as wood on the island became scarce.[70]

Statuettes in particular seem to have been associated with certain rituals. An English visitor to the island in 1827 noticed how, upon relinquishing to their purchasers 'idols' in the shape of men and fishes, the Easter Islanders would 'set up a great Shout lifting up the figure above their Heads several times all joining in Chorus and when upon delivery they would prop it against their brest [*sic*] several times . . . whether they where [were] Household Gods or Toys for their amusement I could not discover'.[71] The island's first known European resident, the French lay missionary Eugène Eyraud, similarly reported in 1864 that in all the houses many statuettes are seen, about thirty centimetres high, representing male figures, fishes, birds etc. They are undoubtedly idols, but I have not noticed that they have been attributed any kinds of honors. I have occasionally seen the natives taking these statues, lifting them into the air, making some gestures, and accompanying all of it with a sort of dance and an insignificant song.[72]

Some carvings were symbols of individual status, others probably amulets 'used as protection against the ancient world's constant concern with sorcery'.[73] Statuettes appear also to have played some significant part in *ahu* ceremonies, perhaps as offerings to deified ancestors or as companions to the deceased. Pre-contact and early contact Easter Islanders produced wood carvings that were among the most expert and imaginative in all Polynesia. Their particular penchant for objectivity was unique.[74] The few exemplars that survive in the world's leading museums are today celebrated as ethnic masterpieces.

Bodily art, in particular tattooing, was an especially favourite art form on pre-contact Easter Island. The tattooer's *ngarahu* or 'pigment' was made from burnt ti leaves, then applied by an adze-like *'uhi* (bone comb) and *miro pua 'uhi* (wooden mallet).[75] In 1722 the German marine Carl Friederich Behrens noted how the Easter Islanders were 'painted on their bodies with all sorts of birds and strange beasts, each lovelier than the other'.[76] In 1774 James Cook remarked that 'Tattowing . . . is much used here, the Men are coloured in this manner from head to foot, the figures they mark are all nearly alike only some give them one direction on the boddy and some nother according to fancy'.[77] Cook also observed that the Easter Islanders liked to paint their faces and other parts of their body red (using turmeric) and white (shell-lime). George Forster similarly noted in 1774 that 'the women were seldom satisfied with their natural brown colour, but painted the whole face with a reddish brown ruddle, over which they laid on the bright orange of the turmeric root; or ornamented themselves with elegant streaks of white shell-lime'.[78]

Women, too, were highly tattooed, from head to toe. Pattern and motif appeared to vary according to one's rank and status. These might also convey information. An old woman related in 1911 that the *rapa* or 'dance-paddle' tattooed on her back had been done when she had lost her virginity in early youth: for her, the tattoo 'represented' one of her first lovers.[79] In 1914 the British anthropologist Katherine Routledge was told on Easter Island that members of the Ra'ā *mata* had once tattooed themselves with a sun motif: *ra'ā* means 'sun'.[80] (Here, the tattoo was both emblem and writing.) The island's sacred site of Mata Ngarahu at 'Orongo must have been associated with tattooing at a very early date, since Tahiti's mythical originator of tattooing – Matamata 'Arahu – is cognate with the ancient Easter Island name.[81]

If Easter Islanders excelled in wood carving and tattooing, then they veritably transcended all Polynesian paradigms in their rock art, their *ahu* ceremonial architecture and their *mo'ai* anthropomorphic statuary.

The island's rock art is peerless. 'The astonishing technical skill and artistic ability reflected in the rock art of Easter Island', asserted the petroglyph expert Georgia Lee, 'is found nowhere else in Polynesia'.[82] Around 1,000 island sites, with more than 4,000 petroglyphs, contain a rich treasury of motifs and designs – symbols of power, prayers to the 'gods', as Lee astutely deemed them. Because of the stones' rapid weathering, much of what remains today is of recent date. But this vestigial library draws from a tradition that pre-dates island settlement. Designs and images were always incised into, or carved out of, rock for a variety of reasons: to create totems, mark territory, memorialize a person or event, or to accomplish any number of other things. Besides such invasive treatment, Easter Islanders also painted cave walls and the inside of stone houses with red-and-white birds, dance paddles and goggle-eyed faces, among other motifs.

Yet it is above all for its incomparable monumental architecture and statuary that Easter Island is celebrated throughout the world.

AHU AND MO'AI

Today it is primarily in the majestic *ahu* ('ceremonial stone platforms') and monolithic *mo'ai* ('anthropomorphic statues or statuettes') that the complexity of Easter Island's ancient culture is measured. (Here, original *mo'ai*, with glottal stop, takes precedence over the spelling *moai*, without the glottal stop, that was introduced in the 1880s.) Between the twelfth and fifteenth centuries AD, this complexity was fuelled by interaction with other East Polynesian islands. From the Australs to Hawai'i, similar holy precincts with statuary were being erected that today demonstrate a remarkably homogeneous evolution in use and design. With Easter Island's isolation about 1500, the dynamic waned.

During these three or four centuries the island's entire social impetus, it seems, was focused on erecting colossal platforms and statues – 'the most spectacular religious building compulsion known anywhere in Polynesia'.[83] Although acclaimed almost exclusively for its *mo'ai*, Easter Island deserves like awe for its *ahu*, of which at least 313 encircle the coastline (Map 2). The island's *ahu* is a variant of the East Polynesian *marae* (Hawaiian *heiau*) complex, including this holy precinct's enclosed court with raised altar at one end. (In other East Polynesian societies the word *ahu* refers specifically to this altar.)[84] 'The *ahu* concept was undoubtedly brought to Easter Island by the initial colonists, where it was elaborated and developed',[85] and this to a remarkably sophisticated degree.

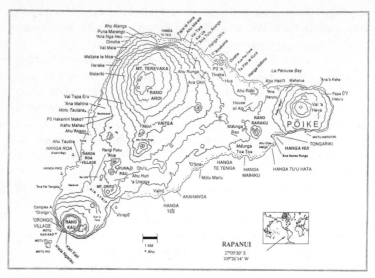

Map 2: Easter Island, with its coastal *ahu*.

Easter Island's original *ahu* began as a simple stone altar. Then early settlers enlarged this at one end, using a rubble core faced with dry-wall masonry; often this was of precisely carved and fitted monoliths. Already these earliest complexes – such as Vinapū 2 on the western south coast – counted among Polynesia's greatest achievements in communal engineering. The earliest platforms might have held ancestral figures of wood, too, as was common in the Marquesas and Hawai'i. About AD 700, *ahu* Tahai on Easter Island's west coast appears to have been a narrow, flat, rubble-fill platform enclosed by simple masonry; once it received its lateral extension, a small red-scoria statue may have adorned it. Many sites, such as *ahu* Naunau at 'Anakena, experienced several eras of building activity, with superimpositions and enlargements. Often, old discarded *mo'ai* served as masonry fill.

In this way, over centuries, small platforms expanded in a continuity of development 'characterized by gradual introduction of new ideas, expansion of themes and improvement of capacities'.[86] Consequently, Easter Island's *ahu* sequence reflects an 'unbroken chronological progression such as might be expected from the architectural reflection of the activities of a single continuously developing society'.[87]

A recent 'spatial distribution analysis' of Easter Island's *ahu* has determined that nearly all the structures are situated by the coasts and that very few are in the interior or at the extreme corners, Pōike and 'Orongo. Every 0.7 kilometre, it seems, an *ahu* punctuates the coastline, delineating descent-group areas and marking centres of socio-religious activity. 'Large structures are more evenly distributed over the island than small and middle sized, which mainly are found on the south and north coast.'[88]

Ahu were the product of local groups. Nowhere in ancient Polynesia did a central authority ever undertake the construction of local monuments: 'Easter Island could hardly have been the exception to this rule'.[89] The 'Golden Age' of *ahu* construction, *circa* 1250 to *circa* 1500, witnessed their adornment with large monolithic statues standing in tall rows, with platform wings gracing either side. It is possible that no stone statues at all were mounted on *ahu* until the thirteenth century or even the fourteenth.[90] And no further statues – or only very few – were erected on *ahu* after about 1500.

Those major subsistence projects of other prehistoric Polynesian societies – stone aqueducts, breadfruit pits, great fishponds, huge taro terraces and other things – are missing on Easter Island. Here, nearly all community effort was instead funnelled into the construction and erection of ever larger *ahu* and *moʻai* (and their connecting kerbed roads). Monuments in stone were the Easter Islanders' group expression, a voluntary effort performed for its promise of supernatural returns: 'rather like the medieval cathedral builders of Europe'.[91] Eventually, more than 125 *ahu* came to carry statues, most of these constructed between 1300 and 1500. The glorious fifteenth century finally witnessed Easter Island's 'cultural peak'. Whereupon, 'Economically and demographically, it was all downhill after that'.[92]

Yet it is Easter Island's *moʻai*, its monolithic statues, that will forever remain not only the island's emblem, but the quintessential Polynesian icon. At least in historic times, these *'aringa ora* ('living faces') 'served to maintain alive the memory of the ancestors'.[93] Their original significance remains unknown. In 1722 the island's European discoverer, the Dutchman Jacob Roggeveen, recorded that the Easter Islanders 'kindle fire in front of certain remarkably tall stone figures they set up; and thereafter squatting on their heels with heads bowed down, they bring the palms of their hands together and alternately raise and lower them'.[94] In 1774 James Cook collected the names of various statues and heard the word *'ariki* used in connection with some.[95] Twelve years later, the Frenchman La Pérouse noted only that 'the islanders show them respect'.[96]

Evidently the *moʻai* 'personified' in some fashion the living essence of high-ranking ancestors, maintaining a custom known in various forms throughout East Polynesia. Significant in this regard is the fact that, on Easter Island in 1770, the Spanish pilot Moraleda noted that the statues represented people of particular merit, worthy of being commemorated.[97] Further, the bas-relief designs on the back of several *moʻai* probably reproduce tattooed signs of rank.

Easter Islanders of every era apparently believed that the *moʻai* held special attributes and possessed great powers. In 1882 the German Wilhelm

Geiseler reported that 'even today every older Rapanui man knows well the name of each of the many idols, whether standing or fallen, [and] he shows great respect to the same'.[98] Since the concept of realistic individualized art did not exist in ancient Polynesia, no *mo'ai* bore an individualized appearance. All the same, each elicited a highly personal veneration. Indeed, this was perhaps the entire point of erecting a statue in the first place. Carving and erecting *mo'ai* between about 1250 and 1500 reflected the Islanders' surprising reinterpretation of what a ceremonial structure should comprise, marking a significant rupture with the ethos behind the older tradition of (assumed) imageless *ahu*. For the innovation signalled, above all, a shift in the island's style of authority:

> The unadorned *ahu* stand for a generalized religious authority, the images – if they are definitely not of gods – for a more personalized authority. The change in architectural interest from meticulous masonry work to a cruder construction suggests that the more personal authority lacked the stability of office of its predecessors. An apparent preoccupation with numbers of images rather than with quality of masonry is consistent with the assumption that military chiefs had begun to replace the exclusive authority of a religious ariki.[99]

That is, the individual personality had become a force to be reckoned with on Easter Island. The *ahu* Tongariki, with its fifteen towering *mo'ai*, is an extraordinary display of this shift of authority. Perhaps dating from the fifteenth century, it epitomizes better than any other monument on the island the emphasis of this cultural peak on personal aggrandizement and quantitative pomp – as then flaunted foremost by the three *mata* of the eastern 'Otu 'Iti *hānau*.

Nearly all erected *mo'ai* stood atop coastal *ahu*, their backs to the sea. The still-powerful ancestors were each facing their respective village, their immediate *ure*, and while working in their fields all Easter Islanders would look up to see them, the *ahu*, the entire holy precinct and the boundless sea beyond. The prospect oriented their existence, staked a claim to ancestral land. On a psychological level, the *mo'ai* 'probably provided considerable reassurance and [a feeling of] protection' as well.[100] On the larger social level, each row of *mo'ai* heralded economic strength: the difference between the east's colossal Tongariki and the west's small, though dignified, Tahai comprised a political statement of the first magnitude. Social hierarchy, too, was petrified in the island's *mo'ai*, since they were ever-present symbols of competing descent groups. The *mo'ai* were *mana* turned to stone.

So far, approximately 887 statues have been inventoried by modern researchers.[101] Nearly half of these – 397 – seemingly still await their transport (if the interpretation is correct), and this from where most were quarried: Rano Raraku ('Quarry Lake') in the east, in 'Otu 'Iti territory. All but 55 *mo'ai* are of Rano Raraku's porous, yellow-brown, volcanic tuff of ash and lapilli. (Non-tuff *mo'ai* were of basalt, trachyte or even red scoria from Puna Pau in the west.) Steel-hard on its exterior, the tuff is only slightly harder than chalk in its interior. It has been estimated that six men, working daily with *toki* or basalt hand adzes, could complete a 5-metre tuff *mo'ai* in twelve to fifteen months. Indeed, the actual carving was apparently far simpler than the transporting and erecting. More than 230 *mo'ai* found a place atop a village's *ahu*, and the respective wealth and power of each *ure* permitted it to erect from one (such as the west's graceful Ahu Huri 'a Ū Renga) to fifteen (the east's regal Tongariki). Each differs in height, width and / or weight. At some *ahu*, such as the west's 'A Kivi and north-east's Naunau at 'Anakena, the *mo'ai* are surprisingly homogeneous in all three aspects. At others, such as the west's Tahai, evidently the island's oldest, differences are striking.

More details about these wonders can be read in any one of several recent studies.[102] Important for a general history of Easter Island is the fact that for several centuries, without apparent interruption, everyone of both the Tu'u and 'Otu 'Iti *hānau* participated, either directly or indirectly, in such discrete competitive undertakings at eastern Rano Raraku. Later, perhaps in the fifteenth and sixteenth centuries, both quarried western Puna Pau for the red-scoria *pukao* or 'topknots'. Such island-wide co-operation, over centuries, would not have been possible in a society wracked by war or divided by territorial isolationism. So at least the island's *mo'ai* phase – the 'Image *ahu* Period' as it is sometimes called – had to be one of relative peace (perhaps periodically punctuated by minor conflict). During this same period, however, the Pōike Peninsula's population, in the far east, apparently kept apart from everyone else (see below).

The facts surrounding certain social dynamics of *mo'ai* production are only now becoming clear, such as that, just as with *ahu* construction, competition lay primarily in size and numbers.[103] Especially in the 1400s, both *ahu* and *mo'ai* increased tremendously in size. Certainly, prestige was a motivating factor here. Kin-group teamwork in design, management and engineering had suddenly prompted an island-wide synergism of creativity, producing ever larger and more imposing platforms and statues. Each *ure*, in fact, was vying with immediate neighbours, even within the same *mata*, to raise quality and quantity of production. In other words, Easter Island's was a positive society, targeting visible growth. For the phenomenon was tapping that essential resource of all early East Polynesians, one that enabled the successful colonization of nearly every inhabitable island there: communal enterprise.

Forming a highly specialized profession, expert Easter Island sculptors, like the legendary U'u Rata Hui, were highly privileged *tuhunga*, their status an inheritance through the male line, their name defying the centuries. Apparently, while carving at Rano Raraku's '*mo'ai* factory', the image sculptors would be supplied with food by farmers and fishermen. An informant in the 1930s related that elders had earlier recalled how 'expert stone carvers ... received orders from people who wanted a monument for their *ahu*. They worked under the leadership of a master ... and were paid in fish, lobsters, and eels'.[104] These were no 'guilds', but kinship-based groups of labourers working together 'for the benefit of their own kin groups and invoking their own '*atua* or *akuaku* for assistance'.[105] The figures were hand-carved out of Rano Raraku's higher rock face, then lowered down the slope with thick fibre cables into prepared pits, to stand erect awaiting transport to a distant *ahu*. (Some scholars believe that at least some of Rano Raraku's standing *mo'ai* might have been meant for permanent display there.)

A variety of transport methods was probably used. This was enabled through a sophisticated road system of cut-and-fill construction, with kerbstones and post holes at crucial points. Some *mo'ai* might even have been floated to a coastal site on large timbers. Statue size, above all, appears to have determined method. Once at the *ahu*, the erect *mo'ai* would have been tilted by timber levers on alternate sides as logs or stones were inserted underneath, gradually raising it to the desired level. Then it was slowly edged into position. Probably in the fifteenth (but perhaps also in the sixteenth) century, the cylindrical red-scoria *pukao* or 'topknot' – this might have represented a distinguishing headdress – that topped only statues on the largest and most important *ahu*, were most likely pulled atop their tall *mo'ai* on wooden beams.[106] Once erected on the platform, the *mo'ai* finally had their eye sockets carved out. These, perhaps only at special times, were garnished with white-coral 'eyes', their red-scoria pupils directed heavenward. (Mangareva's traditional name for Pitcairn – 'Mata ki te Rangi' or 'Eyes Towards the Heavens' – possibly recalls identical statuary there.) Finished *mo'ai* on platforms ranged from 2 to nearly 10 metres in height. Particularly with eyes in place, such an occupied *ahu* had to be awe-inspiring.

Once lack of resources hampered transportation and reduced food supplies, *mo'ai* production ceased. (Socio-religious targeting came only later; see chapter Two.) Even during the island's 'cultural peak', it appears that things were rapidly winding down. Island traditions indicate that quarrels over food became a frequent problem. When a *nuahine* or 'crone' who cooked for the carvers was denied her rightful share of a fine lobster, as one story relates, she avenged herself by telling 'all the images to fall down, and thus brought the work to a standstill'.[107] Such traditions are today generally assumed to

indicate that it was a breakdown of the system of distribution, the exchange networks and the feeding of the craftsmen by the farmers and fishermen that finally halted the group co-operation that was so vital to the enterprise. The abandonment of work at Rano Raraku was not necessarily the sudden dramatic downing of tools so beloved of the mystery writers, but is more likely to have been a more gradual winding down and disintegration of the system: in short, work quickly ground to a halt because of an ever-increasing imbalance between the production of essentials (food) and that of non-essentials (statues).[108]

This occurred most pronouncedly towards the end of the fifteenth century, so that, by the sixteenth, few, if any, *mo'ai* were being carved and moved.

In a related social phenomenon, the offshore islets of Motu Nui and Motu 'Iti in the south-west were always prized for their obsidian and, later, once land birds had been annihilated, for their bird life as an important source of protein. In apparent veneration of this bounty, a special centre was established on the south-western cusp of the Rano Kau volcano: 'Orongo. Originally consisting of one or two *ahu*-like 'terraces', the site also held an attendant holy precinct. Most prominently, it overlooked the islets and especially Motu Nui's bird life. Long a site imbued with *mana* and laden with *tapu*, 'Orongo's original purpose remains unknown. (An analogous myth from the Society Islands would suggest that Mata Ngarahu, 'Orongo's holiest area, might have commemorated East Polynesia's creator of tattooing.) Since frigate birds undoubtedly nested on Motu Nui and were also venerated in some way, these became forever connected with 'Orongo as an identifiable icon. Shortly after 1400, the terraces were abandoned. Islanders then constructed oval stone houses at the same site for some unknown purpose.[109]

Certainly 'Orongo hosted an early ritual associated with Motu Nui, first eggs and perhaps even a human-bird concept. Possibly this obtained as early as the sixteenth century, once the voyaging sphere had collapsed and Easter Island had become isolated from Mangareva. (The later Birdman ritual incorporated and expanded this original concept; see chapter Two.) After about 1540 'Orongo comprised approximately 50 stone houses of corbelled roofs, aligned in a half-ellipse facing the offshore islets. Probably the site's function then was to accommodate participants at periodical rituals in which birds and fertility played a central role.

Before the eighteenth century, two such rituals apparently dominated Easter Island culture: the *pōki manu* ('Bird Child') and the *pōki take* ('White Tern Child'?), both 'rites of passage' initiating the island's young into adult society. Boys of between 13 and 15 years of age were secluded on Motu Nui for three months. Then a ceremony was held at 'Orongo with a *tangata tapu manu* or 'Bird Holy Man': the boy had his head shaved, then gave the holy man an egg, whereupon the latter bestowed on the boy a name for insertion in the ritual. Singing and dancing then took place in front of the stone houses.[110] Girls, on the other hand, had had their clitoris or labia majora lengthened from an early age, a practice common throughout pre-missionary East Polynesia. Between 13 and 15 years of age they, too, would then participate at an equally important ritual at 'Orongo, whereby a *tuhunga* would inspect the girls' genital enhancement as they stood spread-eagled between two boulders. If their enhancement was deemed successful, a special ceremony then initiated the candidates into womanhood. Whereupon the same *tuhunga* immortalized the girls' *komari* or labia as a petroglyph on a nearby boulder. (Wooden *mo'ai* or statuettes that prominently featured lengthened labia were also carved.) Easter Island's 'passport to womanhood' survives today ... as the island's most frequent petroglyph motif.[111]

EXPANSION

The cumulative weight of principally the archæological and palæobotanical evidence from Easter Island 'points to an early centre of habitation on the island's south-west corner, more or less where the population is gathered today'.[112] Island tradition relates how each new 'ariki mau first occupied *ahu* 'A Kapu, just north of the Tahai complex on the west coast. Further north, at *ahu* Te Peu, can be seen the island's largest *hare pa'enga* (a stone-kerbed boat-shaped structure for high-status individuals), that of Tu'u ko Iho, mythical co-founder of the island population, who also 'brought the statues to the island and caused them to walk'. Tahai, 'A Kapu, Te Peu (and perhaps also Vinapū 2, on the western end of the south coast): probably these were the salient population centres in the first centuries of settlement. The general territory was also the cradle of the royal Miru *mata*, which gave rise to the dominant Tu'u *hānau*.

Perhaps every 150 years, the population doubled. Since food and water were abundant, epidemic diseases unknown and dangerous neighbours non-existent, an even more rapid expansion was possible. With increased population, migration to other attractive island locations followed. 'Anakena in the north-east possibly received its first colony from the west coast in the late eighth or early ninth century AD; by 1100, an elaborate *ahu* – precursor of the presently visible *ahu* Naunau (today boasting re-erected *mo'ai*) – had been constructed there (illus. 3).[113]

The *kumara* or sweet potato (*Ipomoea batatas*) added an alimentary boost to a population already beginning to suffer from the first dearth of certain island resources. About AD 1100, if not a century earlier, Easter Island scouts probably sailed east to South America, acquired there the *kumara* and possibly also the *hue* or bottle gourd (*Lagenaria vulgaris*), then returned to central East Polynesia – probably to the eastern Tuamotus – with these valuable introductions, which, in time, also found their way to Hawai'i and New

3 *Ahu* Naunau at 'Anakena, Easter Island's last indigenous capital.

Zealand.[114] The scouts would then have returned to Easter Island by way of Mangareva, Pitcairn and Henderson – that is, using the then still-active voyaging sphere. Because of their temperate climate, both Māoris and Easter Islanders would eventually make the *kumara* their staple food crop; Easter Islanders even let *kumara* eclipse taro, until then their main cultivar, at a time when sources of running water, essential for abundant taro production, were beginning to diminish. (In 1774 James Cook praised the Easter Island sweet potato as the best he had ever tasted.)[115] By the beginning of the twentieth century, 25 varieties of *kumara* were still being cultivated on the island.[116]

It appears likely that, in or around the thirteenth century, Marquesans swept down into the eastern Tuamotus, then on to Mangareva (and perhaps Pitcairn and Henderson as well), subjugating resident populations and replacing dominant descent groups with Marquesan-speaking colonists. Although still connected at this time to the South-east Polynesian voyaging sphere, Easter Islanders seem to have escaped this Marquesan incursion. The upshot of the Marquesans' arrival was to render Easter Island society, which had remained 'original' South-east Polynesian, even more archaic and vestigial than that of its (probable) home island Mangareva, which was forced to adopt Marquesan innovations. (About a century later, Marquesan-influenced Mangarevans went on to establish the first-ever settlement at Rapa in the Austral Islands in the distant south-west; Rapa's name, in the Rapan language, means 'Extremity'.)

For their first few centuries on the island, the Easter Islanders had concentrated their agriculture on the western coastal zone. Only about AD 1100 were upland areas cleared and settled.[117] At the same time, the Pōike (lit. 'Hill') Peninsula, comprising the island's eastern terminus, was settled by migrating villagers seeking new farmland. Throughout the 'Golden Age' of *ahu* and *mo'ai* production, Pōike's descent group refrained from participating in the communal quarrying at Rano Raraku. (Only two of Pōike's dozens of statues are of Rano Raraku tuff.) For reasons still unknown, they always remained a people apart. By the latter part of the thirteenth century, however, Pōike's population had already grown to such an extent that the rich forestland there was beginning to suffer: about 1280, eastern Pōike experienced a dramatic change in its ecosystem, with an obvious expansion of local agriculture.[118] Its *Jubæa* palm forest was cleared in a short period of time 'to open the landscape in the down-slope areas for new ceremonial places, dwellings and agriculture. Less than 200 years later the deforestation and the beginning of agriculture reached the upper slope' of Pū'a Katiki crowning the hill.[119] Great sheet erosion ensued, first ruining the cultivated soil then burying the *ahu* and dwellings. As a result, eastern Pōike's land use ceased by 1400. The forest of south-west Pōike was cleared about 1380–1480. The *Jubæa* palms of north-west Pōike were annihilated about 1440. Within a space of a couple of centuries, the entire peninsula had become treeless. By 1500 it lay denuded and eroding. The people of Pōike were left no alternative, and 'back-migrated', that is, they returned to ancestral lands in the west and north. Pōike 's fate was an omen for all Easter Islanders.

By 1500, however, the island's eastern territories had never known greater power. For after *circa* 1300 the 'Otu 'Iti 'confederation' of *mata* had grown populous, producing surpluses that enabled extravagant construction projects flaunting affluence and authority. Rano Raraku itself, the statue quarry, lay within the *kāinga*, the territory, of the 'Otu 'Iti. The western and northern Tu'u were no longer wielding absolute power on Easter Island. Above all, it had become the Tūpa 'Otu (Tūpahotu) *mata* of the 'Otu 'Iti, who were heralding in stone that they were now a force to reckon with on the island. The visible symbol of this new socio-economic focus was their own Tongariki, Easter Island's largest *ahu*, boasting fifteen gigantic *mo'ai*.

Today, Tongariki still emanates majesty. Its central platform, nearly 100 metres long, flaunts two wings at either side that extend its total length to approximately 220 metres. In all, the site holds more than 800 (crudely fitted) basalt blocks. The seaward wall averages 4 metres in height. The fifteen exceptionally tall statues – from 5.6 to 8.7 metres – weigh, on average, more than 40 tonnes. Together with their *pukao* 'topknots', they would have brought the complex to a height of 14 metres. In AD 1500 the holy precinct would have been the island's fulcrum.

This most dynamic century of island history witnessed not only the accelerated construction of such imposing *ahu* as Tongariki, with ever more and larger *mo'ai*, but also the implementation of larger field systems of agriculture, accompanied by intensive upland occupation (after about 1425). Yet in the riot lay the rot. Already by about 1400 the Little Ice Age had begun, which progressively impeded inter-island voyaging. (By about 1500 Easter Islanders would have lost contact with their neighbours on Henderson, Pitcairn and Mangareva, after which their memory – as a collective 'Hiva' or 'Out There' – became legend; the few Polynesians on Pitcairn and Henderson still continued to trade with the more populous Mangarevans well into the sixteenth century, but then they abandoned both islands forever.) It is possible that timber for voyaging vessels, as well as for deep-sea fishing, was no longer to be had on Easter Island. The island's caves and rock shelters began to be used regularly, indicating increased shore fishing – presumably to feed a larger population, but perhaps also to compensate for declining land resources because of deforestation and soil leaching.[120]

For, from the 1300s, when the Islanders had begun rapidly to colonize the south coast, soils there had become excessively drained. Soon, moisture was lacking. So farmers started using lithic mulch – skull-sized rocks placed apart in order to protect the soil base and enhance its moisture content (a practice still witnessed, and praised, by La Pérouse in 1786).[121] Because of the swiftly growing population, Easter Islanders everywhere were then forced to occupy areas of ever-poorer soils, as forest degradation continued apace. Finally, by the late 1500s, upland farms were simply no longer productive: they were abandoned. Whereupon even greater dependence was made on marine resources, which, in turn, then experienced serious depletion.

All this led to social conflict. Of course, this was not the island's first. It is perhaps naïve to trumpet Easter Island's 'amazing peace of a thousand years',[122] if only for the fact that the Old Rapanui language abounded with the Proto-Polynesian vocabulary of war, warriors and weapons. Doubtless there had been many conflicts over many centuries. But overall, exchange systems continued, or were always resumed. Even when *mo'ai* carving and transport ceased almost entirely, about 1500, island exchange systems apparently remained in place and large-scale warfare was still unknown. Easter Islanders abandoned the large communal projects only because they lacked the necessary resources for these, not because their society collapsed into anarchy. Yet trouble was brewing.

For those tall *mo'ai* atop Tongariki's *ahu*? the ones so pompously adorned with 2-metre-high 'topknots'? – they were not royal Miru of the leading Tu'u *hānau*. They were *'urumanu*, 'commoners', of the inferior 'Otu 'Iti. And they were flamboyantly lording over a landscape all but denuded of palm forests and larger scrub. Gone was the absolute secular authority of the *'ariki mau*, as well as the territorial supremacy of the Miru *mata*. Shortly before this period, the Miru may have established north-eastern 'Anakena as their new royal capital, provokingly bordering the 'Otu 'Iti *kāinga*. But new wealth and power – and, with it, temporal authority – lay with the eastern 'Otu 'Iti, who perhaps had long resented Tu'u absolutism. The first break between the Tu'u and the 'Otu 'Iti came perhaps already in the 'glorious' fifteenth century, which, as it heralded in stone the rise of the eastern 'upstarts', also announced the descent of the white-skinned *'ariki* and his kin.

Evidence for this abounds in island lore. The famous legend of the battle between the *hānau momoko* or 'slim tribe' and the *hānau 'e'epe* or 'stocky tribe' (later erroneously translated as the 'Short Ears' and 'Long Ears'), the first allegedly of a western *ahu* and the second from Pōike,[123] recalls the division of the island into the two competing *hānau* of the Tu'u and the 'Otu 'Iti. It is possible that the legend recalls an actual conflict that took place north of Tongariki between these two 'nations', perhaps as early as the sixteenth century. Later traditions specifically identify by name the Tu'u and 'Otu 'Iti (Hotu 'Iti, Hotuiti), recalling a 'war' that probably occurred in the eighteenth century (see chapter Two).

Between 1500 and about 1675, in the down-slope area of south-west Pōike, renewed efforts at agriculture continued apace on open land. Yet even here cultivation was difficult. As with so much of the island at this time, reduced soil fertility was leading to the wholesale abandonment of fields, gardens and even ceremonial *ahu*. Nearly everywhere on Easter Island, grass had replaced wood as fuel. Over time, centuries-old villages lost entire populations. The erstwhile 'garden paradise' had become a crowded desert isle.

ENVIRONMENTAL COLLAPSE

By the end of the seventeenth century things were critical. Ironically, it had possibly been the *kiore*, the tiny Polynesian rat, and not humans, that had wreaked most havoc. Their eating of the small *Jubæa* nuts had prevented the giant palm's regrowth. So whenever Islanders felled a palm – primarily for their earth ovens, but also for cropland clearance, construction and *mo'ai* transport – no seedling would replace it. Over centuries, vast forests shrank to nothing. (Fragments of palms from Ma'unga Tari suggest that some might have survived into the sixteenth century, perhaps even into historic times; but no eighteenth-century visitor witnessed them.)[124] The removal of the forest cover had increased local temperature and humidity, causing greater erosion and leaching of the soil. As the evaporation rate increased, the soil became more porous. Drainage worsened; water was poorly retained. Perennial and intermittent streams – even important springs – dried up entirely. (Puna Pau, the red-scoria quarry, means 'Exhausted Spring' in Old Rapanui, a name perhaps dating from this time.) Only the three crater swamps, isolated pools in lava tubes and a handful of springs – such as Vai Tapa Eru, inland from Te Peu

– provided fresh water. Indeed, water access and management became major issues, leading to greater competition, perhaps even to sporadic conflict. Agricultural practices had to change dramatically. Gone were the large taro paddies in well-watered ravines, such as those just east of Vaitea in the middle of the island. They were replaced everywhere by dry-field cultivation of kumara, yams and sugar cane using lithic mulch, as well as *manavai* or 'stone garden enclosures' for bananas and paper-mulberry.

Yet it got even harder. To retain rainwater, stone basins were adzed out of rock faces. Once Easter Island's bird resources were wholly depleted, occasional voyages in patched-together canoes to Sala-y-Gómez, a small reef 415 kilometres to the north-east, were hazarded in order to gather seabird eggs and young – an extremely perilous journey, something only near-famine might prompt. But even this lifeline broke when wood for seagoing vessels disappeared. By about 1700, if not already a century earlier, the island was indeed like a desert, its flora almost wholly destroyed. (And so it would remain until the present day.) 'There is no other oceanic island of comparable dimensions, geology and climate with such a poor native flora.'[125]

Yet the Easter Islanders coped, somehow maintaining their production of essential crops. Soon, short-term visitors would even find the island 'fruitful'. Indeed, in 1722 the Dutchman Roggeveen held the island to be

exceedingly fruitful, producing bananas, potatoes, sugar cane of remarkable thickness, and many other kinds of the fruits of the earth, although destitute of large trees and domestic animals, except poultry. This place, as far as its rich soil and good climate are concerned, is such that it might be made into an earthly Paradise, if it were properly worked and cultivated; which is now only done in so far as the Inhabitants are obliged to for the maintenance of life.[126]

At least outwardly, there was no exigency, no warfare. Although not thriving, Easter Islanders were at least managing food production and so surviving their reduced circumstances. Their life held no immediate desperation. The first visitors to the island even witnessed a surplus of food. Indeed, the place seemed blesssed with 'rich soil and good climate'. If anything, these visitors met a vigorous, healthy, dynamic people with seemingly everything they needed to survive. [127]

But appearances might have been deceiving. Being produced in the eighteenth century, in great numbers, were statuettes of an emaciated male with ribs showing – the famous *mo'ai kavakava* that now grace the world's leading museums – that might have mirrored the factual Easter Island, the one that knew frequent famine. The extremely high incidence of dental caries and bone porosion, now being measured by osteologists in the skeletons of early

Islanders, resulted from a carbohydrate-rich diet seriously insufficient in iron and calcium.[128] Not only seabirds, but even fish were becoming scarce, it seems. Local marine resources begin to show early signs of depletion about 1400. About a century later, fewer hook manufacturers were using the island's rock shelters: this is because the lack of large timber trees had limited the number and size of canoes for offshore fishing. All fishing was reduced to near-shore activities, in small two-man canoes of sewn-together planks. Dolphin bones begin disappearing from the archæological record at this time.[129] An abundance of fresh fish was a thing of the past – and as a result Easter Islanders were suffering.

The last forest on Easter Island may have been cut – probably for firewood – about 1640.[130] After this, among the most precious things on the island was wood. Driftwood became a gift of the 'gods'. The pan-Polynesian word *rākau* ('tree, wood, timber') came to mean 'riches' or 'wealth' in the Old Rapanui language of Easter Island, a meaning attached to the word nowhere else in Polynesia.

Perhaps there had been a population crash. By the second half of the seventeenth century entire villages might already have starved to death. Or, because of malnutrition, many Easter Island women might have become infertile. Both possibilities would have given the reduced number of their descendants in the early eighteenth century better chances for survival – giving the short-term visitors who encountered them and their ways the impression of 'plenty'. The noticeable decline in food remains, in particular marine foods, in island shelters from this time might indeed reflect a sudden and drastic population decline. Similarly, obsidian or volcanic glass, traditionally used for cutting all sorts of things, all but disappears in the archæological record for some fifty years.[131]

Certainly no cultural collapse occurred, however. Although under mounting pressure from the eastern 'Otu 'Iti's more aggressive *matato'a* or 'professional warriors', at the beginning of the eighteenth century the *'ariki mau* apparently still wielded most, but not all, secular and religious authority. Periodically, the ten *mata* still met at 'Orongo to observe such time-honoured traditions as the *pōki manu* and *pōki take* initiations. And though *mo'ai* production had long ceased, the *mata* were nevertheless actively constructing or renovating everywhere but at Pōike, albeit under material constraint that limited style and size. Above all, no significant warfare disturbed island-wide exchange systems. For it was still the revered ancestral deities of old – Tangaroa, Tāne, Rongo, Tu'u, Hiro – that ultimately ruled Easter Island.

But suddenly aliens landed.

two

White Men and Birdmen

In the second century AD, the Alexandrian mathematician and geographer Ptolemy depicted on his celebrated maps a *Terra Australis Incognita* or 'Unknown Southern Land' some ten degrees south of the equator. Yet it was not until the 1500s that Europeans finally had the climate, funds, technology and motivation to ply the Pacific in order to discover what actually lay there. The rivalry between Portugal and Spain for control of the 'Spice Islands' (now part of Indonesia) in the early 1500s had inspired, in particular, Spain's historic voyages of Pacific exploration; her acquisition of the Philippines; and her 'Acapulco Run' between Mexico and Manila that, for many centuries, rendered the Pacific the 'Spanish Highway'.

With the establishment of the Dutch East Indies Company in 1602, the Dutch took the lead in Pacific exploration. All through the century, the Company actively sought out new lands to exploit commercially: in 1642 Abel Tasman, for example, 'discovered' Van Dieman's Land (Tasmania) and New Zealand on behalf of the Company. The Company, however, resented any non-Company Dutch presence in the region. Schouten and Le Maire's historic voyage of 1615–16, they believed, had been interference. Once the Netherlands had wrested jurisdiction from Portugal in the 1670s, Batavia (Jakarta, on the island of Java) became Company headquarters. From there, the Dutch East Indies Company was similarly to describe Jacob Roggeveen's epic Pacific callings in 1722 as 'criminal trespass', although the Dutchman's firsts included Samoa, Bora Bora – and Easter Island.

On Easter Island itself, by the early 1700s the peak population of approximately 12,000 that might have been attained in the fourteenth and fifteenth centuries had perhaps shrunk, because of possible starvation and malnutrition leading to sterility, to as few as 6,000 souls. Certainly Easter Islanders had never forgotten the outside world. Perpetuated in legend were the names of islands and villages still on the tip of everyone's tongue (only to be lost in the nineteenth century). But because the voyaging sphere that once had linked them to Mangarevans, Pitcairn and Henderson Islanders and others had been defunct for some two centuries, 'Out There' – always the *Hiva* of Easter Island tradition – was no longer simply a physical destination: it was also a metaphor for otherworldliness, the range of sacred migrating albatrosses and frigate birds that nested at Easter Island.

Hiva was the tangible correlate to intangible Pō, the realm of night where the dead went. Pō was simply the supernatural extension of Hiva, and was just as real. Both Hiva and Pō, fact and fiction, were one conceptual unity in the prehistoric Easter Island psyche. As the albatross and frigate bird arrived from Hiva, so, too, could Easter Island's *tangata tapu manu* or 'Bird Holy Man' fly to Hiva, to Pō, to visit the ancestral spirits. Only he could leave Easter Island – albeit in a trance.

Many an Islander possibly wished to accompany him, in order to escape. For human-induced ecological disaster had brought Easter Island to the brink of collapse. Although the *'ariki mau* was still wielding most temporal and religious authority by the beginning of the eighteenth century, his *mana* had been seriously eroded. The eastern *matato'a* – the professional warriors and warrior-leaders – were swiftly usurping all secular power on the island. They were even encroaching on the *'ariki mau*'s sacral privilege. By 1722 it had clearly not yet reached open warfare between the upstart 'Otu 'Iti warriors and traditional Tu'u *'ariki*. But Islanders were in desperate straits. Above all, there was universal alarm about the apparent supernatural desertion: island resources were exhausted, society was teetering. At which moment the white men arrived.

THE DUTCH

Some early accounts allege that the Spanish explorer Alvaro de Mendaña (1567) or the English buccaneer Edward Davis (1687) were the first Europeans to reach Easter Island. Proof exists for neither visit, however; the cumulative weight of evidence even gainsays both. Rather, the first non-Polynesian visitors to Easter Island were certainly Jacob Roggeveen's three cosmopolitan crews in the year 1722, who then introduced the island to the world at large.

Fulfilling a plan devised by his father already in 1671, Jacob Roggeveen – a doctor of law who had served in Batavia as Council of Justice to the Dutch East Indies Company – on his return to the Netherlands secured the backing of the partially competing, but vastly smaller, West Indies Company for a grand voyage of discovery.[1] By then aged 62, Roggeveen commanded the fleet of three ships – the *Arend* (Captain Jan Coster), *Thienhoven* (Captain Cornelis Bouman) and *Africaansche Galey* (Captain Roelof Rosendaal) – that departed from Holland's island of Texel on

1 August 1721 bound for the South Pacific to seek the legendary Terra Australis, for the glory and profit of the Netherlands.

In the late afternoon of 5 April 1722 – Easter Sunday – Captain Rosendaal of the smaller and faster *Africaansche Galey*, sailing ahead as ever, sighted an island 'to west by south'. It was not on Schouten and Le Maire's chart, but, as Captain Bouman later penned, 'at this last position we found an island on van Ceulen's map'.[2] Whereupon the *Africaansche Galey*, as Roggeveen himself wrote,

> headed into the wind in order to wait for us, giving a signal of seeing land . . . we asked what she had seen, whereupon it was answered that they had seen very distinctly ahead to starboard a low flat island . . . Hereupon it was found fitting . . . to let drift so as to wait for the coming of the day. All three ships grouped and waited offshore until the following day. This being thus decided, we gave to Captain Bouman, who was astern, the relevant information and to the land the name of Paasch Eiland [Easter Island] because it was discovered and found by us on Easter Day.[3]

On 6 April Roggeveen finally saw the island for himself. The fleet cruised along its coast, sighting smoke – a clear indication of habitation. It was decided to venture ashore the next day in order to acquire fresh vegetables and fruit from these 'natives'. But 7 April brought lightning, thunder and rain. The landing was postponed for one more day.

Yet as the fleet abided in the middle of the storm, a lone Islander in a canoe approached the *Thienhoven* while still 3 nautical miles distant from the middle of the north-east coast – possibly just outside Hanga 'o Honu (now called Hanga Ho'onu), off *ahu* He Ki'i. Captain Bouman immediately brought the emissary to Commander Roggeveen in the *Arend*. This first Islander to welcome Europeans was

> a man well into his fifties, of the browns, with a goatee after the Turkish fashion, of very strong physique. He was much astonished at the make of our ship and all that belonged to it, as we could perceive from his expressions. As we could not in the least understand each other, we had to make it out from his expressions and signs. We gave him a small mirror, wherein he looked at himself, at which he was very frightened, as also at the sound of the bell. We gave him a glass of brandywine, which he poured over his face, and when he felt the strength of it he began to open his eyes wide. We gave him a second glass of brandywine with a biscuit, none of which he used. He had some shame because of his nakedness when he saw that we were clothed. He went therefore and

put his arms and head on the table, appearing by this to make a speech to his deity, as was evident from his actions, and raised his head and hands many times to the sky, used many words in a loud voice, being engaged thus for half an hour, and when he stopped this he began to leap and sing. He showed himself very merry and gay. We tied a piece of sailcloth in front of his private parts, which wonderfully pleased him. He was naturally cheerful of face.[4]

Captain Bouman also sensed that the man

felt ashamed because of his nakedness as he saw that we were all dressed. Therefore he put his arms and head on the table and it seemed he addressed his gods about this, as we could clearly see from his movements: he raised his head and hands many times toward heaven, and used many words in a loud voice. He was busy in this way for about a half an hour.[5]

Yet no Easter Islander would have felt a Christian sense of 'shame' at being naked: most males, and all girls before puberty, nearly always went naked. If anything, the Islander would have been most struck by the fact that just about every single one of these visitors had skin as white as that of the *'ariki mau* and his immediate family: a manifest sign of royal lineage. Almost certainly he was reacting to a perceived *tapu* – something that the crew on the *Arend* clearly did not understand. The man's loud and long chanting was effected to remove this *tapu*. This identifies him as a *tumu ivi 'atua*, a shaman. As the right hand to *tangata hōnui*, he was the perfect emissary to the first visitors to Easter Island in probably more than two centuries. When the Islander afterwards demonstrated great gaiety, singing and dancing, this undoubtedly denoted his having successfully removed the first immediate *tapu*, that of initial contact, which result always demanded a public display. 'Then we ordered the violin to be played for him', noted Bouman further, 'and he danced with the sailors.' The comico-pathetic interface of two mutually ignorant cultures.

The German Carl Friederich Behrens observed it all, noting how their guest was 'very peculiarly painted' – meaning tattooed – and was brown, with long stretched ears hanging down to his shoulders.[6] He was 'rather tall, rather strong of limb and pleasant of face, sprightly of figure, agreeable in speech and gestures'. He had danced together with the sailors only after they had taken him by the hand (for this dancing was different from the ritual lifting of the first *tapu*).

Yet he departed reluctantly from us, and raised his hands, turned with his eyes towards the land and forcefully started to cry out these words: O dorroga! O dorroga! and wished no return to his skiff, but made to believe he would remain with us, that we ourselves with our ship should bring him to land. I wholly believe, through the aforementioned forceful cry he was invoking his God, as one then could discern and see on the beach very many of their erected idols.[7]

'O dorroga!', the first indigenous words recorded on Easter Island, was actually Old Rapanui *otoroka* ('welcome!'), a now-extinct salutation.[8] The shaman was still enacting his official welcome: he was letting them know in no uncertain terms that he was performing a prescribed ritual – perhaps one that had been commonplace during the voyaging-sphere era. (Such welcoming rituals are still customary today among the Māori, Tongans, Samoans and others.) That is, the *tumu ivi 'atua* was trying to inform the white men that he personally had to escort them to land, in order to uphold traditional etiquette and to avoid violation of the arrival *tapu*.

The Dutch were having none of it. The wind had increased, the island now lay only two nautical miles south-southwest. They had to win distance, and so their guest had to leave. 'He showed little inclination to leave', penned Bouman later. 'In order to get rid of him we had him brought to his boat but he kept paddling next to our ships until he saw that we were moving away from the coast. Only then did he return to the island.'[9] Roggeveen had given the man the mirror, a pair of scissors and some small gifts, and the Islander had seemed pleased with these.

By 8 April the weather had improved, and so two sloops of marines rowed near the shore, probably in Hanga 'o Honu just off of He Ki'i. Intimidated, however, by the great number of 'very properly dressed' Islanders – who were evidently fitted out in their finest feathers and *tapa* for the extraordinary event – beckoning to them to land and be welcomed, the marines grew afraid and returned to the fleet. They made a full report of what they had seen to Commander Roggeveen and the three captains. Evidently the *tumu ivi 'atua*'s own report of what he had experienced aboard the white men's ship had been favourably received, for Islanders began arriving off all three ships in small canoes and 'swimming on bundles of tied reeds'. Climbing aboard, the Islanders appeared not in the least frightened of the foreigners, as if they had been receiving overseas guests for years. As gifts, they presented living and roasted chickens as well as bananas, which the Dutch gratefully accepted.

Nonetheless, 'they were big thieves, taking everything that they could lay their hands on', noted Bouman. Above all, they grabbed anything of wood: 'worn brooms, broken spokes, firewood and such things, and jumped overboard with them and swam to the coast'.

The Islanders returned the next day, eagerly boarding the ships with chickens, yams and bananas. Whereupon they began snatching hats and caps off the sailors' heads and springing overboard with them. One Islander climbed straight from his canoe into a porthole of the *Africaansche Galey* to pilfer a tablecloth. Yet the Dutch remained unruffled, having received from their robbers direly needed fruit, vegetables and chickens. If anything, they were bemused by the thieving, especially by the Islanders' odd coveting of 'wooden trash'. All the more inexplicable, then, is Behrens's comment that 'one of those who were in the vessels was suddenly shot, whereupon they all sprang into the water and swam away'.[10]

The Dutch spent only one day ashore: 10 April 1722. Although Behrens claimed that 'I was the first, at the landing of our people, to set foot on the island', the declaration cannot be taken at face value; elsewhere in his account Behrens exaggerates wildly. The cosmopolitan crew landed at 7 o'clock in the morning with 137 men in five sloops at 'high cliffs', probably in Hanga 'o Honu. Bouman observed that the Islanders carried no weapons of any kind, but rather approached in masses to welcome them, 'hopping and jumping for joy' – perhaps a ritual dance to welcome the visitors.

Twenty men remained on shore to guard the sloops. The main landing party ascended the slope and began marching inland. Suddenly, back on the beach, a single musket shot split the air. Whereupon a cascade of musketry followed (illus. 4). At once the officers, including Roggeveen, turned back to investigate: some ten to twelve Islanders (Bouman later wrote 'nine to ten') lay dead, around them a larger number of wounded; not one European seemed to be harmed in any way. All the remaining Islanders had fled 'into the mountains'. Roggeveen was hurriedly told that an Islander had tried to steal a musket while another had attempted to rip a shirt off the back of its wearer, at which moment a scuffle had broken out and the landing party, fearing for their lives, had started shooting Islanders at random.

Despite his grave concern not only for the safety of his landing party but also for the dead and wounded Islanders, Roggeveen proceeded to the closest village in order to inspect the Islanders' dwellings – 'in which we found absolutely nothing', Bouman later logged.[11] All the entrances lay on the north-east, facing the shore. And he saw some 'small coconut palms' (perhaps remnants of *Jubæa*). The Dutch were preparing to quit the village for the beach when, as Bouman noticed,

> an inhabitant approached us quietly, wearing a crown of white feath-
> ers on his head, a white dress and a white shell hanging on his breast.
> Even when still walking he showed homage by stooping. He laid a
> bunch of bananas down on the ground at least thirty steps from us
> and then galloped away like a horse. But when he saw that this was

4   This earliest known depiction of Easter Island highlights the bloodshed that occurred during Roggeveen's landing, 10 April 1722.

agreeable to us, he returned together with other inhabitants, bringing more chickens, bananas and young plants. They again laid them down together with sugar cane. We only took the chickens and the bananas.[12]

Bouman described how, while they were walking back to the beach, this 'chief', evidently terrified by the musketry and the deaths it had caused, made others bring the Europeans more chickens and bananas. But few of these foodstuffs were to be found ('they were not very well provided with these'). Finally recognizing the Islanders' poverty, the officers compensated them with 'half a piece of Haarlem cloth of 5 to 6 penny per yard, which they accepted with gratitude'. Here the Europeans were finally able to make fleeting observations about the people and their circumstances – the earliest eyewitness information from Easter Island. But when the 'chief' invited them to visit the opposite side of the island, where intensive agriculture was apparently being practised, Roggeveen, noticing that a northerly was blowing up, declared that they had to return at once to the beached sloops.

Whereupon a number of 'chiefs', probably a formal escort of local descent group leaders publicly displaying their fearlessness and *mana*, accompanied the landing party back to the beach. Here everyone bided until the entire landing party had successfully boarded the five sloops. No further incident occurred. 'So we left like good friends', opined Bouman. Nothing was further from the truth, of course. Only fear, suspicion and murder had followed the first European footfall.

For his part, Behrens enthused about the Easter Islanders. 'These inhabitants', he later wrote, 'were universally hearty, well-proportioned, strong of limb, not wholly lean, and yet nimble afoot, friendly and graceful in their gestures, humble, but thereby also very timid: for the majority of the same, when they were bringing something, threw everything down and ran away again with greatest alacrity.'[13] Behrens failed to appreciate the *mana* of the musket – to the Islanders a thing of wonder and terror that determined their every move.

The following day, 11 April, high seas and winds kept the fleet offshore; the *Thienhoven* even snapped her anchor line, causing a moment of alarm. On 12 April the strong winds continued to blow. Another anchor line snapped, and there was danger of wrecking on the rocky shore. So Roggeveen ordered the fleet to range the coastline, after which they quit the island for the west to continue their search for the Terra Australis.

On the same day, Roggeveen held a shipboard inquiry with his three captains in order to determine the exact circumstances surrounding the killings ashore. It had been Bouman's officer, Cornelis Mens of the *Thienhoven*, who had started the incident, everyone alleged. The man had evidently panicked. Called to declare himself, Mens claimed his gun had been seized, and the Islanders had threatened him with stones. So he had fired, without waiting for Commander Roggeveen's order. Once he had fired, others did so too, wrongly assuming that the order had been given. The Commander and Captains Coster and Rosendaal, as well as Bouman's own lieutenant, ensigns and sailors who had been present, to a man did not believe Mens's account. Equally dubious, Bouman highly disapproved of Mens's conduct

> because we landed first and passed through a great number of inhabitants who made room for us, showing great friendliness. The officer [Mens] maintained that he had been assaulted, but all other officers were of the opinion that he had acted out of cowardice. When we landed he had been difficult because, as second of my company, he should have landed immediately after me; however, he remained in the sloop up to the last and then chose another way to go on land where he saw fewer people and that is where he started firing.[14]

If Mens was ever punished for the offence, it was never recorded. Perhaps the affair's most poignant irony was what Behrens happened to note: 'There were many shot dead here, among them also the man who had earlier been by us, which grieved us sorely.'[15] That is, the *tumu ivi 'atua* 'emissary' himself – the first Easter Islander to welcome the outside world – lay dead. The outrage carried a disturbing symbolism.

After this, tragedy pursued the Dutch fleet: the *Africaansche Galey* was lost in the Tuamotus; the Terra Australis was never discovered. With most of his two remaining crews suffering from scurvy, Roggeveen resolved to return to the Netherlands by the safest possible route: that is, sailing west – through the exclusive territory of the rival Dutch East Indies Company. Perhaps predictably, once the *Arend* and *Thienhoven* arrived at Batavia, the governor general of the Company, charging 'breach of privilege', arrested Roggeveen and his crews, confiscated both ships and sold their cargo. Roggeveen and his men were then sent back as prisoners to the Netherlands on a Company ship. They were soon set free, but only after much litigation was a settlement finally reached whereby the Dutch East Indies Company handsomely compensated the West Indies Company for their two ships and paid both crews all outstanding wages.

After this debacle, the Netherlands in general showed no further interest in Pacific Islands, concentrating her regional activities instead in the Spice Islands and the Dutch East Indies Company in Batavia.

WAR!

The Dutchmen's visit was seemingly the grain that set the sandpile toppling. That the Easter Islanders evidently experienced little surprise at being visited from abroad – and for the first time in perhaps more than two centuries – was not wholly atypical for Polynesia. (James Cook's visit to the Māori of Hauraki, New Zealand, in 1769, for example, was similarly to prove 'no more than a fleeting, if memorable, distraction from [the Māoris'] own compelling affairs'.)[16] A profound shock, however, certainly attended the witnessing of the foreigners' power. Felled by a musket-magic none could explain, the lamented dead would have long filled fireside conversations. No ancestral spirit could summon such force. Yet these *tangata hiva* – 'men from beyond' – were neither returned spirits nor 'gods'. They were white men with lethal *mana*. And Easter Islanders were vulnerable in a way they had never been before.

There is a possibility that the Dutch contaminated the Islanders with a pathogen against which their kind had no immunity. In coming years, initial contact with Europeans would often kill Islanders in this way throughout the Pacific.[17] By 1723 or 1724 two or three thousand Easter Islanders might have perished, further reducing the island's population and reinforcing the impression that their traditional deities were refusing to heed the *'ariki mau* and his *tumu ivi 'atua*. As a result of the *tangata hiva*'s visit, Islanders were not only vulnerable: they were possibly dying in large numbers (perhaps for the second time in living memory).

At this juncture the Tūpa 'Otu *mata* of the eastern 'Otu 'Iti *hānau* made its move. Perhaps a sudden population crash had brought new claims on hereditary lands, leading to larger conflicts that, in turn, destroyed the newly revived exchange systems. A revolutionary change on Easter Island had long been in the offing. Already from about AD 1250 the new erect *mo'ai* atop the *ahu* were signalling the rise of individual authority: the first *matato'a* or warrior-leaders meant the simultaneous weakening of the once omnipotent *'ariki mau*, the island's paramount chief. By the beginning of the eighteenth century, this chief's secular power had been exhausted as forests disappeared and soils washed away. The almost complete lack of wood prevented canoe-making for deep-sea fishing, the privilege of the all-powerful Miru *mata* whose leader, the *'ariki mau*, was responsible for upholding resources and distributing wealth.[18] As the secular power of the *'ariki mau* had waned, that of the *matato'a* – in particular those warrior-leaders of the eastern Tūpa 'Otu – had waxed.

So it was *matato'a* who now distributed the intensive dry-field cultivars (sweet potatoes, yams, taro and bananas) and scanty catches of fish. It was to the leading *matato'a* that Islanders increasingly looked for their resources, their safety, even their good fortune. The *'ariki mau* still held supernatural power and certain personal privileges, but even these were now being challenged by the eastern *matato'a*.[19] The traditional hereditary prerogative was being disregarded wholesale for achieved status.[20]

It was not a revolt of lower against upper classes – an absurd concept in ancient Polynesia. Rather it was a struggle between rival forces of equals, as had always occurred on Easter Island. For warfare was endemic, part of the first settlers' cultural baggage: the Old Rapanui word *tau'a* ('war, warrior') was of Proto-Polynesian origin, nearly 3,000 years old. For most of the island's history, the ordinary soldiers, the *paoa*, probably served only when needed. But the *matato'a* – a compound word consisting of *mata* ('grouping') and *to'a* ('warrior, courageous') – were something special. The *matato'a* formed a warrior class. *Matato'a* were both leaders in war and 'the actual rulers of the tribes'.[21] Local legends suggest that, at least temporarily in the eighteenth century, some *matato'a* actually came to wield absolute authority on Easter Island – despite the hereditary *'ariki mau* who still held all religious power. (Such a division of authority in prehistoric Polynesia, whereby warriors succeed in overcoming the authority of a traditional *'ariki* whose *mana* nevertheless endures, is known from only one other island: Mangaia in the Cooks.)

Shortly after the Dutch visit, for whatever cause, the *matato'a* of the Tūpa 'Otu of the eastern 'Otu 'Iti seized control of the island – and were fiercely resisted by the western and northern Tu'u, especially by the Miru, the traditional aristocrats, whose thousand-year pre-eminence had effectively ended. Continual conflict ensued between the two eastern and western confederations of 'clans'. The war raged for an entire generation, from about 1724–5 until after 1750. (Only the eastern headland, the Pōike

Peninsula, was seemingly spared the carnage – but it had already been abandoned, because of soil erosion.) Even then, intermittent fighting would flare up again and again, into the 1860s. Nonetheless, the Miru *mata* of the western and northern Tu'u managed to retain their traditional rank and sanctity, while the chiefs of the plebeian eastern *mata* wielded all effective power.[22]

While war raged, huts were burnt and fields were plundered. Famine followed. Chaos alone ruled Easter Island, and this for an entire generation. Earlier a rare item, the *mata'a* – large stemmed flakes of volcanic glass, shaped and hafted to staffs to form spears, and to handles to produce daggers – now became the island's most common artefact. (In 1770 the Spaniards marvelled at the grotesque *mata'a* wounds on several Islanders.) Apparently tens of thousands of these were produced in the eighteenth and nineteenth centuries.

Certain encounters were forever etched on island memory, later to be embellished and manipulated. The infamous battle between the 'stocky' *hānau 'e'epe* versus the 'thin' *hānau momoko* has long explained the so-called Pōike Ditch – in fact, a 3.5-kilometre series of elongated trenches in the east, just above Tongariki, which were probably used for growing crops. The legend possibly recalls an eighteenth-century clash of some consequence there between the Tu'u and the 'Otu 'Iti.[23]

In fact, battlefield 'butchery' appears to have remained minimal.[24] But the consequences of a defeat could be devastating. Victors pursued the vanquished back to caves and rock shelters; defeated warriors often fled to the safety of offshore islets, but children and infirm elders were brutally murdered, it appears. Women and girls were frequently spared, if only to be given as wives to unmarried warriors. Some defeated tribespeople sought refuge among victorious relations. The menfolk cowering on the islets were not allowed ashore, and lived wretched existences in utter deprivation.

Perhaps they still fared better than their fallen comrades. At the end of the nineteenth century many Islanders were still recalling stories of cannibalistic meals by triumphant warriors – always in a secluded spot away from women and children – whereby defeated enemies of rank were devoured.[25] The skulls of these were then burnt, as a special insult. It should be pointed out, however, that the occurrence of cannibalism on Easter Island is 'entirely narrative, and not archæological'.[26] Cannibalism is not only unproductive for victors, it is self-defeating. Although rare instances of cannibalism might have occurred on Easter Island – to be exaggerated by later generations – it is more probable that nearly all defeated warriors, once caught, were made *kio* or 'slaves'.

A *kio* in Mangareva was a simple farmer who voluntarily placed himself under a wealthy landowner's protection, or who was a yeoman working leased land.[27] Similarly, in early Easter Island society *kio* were simple tenant farmers, who probably comprised a large proportion of the population. By the eighteenth century, however, the *kio* formed the lowest rung of society there. They often comprised conquered enemies who worked their victor's land as 'slaves', in abject circumstances, penned in caves that they were allowed to leave only to cultivate their master's lands. Yet their condition was not immutable, which meant that they were not actual slaves. Old age or infirmity usually compelled their 'freedom' – which meant that, unless relations rescued them, they were free to fend for themselves in utter poverty. Their wives and daughters had already long been married off to enemy warriors.

Easter Island's ancient society was rapidly disappearing. Up to that time, the sources of social control had been provided through the *mana* of the *'ariki mau* and his *tumu ivi 'atua*.[28] Now, only the *matato'a* and their *paoa* ranged the land, and all social control was lost. Even those villagers not directly involved in warfare had retreated to the safety of caves and rock shelters. Islets also became welcome, if bitter, refuges. Everywhere defensive walls rose; these were then camouflaged and highly fortified. Spanish visitors observed in 1770 – probably twenty years after most fighting had ceased – that most Islanders were still living in underground caves with narrow entrances. Four years later James Cook's party, surveying from a hill near Hanga Roa, 'did not see above 10 or 12 huts, though the view commanded a great part of the island'.[29]

The generation of lawlessness had spawned a generation of homelessness. Easter Islanders had become exiles on their own desert isle. In consequence, 'the various communities scattered over the island became more and more like predatory bands, and much of the older, more ordered way of life gradually vanished'.[30]

MAKEMAKE

Evidently the 'gods' were dying, too, on ravished Easter Island. Similar to Mangaia, where the island's warrior class had succeeded in overcoming the authority of the traditional paramount chief, on Easter Island the *'ariki mau* now lost nearly all eminence. In fact, this was the only place in Polynesia where the commoners, the *'urumanu*, took upon themselves not only the land's secular power, but also the complex of *mana* and *tapu* that was, throughout Polynesia, manifestly not theirs to take. 'The warriors' supremacy had gone even further on Easter Island because here they had gained not only the political power, but had achieved an ascendant religious position as well.'[31] These new secular rulers of Easter Island, the *matato'a*, were now challenging the legitimacy of the *'ariki mau*, attempting to wrest all power – secular and religious – away from the Miru *mata* and thus breaking from the core of ancient Easter Island custom.

The extraordinary challenge toppled the island's ancient 'pantheon' of leading ancestral deities, replacing these with a single, all-embracing godhead. It also brought about a remarkable ritual that, through an annual 'sports' competition, heralded a new socio-religious culture. Yet ultimately, neither innovation was to succeed wholly in wresting complete authority away from the *'ariki mau*.

Deified ancestors – all of them of venerable East Polynesian origin, as we have seen – had comprised the most important cultural baggage of Easter Island's settlers. But these ancestors had obviously failed to protect the settlers' descendants from ecological disaster, famine, dangerous foreigners, pandemics (possibly) and now the chaos of continuous warfare. The island was dying, and drastic new measures were needed.[32] Or so judged the ruling *matato'a* who, convinced that a single deity could save the island, at this time advanced ancient Makemake – who came to incarnate Tangaroa, Tāne, Rongo and Tu'u in one. (For some reason, Hiro remained independent.) The island's *'ariki mau*, dedicated to the gods of old, of whom he was the chief mediary, would never have proposed the religious revolution. Only a powerful, temporal ruler would have dared: a *matato'a*, who had emerged victorious from the chaos of intertribal warfare. Whereupon all traditional deities, no longer venerated, were relegated to myth and legend: they survived only in chants and in the names of places and of nights of the moon calendar.

Ancient Makemake might actually have begun as an epithet – Old Rapanui *makemake* means 'tumescent (of the phallus)' – of the leading deity Tangaroa, who, on Easter Island, appears to have usurped the creator role of Tiki te Hatu and / or Tāne. (At the end of the nineteenth century, Islanders declared Makemake to be 'the great spirit of the sea', formerly Tangaroa's realm.)[33] Foremost a fertility deity, Makemake originally appears to have been a more generalized figure. But he soon became the focus of the so-called Birdman cult (see below) and, consequently, of its warrior patrons. Most importantly, Makemake was proclaimed to be the primary source of the island's *mana*.[34]

Almost immediately, Makemake was venerated in the form of the frigate bird – that 'messenger' from Hiva – which was often carved, in relief, as a seated human figure in profile, with a bird's head and egg in hand, on the boulders at the ritual site of 'Orongo, or colourfully painted on cave and house walls. Makemake was never worshipped, but 'receives his veneration through a series of carved wooden idols which are carried about in honour of the god at the principal festivities'.[35] Makemake's constant companion was the deity Hauā ('Twin'), with whom he also appeared in statuary.

Yet if the anonymous *matato'a* who installed Makemake had as his chief aim not so much the Islanders' welfare as his own religious elevation, he was to be sorely disappointed. For it appears that within a short time the *'ariki mau* also became mediary to Makemake as well. And this curious turn, at first sight perhaps a betrayal of the ancestral patrimony, was apparently accepted by all Islanders, who continued to seek out their paramount chief for religious intervention. Similarly, the *'ariki paka*, the noble Miru *mata*, on behalf of all Islanders continued to address their prayers and offerings to Hiro, Tare, Tive, Tiki te Hatu, Hiva Karā Rere and to other minor deities as well. Makemake may have supplanted most deities in the island's new power structure, but not in popular piety. Whereupon the *matato'a* apparently responded with a radical revamp of the ancient 'Birdman' ritual – and stood Easter Island society on its head.

THE TANGATA MANU

With island beliefs now focused on fruits, fertility, procreation and their related rituals, the 'imperious' *matato'a* now expanded the warrior-chief's prerogative. (Only an exceptional personality could have achieved this, his name perhaps preserved in the confusion of later contradictory 'king' lists.) Cleverly cannibalizing the old *tangata tapu manu* or 'Bird Holy Man' ritual, held since time immemorial in conjunction with coming-of-age rites at 'Orongo, this public figure instituted an annual competition to dictate the island's temporal and religious stewardship for each respective year. The winner of each year's competition – now simply called the *tangata manu* or 'Birdman' – would be Easter Island's temporary secular and spiritual leader. He alone would also be the sole mediary to Makemake. With this manoeuvre, ancient ritual became political cult. It was also one of those rare instances in human history when competitive sport determined local governance.

Of course, the *matato'a*'s ultimate design was to wrest all religious authority away from the *'ariki mau* of the Miru. 'Orongo was the perfect choice for the inspired conceit. It had been where the old *tangata tapu manu* had imitated the frigate bird and had flown to Hiva, even to Pō where the Islanders' ancestral spirits dwelt. Closely associated with this was the 'holy egg' given to him by the *pōki manu* or 'Bird Children' during their initiation to adulthood, forever one of the year's special events.

The egg ritual had arisen from an early awareness of vanishing island resources: both bird and egg had since become fertility symbols. The bird was also venerated as the creature that could regularly communicate between Easter Island and the outside world. In the eighteenth century, some birds – such as the noddy – were treated with such respect that they would freely land on Islanders' shoulders, like domestic pets, which surprised European visitors to no little effect.[36] (The custom defied the rapacious exploitation of previous centuries.) Easter Islanders' relationship to birds had changed profoundly. Makemake himself was a bird, the egg in his hand the symbol of *'ao* – of temporal power.

If earlier the albatross and the frigate bird had been the most greatly respected, it appears that by the eighteenth (or nineteenth) century the *manu tara* or 'sooty tern' had replaced them. Sooty terns migrated annually to Easter Island about September to nest along 'Orongo's cliff and also on the three offshore islets just below, especially on Motu Nui. (The preferred petroglyph of Makemake, or of his representative the 'Birdman', remained the frigate bird, however, a fossilized icon of fertility, often with egg in hand.)

All the abovementioned phenomena now combined to create the 'Birdman cult'. The scheme was as simple as it was ingenious.[37] It installed a rotating leadership, a fixed-term Birdman, who was chosen by open competition – by 'sport'. This occurred in the form of an egg race at 'Orongo that drew various elements from the time-honoured rituals always held there. Each leading *matato'a* either competed himself – it is possible that all early Birdmen were genuine victors – or used a proxy. (As time went on, it seems that nearly all competitors were proxies.) Anticipating the sooty terns' September nesting, competitors first threaded down an ancient narrow trail on Rano Kau's sheer 300-metre rock face, then paddled on reeds 2 kilometres out to Motu Nui, where they camped and waited. Once the terns arrived, competition become fierce to find the first egg, probably on Motu Nui's high sheer cliffs. The one who found it – possibly using self-made crampons and finger extensions, risking death from falling to the rocks below – hurriedly tied it to his headband, took again to sea, paddled to shore and then scaled the high cliff to 'Orongo where, if he was a proxy, he handed the egg – symbol of the *'ao* or temporal power – to his leader, a *tangata hōnui*. Everyone who was gathered about then acknowledged this man to be the new *tangata manu*, the Birdman, for the next twelve moons: the incarnation of the bird deity Makemake. For having lost, his opponents had to lacerate themselves ritually with *mata'a*-tipped spears.

The new Birdman then shaved his head, eyebrows and eyelashes, whereupon his head was painted. Retiring to privileged isolation at a special Rano Raraku residence, for the next full year he lived a life of luxurious seclusion, with all bodily needs and wants fulfilled by loyal 'subjects'. For twelve moons, the *tangata manu* could not wash or bathe himself, or cut his nails, which grew conspicuously long – like talons.

Just before the Birdman competition, the ceremony known as the *mata veri* – literally, 'grand assemblage' – had taken place just down the hill from 'Orongo, towards Hanga Roa. Eventually this venue came to be called, after the ceremony, Mataveri. (It is now the site of the International Airport.) It was held by, and for, the *'urumanu*, the commoners. While it was going on, a general armistice remained in force throughout the island.

The Birdman cult was never a solution to Easter Island's problems: from its inception it was a *coup d'état*. The Birdman was meant to reign as the island's ersatz *'ariki*. Yet the manoeuvre only partially succeeded. Its enduring legacy was the cessation of the most grievous hostilities, probably shortly after 1750. The price, however, was permanent tyranny by each respective Birdman's *paoa*, thugs who now 'lawfully' ranged the island sowing terror. For until the following year's competition, the *paoa*, enjoying Makemake's patronage, were free to punish all Islanders who, in their opinion, failed to acknowledge the sanctity of the new *tangata manu*, burning down offenders' huts. (In later years these *paoa* resided permanently at Mataveri.) In the early nineteenth century some Islanders recalled elders telling them that the Birdman's *paoa* terrorized and plundered all *mata* who were simply not strong enough to resist. The Birdman cult might have ended open warfare. But it frequently resembled this, with its own flavour of punctuated butchery and intermittent mayhem. (At the Spaniards' visit in 1770 and Cook's visit in 1774, most Islanders were still inhabiting fortified caves – despite this innovated 'solution' to social unrest.)

Although the Birdman cult superficially stemmed the island's chaos, the local social order remained 'as fragile as the shells of the eggs that were the focus of the annual quest'.[38] Perhaps most importantly, the scheme, which was to continue for more than a century, failed to take supreme religious authority away from each successive *'ariki mau*, who still reigned as paramount chief – irrespective of the self-styled 'sanctity' of any Birdman from the upstart eastern *'urumanu* ('commoners'). To the Miru and their loyal confederates, it brought only sorrow and distress.

THE SPANIARDS

Alarmed by Britain's and France's increased attentions in 'her' sphere of influence, Spain was prompted to explore the Pacific even more assiduously, both for the sciences and to discover the still elusive Southern Land. While James Cook was busily charting the Pacific on his first magnificent voyage of discovery, in 1770 an expedition led by *capitán de navío* Felipe González de Haedo set out from Peru in two ships, the *San Lorenzo* and *Santa Rosalia*, with the express objectives from Peru's Viceroy, Don Manuel de Amat,

– of finding and exploring the land or island of David, or Davis (the isle English buccaneer Edward Davis reputedly sited in 1687), and the New Island of (Silvestre) Luján, and of recording that of the Madre de

Dios; and – of looking out for foreign troops and / or colonies in said islands and on the coasts of the South Pacific.[39]

The expedition was ordered to locate precisely the whereabouts of the first two, and to determine whether they had any European posts or colonies or whether the natives had any contact with Europeans. If no foreign power was present, the *capitán* was to take possession for King Carlos.

The Spaniards arrived at Easter Island on 15 November 1770, anchoring again in Hanga 'o Honu. González was certain that this was not the 'Isla de Davis', but a hitherto unknown island. (He seems to have been unaware of Roggeveen's visit here in 1722.) As a result of wars, deadly raids and perhaps pandemics, by this time the island's population might have sunk to as low as 3,000 (a little lower than today's). The Islanders' curiosity was keen. Again, a small party came out to welcome the foreign visitors, and within two days of initial contact men and women in large numbers were swimming out to the Spanish ships, where they began trading for trousers, shirts, ribbons, seamen's jumpers, as well as for tiny metal crosses. Islanders even accepted salt pork, rice and biscuits – things they had never tasted before. An officer in charge, Don Cayetano de Lángara, had issued orders that no one, 'under pain of severe flogging', was to accept any article from the Islanders without giving something equivalent in return, or even something of greater value.[40]

The Spaniards were amazed by the 'standing idols', the *mo'ai*, all of which were still erect (at least those that they could see). As the island's apparent 'discoverer', González resolved to chart it and so he dispatched an armed party in two pinnaces to circumnavigate the isle for this express purpose. The party sailed all day, camped the night at Vinapū on the western south coast, then returned to Hanga 'o Honu and to the two ships. On 20 November 1770 a shore party led by Lieutenant Alberto de Olaondo – comprising 125 soldiers, a number of seamen and a few officers from both ships – landed ostensibly to reconnoitre the interior and make cartographic measurements, but primarily to draw attention away from the main shore party. This main party – led by González's second-in-charge, *capitán* José Bustillo, and including infantry captain Buenaventura Moreno, further officers, chaplains and 100 armed seamen – partially ascended Pōike in the east to plant three Christian crosses atop the three parasitic cones just north-northeast of the summit of Pū 'a Katiki.

Several hundred Islanders – probably members of the Koro 'o Rongo *mata* of the eastern 'Otu 'Iti – observed the elaborate ceremony that was then staged, not far from Pōike's northern cones. Following three boisterous 'Viva el Rey!' for each cross, the shore party let off three salvos of musketry, whereupon the two Spanish vessels at anchor below responded with 21-cannon salutes.

The spectacle must have been awe-inspiring for the islanders. The parade of uniformed soldiers; the fluttering flags; the chaplains in their surplices chanting out the litany; the beating of the drums and the trilling of fifes must have left a lasting impression on all the natives who witnesssed the procession.[41]

At this point Bustillo took formal possession of the island 'in the name of the King and of Spain, our Lord and Master Don Carlos the Third', naming the island San Carlos in honour of *Su Majestad.*

Just before this, however, a curious ritual had taken place. Three island elders had been persuaded to take feather in hand, dip it into a black liquid, and then scratch marks on a *tapa*-like material white as sand and thin as a leaf. The Islanders drew scribbles – like the ones the foreigners had just drawn that ran in stacked lines from left to right – and also geometric designs and a couple of petroglyph signs. Only the Spaniards knew that this was the official record of the event, already signed by their officers and paymasters, and that the three elders were 'signing away' all Easter Islanders' rights to their home. The Islanders hadn't a clue what the ritual meant. None even knew what writing was. Nevertheless their 'signatures' were to have historic consequences.

No violence occurred on either side during the Spanish visit. Indeed, one Spaniard wrote: 'They [the Islanders] have a docile disposition and an utter horror of firearms, to such an extent that, even when some distance away, after hearing a shot they run off in terror'.[42] Petty thievery took place, and some begging, which annoyed the Spaniards, who were under strict orders to maintain peace. Girls freely offered themselves, their men often acting as panders. (This occurred with every subsequent visit to Easter Island, and was still the object of censure in the early twentieth century; Polynesian sexual behaviour in general was always something remarkable to nearly all Europeans.) Seemingly hesitant to engage the Islanders more than was absolutely necessary, the Spaniards refrained from exploring the island's interior. Their immediate mission carried out successfully in every way, after six days at Easter Island they left again, sailing on 21 November, to search for the other designated islands. They found none.

After this, Spain failed to assert its claim to 'San Carlos'. Instead, subsequent Spanish voyaging focused on Tahiti and other Society Islands, as well as on Tonga and New Zealand. Evidently barren and isolated, 'San Carlos' lay forgotten in the larger arena of Pacific competition. As for the Islanders, after the visit they frequently wore Spanish articles of clothing, seemingly a prestige apparel. Calling with Cook four years later, Georg Forster remarked, for example, how his landing party had 'observed some [Easter Islanders] who had European hats and caps, chequered cotton handkerchiefs, and ragged jackets of blue woollen-cloth, which were so many indubitable testimonies of the visit which the Spanish had made to this island in 1770'.[43]

But fashion was not the Spaniards' real legacy.

RONGORONGO[44]

Once Easter Island's most powerful *matato'a* or 'warrior leader' had instituted the Birdman cult, thereby effectively installing an equal and opposite paramount chief, the *'ariki mau* suffered his most serious challenge thus far. For each Birdman was now declaring himself to be the incarnation of Makemake, the island's supreme deity – threatening the very legitimacy of the *'ariki mau*, who was still claiming religious pre-eminence. The *'ariki mau* needed a veritable wonder to withstand the Birdman's offensive. And it was the Spaniards who now provided it: *writing*.

During the Spaniards' visit the Easter Islanders had witnessed writing – human speech conveyed through graphic art – for the first time, and this in a ceremonial, histrionic, even awesome context. Three Islanders themselves had 'written' – that is, they had set ink to paper. Throughout the world in the eighteenth, nineteenth and early twentieth centuries such first encounters with writing frequently led almost immediately to the local elaboration of invented scripts: the Vai, N'ko, Mende, Bamum of Africa ; the Cherokee script of Sikwayi (Sequoya) and Cree script of the Hudson Bay Territory; the Caroline Islands' scripts; and many more. In similar fashion, Easter Island's first encounter with writing in 1770 apparently led to the elaboration of the *rongorongo* script (so-called from the 1870s, from the Mangarevan word for 'ritual chanters'). It was Oceania's only indigenous writing before the twentieth century.

Borrowing merely the idea of writing, linearity and a left-to-right reading direction, Easter Islanders drew from their corpus of rock art to incise a limited number of standardized, codified, contour signs first into thick wooden battle staffs, then later into driftwood boards (creating 'tablets') and other things. The long regular lines of this genuine script – each 'hieroglyph' of which reproduced a whole word, action or even complete phrase – conveyed traditional and invented serial procreation formulæ ('x copulated with y: there issued forth z'), serial pæans to the *'ariki mau*, rhetorical calendars and other things to be chanted by *tuhunga tā* ('writing experts') in the Old Rapanui language.

Having grasped the principle of writing (but not the Latin alphabet) after having witnessed the Spaniards, whose demonstration had evinced a powerful *mana*, resourceful Islanders – perhaps Koro 'o Rongo of the eastern 'Otu 'Iti – at first developed the *rongorongo* quite independently of any hierarchical privilege. But in time the *'ariki mau* monopolized the practice, declaring it *tapu*. At the Miru's religious 'capital' of 'Anakena, the island's now only nominal 'paramount chief' was eventually to exploit the innovation for a specific, personal objective: to arrest the Birdman's hegemony and reassert traditional authority. The *rongorongo* was to become the *'ariki mau*'s very legitimization – and his last crusade.

Soon after its elaboration, an entire complex of associated rituals emerged, with *rongorongo* feasts, 'schools' and ceremonies conducted principally by the *tuhunga tā*. Nearly all of the surviving *rongorongo* corpus appears to focus on fertility, the all-embracing concern of eighteenth-century Easter Island society: copulation, procreation, what the *'ariki mau* (not Makemake) makes fertile, and other related themes. Although the *'ariki mau* was apparently barred from attending the annual Birdman competition at 'Orongo, he sent his *tuhunga tā* to its holy site of Mata Ngarahu where, during the 'egg-wait', these experts loudly chanted while holding *rongorongo* staffs and tablets. (This custom might have taken three generations to develop; it is first alleged under the famous *'ariki mau* Nga'ara.)

Through the *rongorongo* phenomenon the *'ariki mau* did manage to legitimize a separate entitlement to religious authority on the island. (By the 1850s the *rongorongo* constituted nearly an *'ariki mau*'s sole remaining claim to authority of any kind.) The custom of *rongorongo* ceased in the 1860s because of labour raids, pandemics, Christianity, the loss of *tapu*, the abandonment of the *rongorongo* 'schools' and the introduction of the Latin alphabet. Once, there had been hundreds of incised staffs and tablets; today, merely 25 *rongorongo* artefacts grace the world's museums, from Tahiti to St Petersburg. Not one authentic *rongorongo* artefact remains on Easter Island.

THE ANCESTORS TOPPLE

Easter Island's *mo'ai*, the ancestral statues, were apparently still standing when Roggeveen visited the island in 1722 and González de Haedo in 1770: neither explorer saw one fallen statue. By James Cook's visit in 1774 (see below), however, many lay prostrate; skeletal material littered the *mo'ai*'s beds; and monuments were no longer maintained. Between 1770 and 1774 something had happened, something extraordinary that toppled even deified ancestors. It was not erosion, earthquake or tsunami. Another break with tradition had occurred, whereby even ancient *tapu* was no longer sacrosanct.

For two full generations, from the 1770s until the 1830s (or even later), what has been called 'the wars of the throwing down of the statues'[45] – the *huri mo'ai* ('statue-toppling') – brought targeted destruction everywhere on Easter Island. In the end, not a single statue remained erect on its *ahu*. Eyewitness informants told the French in the 1870s how 'during their intertribal wars the victorious party toppled the statues of the defeated'.[46] Yet when the statues began toppling, the great wars had long been over. It actually occurred during this later, more contentious, era of the serial Birdmen and their henchmen, the *paoa*, who 'indulged in the barbarous pleasure of toppling each other's images', as other informants told the Roman Catholic bishop of Tahiti.[47]

Each Birdman's followers had set about destroying their competitors' *mana*, whose most conspicuous manifestation was their *mo'ai*. And as most marauding bandits belonged to the eastern 'Otu 'Iti *hānau*, the most frequent early targets were the prominent ancestors of the western Tu'u, in particular those lording over the *ahu* of the Haumoana, Marama and especially the chiefly Miru who traditionally provided the *'ariki mau*. Shortly after the departure of the Spaniards, the western *mo'ai* were the first to fall, whereupon the entire region was apparently bitterly plundered.

The methods that the *paoa* used to topple the behemoths is significant. They not only slung ropes about the *mo'ai*'s heads and yanked them down, or removed the foundation slabs from underneath to let them crash to earth, but, nearly always tipping the statues forward towards the court, they precisely positioned large boulders there with the intention of decapitating the statue through the thunderous fall.[48] This was the specific purpose, since 'only the broken ones [are] dead and without any power', as Islanders told German visitors a century later.[49] To decapitate the ancestors was to destroy their supernatural power. The *mo'ai* themselves were not the primary target, then, but their inherent *mana* – which, aiding rivals, could threaten the *paoa*'s descent group. Even the dressed stones of the respective *ahu* were then pried apart and strewn, to desecrate further the sacred site.

The statues had been cannibalized for building platforms for many centuries – especially their heads, which then incorporated the *mana* of the local group's ancestors into renovations and expansions. But this was something drastically different. This was not construction, but destruction. It was not only that the 'outrages inflicted on these ancestral figures were symbolically inflicted on the whole group'.[50] Perpetrated island-wide in tit-for-tat raids, their cumulative effect struck Easter Island society more deeply than anything before: it was the disintegration of an existential dimension, the switching off of Easter Island's 'power supply'. That the ancient magic was gone could be seen with one's own eyes, strewn over the island's barren landscape like so many gravestones. No class revolt, no mere 'intertribal conflict', this. It was wholesale apostasy. And, once started, it would not stop until all were prostrate.

Traditional, but curiously altered, practices nevertheless persisted. Toppled *mo'ai* were covered with crude *ahu* and, in between the fallen and broken heads, burial crypts were set. Some 70 'semi-pyramidal' platforms were constructed atop, or near, wasted *ahu* as well and used as sepulchres, perhaps largely for '*urumanu* or 'commoners'. (None bore a statue.) A respect for the immediately deceased endured, but this was seemingly now disassociated from the rank reverence of earlier generations – something inconceivable before 1722.

When the Russian Lisjanskij visited in 1804, four statues yet loomed in Cook's Bay, seven at Vinapū; in all, Lisjanskij saw at least 20 standing *mo'ai*. But twelve years later his landsman Kotzebue found these toppled, with only two still standing at Vinapū. By 1825 all monuments on Cook's Bay had been demolished.[51] The French admiral Dupetit-Thouars was the last to give eyewitness testimony of a standing *mo'ai*: in 1838 he saw on the west coast 'a platform on which were set four red statues, equidistant from one another, their summits covered with white stones'.[52] By the time French missionaries arrived in the 1860s, however, every platform *mo'ai* lay on the ground. Most of their necks were broken.

JAMES COOK

Of all the early visits to Easter Island probably the most important – at least for its wealth of observations – was that made by the British explorer James Cook in 1774. Great Britain had arrived late at regular Pacific exploration, its primary aim in the region being to wrest control from Spain and France. In this, the search for the Southern Land and, later, for the North-West Passage became paramount, prompting the voyages of John Byron, Philip Carteret, Samuel Wallis and, above all, James Cook. Cook's first voyage, in the years 1768–71, in the celebrated *Endeavour*, mapping first New Zealand then Australia's eastern seaboard and collecting specimens and scientific data, was an epochal success. In 1772 Cook left England again, this time on the *Resolution*, another former Whitby collier barque, to search once more for the Terra Australis, and in 1773–4 he ranged the Pacific's southern latitudes, serendipitously becoming only the third known European to reach Easter Island.

It was 13 March 1774, and Cook and his crew had been searching in vain for the Southern Land for two long months. Aware of the earlier reports of 'Davis's Land', as well as the Dutch and Spanish visits, Cook hove to in order to procure fresh supplies and water. He was in dire need of both: his men were already showing signs of scurvy. Aboard were the German naturalists Johann Reinhold Forster and his 19-year-old son Georg (also known as the English 'George'), both of whose accounts of Pacific island callings were to be among the most significant in history.

Cook encountered a different island from González's: it was obvious that something terrible had happened in the interim, probably a war. Little fresh food was to be had, and only brackish water was available. The *Resolution* anchored off Hanga Roa. Young Georg wrote the observation in his journal: 'the surface of the isle in general appeared to be extremely dreary and parched'.[53] Two men approached in a canoe; the Britons threw down a rope. The Islanders then tied 'a great cluster of ripe bananas to it, making signs for us to haul it up. The sudden emotions of joy in every countenance at the sight of this fruit are scarcely to be described.' An Islander came aboard, indicating that his name was 'Maroowahai' (Maru Vahe?). Mahine, a Tahitian who was sailing on Cook's ship as 'translator', was pleased to find people on this distant island speaking a kindred tongue. But since the Old Rapanui language of Easter Island was as distant from Tahitian as German is from English he could understand only isolated words here and there. (Apart from rare drift accidents, this was perhaps the first encounter between Easter Islanders and another Polynesian since the collapse of the voyaging sphere about 1500.)

The next day, Cook went ashore with 'Maroowahai', who had spent the night on the *Resolution*, and Mahine (for 'translating'), Forster father and son, and the ship's surgeon, Dr Sparrman. Young Georg was anxious to see the island, 'though my feet and legs were still swelled excessively and I was hardly able to walk', because of scurvy. Some 150 Islanders had gathered on shore to greet them – apparently at Hanga Piko, a natural cove. (Today it is the island's goods port.) 'The people did not make the least unfriendly motion at our landing, but expressed a prodigious dread of our fire-arms, of which they seemed to know the deadly effects.' (This was 52 years after the Roggeveen murders, and three-and-a-half years since the Spaniards' peaceful visit.) 'We saw but few arms among them', Georg noted.[54]

They traded their coconut shells, Tahitian *tapa* cloth and other small articles for small wooden 'idols'. 'There was something characteristic in them', wrote Georg, 'which showed a taste for the arts.' For the smallest trinket, it seemed, the island girls would again make themselves 'available'. Chickens and other provisions were very scarce; the Islanders of the west coast had little to eat, evidently the effect of some calamity they had just suffered. It appeared that Cook's arrival 'coincided with a destructive war which went against the people of the Tu[']u district, decimating the population of the south and west coasts'.[55]

Cook returned to shore a second time, in the afternoon of 14 March, landing again at Hanga Piko. Here he met a commanding figure, either an *'ariki* or *tangata hōnui*. Pockets were picked, hats and caps snatched off the Britons' heads. Even Mahine was victimized. As Cook's party walked along the shore, they were surprised to see 'two or three noddies [dark-plumed terns], which were so tame as to settle on the shoulders of the natives'. (This contradicts some modern theories of total ecological depredation on the island at this time; that is, at least some birds were *tapu*, even to the point of tameness.) As the sun set and they were returning to the cove, they noticed to westward a very large *ahu* with three standing *mo'ai*. Asking its name, the Britons were told: 'Hanga Roa'.

The following day, Lieutenants Pickersgill and Edgecumbe, with the artist Hodges, Dr Sparrman and Johann Forster, were sent to reconnoitre the island's interior. Cook again returned to shore, with Georg Forster and some officers. Some of these proceeded inland in 'violent' heat in order to hunt game, but found none. Cook remained on shore, evidently at Hanga Piko again, trading with about 200 Islanders (but only 14 or 15 females). The Islanders prized empty coconut shells from Tahiti and Tonga in particular, so long as the hole in them was small or they had a cover. Tahitian *tapa* and English cloths came next on the shopping list, followed by ironware (nails). Beads were tossed away as worthless. In exchange, the Islanders' caps, head-dresses, necklaces, ear ornaments and especially wooden statuettes were acquired. 'Mahine was most pleased with these carved human figures, the workman of which much excelled those of the *e Tees* [*ti'i*] in his country, and he purchased several of them assuring us they would be greatly valued at Taheitee [Tahiti]', observed Georg. The *tapa* introduced Tahitian design to Easter Island, which changed local design forever.

At the same time, Lieutenant Pickersgill and party, in the company of some 100 Islanders, were proceeding under Rano Kau and Orito to the island's western south coast, arriving at Vaihū, whose chief 'Ko Toheetai' (Tao Hite?) they met: 'He was a middle age man', recorded Johann Forster, 'rather tall; his face and whole body strongly punctured [tattooed]. He wore a piece of cloth made of mulberry bark, quilted with threads of grass, and stained yellow with turmeric; and on his head he had a cap of long shining black feathers, which might be called a diadem.'[56] The imposing personality, perhaps the *tangata hōnui* of the Ngā Timo *mata*, accompanied the shore party on their march as they turned north towards the interior.

At that moment an Islander snatched Forster's plant bag from a sailor and ran off. Immediately Lieutenant Edgecumbe fired small shot. Wounded, the Islander dropped the bag – the Britons hurriedly recovered it – then he

> fell soon after; his countrymen took him up, and fled to a little distance, till we beckoned to them to return, which almost all of them did. Though this was the only instance of firing at a native during our stay at Easter Island, yet it is to be lamented that Europeans too often assume the power of inflicting punishments on people who are utterly unacquainted with their laws.

The shore party then marched through 'the centre of the island', evidently proceeding north-west between Puna Pau and Ma'unga (Mount)

Tuʻu. In the searing heat of day, the elder Forster found 'the path more rugged and fatiguing than ever, the country being strewn with volcanic cinders, and desolate all round us, though we found many remaining proofs of its having been formerly cultivated'. Here the party divided, and Forster, Dr Sparrman, a sailor and two Islanders ascended the summit of a hill: to the west they could see the sea and the *Resolution* at anchor. Soon after, the sun set and both parties spent two disorienting hours in the dark returning to where they had landed.

In the meantime, Georg Forster had returned with Captain Cook in the late afternoon to the ship, where, though the *Resolution* was more than a kilometre offshore, they found a few Islanders had swum out. 'Among them was a woman who . . . carried on a particular traffic of her own', Georg did not fail to notice. (Possibly since 1722, probably since 1770, and certainly since 1774 there has been a European admixture to the Easter Island genome. It was the end of the 'pure' Easter Island stock – that is, at least its exclusively East Polynesian heritage. Today no Easter Islander is without European ancestry.) On the whole, Easter Island women were, Georg found, 'neither reserved nor chaste, and for the trifling consideration of a small piece of cloth, some of our sailors obtained the gratification of their desires'.[57]

After being apprised of what the shore party had seen and experienced, Cook wrote in his journal:

On the East side near the sea [the western south coast], they met with three platforms of stonework, or rather the ruins of them. On each hand stood four of those large statues, but they were all fallen down from two of them, and also one from the third; all except one were broken by fall or in some measure defaced.[58]

Despite the shore party's inability to explore all of the island, the Britons had seen enough to convince Cook that some cataclysmic event had happened: much cultivation here had been destroyed or abandoned. All of them had been very impressed by the monumental *ahu* and tall *moʻai*, and several observers furnished detailed descriptions of these. James Cook and both Forsters correctly attributed the architectural phenomena to an earlier, more favourable period of island history.

On 17 March the Britons sailed off. They had found the Islanders 'exceedingly civil'. These had welcomed Cook's shore parties, showing no fear, but had practised all types of thievery. Hats and caps were snatched off heads. At a time of utter deprivation, unwitting neighbours' bananas, sweet potatoes and yams were wantonly pilfered and traded. Demanding payment in advance, Islanders grabbed it then ran away. Underneath piles of delivered sweet potatoes lay stones.

Still, Mahine approved of his Easter Island cousins. 'Ta'ata maita'i, fenua 'ino', he reckoned in Tahitian, with nice understanding: 'People fine, island bad'.[59] Georg Forster was similarly sympathetic. 'The disposition of these people is far from being warlike; their numbers are too inconsiderable, and their poverty too general, to create civil disturbances amongst them.' (Here the teenager was tragically wrong.) He found it 'extraordinary that they should have different kinds of offensive weapons, and especially such as resemble those of the New Zealanders; and we must add this circumstance to several others, which are inexplicable to us in their kind'. In the end, the young German had to grant that, although the Easter Islanders were terrified of the Europeans' weapons, 'it is not to be doubted, at the same time, that there is a mildness, fellow-feeling and good nature in their disposition which naturally prompts them to treat their visitors kindly and even hospitably, as far as their wretched country will permit'.[60]

In general, the British and German accounts of the visit of 1774 drew attention to the breathtaking barrenness of the island and bitter destitution of its few inhabitants – in striking contrast to the majesty of their monolithic *mo'ai* and the grandeur of their monumental *ahu*. So began the 'mystery of Easter Island'.[61]

Although James Cook hereby founded the scientific study of the island, which continues to this day, he himself was scathing about the place: 'No nation need contend for the honour of the discovery of this island', he wrote with peerless authority, 'as there can be few places which afford less convenience for shipping than it does'.[62] The epochal judgement condemned Easter Island to flotsam.

THE FRENCH

In 1785, just four years before the French Revolution, Louis XVI personally commissioned – and himself financed – a major expedition to the Pacific. It was led by a nobleman, Jean-François Galaup, Comte de la Pérouse, who commanded the two ships *Astrolabe* and *Boussole*. For the race was now on in earnest between Britain and France to discover the North-West Passage – now that James Cook had proved to the world that the Southern Land, the Terra Australis, did not exist after all. Prominent among La Pérouse's instructions was also the collection of scientific and ethnographic information about the Pacific, and the gathering of animals and plants from the region. La Pérouse's first destination was Hawai'i, 'discovered' by Cook only seven years earlier. But while en route, the *Astrolabe*, La Pérouse's flagship, navigated towards Easter Island as well in order to confirm Cook's position and estimation of the place. The French sighted the island on 8 April 1786, and landed two days later.

Coming from Chile's principal port of Valparaíso fully stocked, La

Pérouse, unlike Cook, suffered no material or medical want when he anchored at Hanga 'o Honu – that is, where the Spaniards had anchored nearly sixteen years earlier. Once ashore, the French marines formed a large circle to indicate their inviolable 'camp', as was French naval custom. Whereupon they brought ashore animals (sheep, goats, pigs) and other gifts for the Islanders. Monsieur de Langle was sent with a small armed party to explore the island's interior. As had happened with Cook's shore parties, pilfering abounded, especially once the Frenchmen's 'passivity' was perceived. (Each shore member had been ordered not to fire his musket at an Islander unless direly threatened.) Astonishingly, some 800 Islanders had soon amassed around the 'camp' – approximately 150 of them were even women and young girls. The purpose of the latter's presence soon became apparent.

'Several of these wenches', penned La Pérouse later, 'had a pleasant countenance and offered their favours to each who wished to give them something in exchange . . . During the time that the females impressed their caresses on us, our hats were stolen from our heads and our handkerchiefs from our pockets.'[63]

At one o'clock in the afternoon, La Pérouse returned to his command tent so that Monsieur de Clonard, his second, could come ashore. By then, all the French had lost their hats and handkerchiefs. Once La Pérouse was back on board the *Astrolabe* and De Clonard was ashore, a boat's grapnel was stolen. An armed party of French marines pursued the thief, but then they were pelted with stones by others to such a degree that they were forced to fire their muskets in the air. To no effect: the Islanders continued stoning them. So the French fired small shot directly into their assailants. The thief got away.

At this point the Easter Islanders apparently wished to make up for any seeming inhospitality and returned to the French camp, pandering their women and girls again as if nothing had happened.

By six in the evening all the French were aboard the *Astrolabe* and the ship's boats were hauled up. Just before setting sail, La Pérouse heard Monsieur de Langle's report of the march to the interior. He had made it perhaps as far as Ma'unga Pu'i (the hill for traditional banana-stem 'sledding'), De Langle related, planting seeds along the route. On the way he had met a 'chief', whom he had politely presented with a ram and goat: whereupon the 'chief' had taken the animals with one hand and stolen De Langle's kerchief with the other.

La Pérouse himself had several salient observations to share. Perhaps most importantly, he was the first visitor to lament the Islanders' own 'imprudence' for having felled their forests, creating a wasteland. The French nobleman also identified Easter Island's social collapse:

Nothing is more certain than that this people's present form of governance has made all classes and stations so similar to one another that one no longer encounters a chief among the same whose influence would be of such importance that a large number of people should take pains to immortalize his memory through the erection of a statue. Instead of those colossi, in the present day one accordingly erects small pyramid-shaped stone mounds whose tips are painted with a type of limewater.[64]

(La Pérouse had not been on the island long enough to discover that it had not one chief, but two: the permanent *'ariki mau* and the pro tem Birdman.) Above all, La Pérouse was disappointed in the Easter Islanders' characters:

All their flatteries and caresses were nothing more than dissimulation. Never did their facial features express a truly felt emotion . . . They permitted themselves obvious acts of violence in dragging to us girls of thirteen to fourteen years in the hope of being able to appropriate for themselves what these might earn.[65]

He was adamant that no Frenchman 'took liberties' with these girls or with other females, and there is no reason to doubt this – there was little time ashore and no privacy. His verdict of these people, as recorded in his log: we French came to them with benevolence, gifts and peace; yet 'they pelted us with stones and stole everything that they could carry away'. He estimated their number to be about 2,000.

Apparently none of La Pérouse's animals had time to breed. (Later visitors would leave swine, too, which were fed on bananas and sweet potatoes then devoured with their litter.) His gift to island ethnography was profound: his geographical engineer Monsieur Bernizet effected a detailed and accurate description of the monuments and houses they encountered, which the expedition's artist immortalized.

Having spent only one day on Easter Island, the French sailed off.

'SUCH A FAVORABLE APPEARANCE'

Foreign ships began descending on Easter Island after the French visit (illus. 5). Although there is certain documentation of more than 50 vessels visiting or sighting the island before the calamity of 1862–3,[66] the real figure is probably much higher than this. Roughly half of these known visitors were New England whalers. The rest were international explorers, naval personnel, traders, sealers and perhaps one group of French Catholic missionaries. After James Cook's visit, Hanga Roa became the customary anchorage; for this reason it has been called Cook's Bay to the present day.

5 The Imperial Russian Navy approaches the shore from Capt. Otto von Kotzebue's *Rurick*, 28 March 1815.

(Chile prefers 'Hanga Roa'.) Those who landed on the island came primarily to get fresh water and replenish their ship's stores, which they did above all with the Islanders' sweet potatoes, yams and bananas. Like La Pérouse, in 1821 the captains of the *Foster* and *Surrey* left behind seeds – perhaps to encourage the Islanders to cultivate crops for future ships' needs, as was common at the time throughout Polynesia. (Again, there is no evidence that the attempts were successful.)

Until 1805 the only outsiders to call were explorers, naval personnel and traders with their crews. With the first sealer came the first (known) outrage of the nineteenth century. James Cook's third expedition to the Pacific had discovered fur seals along America's north-west coast. Once news of this spread in the 1780s, sealers began voyaging from Canton (Guangzhou), the first Chinese port to open European trade, to hunt the seals, then replenish and winter over in Hawai'i, whereupon they would return to Canton to sell their sealskins for small fortunes.[67] The trade involved mostly Hawai'i and New Zealand's South Island, but it affected islands off Chile as well. This latter development proved fateful for Easter Island.

In 1805 (another source cites 1808) the crew of the *Nancy*, perhaps captained by the hard-driving and ruthless J. Crocker of Boston, whose infamy was already known to the Russians, allegedly fought a bloody encounter with Easter Islanders, then kidnapped twelve men and ten women.[68] These were intended as 'labourers' for a proposed seal-hunting colony on Más Afuera (now Chile's Isla San Ambrosio), but when after three days' sailing the 22 captives were allowed on deck for the first time, all the men sprang overboard and began swimming back towards Easter Island, well over 200 nautical miles astern. The captain tried to recapture them, but failed. (None would have survived.) The women were taken to Más Afuera, from where they and / or their descendants perhaps emigrated to Chile, Peru and elsewhere. Allegedly the *Nancy* returned, under the same captain, several times to kidnap more Easter Islanders for the Más Afuera colony.

Once word of the incident had circulated in Pacific ports, outraged captains thought that this would explain why Easter Islanders had violently prevented Captain Adams of the *Kahu-manu* from landing in 1806; Captain Winship of the *Albatross* apparently met the same animosity in 1809.[69] (Curiously, Captain Page of the *Adventure* had reported no violence after his visit to the island in 1806.) Europeans and Americans, not Easter Islanders, were to perpetrate all subsequent atrocities that occurred there as well. Before the 1870s only one foreigner died at the hands of Easter Islanders (in 1856; see below), whereas from 1722 to 1863 more than 1,000 Islanders were gunned down or transported to their deaths by Europeans, North Americans and South Americans.

Although a few isolated whalers had begun calling at Tahiti and Tonga by 1800, none had hitherto arrived at Easter Island. Pacific whaling was far from North America's and Europe's markets; each whaling venture to the Pacific required, on average, three years. This made the undertaking too costly, and therefore unprofitable. But times were changing. Generations of North Atlantic whalers had all but eradicated entire populations of sperm whales that were the developed world's most valuable and applicable source of oil for lighting and industrial lubricants (until the discovery of petroleum in the 1850s). The Americans, Britons and French realized that the only way to maintain a steady supply of whale oil was to turn to Pacific stocks, despite their distance. With the demand for whale oil soaring as Atlantic sperm-whale numbers dwindled, Pacific whaling at last became profitable. Whalers now descended on the Pacific Islands in droves – and stayed for decades.

The Pacific's whaling trade was briefly interrupted by the American-British War of 1812–14, but then dramatically increased at exactly the same time that the sandlewood trade in the region was starting to decline. In Pacific islands, the whaling trade became the whaling industry: for 40 years (1820–60) it was the backbone of Pacific commerce. Whaling was the stimulus for the Europeanized Pacific. In most places, it was New England American: in 1828 the USA had 200 whaling vessels, nearly all from New

England, ranging the Pacific; sixteen years later, there were 571. (Britain and France together had only a few dozen whaling ships in the Pacific in the 1840s.) New Englanders from the new United States dominated whaling in the Pacific, commonly sailing with half their crews Polynesian – usually Hawaiians and New Zealand Māori who further complicated local gene pools.

From the 1820s Easter Islanders, too, began to profit in several ways from the whaling trade, as ever more ships called to replenish stores, take on fresh water, trade and 'mix'. The Islanders created a local demand around items at first merely fortuitously given to them: metal ornaments, coins, empty bottles, but especially wood, items of clothing (particularly hats and caps) and fishhooks.[70] In exchange, visitors sought above all the Easter Islanders' wooden carvings: especially the statuettes or 'small idols' that, since James Cook's visit, had become collectors' items.

Yet sex was perhaps even more frequently trafficked. If a crew were denied shore leave, women and young girls were frequently brought on board where they earned trade items for their menfolk. In 1830 Captain Waldegrave of HMS *Seringapatam* logged that 'the women admitted the embraces of the sailors in the most unreserved manner'.[71] Of the same crew, Midshipman John Orlebar confessed: 'We found that chastity was not in their catalogue of virtues, but certainly, proved with us, I am ashamed to say, their best article of traffic.'[72] Again, this ostensibly meretricious conduct, witnessed at this time throughout Polynesia, was not 'prostitution' in the Western sense, with all its social and moral connotations. It probably originated in, and in part was continued out of, the combined necessity to increase the respective descent group's holdings and to enrich its gene pool – the latter an especially enduring and status-enhancing prospect on small Pacific islands. Its ultimate upshot on Easter Island and elsewhere, however, was not only the birth of many children of mixed (mainly New England American) pedigree, but also the prevalence, already by the 1830s, of venereal disease.[73]

Such associations necessarily altered island life further. Although the old culture was being lost, no new replacement was being consciously fashioned. Islanders simply reacted to the series of intrusive events, creating in the process a 'jury-rigged society' beating towards an unknown horizon. In time, Easter Islanders would be building long mounds, called *miro 'o'one* ('earthen ships'), and re-enacting, with singing and dancing, a European crew. Sometimes mock boats were constructed in which Islanders performed in actual crew garments, with European gifts as stage properties.[74] So much contact with English-speaking crews was taking place that many words of 'Whalers' Pidgin' were now entering the Old Rapanui vocabulary: *manuā* ('man 'o war'), *poti* ('boat'), *moni* ('money'), *tara* ('dollar') and many more.

Predictably, many island youths wished to become 'real birdmen' and fly from Easter Island on a foreign vessel. As early as 1795, two of them begged Captain Bishop of the *Ruby* to bring them to 'Britanniee'. But at least in this one instance, the English merchantman sailed without them.[75]

One of the more fascinating tales in this regard has to be that of the teenager 'Henry Easter'.[76] When Captain Benjamin Page of the south whaler *Adventure* put in at Easter Island in 1806 to refresh his scurvy-ridden crew, the youngest son of 'King Crang-a-low' (Kura Ngaro?) – perhaps a *tangata hōnui*, since no Kura Ngaro figures among the preserved names of *'ariki mau* – secured a hammock for the return voyage to England. When his son left the island, according to the Massachusetts *Worcester Gazette* of 8 January 1812, quoting a London paper, 'King Crang-a-low was supposed to be 125 years old, scarcely able to walk, and his hair as white as milk, and father of twenty three children, all of whom were alive.' Six years later, in 1812, the Easter Island immigrant was baptized 'Henry Easter' at Rotherhithe church in London. 'This young Prince', continued the *Gazette*, 'is, in every respect, a handsome man, about 22 years of age, five feet eight inches high, is very tractable, and will, in a short time, be able to civilize his countrymen, if an opportunity should offer.' There is no record of Henry Easter's fate: whether he did indeed return to Easter Island, or fathered a family in England instead.

Only a few other names, or nameless cases, are known of Islanders who managed to depart. There was a certain Toroveri 'who went to sea in a whaler sometime in the [nineteenth] century'.[77] A famous *rongorongo* expert was U'i Hiva (literally 'Seen Foreign Land'), born about 1780, who perhaps had spent a few years on an early whaler.[78] Miguel Kere Muti Hea (Timikore Keremuti) of the Tūpa 'Otu, born about 1828, claimed that he had been taken to Tahiti when he had been 20 years old (*circa* 1848); 'White men made [a] mark on his hand', it was noted, suggesting slavery or penal servitude.[79] Doubtless many left the island, their names never recorded.

Their return to Easter Island, for the few who succeeded in this, could prove dangerous. Several years before 1866, a vessel approached the island and a few Islanders swam out to it, one of whom, though married, expressed his desire to join the crew. The captain – 'probablement améri-cain', as the French account relates – consented and the Easter Islander sailed away on a voyage that lasted 'nearly two years'. Finally back at Easter Island once again, the young man was sent ashore, alone, in a ship's boat, by his remarkably generous captain. When he entered Hanga Roa, he was recognized by friends and family, but they thought him to be 'his shadow' – that is, a spirit. So they chased him with stones. He fled for his life back to the small ship's boat. But his Easter Island wife, who had jumped into the sea, then into the boat, embraced him publicly, convincing the crowd that it was not a spirit but her living husband. At which point the crowd battled over the boat instead: two men were killed and several wounded, the boat itself being destroyed in the chaos.[80]

On his way from Valparaíso, Chile's main port, to Hobart, Tasmania, in 1821, Captain Raine of the *Surry* called at Easter Island and was most taken by the pleasantness of the Easter Islanders and their lovely isle. Accordingly, he 'entertained an idea of bringing one of them with him, who seemed anxious to forsake his country and friends'.[81] But fearing for the fellow's prospects abroad, Captain Raine then retracted his offer. As a result, 'the native that was selected on this occasion, was not well satisfied with the determination of Captain Raine; on the contrary, he seemed to feel the denial of his wishes rather acutely'. Captain Raine had been unduly impressed with Easter Island, which 'has a much more inviting appearance than when Cook visited it . . . It now wears the cheering aspect of industry, the land seemingly well cultivated, and the fields are laid out with surprising regularity, and the allotments of ground with peculiar neatness'.

By 1821 the island had evidently recovered at least somewhat from the ravages of the eighteenth-century wars and possible pandemic(s). The population was perhaps back up again to approximately 5,000 or 6,000 souls (many of the younger women still facing venereal sterility); cultivation was conspicuously abundant and well managed; and trade with visiting vessels circulated a certain local wealth. Several brief visitors wrote highly of Easter Island and its people at this time. In January 1821 Captain Chase of the whaler *Foster* was the first to mention the dual division of Easter Island society (that is, the Tu'u versus the 'Otu 'Iti) and an annual ritual that unmistakably referred to the Birdman competition at 'Orongo.[82] An account written on Captain Raine's *Surry* in April of the same year, probably by one Edward Dobson, captures the era in exemplary fashion (here published for the first time):

> running along the NE side of the Island, the appearance very beautiful, and as we approached the NW Point, which we rounded at 1 Mile distance, saw a number of the Natives, running hallooing and saw some swimming off to the Ship which was going 4 knots at least through the Water. Hove Ship too with her head off the Shore, but before this was done, they were alongside and had caught hold of the Ropes that had been thrown to them and held on surprizsinly, we hauled six of them up and then hauled the Ropes inboard or we should soon have had too many. As soon as they were on board they began to caper and Dance about, with every Appearance of being very much pleased, they got up the rigging and hallooed and waved to their Friends, which was answered with loud cheers on shore by thousands, nor did they evince any Symptom of fear, but ran about like madmen dancing, Singing +

making all manner of Anticks, their attention hardly being engrossed for one Moment upon the same thing. We offered them Spirits, Wine etc., but they had no sooner tasted it, but threw it out with every appearance of disgust. The Looking Glass particularly excited their curiosity.

They all of them brought a Bag with them either in their hands or tied round their loins, made of the Plantain Leaf containing some beautiful sweet Potatoes. By their signs they were very anxious for wearing Apparel, the Captn and Officers soon continued to rigg them out with Shirts and Trousers, they also gave them Knives, Handkerchiefs, some old Iron Hoops and some Razors, the last they understood the use of, for one of them had a very long Beard, who made frequent signs for to be shaved, which favor was soon granted him by our Gunner.

They Several times amused us with a Dance and Song, each of them taking his part as regular as possible which was far from being a disagreeable or disgusting Performance.

Upon the whole these Islanders appeared a very friendly and inoffensive race of People, their colour Copper, their Hair Black and dark brown, but not woolly, they were well made and had neither the thick lip or flat nose, but their countenance resembles Europeans. their Bodies were tattooed, but two more than the rest who appeared to be chiefs, the Figures about their arms thighs etc. were well executed.

From what could be seen of the Natives ashore, they did not seem to have any offensive Weapon whatever, the Shores were lined with them Cheering, Hallooing and Waving to us.

Before they left the Ship, they measured her from Stem to Stern and from Side to Side, measuring in fathoms and at every fathom one of them would count in a high voice, Stamping with his Foot and throwing his Arm up and down, and they also counted the Number of People on Deck. When they were going to leave us, they tied these cloaths and Presents, every Man his own, in a Bundle and tied it round their loins, and then shook hands with all of us, they having as we supposed taken notice of our doing so, as a Mark of Friendship and so returned the comple[me]nt and overboard they jumped, they were excellent swimmers . . . The Island had such a favorable Appearance, that we were all quite delighted, the Valleys and slopes of the Hills showed to us the Industry of the Natives, as they were all under Cultivation and the fields of Potatoes and Plantains, in such regularity surpassed any thing that could be expected from such a class of People . . . At 3 p.m. our Visitors having left us we made Sail, every one on board much pleased with the occurrences of the day and entertaining the highest opinion of Natives and the Island[83]

Still, the foreign outrages continued, despite the Islanders' obvious harmlessness. The American whaler *Pindos* called the next year, in 1822. Second Mate Waden went ashore and gathered a number of girls, then brought them back to the ship. All night long the crew revelled, then next morning they tossed the girls overboard to swim to shore, where a crowd had congregated. Suddenly Waden shot randomly into the gathered people, seemingly for 'sport'. An Islander fell.[84]

One thing was certain. Easter Islanders were anything but the hostile 'cannibals' of Pacific lore. At worst they could be incited to stone-throwing (1786, 1806, 1809, 1816). Most Mangarevans, the Easter Islanders' closest Polynesian relations, were (and still are) shy and retiring in their behaviour. But the Easter Islanders, in contrast, were always known – as early as Roggeveen's visit in 1722 – to be generally loud and gaily gregarious, a natural proclivity. Exceptional violence did erupt, however, in 1825 during the visit of Captain Beechey of the *Blossom*. When the Welshman's crew went ashore at Hanga Roa, serious pilfering was followed by general pandemonium. Returning to the ship's boat under an assault of stones, some of Beechey's crew opened fire – one Islander, perhaps a 'chief', was killed. One of the *Blossom*'s own officers later surmised that the Islanders had feared the Britons were about to depart 'without making them the presents they had expected'.[85] As a rule, however, trading proceeded on Easter Island calmly and with mutual satisfaction, punctuated now and again by such events as 'the mysterious outrage committed by Captain Rugg in 1838', of which no details are known.[86]

A particularly enigmatic calling – if it occurred at all – was Captain O'Sullivan's of the *Marie-Joseph* in 1843. On board was Monseigneur Etienne Rouchouze of the Catholic Congrégation des Sacrés-Cœurs de Jésus et de Marie, together with seven priests, seven lay brothers, ten nuns, one Polynesian catechist and twelve crew members. It is alleged that, on landing at Easter Island, all were 'massacred' there.[87] But evidence for this is sketchy, at best. It is true that, while en route to do missionary work on the Pacific islands, the vessel disappeared. But if the *Marie-Joseph* had landed at Easter Island and encountered difficulties there, it would probably have simply sailed away again.[88]

Uncontested is the inexplicable tragedy that befell Robert F. Weeks of Captain Hamilton's whaling barque *President* (or *Prudent*) of Westport, Connecticut. Arriving at Easter Island in May 1856, the crew had just stepped ashore to trade when the pilot Weeks was promptly murdered. Islanders captured another crewman, but he managed to escape.[89] The extraordinary incident – the only known case on Easter Island before the 1870s of an outsider's murder – has no explanation.

Many white men had come; none appears to have stayed. It is not impossible that a small number of crewmen might have deserted from, or been abandoned by, their whalers there. (One Easter Island family alleges a Tuamotuan connection from this era.) Still, there was certainly none of the settlement that one witnessed at the same time in New Zealand, nor the commercialization that was rapidly altering Hawai'i, Samoa and Tahiti, all of these lying on important trading routes and thus enjoying the benefits of lucrative commerce. Easter Island was literally at the end of the known world, offering only sweet potatoes, bananas, 'idols', brackish water – and sex. While in the vast caverns of European admiralties and American secretariates James Cook's damning verdict still echoed.

THE SHATTERED WORLD OF NGA'ARA

Behind the peaceful façade of most foreign visits – for Easter Islanders, fleeting punctuations of entertainment and gain – lay daily want, with frequent bloodshed and terror. Life was hard and brutish. Time-honoured rituals that had miraculously survived the eighteenth century – such as 'Orongo's *pōki manu* and *pōki take* coming-of-age rites – were now being abandoned. The difficult era generated a wealth of traditions relating of murder and mayhem: not from outsiders, but from one's own neighbours. The main cause of these troubles was still the marauding *paoa*, who upheld, and were fomented by, each respective Birdman who was the island's reigning *matato'a*. The stench of burning huts was Easter Island's most common visitor.

By now it was the *matato'a* who were receiving the tuna offerings that in the past had always been the privilege of the *'ariki mau*. Many plants were vanishing from the island. This was because the *rāhui* ('periodic and temporary restriction') laid on plants for ecological management had always been the prerogative of the *'ariki mau*. Challenged by the *matato'a* and their thugs, a weak paramount chief failed to maintain the venerable custom. Most Islanders still held their *'ariki mau* in highest regard, considering his person to be sacred. But his temporal authority had gone completely. It was the *matato'a* alone who now 'governed' Easter Island.[90]

Between 1838 – when the French admiral Dupetit-Thouars had caught sight of statues still standing atop an *ahu* on the north-western coast – and 1864, the last *mo'ai* fell (illus. 6). Probably already by about 1840 all *mo'ai* at *ahu* were down.[91] (No one alive in the early 1900s could recall seeing a statue standing on an *ahu*.) It appears that the last to be toppled was the giant Paro – the tallest to have been erected on an *ahu* – which solitarily crowned the famous *ahu* Te Pito te Kura on the mid-north-eastern coast. The vandals this time had been the 'O Uta of the Tūpa 'Otu *mata*, who bore a grudge against the 'O'one of the same *mata* 'who had eaten one of their women'. The woman's son had then trapped 30 of the 'O'one in a cave 'and consumed them in revenge'. In the resulting clash, Paro thundered to earth.

6 Fanciful late nineteenth-century depiction of the *huri mo'ai* or 'toppling of the statues'.

It was like the last palm to be felled on the island. With the deafening thud, an entire way of life suddenly came to an end. Ironically, it coincided with the begin of the reign of Easter Island's final great *'ariki mau* – 'the last man to fill the post of ariki with its original dignity'.[92]

Many names of *'ariki mau* have survived in confused and contradictory 'kings' lists' that are as much myth and legend as they are faulty memory and invention.[93] Nga'ara's father appears to have been Kai Mako'i, perhaps son of Te Rahi who was son of Mata Ivi (although this is disputable). It appears that Nga'ara's reign as Easter Island's paramount chief began about 1835; his death came in about 1859 ('shortly before the Peruvian raid').[94] More than 50 years after his death he was still well remembered. Short, corpulent, with 'white skin, as had all his family', he was so heavily tattooed that he looked black. He wore feather hats and, front and back, little wooden ornaments. His wife having died early, he lived with his son and heir Kai Mako'i 'Iti ('Junior'). His capital was 'Anakena, on the north-eastern coast.

'Nga['] ara held official position for the whole island', wrote the British anthropologist Katherine Routledge from eyewitness statements more than half a century after the fact, 'but he was neither a leader in war, nor the fount of justice, nor even a priest; he can best be described as the custodian of certain customs and traditions. The act most nearly approaching a religious ceremony was conducted under his auspices, though not by him personally.'[95]

In times of drought, Nga'ara sent a younger son – not Kai Mako'i – and other *'ariki paka* of the Miru up to a hilltop to ask the still-revered

Polynesian deity Hiro (not Makemake) for rain. Nga'ara also increased the fertility of chickens, it was believed, and he was often approached to perform this ritual. He dedicated any new house boasting stone foundations: after placing wooden lizards at either side of the entrance crawl-hole, Nga'ara and his *tumu ivi 'atua* were the first to eat in the new residence. Significantly, despite the simultaneous rule of terror by the pro tem Birdman and his *paoa*, Nga'ara 'was visited one month in the year by "all people", who brought him the plant known as pua ['turmeric', *Curcuma longa*] on the end of sticks, put the pua into his house, and retired backwards'.[96] At such a sacred moment, his *rongorongo* experts would intone the reverential chant 'What does the king make fertile in the country?'.[97]

For the *rongorongo* had become Nga'ara's trump card. It was his weapon to counter the Birdman's challenge to the *'ariki mau*'s religious authority. Before Nga'ara, it is a moot point whether the *rongorongo* had constituted a prerogative of Easter Island's paramount chief. But Nga'ara, from his seat at 'Anakena, brilliantly exploited the 'sacredness' perceived to be inherent in the invented script in order to render it an exclusive expression of the royal *mana*. With this, he won power from each performance, while simultaneously expanding the phenomenon's social domain.[98] The annual gathering at 'Anakena, for example, to read the *rongorongo* tablets and staffs – this event took priority even over war – asserted the pre-eminence of the *'ariki mau* in all matters sacral. (At this, Nga'ara and his son heard the readings, rewarded the successful and punished the unsuccessful.) There were also minor asssemblies at each new moon, when Nga'ara 'walked up and down reading the tablets, while the old men stood in a body and looked on'.[99]

Nga'ara even sent his *rongorongo* experts to chant at the holy site of Mata Ngarahu at 'Orongo during the 'egg-wait', although Nga'ara himself dared not trespass; through his experts' loud chanting, the *'ariki mau*'s presence there would have been tangible. (Nga'ara came only as far as Mataveri, which had earlier been a lair of the Birdman's *paoa*.) Nga'ara also travelled round the island visiting each local *rongorongo* expert for a week or two. The *rongorongo* not only figured among Nga'ara's most public responsibilities: he himself was acknowledged to be the island's greatest expert.

Whereupon Nga'ara's fragile world suddenly shattered. His related kin of the Marama *mata*, 'inspired with jealousy because the Miru had chosen the Ngaure [Ngā Ure *mata*] as their successors',[100] burnt down Nga'ara's house at 'Anakena. The royal Miru had deferred to the Ngā Ure not only because these had been the island's ascendant power in the 1850s, but because they had been carrying off Miru to be their *kio* serf farmers. When the conflict escalated, the Ngā Ure, in retaliation, captured Nga'ara, his *atariki* son Kai Mako'i 'Iti and grandson Mau Rata and carried them off to their centre at Akahanga on the south coast. For five long years the Miru were powerless to free the royal family, in whom all island *mana* was traditionally vested.

Finally, in a remarkable twist of history, the Miru joined forces with their traditional foe the eastern Tūpa 'Otu and rescued Nga'ara, his son and grandson. But by then the paramount chief was old and ill. He went to live with his daughter, who had wed a Marama, and while there at 'A Kapu on the western coast he died. Six men carried the illustrious chief's ponderous corpse on three large *rongorongo* tablets one kilometre south to Tahai, where he was sepultured within the island's most venerable *ahu*. Fittingly, the sacred *rongorongo* tablets were then envaulted with him.

Old Easter Island society survived well into the nineteenth century – though with substantial changes – until its final annihilation in the 1860s. (The last members of this society died in the 1910s and 1920s; see chapter Four.) By 1862, primarily because of venereal sterility, the island's population had probably again dropped back to 3,000 to 4,000. By this time Easter Islanders had regulated their trading customs with the frequent visitors, fixing local 'prices' and appreciating the true value of outsiders' goods. There was no more pilfering. Islanders now understood foreigners' sensitivities and usefulness, and this had rendered nearly every encounter a mutually satisfying exchange.

Significantly, no Easter Islanders sold their pubescent daughters for muskets and powder, so the island avoided those 'Musket Wars' that decimated New Zealand's Māori at this time. Nor did the Islanders make any attempt to seize a foreign ship, as happened so often at other Polynesian ports. Not merely was a collective desire to wage modern warfare or to 'escape' the island's isolation in such a way totally lacking here, no central authority existed either to imagine or to organize either enterprise. The *tangata hiva* – the 'outsiders' – forever remained the providers of a serendipitous and individual bounty: rare wood, clothing, fishhooks . . . and, increasingly, hard *tara* ('dollars').

Certainly, the 'fatal impact' of repeated encounters with Europeans and Americans had, through cultural contamination and possible pandemic(s), permanently altered Easter Island society. But already by the early nineteenth century it was the Easter Islanders themselves who were transforming local life through their increasing reliance on the outsiders' goods, 'cultemes', genes. Although over succeeding years the Islanders would attempt to continue to control their own fate, the island's small population and extreme isolation meant that it could never be anything more than a pawn in a much larger, fiercer game of imperialist exploitation. Easter Islanders were never to attain to that degree of self-control exercised by larger Polynesian populations such as the Māori, Hawaiians, Samoans and especially Tongans. European and

American unilateral 'impact' then came to play a much larger role on Easter Island than the outcomes of such contact on other islands. Easter Islanders were to share, then, little initiative in all subsequent island developments; they also held little responsibility for these, from 1866 to 1966. The concept of 'dual agency' was hardly to figure in the approaching century of oppressive neglect.

Yet this was still to come. The discovery of petroleum for lighting and for industrial lubricants in the 1850s was ending whaling – with all its commercial benefits and social repercussions – everywhere in the Pacific. At the same time, Britain and France were competing with one another as never before in order to realize openly imperialistic designs in the region. Tiny, isolated Easter Island? It was again teetering. Its declining population was suffering from increasingly limited natural resources, from more frequent inter-*mata* conflicts (even Tu'u were fighting Tu'u now), from the renewed terror of the Birdman's marauding *paoa*, from the uselessness of local exchange systems, from the apparent impotence of Makemake, from the obvious futility of all religious ritual now that the *'ariki mau* Nga'ara was dead. It was once again an island on the brink of collapse.

In February 1862 Captain Smalley of the New England whaler *Edwards* approached to within several kilometres of Easter Island, but sailed away again without calling. On 7 September Commander Joseph Laurent Lejeune of the French frigate *Cassini*, after having spent three months flaunting the French presence along the Peruvian coast and in the Chincha Islands, ranged Easter Island for several hours, sighting on shore between 1,200 and 1,400 Islanders. Dispatching two launches to make closer observations, Lejeune welcomed aboard several Islanders from whom he acquired sweet potatoes, taro and one chicken in the most harmonious manner. Greatly impressed by the 'hale, robust and well-looking' Easter Islanders, when Lejeune visited Valparaíso in mid-October he stopped in at the regional headquarters of the Congrégation des Sacrés-Cœurs de Jésus et de Marie (sscc), France's leading Catholic missionary society. Here he praised Easter Island's qualities to its Vice-Provincial, Father Pacôme Olivier, and to Father Albert Montiton, then on his way home to France after having missioned for the sscc for thirteen years in the Tuamotus.

In 1825 the Congrégation pour la Propagation de la Foi had petitioned Monseigneur Coudrin of the sscc to send missionaries to the Pacific, and at the end of the following year the first Catholic missionaries had embarked for Hawai'i.[101] Father Honoré Laval had established the Mangarevan Mission in 1834; a Marquesan mission had followed in 1838; and in 1841 the first Catholics had at last been allowed, as a result of intense French political pressure, to carry out missionary activities in the Kingdom of Tahiti, which then became an apostolic vicariate seven years later, responsible for Tahiti (the Windward Islands), the Marquesas, the Australs, the Tuamotus and the Gambiers (Mangareva).

Father Montiton was so impressed by Commander Lejeune's report about Easter Island that he immediately suggested to Father Olivier that they bring Christian salvation there, too, and he volunteered himself as leader of the historic mission. Unknown to the French commander and priests, however, Peruvian 'blackbirders' were at the same moment planning their own special mission.

Not to save Easter Island, but to ravish it.

three

Pirates and Priests

The period 1862–88 is the second most important in Easter Island's history.[1] In the first nine years, approximately 94 per cent of the population perished or emigrated – one of the Pacific's greatest human losses. It was also then, in blood and anguish, that ancient 'Easter Island' crumbled – and *Rapa Nui* was born.

For most of the nineteenth century, the world's two leading colonial contenders – Britain and France – harboured little interest in Pacific Islands: the region was too poor and too far away to be of any true advantage in the greater scheme.[2] To be sure, in the 1840s France had acquired important islands in east Polynesia – Tahiti, the Marquesas, the Tuamotus – in order to profit from trans-Pacific trade and the robust whaling industry. And Britain had colonized New Zealand, mainly to supply its larger Australian investment. But by the 1860s the robust Pacific promotion was over, chiefly because whaling had collapsed. East Polynesia's dominant foreign power – France (only tiny Pitcairn lay in British hands) – certainly had no immediate plans for the area; profits from the fledgling coconut oil and pearl-shell industries were appallingly small. Easter Island's role in the area? It epitomized the end of nowhere, as Cook himself had famously decreed.

Suddenly things changed. Whereas the French man-of-war *Cassini* had ranged the coast of Easter Island in 1862 with no specific orders, by 1868 the British man-of-war HMS *Topaze* was assessing the island as a potential British protectorate. By then, the South Pacific had become an extension of the 'Great Game': Pacific Islands had evolved into an international arena. In the ideology of the time, Easter Island, for its part, was also 'up for grabs'. Each subsequent naval visit to the island – in the 1870s and '80s – must be seen in the light of this infinitely larger contest. For every global power, and would-be global power, was by this time mindful of the immediate challenge: how to make Easter Island a national asset.

As it happened, Easter Island's second colonization did begin as French after all. 'The foundation from France came in the form of missionary priests and lay commercial exploiters, from 1863, until France abandoned the place to Chilean influence in 1888.'[3] From 1871 especially, when most Easter Islanders became exiles struggling to survive abroad, the few indigenous people left on the island began fading into the background, metamorphosing from prehistory's 'active doers' and history's 'co-directors' into modern 'passive receivers'. For the *tangata hiva* or 'outsiders', those who had shipped them offshore, replaced their 'gods', stolen their patrimony then exploited the landscape, were now wielding history's plume. The rude intrusion – by all manner of pirates and priests – heralded that 'relentless process of modernization by Western agencies'[4] that quickly transformed both population and island beyond recognition. But first came . . .

THE RAPE (1862–3)

'Blackbirding', or kidnapping, was the most heinous series of crimes ever perpetrated against Easter Islanders.[5] Peru was to blame, its name still anathema to most East Polynesians because of the outrage. Like most South American countries, Peru had abolished slavery and was suffering serious labour shortages. It had also exhausted its labour force of Aymara, Quechua and other indigenous peoples of the Andes. More than 500 Chinese labourers had promoted the Peruvian economy in the 1850s, working in mines, plantations and private residences; but then Britain had halted Peru's access to the Chinese labour trade by blocking entry to Chinese ports. Commercial enterprises had turned to other sources of labour: African blacks, even poor south-western Germans and Austrian Tyrolians. But this had not sufficed. The Peruvian economy desperately needed more workers – and the cheaper the better.

At this point a Dubliner, Joseph Charles Byrne, arriving in Peru in 1861, suggested to the Peruvian government something rather novel: why not simply trade in indentures instead of people? 'It would be these contracts, not the people . . . that would be sold to the highest bidder at public auction.'[6] So it would not be slavery, at least not formally. And a harvest of cheap labour was waiting just next door, in the Pacific Islands, he assured the country's leaders in Lima. Primitive Islanders, with nothing to lose, would be eager to become 'immigrants' to civilized Peru. The government agreed, and issued Byrne a licence to recruit such 'immigrants', under long-term indentures. Ironically, Byrne died in October 1862 on the first voyage of his 'immigration' scheme, while returning from Tongareva in the Cook Islands.

Byrne's death did nothing to discourage other entrepreneurs, however. Convinced of the financial soundness of the scheme, they had already organized their own expeditions. A number of international vessels had been chartered and outfitted, targeting in particular those Polynesian islands that still lacked the immediate protection of some European power and which lay closest to Callao, Lima's port. At the top of their list was Easter Island, closest to Callao and still unclaimed. In time, Easter would even become the blackbirders' rookery.

One of the first to recruit 'immigrants' at Easter Island was Captain Martínez of *La Serpiente Marina*, who arrived at Pape'ete, Tahiti, on 8 November 1862 with, among other booty, two Polynesian prisoners who announced to shocked French authorities that they were from the 'island of 'Anakena'[7] – the first documented time that Easter Islanders identified their island to others abroad. Outraged at the 'immigration scheme', the French officials immediately freed the indentured Islanders.

But it was only the beginning. In December 1862 perhaps a total of eight vessels crowded the Hanga Roa roadstead off Easter Island to collect 'immigrants' there. A few captains held close to the initial scheme of legal recruitment: with each 'immigrant' they insisted on signed, witnessed and later confirmed contracts of indenture, wherein all duties and benefits were clearly spelled out for the concerned parties and legal authorities. Captain Sasuategui of the *Elisa Mason* representing Callao's Sociedad de los Seis Amigos, for example, even used a Polynesian interpreter, brought from Callao, in order to explain to the Easter Islanders, if at all possible, their potential benefits in return for bonded labour under specified conditions.

One typical contract, entitled 'Emigración' in bold letters, is Sasuategui's of 20 December 1862. In it, the respective Easter Islander is contractually promised passage and food to 'whatever part', clothing, a blanket, 5 pesos in gold or silver, medical care when sick (but docking pay), a monthly wage of 5 pesos (4 in cash minus 1 for passage, clothing and food in the port), and two changes of clothing each year. For this, the Easter Islander indentures himself / herself for eight years, in a place to be designated, free to practise his / her religion, holidays to be exempt from forced labour except in domestic service, whereby he / she must show respect and obedience towards superiors. In this case, the Islander signed with an 'X', the Polynesian 'interpreter' signed as well (though no interpretation was possible, since no outsider yet knew the Easter Island language), and then Captain Sasuategui signed. Later at Callao the contract was endorsed with yet another signature.

In this way, legally and humanely, Captain Sasuategui enlisted, on their own volition and without violence, no fewer than 238 Easter Islanders. And the contractual promises were kept. More than a century later, one Easter Island family recalled how two brothers had been given time before embarking to take leave of their relatives and, later in Peru, had managed to send Easter Island's first 'remittances': woven blankets and South American trinkets.[8] This was not slavery.

However, most of the eight recruiting captains in that terrible month of December 1862 were of different ilk. One allowed Easter Islanders to board for trade, then suddenly locked them below and sailed off. Most of the captains simply anchored their vessels close together in Cook's Bay then sent in armed parties, who, once arriving on shore, spread out mirrors, clay pipes and other small goods. When the Easter Islanders approached to collect these apparent tokens of friendship, they were seized, tied up and thrown into waiting launches. Specifically targeted for labour were males in their twenties. Fleeing Islanders were pursued and caught – or simply shot and left for dead.

Many Islanders resisted. Six years after the event it was related to the visiting British officers of HMS *Topaze* how three Peruvians[9] – a much later account claims only two[10] – were killed, cooked and eaten. (If true, this would be the only known case on Easter Island of cannibalism directed towards outsiders.) The response of one British officer was: 'with such provocation it is not surprising'. Nearly all resistance was futile, however, and the Islanders fled yet again to family caves. Within weeks, the island had become 'a staging area where Polynesians collected from other islands were brought'.[11]

The horror lasted for several months, well into 1863. Apparently as many as 1,500 Easter Islanders were abducted or killed during this time. Perhaps even more: after the Peruvian government's crackdown, unscrupulous captains might have diverted their wretched cargoes to the ports of Huacho, Islay or, as one Chilean Consular record suggests, Lambayeque.[12] Half of the island's population was gone.

They were dying in Peru. By June, 1,408 Easter Islanders were registered there (of whom 1,054 had 'signed' legal contracts of indenture).[13] Of these, 1,282 were working as agricultural labourers or domestic servants, most of them having been sold, like slaves, at public auction with fellow Polynesians. Crammed into Callao's huge quayside warehouses, many were still waiting to be sold. A very small number ended up shovelling guano in the hellish summer heat of the Chincha Islands, where Polynesian labourers were dropping like flies. This was allegedly the tragic fate of Nga'ara's son Kai Mako'i 'Iti – Easter Island's current *'ariki mau* – and grandson Mau Rata.[14]

Easter Islanders in Peru and the Chinchas experienced only death. Tuberculosis, smallpox and dysentery proved to be civilization's strongest gifts, to which the Polynesian 'immigrants' quickly succumbed because of poor nutrition, overwork, lack of hygiene, crowded accommodation, the harsh climate of plantation heights and especially 'nostalgia' (clinical depression), all of which challenged already weakened immune systems. Most labourers were males in their early twenties. Many worked as domestics in middle-class Lima households, further exposed to simple childhood contagions against which they had no immunity. Their Peruvian adventure was soon over, however. Of the 322 Easter Islanders who had arrived to work in the Chillon and Chancay Valleys, for example, only 119 were still alive six months later.[15]

International protests began almost immediately. When he learnt that his Catholic converts in the Marquesas, Tuamotus and Australs had been blackbirded to Peru, Bishop Jaussen of Tahiti, for one, did everything in his power to effect their immediate repatriation. In time, Monseigneur Florentin Etienne 'Tepano' (Tahitian for English 'Stephan') Jaussen – first Apostolic Vicar of Tahiti and titular Bishop of Axiéri *in partibus infidelium* – would become one of the Easter Islanders' historic champions. Born in the Ardèche, France, in 1815, he entered the Congrégation des Sacrés-Cœurs de Jésus et de Marie (sscc) in 1845 and was sent to teach at their mission school at Valparaíso, Chile.[16] Four years later he left for Tahiti as East Polynesia's first apostolic vicar, and remained there at the sscc's Catholic Mission at Ha'apape (now a suburb of Pape'ete called Mission, only ten minutes' walk south-east of the city centre) until his death 42 years later. At a period of great political unrest and international power struggles in East Polynesia – particularly between Britain and France, and France and the Vatican – Jaussen's aspiration was to enrich his Islanders' power base in order to counteract what he believed was a virulent European exploitation in the area. 'Tepano' Jaussen would soon come to identify with the Easter Islanders, too, whom he took under his wing. For him, their cause was always paramount: for the very survival of the Islanders lay at its heart.

Receiving the full support of the Vatican, which also resented Catholic converts being kidnapped with official Peruvian sanction, Bishop Jaussen put pressure on the French minister in Lima to halt the fraudulent 'immigration' scheme. Lima's leading newspapers, and even some important government officials, had already dared to challenge the morality of the business, but their censure had largely gone unheard. Now France, which at that time was opposing Peru's support of the rebels in the Mexican Civil War, exploited this latest outrage to ally Britain to its larger cause. Against such a powerful coalition, the Lima government had no choice but to cancel all 'immigration' licences, which occurred with the decree of 27 April 1863. Orders were then issued to assemble all Polynesian immigrants at Callao and other minor ports in order to return them to their respective islands as quickly as possible.

If anything, the resultant 'repatriation that wasn't' triggered an even greater tragedy. For in April 1863 the quarantined crew of the American whaler *Ellen Snow* were allowed ashore at Callao. This was where most Polynesians were now gathered – initially for auction, but then for repatriation – and more were arriving daily from distant valleys to overcrowded quayside depots. Once ashore at Callao, the Americans eventually spread 'one of Lima's worst smallpox plagues in decades'.[17] Peruvians were hurriedly vaccinated. Polynesians were not, and so within days they began to succumb. What was worse, with repatriation the small numbers who survived the voyage home imported the smallpox bacillus (and other contagions) with them. The consequence for small, crowded, island populations was devastating. Returnees to Nuku Hiva in the Marquesas, for example, immediately infected the 3,800 locals there: in consequence, nearly half the island's population – 1,560 Nuku Hivans – were dead within a few weeks.

Easter Island was not spared. It is claimed that of the approximately 1,500 Easter Islanders who had been blackbirded to Peru, nearly all soon perished there. During repatriation 85 survivors died, perhaps aboard the French vessel *Diamante*, which was returning Polynesians to the Marquesas around September 1863. And only about a dozen Easter Islanders actually disembarked at their homeland again. (Among the returnees was Ure Kino, later baptized 'Pakomio' [French 'Pacôme'] Māʻori.) One was infected with smallpox.[18] The subsequent epidemic decimated the island's remnant population of about 1,500. Three years later, a missionary was told that so many had died at this time that it had not been possible to bury them all.[19] The outbreak appears to have carried off all the *tumu ivi ʻatua* – the island's priests and bearers of traditional chants and genealogies – as well as all the *rongorongo* experts.

In this era of death, the island's new name was born.[20] In December 1862 the Peruvian schooner *Cora* had taken several Easter Islanders, among them Mau Rata's son Manu Rangi ('Heavenly Bird') – the next *atariki* or 'heir apparent', who was then about eight years of age – and had then sailed to Rapa in the Australs to recruit more 'immigrants'. But the Rapans had seized the *Cora* and sailed in her to Tahiti. Under way, Manu Rangi and the other Easter Islanders had apparently compared geographical notes with their Rapan saviours and hosts, thereby discovering that Rapa ('Extremity') was indeed only Rapa 'Iti ('Lesser Extremity'), whereas Easter Island was Rapa Nui ('Greater Extremity / Land's End'). The name being incomprehensible as such in the Easter Island language, it was simultaneously translated into this as Te Pito ʻo te Henua ('The End of the Land'). Whereupon Manu Rangi's *mana*, as heir, ensured that the new Polynesian name 'Rapa Nui' was adopted by all Easter Islanders once the young *atariki* returned to the island in January 1864, on the same vessel bringing the first missionary. In writing, the name first appears as 'Rapa-nui' in the 1863 handwritten memoirs of Father Honoré Laval of Mangareva. The new name Rapa Nui fittingly defined both the place and the fate of Easter Islanders in the new Polynesia that was then emerging. (From this point on in the present history, following current usage, the spelling 'Rapa Nui' will be used to designate the island, 'Rapanui' to designate its people and their language.)

What was the result of the blackbirding and then the pandemic on the remnant Easter Island population? Besides sudden depopulation, it brought heated disputes over lands that had once belonged to the deceased and disappeared. The years 1863 and 1864 were marked by intermittent hostility, persisting dearth and continuing mortality. When crops were to be allocated, violent quarrels broke out. These then escalated into larger 'tribal' conflicts that eventually resulted in 'looting, devastation and famine'.[21] Into this chaos Rapa Nui's first missionary naively interloped.

EUGÈNE EYRAUD[22]

Easter Island's first Christian mission was not directly the result of the labour raids. The French commander Lejeune's favourable report of 1862 had prompted Father Olivier of the sscc in Valparaíso to charter the schooner *La Favorite* so that Father Montiton, Father Rigal and the novice Joseph-Eugène Eyraud might establish an sscc mission there. But on its way to Easter Island in May 1863, *La Favorite* stopped first at Pape'ete, where, during Bishop Jaussen's absence, the Superior of the Missionaries of the Apostolic Vicariate, Father Fouqué, informed the three would-be missionaries to Easter Island that their chosen island had been the victim of terrible labour raids. He was sorry, but the Apostolic Vicariate of Tahiti had decided that it was not an appropriate time to mission there after all.

The novice Eugène Eyraud refused, however, to abandon the project. From his Bolivian mining interests the Frenchman had become modestly well-to-do and, emulating his missionary brother Father Jean Eyraud of China, now wished to dedicate his fortune and talents to the sscc.[23] Despite the fact that he was still completing his noviciate, Eugène Eyraud argued passionately to Fouqué that if the sscc would let him go to Easter Island alone he would be able to 'prepare the way' for a later, official mission once conditions improved. Despite the obvious dangers this involved, Fouqué saw the logic of the proposal and chartered the schooner *La Suerte* towards this end.

Thus it happened that, on 9 December 1863, *La Suerte* sailed out of Pape'ete, bound for Easter Island. Aboard were several Easter Island returnees who had miraculously escaped the labour raids: Pane 'a Paohu, 'Adrien', Tama Teka, another man, a woman and a child – Manu Rangi, Easter Island's next *atariki*, who was now returning as the apparent *'ariki mau*. They first called at Father Laval's mission at Mangareva, where 'Daniel', a local Christian Mangarevan, boarded as second pilot and as Eugène Eyraud's personal assistant for the Easter Island Mission. As the voyage continued, Eyraud taught the Islanders the Tahitian catechism and some Christian doctrine, aided by Daniel and Pane 'a Paohu.

La Suerte arrived just off 'Anakena's white sandy beach on 2 January 1864 – Pane, a Miru who hailed from 'Anakena, had urged them to land there.[24] But the captain objected and in the afternoon they sailed around to Hanga Roa, where on 3 January Eyraud and the Easter Islanders disembarked. The Mangarevan Daniel accompanied them towards shore in the launch, but then became horrified at the prospect of so many Easter Islanders there. They were armed with *mata'a*-tipped lances and heavily tattooed: all seemed on guard, fearful of *La Suerte*'s intention. Daniel made the launch return, saying he feared the Islanders and their smallpox and would not go ashore 'for 1,000 francs'. Whereupon the captain then offered to take them all back to Tahiti, without payment. But Eyraud was not so easily frightened, and set out with the returnees in the launch a second time after the captain had agreed to deliver his effects to 'Anakena's beach the following day – if Eyraud turned up alive. (Daniel never did set foot on Easter Island, but returned to Mangareva.)

At this point Eyraud suddenly found himself on shore at Hanga Roa – facing some 1,200 men, women and children, many armed with lances. The returnees were not celebrated at all. Instead, the Islanders were after Eyraud's and the returnees' personal effects. Eyraud set off at once with Pane for 'Anakena and safety, but both were halted and manhandled. They tried to flee, then hid behind rocks. Eyraud was pulled out again into the middle of the crowd. Presently Pane extricated him and offered *kumara* from an earth oven – Pane's immediate intervention might well have saved Eyraud's life – and only after a harrowing night both of them finally reached 'Anakena.

Here Eyraud signalled to *La Suerte*, which was waiting offshore. But the schooner simply sailed away: it hadn't seen him. Eyraud was devastated. 'It was for me a moment of profound sadness when I saw myself abandoned in this island, without recourse to any goods and deprived for some time perhaps of the means of being able to speak of religion to these unhappy natives.' Most of all Eyraud lamented the loss of 'a Tahitian catechism that was indispensable to me in instructing the natives the prayers and first truths of the faith' – Bishop Jaussen's small *Ui Katorika* printed by E. Dubuisson at the vicariate's press at Ha'apape.

But only hours later Pane came up with a fellow Miru just arrived from Hanga Roa, saying that *La Suerte* had unloaded all Eyraud's effects on the Hanga Roa beach – and the locals there had stolen the lot. Shocked a second time, Eyraud spent the night at 'Anakena in Pane's hut, then returned to Hanga Roa the next day to face the same hostile crowd. Only his locked trunks and prefabricated building material still lay on the shore. At once Eyraud set about erecting his shack, just above the small bay of Apina 'Iti, using the hammer and nails from his trunks while being harassed incessantly by Hanga Roa locals. But soon he was finished and able to spend his third night ashore – behind a locked door, relatively safe from assault for the first time.

Close by stood the hut of Torometi, the *tangata hōnui* or 'leader' of the local Miru, who was to confound utterly the Frenchman's many months there. The problem lay in Eyraud's building his hut within Torometi's terrain. In the Easter Island way of things, Eyraud and all his possessions were then Torometi's. In exchange for Torometi's protection, Eyraud would daily receive cooked *kumara* – and no other food (the famine lingered). Despite these circumstances, and though he did not command the Old Rapanui language, Eyraud dedicated himself to Christian tuition. He conducted prayers with the locals three times a day and also held a class to repeat the prayers, instruct the Tahitian catechism and teach reading. (This was the first Western-style instruction on Easter Island.) By the end of his sojourn on the island, five or six Rapanui were reading regularly and Eyraud himself had learnt rudimentary Old Rapanui, 'which is more difficult than one thinks'.

Eyraud had initially started building an adobe chapel as well. But after three months' intense labour its 8-by-4-metre foundation walls were melting under unremitting rain. So he concentrated on teaching the Tahitian catechism instead. Once he went to 'Anakena for a few days to teach, but then the news arrived that Torometi had in the meantime appropriated all his effects. Eyraud rushed back to Hanga Roa: to be sure, nearly everything had vanished. When challenged about this, the *tangata hōnui* replied it had been 'the wind'. This, and the harsh wet southern winter, put paid to Eyraud's missioning outside Hanga Roa.

As September and its Birdman competition approached, Torometi even stole Eyraud's clothing, among other possessions, telling the Frenchman that it was to guard them in a safe place. Torometi then began to oppose Eyraud's freedom of movement, hampering the baptism of the dying who had received Christian tuition and had requested this. (Pane had been one of those who had died, at 'Anakena.) In consequence, Eyraud tried to flee, and made it as far as the Hanga Piko cove with a simple bag of belongings. But once there, the locals began stealing even these. Suddenly Torometi appeared with several of his *paoa* and, by force, hauled Eyraud back to Apina 'Iti.

It was soon after this that the *La Suerte* returnee Tama Teka, Torometi's enemy, arrived from nearby Mataveri with his own *paoa* to gather between Eyraud's shack and Torometi's hut, shout and threaten. When Torometi failed to attack the intruders, fearing their numbers, Tama Teka's *paoa* set fire to the *tangata hōnui*'s hut but spared Eyraud's shack; indeed, they even protected this and Eyraud's person, too, with their lances. But Torometi fled to Mataveri, taking Eyraud with him, and an angry crowd followed who tore off Eyraud's clothing and shoes along the way. Once arrived, the Frenchman thought his ordeal over, but then Torometi forced him back to the shack in the dark. Eyraud was now fearing the worst. Torometi demanded he give him everything in the shack. Eyraud told him truthfully that his keys had been stolen with his clothing. So Torometi forced entry through the roof and stole its entire contents but for an old pair of shoes and a blanket. The two of them then spent the night at Torometi's brother's hut at Hanga Piko cove.

After this, things changed for the better. For the very next day Torometi, apparently realizing his role towards Eyraud had to change or he would lose his control over him, led the Frenchman to Vaihū. The village seemed not only less hostile, but eager for Eyraud's instruction. Greatly encouraged by this, Eyraud set about teaching them the Tahitian catechism – dressed in the one blanket and old pair of shoes that was all that remained of his personal effects. He had been at Vaihū for only eight days, however, when all the boys in his class cried out 'Poti!' ('boat' in Whalers' Pidgin) and ran down to the shore. It was 10 October 1864, and Eyraud had been on Easter Island for nine months.

Father Pacôme Olivier, Vice-Provincial at Valparaíso, had chartered the schooner *Teresa Ramos* and sent Father Barnabé Castán and Brother Hugues Delpech to find Eyraud and return him to the Chilean regional headquarters of the sscc. It had been a tempestuous voyage: with a sick captain and a malfunctioning chronometer they had been unable to locate Easter Island and were only one day away from turning back. Eyraud had thought the vessel would simply pass by, as several had done over the many months. But on 11 October a boy arrived from Torometi saying that the ship had anchored at Hanga Roa. Curious, Eyraud came to see for himself, and met Torometi halfway there with his *paoa*. The party led Eyraud down to Hanga Roa's beach. Everyone was fearing that it might be the Peruvian blackbirders again. But as soon as Eyraud saw the French flag, he reassured the Rapanui. Many plunged into the water and began swimming out to the vessel, just as in earlier days.

A woman was first to arrive on board. She headed straight to Father Castán, made the sign of the cross and recited in Tahitian-Rapanui the Lord's Prayer, Ave Maria and Creed. Castán was bowled over. Other Rapanui then did the same. A launch was sent to fetch Eyraud, who was soon aboard the *Teresa Ramos* where he was given food and clothing. (The fathers were shocked at his state of undress and physical condition.) Eyraud declared that he wished to return to shore to continue his missioning. But Castán convinced him of the advantage of returning temporarily to Valparaíso, in order to regain his health and secure the necessities to establish the first official mission. Only reluctantly did Eyraud agree. Having anchored only four hours at Hanga Roa, the *Teresa Ramos* sailed off.

Eyraud thought he had been a missionary. In reality, he had been merely Torometi's *kio*, his serf. The Rapanui had had changing attitudes about this first foreign resident on their island: at first they were openly hostile, then merely curious, then amused and, finally, generally indifferent. There was nothing in it for them, so they left him alone to do what he wished – as Torometi's possession. A few Rapanui liked the chanting, a pleasant diversion. A small number were fascinated by Western writing, and five or six even learnt to read, though they hardly could have understood what they were reading. Lacking a corresponding vocabulary, the Old Rapanui language could not conceptualize Christian theology and so the real message was lost. Everyone saw, though, that at least not all *tangata hiva* were rapacious – only very strange. Doubtless Eyraud's celibacy (he was a devout novice) would have caused them the greatest wonder and hilarity, probably prompting them to think he was *mahū*.

Eyraud wrote an exciting account of his sojourn, which, in 1866, was translated into several languages and printed in European journals and magazines. It was probably the largest reading audience that Easter Island had enjoyed until then.

In the nearly eighteen months between Eyraud's departure in 1864 and the landing of the first official mission to the island in 1866, a major upheaval brought renewed fighting, house burnings en masse, the destruction of crops and yet again widespread famine – a level of violence and desolation Eyraud had never experienced. Nearly all of the hundreds of *rongorongo*-incised staffs and tablets he had seen with his own eyes were destroyed in hut burnings at this time; only a few survived, hidden away in damp caves subsequently to rot. The interval was one of death and destruction, one of the worst in island history. At the exact causes one can only surmise. One thing was clear, however. In 1865 Easter Island was dying – as a place, a culture, a people.

'A GOVERNMENT IS ESTABLISHED'

At the end of 1864, Eugène Eyraud's enthusiastic report convinced Father Olivier of the sscc that it was again time to try to establish a permanent mission at Easter Island. Olivier encharged Eyraud with all preparations, in view of his intimate knowledge of the island and experience with its people, who were now calling themselves 'Rapanui'. Wealthy Valparaíso businessmen and their wives provided financial and material support for the mission: the port was then still one of South America's wealthiest.

To lead the new mission, Father Hippolyte Roussel was appointed. It was perhaps an odd choice, though understandable. A tall and powerful, even commanding figure, he had arrived in the region from France in 1854 to evangelize in the Tuamotus and Mangareva. But he had been removed from the latter posting 'due to his strident pronouncements and inconvenient actions which interfered with French trading in the area'.[25] Perhaps Roussel was now being exiled to Easter Island as punishment. Or perhaps it was a deliberate challenge by Olivier, who was ultimately responsible for the sscc's missioning in East Polynesia, against the authority of Bishop Jaussen, who happened to be Roussel's most critical opponent. (One scholar has alleged that Jaussen and Roussel were 'bitter enemies'.)[26] In any event, it was to prove a fateful choice. There can be no doubt that the selection of Father Roussel as Head of Mission played no small role in the catastrophic antagonisms that determined Easter Island's later fate.

By this time Eyraud had finished his noviciate at Valparaíso and become a brother of the sscc. Father Roussel and Brother Eyraud arrived at Pape'ete, Tahiti, at the end of 1865 where they were received by Bishop Jaussen at his Ha'apape Mission. In February 1866 the two missionaries sailed with their Mangaian cook 'Pou Koki' (Whalers' Pidgin for 'Poor Cook') on Captain Lauray's *Maria i te Aopu* – also called the *Notre-Dame de Paix*, the vessel of the people of Mangareva[27] – first to Mangareva, where Father Laval entrusted to them for assistance the Mangarevan Christians Araki ('Alaritio'), Akilio ('Achille') and Papetati ('Babilas'), who seemed eager to join the mission to Easter Island. The *Maria i te Aopu* arrived off the Hanga Roa roadstead on 23 March 1866.

The vessel's arrival had again caused great alarm among the Rapanui. A large crowd was waiting on the shore, armed with lances and loudly clamouring. Forceful Roussel, well acquainted with Polynesian customs, lost no time in demonstrating his *mana*. As soon as he landed he positioned himself atop a sacred *ahu* – perhaps Tautira (whose fitted stones were to be cannibalized for the mole in 1932) – and began blessing Easter Island then addressing the crowd in fluent Tuamotuan. Hearing a stranger speak a language so similar to theirs surprised and at once calmed the Rapanui, who acknowledged Roussel's dominant personality and peaceful intent. They had also recognized Eyraud.

Captain Lauray's men started unloading the Mission's effects at once, of which the most important was the galvanized zinc sheeting. Taking five days, the chore occasioned much pilfering. By the time the *Maria i te Aopu* sailed off again on 28 March, Eyraud and the three Mangarevans had already finished constructing two shacks: one for Roussel and Eyraud to live in, the other for the three Mangarevans and the Mangaian cook. After this, the Mission's first few months on the island were harrowing. When a small group of Rapanui would become frustrated at their inability to plunder the newcomers' effects, they would bombard the zinc shacks with stones and shouts. 'It was impossible to close our eyes, day and night', wrote Roussel, 'it was necessary to seal everything hermetically and to light the lamps in full day.'[28] But in time things improved. Roussel would venture out to visit the sick and baptize the dying, and he would oversee all religious instruction, using the Tuamotuan language while learning Rapanui and beginning to write a Rapanui catechism. Eyraud and the Mangarevans were Roussel's labourers: they raised other buildings and planted their imported plants, seedlings and seeds.

The first building of substance to rise was Easter Island's chapel, constructed of planks and situated on Hanga Roa's beach. The Rapanui still directed individual threats against the intruders. Even Eyraud was not spared. He would have been buried alive, for example, by a Rapanui demanding his clothing had not Roussel, storming up with his ubiquitous staff, frightened off the thug. Eyraud was perpetually kind and deferential to the Rapanui. But Roussel was loud, gruff and domineering, it appears, wielding his thick staff which he used to knock sense into unrepenting Rapanui skulls.[29] Yet the attitude of the Rapanui soon began to change towards the outsiders. More Rapanui arrived from outside Hanga Roa, and ever larger numbers began to participate in religious instruction.

The reasons for the Rapanui's rapid 'adoption' of Christianity are unclear. The missionaries, of course, believed it was the recognition and acceptance of a superior belief. But because many of today's Rapanui still have faith in spirits and curses, Christianity might simply have been a 'cultural overlay', as has been more plausibly suggested.[30] That is, the adoption of the trappings and customs of the Roman Catholic faith formed part of a greater complex of behavioural adjustment: with these the Rapanui were signalling to the *tangata hiva* that they wished to be a part of their lives, to profit from their material wealth. Naturally the Rapanui appreciated, too, that a part of this adjustment included forfeiting their belief in, and practice towards, Makemake and other local 'deities'. But they were eager participants in this forfeiture – so long as it brought them food, clothing, shelter and medicinal care.[31]

Seeming proof of the two missionaries' ability to provide – their *mana* – suddenly arrived about 17 June 1866 in the form of a three-masted schooner. For the Chilean millionairess Isidora Goyenechea Couciño had donated to the Catholic Mission a small number of cows, a bull, one or two mares and a colt.[32] To the Rapanui this would have seemed like divine dispensation. Nothing like this had ever happened before: succour and supply from abroad. And so, just as a century earlier they had abandoned Tangaroa and other traditional ancestral spirits for a single powerful Makemake at a time of desperate need, now they turned to a new solitary godhead – but as a supplement, not a replacement. This was no Christianization. (Admittedly, there were also Rapanui who understood the Catholic creed and accepted it knowingly, but these appear to have been a small minority.) On Easter Island, never would the belief in traditional spirits and curses disappear entirely.

A great help in the conversions and general acculturation came from the three Mangarevan Christians Araki, Akilio and Papetati. Their presence was acutely felt by all Rapanui. In addition to this, the Roman Catholic holy office included many Polynesian chants and hymns with which the locals could immediately identify, providing not only entertainment but also much-needed comfort. No *tangata hiva* had ever offered this before. Within a few short months, Roussel in particular was regarded as a strange form of *tumu ivi 'atua* and, with this, had become 'socially acceptable' within indigenous understanding. On Sundays and holy days the small chapel was packed.

As the Catholic liturgy became more familiar, little Manu Rangi, the last *'ariki mau* – now about 12 years of age and 'distinguished by his intelligence and his excellent dispositions'[33] – became an active catechumen, then the first 'adult' to receive baptism on Easter Island. He received the baptismal name 'Kerekorio' (Grégoire).

One still has for him a certain respect, one still brings him the first-fruits of yams, but he in no way intervenes in island affairs. The power is always usurped by several usurpers each more audacious, more wicked, than the other, who succeed one another each year, tyrannizing the population, aggravating its misery and accelerating its complete dissolution.

Manu Rangi's Christian conversion, however, set an example. In September 1866 Roussel and Eyraud attended the proclamation of the last Birdman to be chosen during their Mission's duration. The cross had seemingly replaced the egg – for the moment.

From then on, 'there remain only a few tapus of which [the Rapanui] make little ado', wrote Roussel boldly.[34] All the island's traditional priests, the *tumu ivi 'atua*, had apparently died by 1866 of smallpox and TB; there had certainly been no opposition to Christian conversion from a traditional 'priesthood'. Roussel summarily forbade among his converts at Hanga Roa many non-Christian customs: nudity, tattooing, most sexual practices and, above all, idolatry or ritual performance of any kind. Even the word *ure* ('penis') was replaced by *kinonga* ('wickedness') in the Old Rapanui language. Traditional Easter Island chanting, singing and dancing all but vanished at this time.

Although the *tangata hōnui* Torometi had earlier been driven out of his Hanga Roa terrain by the *tangata hōnui* Roma, he had returned and, in time, persuaded Roussel to base his Mission permanently there, on Miru land. Whereupon he then convinced Roussel of the advantages of shifting the first Mission houses inland from the beach and erecting a large Western-style building on the site of a traditional Miru meeting house. 'The Church, Torometi wanted it to be quite clear, was firmly in Tu'uaro [Tu'u] hands.'[35] As he had done when Eyraud had been there alone, Torometi was attempting to exploit the foreign presence for personal power. As a result, the SSCC Mission eventually came to comprise 635 hectares of land at Hanga Roa, which, through a series of fortuitous circumstances, would eventually become the nucleus of a new Rapanui society. (This explains why Hanga Roa is today's single settlement; the SSCC's title later became Chilean state property.)

In order not only to secure the six-month-old Mission but also to empha-size Valparaíso's direct stake in it, Father Olivier dispatched two further sscc missionaries to the Easter Island Mission: the German father Kaspar (French Gaspard) Zumbohm and the French brother Théodule Escolan. They arrived on 6 November 1866 with one cow and three calves, as well as with other ani-mals, fruit trees and seeds. Captaining their transport vessel, the majestic three-masted schooner *Tampico*, was the Frenchman Jean-Baptiste Onésime Dutrou-Bornier – one the most notorious personalities in the South Pacific.

Grandson of Deputy Dutrou-Bornier of Paris's infamous Etats Généraux of 1789, Jean-Baptiste Dutrou-Bornier was apprenticed at the age of 14 to a mercantile firm at Le Havre, only to become an artillery officer in the Crimean War. By 1860 a master mariner, he then abandoned his wife Valentine and son in Paris and purchased the *Tampico* in 1865 as a one-third owner, sailing to Callao, where he was arrested, accused of arms trafficking. His trial brought a death sentence. But the French consul there, Jules de Lesseps (brother of the builder of the Suez Canal), managed to effect Dutrou-Bornier's release on lack of evidence. Dutrou-Bornier then settled at Tahiti, where he lived with his new partner Mo'o Atare from Mo'orea, sailing in the *Tampico* throughout East Polynesia recruiting labour for the Scots-Tahitian Maison Brander's coconut plantations. (The Scot John Brander and the English-Jewish-Tahitian Alexander Salmon Jr were partners in this trading and plantation enterprise, with lands in Tahiti, the Marquesas and the Cooks for harvesting copra and shipping coconut oil, then the region's prime export.) Bishop Jaussen was later to accuse Dutrou-Bornier of slave-trading in the Tuamotus and of having once boasted in Tahiti of having murdered a man aboard his ship.[36]

The reception that these two new missionaries experienced at Easter Island could not have been more different. Not only were the Rapanui not hostile, but they even offered to carry both missionaries from the launch to the shore so they wouldn't get wet. Soon everyone was congregated in the Hanga Roa chapel down on the beach – large enough to hold 100 persons – chanting Christian prayers and singing Christian hymns in Tahitian, Rapanui and Latin. Roussel's missioning and Eyraud's and the three Mangarevans' hard labour had created a peaceful European-style 'village' with flower and vegetable gardens, several buildings, stone walls and fences. Captain Dutrou-Bornier was quite amazed, as he later confessed to Father Olivier in Valparaíso: 'I cannot tell you what surprised me more, the intel-ligent work of Brother Eugène [Eyraud] or the angelic patience of Rev. Father Roussel . . . Easter Island has, I believe, a grand future.'[37] His curiosity piqued, Dutrou-Bornier began shaping his own plans for the island.

Within two years Eyraud's health was severely compromised, displaying the early symptoms of the TB that he had contracted during his first sojourn on Rapa Nui. He had tried digging a well in Hanga Roa, but the water was too brackish; and so he fetched all the Mission's freshwater himself from Rano Kau's crater lake. The strain was sapping what little strength was left him. Yet he laboured on, despite daily suffering. In this way he built, on Hanga Roa's beach where he and Roussel had begun their mission, two wooden refuges for teaching boys and girls and for housing the many orphans: the labour raids and several pandemics had taken their toll. Once these *pukuranga* ('followers, disciples') numbered 45, Zumbohm assumed responsibility for their care, while Roussel supervised their moral and religious instruction. The children were the first Rapanui to live in Western-style houses and to sleep in real beds.

Dutrou-Bornier had returned in the *Tampico* about 25 March 1867 in order to recruit Rapanui to work as indentured labourers at Tahiti, but he had failed to acquire a single Easter Islander.[38] Perhaps he had been blocked by Roussel, who, alarmed at the many deaths on Rapa Nui, had already been contemplating sending Rapanui to Mangareva, possibly to support themselves by working for the sscc's small copra and pearl-shell industries there. Roussel's Valparaíso support, however, was subsequently lost with the death of Father Olivier on 27 April 1867, which had the immediate result of Bishop Jaussen of Tahiti taking a more active role in Easter Island affairs – and he did not approve of Roussel. From this point on, the two priests Roussel and Zumbohm competed to curry the bishop's favour, creating unnecessary tension within the tiny Rapa Nui Mission. Yet things would go from bad to worse.

For a rapid form of pulmonary consumption (TB) was raging over the island and, in October 1867, 'Kerekorio' Manu Rangi, the island's final *'ariki mau*, the last in the ancient line of East Polynesian royal first-born sons, succumbed. Aged about 13, he left no heir. With his death, Easter Island's royal line was extinguished. At the same time, two of the Mangarevans – Araki and Akilio – perished as well. And Brother Eyraud's health was deteriorating rapidly.

At the beginning of 1868 the wooden chapel down on the beach was dismantled by the surviving Mangarevan, Papetati (Eyraud was now too weak to work), and rebuilt on Mission lands half a kilometre inland. Rapanui children had already been baptized and had received their First Communion; by now these, and also some local adults, were assisting in the holy offices. At the same time, Roussel and Zumbohm were introducing new crops – maize, white potatoes, figs, beans and perhaps also manioc – and instructing in their husbandry. This all had a great impact on local life.

Even inherited traditions were now being abandoned or reinvented, as Rapanui sought especially to adapt themselves to the greater Polynesian culture that the three Mangarevans and the Mangaian had revealed. The legendary Tu'u ko Iho was now being relegated to a minor role in founder tradition, as the Mangarevan founding father 'Atu Motua was adopted as Easter Island's own (later to be called Hotu Matu'a).[39] The aggressive foreign intrusion was forcing a creative reassertion of the island's communal identity. Out of this there eventually developed – mostly in the 1890s – the 'Hotu Matu'a Cycle' of settlement legends, the Easter Islanders' robust attempt to reconstitute their past. At the same time, the new names Rapa Nui and Te Pito 'o te Henua entered 'ancient tradition' as well. Makemake's nimbus, however, remained so strong that even Bible creation texts were reworded in his name. And out at the former 'capital' of 'Anakena, far from the missionaries, many traditional rituals still thrived.

Captain Dutrou-Bornier was now back on Easter Island. He had amassed huge gambling debts and, once some fraudulent deals had collapsed, forfeited his one-third share of the schooner *Tampico* to his main creditor John Brander, co-owner of the Maison Brander. Brander had then made Dutrou-Bornier his recruiting agent and given him the small yacht *Aora'i*. On a voyage first to Mo'orea, then to Rapa in the Australs, with his Mo'orean partner Mo'o Atare and handyman 'Christian Schmidt' (a German on the run who used several aliases and sometimes claimed to be Danish), Mo'o Atare had died after having given birth to a baby girl, Marthe Jeanne. Finally arriving at Rapa Nui about the beginning of April 1868, the *Aora'i* had sunk. But Dutrou-Bornier, the baby and 'Schmidt' had made it safely ashore with their effects – which had included, curiously enough, a small cannon and some rifles.

Initially, Dutrou-Bornier and 'Schmidt' got along very well with the four missionaries, on whom they relied for their immediate survival. Impressed by Dutrou-Bornier's flashy captain's jacket, the Rapanui dubbed him 'Te Pitopito' (Mangarevan for 'The Buttons'). Dutrou-Bornier carefully cultivated cordial relations with everyone, regularly attending the Catholic mass and assisting, with the German 'Schmidt' always at his side, wherever he could. Encouraged by Torometi, Dutrou-Bornier and 'Schmidt' constructed a house for themselves at Mataveri, which they made their permanent base of operations, away from the Hanga Roa Mission. The missionaries soon understood that the pair were not castaways – but colonists.

At this point the TB epidemic was becoming acute. Many of the young *pukuranga* were now dying; women seemed particularly vulnerable. Eugène Eyraud's own life now lay at risk. Passing missionaries from Valparaíso had furnished missing foodstuffs in April 1868, which had temporarily strengthened the brother. But heavy July rains brought horrible attacks of coughing. Eyraud managed a final walk on Sunday, 2 August, together with Father Zumbohm down to Apina 'Iti – where Eyraud had first begun proselyting. Then they paid an amiable visit to Dutrou-Bornier's house at Mataveri, returning to the Hanga Roa Mission in the afternoon.

The very next day, 3 August, while the missionaries looked on, Dutrou-Bornier completed the island's first documented land purchase. From seven Rapanui he acquired approximately 706 hectares of land from part of Rano Kau's crater, the Mataveri slopes and a stretch of the south-western coast including the cove at Hanga Piko.

Only a fortnight later, on 19 August 1868, Brother Eugène Eyraud died of consumption, at the age of 48. Nearly everyone on Easter Island attended his burial in the small church cemetery at Hanga Roa, including his good friend Dutrou-Bornier 'with all his people'. As Zumbohm wrote of Eyraud to the sscc's Superior General in Paris shortly afterwards, 'He sacrificed to the Rapa Nui Mission a good part of his fortune, his labours and his life.'[40]

Only 930 Rapanui now survived, their future bleak. 'If God does not make [this epidemic] stop it will kill off our natives within four or five years', wrote Zumbohm. 'In the last two months [August and September 1868] we have buried 37 dead.'[41] The three missionaries had but one consolation: 'Thanks to God, paganism with its horrors is buried, and we have the sweet and well-founded conviction that, with the help of the Sacred Hearts, no individual is thinking of returning to heathendom.' In fact, Roma, who had once ousted Torometi from Hanga Roa in warfare, was now the Christian 'Tepano', *gendarme* under the Prefect of Police, the Mangarevan Papetati. And Torometi himself was now the Christian 'Kutano' (Gulstan), who tended his garden and no longer beat his wife.

On 15 October 1868 Roussel bought 335 hectares at Hanga Roa from five Rapanui. Dutrou-Bornier, acting as 'President of the Council of State of Easter Island', duly witnessed the *certificat de vente*.

The British man-of-war HMS *Topaze* visited Easter Island from 1 to 6 November 1868, its primary objective being to 'verify [Easter Island's] position on the chart, to search for certain other islands that were reputed to be in the vicinity, and then to make . . . a survey of the island'.[42] International concern about the region had changed since the visit of the French warship *Cassini* back in 1862. Britain was becoming concerned at the strong French presence on Easter Island. Roussel and Dutrou-Bornier personally escorted the British land party to various sites on the island. Underway, Commander Barclay told Roussel of the rumours then circulating in Valparaíso: that Chile was considering the annexation of Easter Island.[43] It was also during this visit that the first act of 'archæological blackbirding' of Easter Island's *mo‘ai* occurred: the famous statue *Hoa Hakananai‘ā* ('Stolen Friend') from 'Orongo, which now dominates the new central court at the British Museum in London. (Similar *mo‘ai*-nappings were to follow in this and the next century, by French, Chileans, Americans, Belgians and others.)

By December 1868 Father Zumbohm could proudly report to Bishop Jaussen in Tahiti:

A government is established, the council of state functions marvellously under the firm and prudent action of the chairman Mr Bornier.

The judicial sessions under the chairmanship of the Rev. Father Roussel are also held regularly every Thursday if there are cases to judge . . .

Our town, Sainte-Marie de Rapanui, is also founded, but there are lacking not only monuments but even the very houses, since there are only huts.[44]

At the same time, Zumbohm requested of Monseigneur Jaussen that if the Mangaia Mission was being started in the Cook Islands then he would wish the Monseigneur to consider sending him there.

For tensions had reached breaking point. Until now, Father Zumbohm and Brother Escolan had remained with Roussel at Hanga Roa. But the differences between the German Zumbohm and Frenchman Roussel, leader of the Rapa Nui Mission, were simply too great. (It appears that Eyraud and Escolan, both being deferential by nature, had had little to say.) Roussel had always been for one Christian centre, to convert and control; Zumbohm believed in missioning afoot. Roussel harboured a deep distrust of 'pagan' manifestations; Zumbohm wanted to use these to ease the Rapanui people into Christianity. To make matters worse, Torometi (of the western Tu'u) and Roma (of the eastern 'Otu 'Iti, by then being called Hotu 'Iti) aligned themselves correspondingly: Torometi supported Zumbohm, Roma supported Roussel. This, in turn, drove an even deeper wedge between the two priests.

Escolan was caught in the middle. 'If I had to judge between the twain', he confessed to Jaussen, 'I would say that the two are wrong, but I would not know which is more wrong.'[45] As a simple brother under two ordained priests, he knew he had no real choice: 'I must serve both.' But at least someone at the Mission was content. Escolan wrote that the Mangarevan Papetati wished to be well remembered to Monseigneur: 'He is very happy with his wife at Rapanui.'

Whereupon Zumbohm and Escolan left Hanga Roa to build themselves a European-style house and church at Vaihū on the south coast. Here they intended to resettle and Christianize the eastern *mata*, effecting the same changes as those already accomplished among the western. 'Anakena, Vaihū, Mataveri and especially Hanga Roa now became the island's main habitations, with nearly all the others lying abandoned. Zumbohm set up his own competing 'native police force', appointing Torometi as Vaihū's chief *gendarme*.

The dying continued. All three missionaries were convinced that one of the main causes of mortality from TB lay in the Rapanui people's poor diet, and so they did everything in their power to improve nutrition: constantly planting, extending the range of cultivars, even importing a wide variety of foodstuffs, plants, seeds and livestock. It was all to no avail. (As we now know, nutrition plays only a minor role in combatting TB.)

In view of what was happening, the sscc, the Maison Brander and their agent Dutrou-Bornier – who had sailed to Papeʻete with the one-year-old Marthe Jeanne – in April 1869 negotiated a contract that, in essence, would render all of Easter Island a sheep ranch.[46] (Wool was fetching a high price internationally.) Brander would charter to the two others the three-masted schooner *Ionia*, under Captain McLean, for their activities at Mangareva and Easter Island. Bishop Jaussen would be sending a shipment of timber to Easter Island, for continued construction. Dutrou-Bornier would be having timber delivered there too, for he would be needing more facilities for the expanded enterprise. He also privately worked out with John Brander that he would slowly begin to acquire legal contracts to Easter Island land from the decimated Islanders – there were only about 700 left – whom he would then send as indentured labourers to the Maison Brander's coconut plantation at Tahiti or elsewhere. This would leave Easter Island vacant for their ranch.

It was perfectly legal. No country held jurisdiction over Easter Island; no international law or court of justice obtained there. John Brander and Dutrou-Bornier certainly realized that, if merely to survive, the Rapanui would have to emigrate anyway: their present mortality rate was simply too high.[47] Roussel had long considered transporting the Easter Islanders to Mangareva to save them, where he had already missioned with Father Laval. The sscc in Valparaíso had received a tract of land in southern Chile and were contemplating perhaps shipping the Islanders there. Dutrou-Bornier now encouraged Brander to press the Bishop of Tahiti to allow the Rapanui to be sent to Tahiti's coconut plantations. With the collapse of the whaling industry, coconut oil would lubricate Tahiti's economy and the market would surely grow apace.

Once everything had been settled and the larger plan for Easter Island was generally accepted by the three parties, Father Zumbohm and the young Rapanui convert 'Petero' Toro Veri – who was 'living proof' to potential donors of the success of the Mission – were sent to Valparaíso in July. There they enjoyed a grand reception, and were inundated with foodstuffs and sewed clothing for the Easter Island Mission. More importantly, they were given two hundred sheep, five cows, two bulls, a horse, six donkeys, four pigs, four dogs, three cats and an assortment of fowl.[48] Zumbohm's conspicuous presence in Chile reawakened political interest in Easter Island. Santiago's daily *El Mercurio* even published an article asking the government to take possession of the island.

On 2 December 1869 Zumbohm and Petero returned to the island not only with their menagerie, but also with two Chilean servants for the Vaihū Mission, Jorge and María Arena – the first Chileans to reside on Easter

Island. (The Polynesian carpenter Kamake and his wife, sent from Tahiti, were already serving the missionaries.) On the same day, with his new cash and goods in kind, Zumbohm purchased 300 hectares at Hanga Roa from the Tahitian or Mangarevan 'Pierre' Mau, who had earlier bought them from various Rapanui. Perhaps the Mission could be saved after all, Bishop Jaussen and the three surviving missionaries must have been thinking at the time, their resolve now strengthened. Their plan was to shear and breed the sheep and sell the wool and mutton in Tahiti through the Maison Brander. Dutrou-Bornier would handle the enterprise's local management and shipping. But 'Te Pitopito' had different ideas.

THE COLONIAL WAR

Immediately upon his return from Pape'ete, Dutrou-Bornier began 'buying up' large tracts of land from pre-literate Rapanui who had signed the 'sales receipt' with an 'X'. If the captain met any resistence, he merely flaunted his rifle. As one such receipt – dated 10 June 1869, but registered by others at Pape'ete only in November 1880 – testifies, purchases took place for something like '150 francs in merchandise'.[49] (The veneer of legality was strictly maintained in the event that France, Britain or even the Vatican might object.) This particular land purchase happened to be for 'Hotu iti and environs' – that is, most of Rapa Nui's eastern half.

Dutrou-Bornier invited Father Roussel to co-sign the purchases as legal witness, since Roussel, as Head of Mission, represented one-third of the contractual party in the enterprise. But Roussel vehemently refused, strongly disapproving of what Dutrou-Bornier was doing. In particular he resented Dutrou-Bornier's wish to transport the Rapanui to Tahiti, of which plan the captain made no secret. At first Dutrou-Bornier was shocked. Then he was furious, realizing this scuttled his venture.

After this, Dutrou-Bornier dropped all pretence. For him there could be no partnership, not even a coexistence, with the sscc on Rapa Nui. He would toss the missionaries off the island, and with them the entire Rapanui population – who would become indentured labourers in Tahiti. He would indeed supply the Maison Brander as agreed: but with his own sheep, confiscated from the Mission. For him there was no alternative. Easter Island had room for only one *ariki*.

Immediately seizing this opportunity to regain lost influence, both Roma and Torometi found the confrontation to their liking: it was very Rapanui. Roma, from Tongariki, a Tūpa 'Otu of the eastern 'Otu 'Iti, now sided with Roussel at Hanga Roa. A western Miru of the Tu'u *hānau*, Torometi left Zumbohm to settle at Mataveri and become Dutrou-Bornier's man. Here, Torometi first led about forty men and women, an improvised *ivi* based on pre-missionary allegiances. Like him, all were western Miru.[50]

For some time already, Dutrou-Bornier had supported a community at 'Anakena as well. But Roussel had always opposed this, preferring centralization at Hanga Roa. Shortly before October 1869, a small band of Rapanui who belonged to Roussel's Hanga Roa Mission attacked the 'Anakena community, destroying some 'old huts' there. It was only much later – once more violence had occurred – that Dutrou-Bornier, in explaining himself to Bishop Jaussen in a letter, accused Roussel of having incited this initial violence. Affirming he was against neither the Church nor the missionaries, the captain declared truthfully that he and Roussel could no longer co-exist on the island.[51]

In the months that followed, a tit-for-tat conflict raged, with few casualties but much grief. In this, the seven resident Europeans (plus one American) were equally the victims of the Rapanui, who were eagerly reviving ancient antagonisms.

Of course, Dutrou-Bornier knew best how to profit from the violent situation, since aggression was his forte. Yet even while Torometi and his *paoa* were harassing the Hanga Roa Mission on his behalf, the captain and Father Zumbohm were amiably exchanging pigs at Vaihū. Despite his utter loyalty to the sscc, Zumbohm frankly got along better with the bold captain than with the offensive Roussel. Dutrou-Bornier's purpose here might well have been to 'divide and conquer', granted. But the priest's open friendship bespoke volumes. It was also at this time that Dutrou-Bornier took by force the wife of Te Hatu Tini ('The Lord Tini') who lived at Rapa Oteo by *ahu* 'A Kapu, just north of Tahai. 'Koreto' – Pua 'Aku Renga ko Reto – was the daughter of Kai Ika Mata of the eastern Tūpa 'Otu from the area of Ma'unga Teatea (Pōike), and she would remain Dutrou-Bornier's partner until his violent end.[52]

From 22 to 29 January 1870 Commander Don José Anacleto Goñi of the Chilean corvette *O'Higgins* led this South American country's first official visit to Rapa Nui, ostensibly to 'train midshipmen and to lend assistance to the natives'. (Aboard was Midshipman Policarpo Toro, who nearly two decades later would almost single-handedly forge the island's political destiny.) The commander assured Zumbohm that the Chilean government had no intention of seizing the island: in everyone's opinion, he said, for any government that might do this there would only be great expense without benefit.[53] But, in truth, the commander's orders, partially prompted by that earlier *El Mercurio* article, comprised the gathering of information about the island's present situation for Chile's consideration of possible annexation. Taking advantage of the naval presence, Dutrou-Bornier at this time exchanged Rapa Nui's most magnificent *rongorongo* artefact – the famous

'Santiago Staff' – for a keg of gunpowder. In their final report, the Chileans remarked that TB was the island's most prevalent disease and that the suicide rate among the Rapanui was abnormally high. (Apparently the deaths of so many loved ones had caused widespread clinical depression.)

Despite everything, the situation on the island was still tolerable for the missionaries in March 1870, when Zumbohm informed Monseigneur Jaussen that, now that timber had arrived, both chapels were under construction; yet there was not enough material to finish them.[54] The TB epidemic was still rampant, however, and the Mission 'is leaving something to be desired'. Zumbohm was quite enchanted with his new carpenter Kamake, who had been trained at Ha'apape, Tahiti, by Brother Aloys Holtrichter (Jaussen's carpenter at the Catholic Mission).

But then the tit-for-tat strikes resumed, with even greater violence. Torometi and his *paoa* now began raiding regularly Hanga Roa for food and poultry. In reprisal, on 15 April 1870 the Hanga Roa locals, led by Roma, plundered Torometi's own personal yam plantation at Mataveri. This prompted a bloody war between the two groups. It raged until the end of July.

Dutrou-Bornier first had his personal strike force attack Hanga Roa and burn down three or four small huts.[55] Then he incited his Rapanui to tear out the Mission's sweet potatoes (whose loss could mean famine). When Roma's men followed them back to Mataveri, Dutrou-Bornier shot and seriously wounded one of the pursuers, forcing everyone to flee back towards Hanga Roa. At this point, for good measure, Dutrou-Bornier loosed his cannon at them: the thunderous explosion in the middle of the village of Sainte-Marie de Rapanui burst a great boulder and knocked a woman off her feet. Outraged, the villagers attacked the cannon's position, trying to seize it for themselves, but failed. So they destroyed Te Pitopito's boat instead and burnt down his thatched hut on the shore. During the mêlée Torometi fired his rifle at his own two brothers, but missed. Whereupon the missionaries intervened and peace was re-established. The missionaries then compensated the people of Hanga Roa for their losses with articles of clothing from SSCC stores.

A few days later, on 28 April, Mini, an ally to Roma, challenged Torometi to hand-to-hand combat at Mataveri in Old Rapanui style. Arriving with his *mata'a*-tipped lance, Mini took up his warrior's stance while Torometi strolled up with his rifle. Mini threw and missed. Torometi lifted up the rifle, calmly took aim – and killed Mini on the spot.

Several encounters followed. On 7 July, after yet another such skirmish, Dutrou-Bornier arrived at Sainte-Marie de Rapanui with his American henchman and his German Schmidt, who was 'inside [the enclosure] with his rifle, this to carry off the girls'. Torometi, also armed, and others (including Tepano Tau Mo'ai) damaged the Mission house and again tore out food plants. Then they proceeded to the new Christian cemetery close to the centre of Sainte-Marie: they smashed to pieces Eyraud's new gravestone that had cost 250 francs (US $50) at Valparaíso, then broke the crosses over the graves. After this they went to a Mission house near the sea, broke down its doors and casements, then unroofed another small building alongside (which later had to be demolished). Then they went on to destroy a stone wall that surrounded two hectares of Church land; ruin a large brick oven, smashing most of the bricks; then fill in, with large stones, a well used for watering the livestock. Dutrou-Bornier attended each offence. During it all, Roussel was guarding a number of orphan girls who were housed close to the Mission enclosure. Once done there, the captain's armed band then attacked Vaihū, setting three fires and destroying Zumbohm's plantations.

That same day, Zumbohm wrote an angry letter to 'friend' Dutrou-Borner:

> How can you answer before God and before humanity for what you do and are having done? Who has ever taught a Frenchman to colonize as you are doing, leading this pitiful population to destruction and to abominations? . . . What a misfortune for the poor inhabitants of Easter Island that you came to settle here! . . . I conjure you by all that is most sacred: make an end to these wars.[56]

(Since the end of April, Zumbohm had been seriously ill with gastritis, unable even to perform mass. His Chilean servants Jorge and María Arena had been tending him there at Vaihū, applying medications. María also cooked and made all clothing; she was, in fact, 'the soul of Vaihū'. Both were eager to return to Chile, however. Zumbohm was willing to let them go, now that local Rapanui had learnt to perform most necessary duties at the Mission.)

During the same night, a woman was disfigured with axe blows; Timone 'a Rikitea received a horrible neck wound, Ioane ko Hara a wounded thigh, Ko Moha a wounded shoulder, the child Ko Penapara a head wound – all this within the Hanga Roa enclosure where the Vaihū population had been enjoined to seek refuge. The next day the captain's men returned to plunder.

Two days later Dutrou-Bornier ordered the torching of all remaining dwellings at Hanga Roa. Several of Roma's people were killed. To end the violence and effect compensation, Roussel arranged that sweet-potato plantations be exchanged between the two warring parties. The people of Mataveri soon squandered the sweet potatoes they had been ceded, however, and began stealing those of the people of Hanga Roa – with the captain protecting their pilfering with his rifle. Roussel's own personal plot lay next to that ceded to those of Mataveri. Only a few days after the exchange, on 22 July, Roussel was there with the orphan girls so they could harvest some of his *kumara* for themselves. But suddenly: 'Here comes the captain with his rifle!' cried the girls.

Roussel watched in silence. When Dutrou-Bornier came within rifle range, he stopped, took aim directly at Roussel and fired. Roussel, who had not flinched, then thundered over to Dutrou-Bornier: 'Monsieur, I think it is in jest what you are doing!', he cried.

Bornier merely opened his hand, showing him the musket ball: 'Here's the ball.' 'Know that the potatoes are mine!' 'I knew nothing of it.'

Brother Escolan's laconic comment to the episode: 'We knew he [Dutrou-Bornier] was angry at him [Roussel] for not having wished to sign his land purchases.'

It was very like the 'Musket Wars' of other Polynesian islands. But here only one side was armed. And it was led not by an Islander, but by a French megalomaniac who wanted the island for himself. Already by September 1870 Dutrou-Bornier 'owned' 13,237 hectares of Easter Island's 16,059 hectares of land. (The sscc Mission had only 635 hectares, in Hanga Roa.) And his Rapanui 'wife' Koreto had borne him a daughter, Caroline. His blood was now mixed with this Polynesian people in a way that the missionaries' could never be.

Te Pitopito's war 'against the poor *canaques*' – Escolan's way of putting it to Bishop Jaussen, still believing the violence was directed against the Rapanui and not against the Mission *per se* – had already lasted a full year. What confounded the missionaries most, it appears, was Dutrou-Bornier's un-Christianlike behaviour: 'He receives married women; he burnt the village at the height of winter; he has re-established paganism; he is giving the *canaques* rifles to shoot at their compatriots, and to the greatest brigands of the island.'[57] Escolan's frank opinion was: 'If he continues, the Mission is lost.' Dutrou-Bornier now had more than 80 people at Mataveri, and all of them had renounced Christianity. Escolan ended his sad letter with a personal complaint: 'Here I am again reduced to serving two masters, for the Rev. Father Gaspard [Zumbohm] had brought a Chilean and his wife, but he has pestered them too much. They are deciding to leave by way of Tahiti.'

Not only Jorge and María Arena were leaving. The Polynesian carpenter Kamake and his wife were joining them on the *Marama* (formerly Dutrou-Bornier's *Tampico*), all of them anxious to quit the troubled island in September. They bore with them Zumbohm's own letter to Bishop Jaussen. The German Zumbohm was, by now, also despairing of the Mission: 'If the Chileans take the island, it is going to depopulate rather quickly.' It would do so anyway, he felt. He therefore deemed it useless to send more building materials for the two rising chapels.

However, for the little that it must last, if Monseigneur [Jaussen] could make Mr Dutrou Bornier leave from here for us, it would be a favour which would be worth paradise for a good number who probably will not have it under his patronage. At Mataveri one refuses the sacraments and all religious assistance to the dying. One does not have the children baptized, one does not come to Mass on Sunday. The Christian prayers and religious instructions [are] replaced by heathen dances, by games and chants, etc.[58]

As Tahiti's Queen Pomare Vahine iv had once turned to the new Queen Victoria of Great Britain as the Polynesian kingdom's ultimate 'authority', the Rapanui of Easter Island now turned to the Bishop of Tahiti, their own 'Tepano' Jaussen, writing fervent letters in Tahitian imploring the bishop to have the Church intervene on their behalf. It was the first time in history that the Rapanui people directly sought foreign intervention. They were certainly not coerced into this by the missionaries, but acted themselves in sincere faith, believing that Bishop Jaussen had their best interests at heart.

Monseigneur Jaussen was understandably moved by the rare gesture, and immediately wrote a letter to Admiral Cloué requesting the French Navy 'to send, if it is possible, a ship in order to put an end to these acts' of the French citizen Dutrou-Bornier.[59] France did not act, but the local government in Pape'ete did apply gentle pressure on John Brander and Alexander Salmon Jr of the Maison Brander to 'rein in' their agent on Easter Island.

By this time Father Zumbohm, confined to bed and deeply depressed, was certain he would soon die. But at the end of 1870 Commander Bridges of hms *Chanticleer* – who for Britain was again 'sniffing out' Easter Island, with a reserved interest in establishing a protectorate there – offered to transport Zumbohm to Callao. And so the German priest left the island. Later recovering fully at Lima, Zumbohm took up service at the convent of Santa Rosa in Santiago, Chile. He never returned to Rapa Nui. His house, mission school and partially completed chapel at Vaihū now stood abandoned.

Father Roussel and Brother Escolan carried on alone at Sainte-Marie de Rapanui, fervently praying that things would improve. They didn't. Now that Zumbohm was gone, Dutrou-Bornier pulled no more punches. It returned to that open warfare that had torn the island apart in 1865. At this time the Frenchman perhaps also began sabotaging visiting ships in order to acquire their timber: the *Huntwell*, a timber ship (from Oregon?), wrecked here early in 1871 with ten surviving crew; none stayed, but sailed on Captain Schaffer's *Mahina* to Pape'ete, where they arrived on 18 March.

Through letters and visitors Bishop Jaussen was kept fully informed of what was transpiring on Rapa Nui. Finally, exploiting the full weight of his office, he challenged John Brander to force Dutrou-Bornier to cease his crimes against the Rapanui people and against the sscc Mission there. Worried for their reputation, Brander and his wife sailed to Rapa Nui themselves, arriving in early February 1871. Roussel lent the powerful Scots merchant Brander – a Pacific magnate – a horse and even rode with him, showing the damage that Dutrou-Bornier had so recently caused, the many burnt dwellings. But Brander thought it all exaggeration, and decided not to intervene. Instead, he and his wife took back with them 28 Rapanui whom Brander indentured to work on his various coconut plantations.

Immediately after the Branders' departure, the 53-year-old Escolan penned yet another anxious letter to Bishop Jaussen. It so happened, he dutifully reported, that Dutrou-Bornier, seeming too enjoy John Brander's carte blanche, had now started kidnapping young girls and married women for his carnal pleasure. He had also again burnt the Rapanui's dwellings at Vaihū and environs. 'In seeing so much abomination, I could not contain myself', he confessed, 'despite my inexperience in the matter of combat. I mounted my horse, staff in hand; I was the sole attacker, on horse, in the middle of all his troop. I was so aroused that I did not at all fear death.'[60] He had struck at the captain, who had merely deflected the blow. At that moment his henchmen had thrown a dart and some stones, but Dutrou-Bornier had shouted at them to stop. It had been the first time, wrote Escolan, that the missionaries had attacked Dutrou-Bornier. Jorge Arena, the Chilean, had always wanted to attack him; but the missionaries had had no percussion-caps for their old rifles. 'Moreover, Father Gaspard [Zumbohm] was very cowardly, he said that peace was needed at any price. We told him in vain that they would erase Father Hippolyte's [Roussel] village and afterwards go after his [at Vaihū].'

And then followed the news that would have stunned Jaussen. Seven or eight days before John Brander's arrival at Rapa Nui, continued Escolan in his letter, Dutrou-Bornier, rifle in hand, had attacked Hanga Roa in the company of an American 'as wicked as he'. They had burnt all the houses, torn up all the sweet potatoes, yams, banana trees and so forth. There had been four attackers in all, each with two or three rifles. They had set fire to one of the chapel's casements. The missionaries had taken refuge in their stone house together with the girls and women whom the captain had wanted to take for himself. Five or six days of terror had followed, during which they were pelted with stones. They had had nothing at all to defend themselves with. It had only been Brander's arrival that had put an end to the terrible siege. Brander had been shown everything. And yet he had chosen to endorse his agent.

Ironically, it was now the quiet deferential Escolan, more than anyone else, who ultimately decided Rapa Nui's fate. For he concluded his letter to Jaussen with the sober estimation:

> To judge humanely, one can say that all is lost at Rapanui, for such a small population decimated by illness and emigration cannot fare long ... I believe that, if Mr Brander wished to purchase the chapels and animals from us, the best would be to remove the rest and the popula-

tion to Ma[n]gareva. I suppose Mr Brander would be satisfied with the island's cession for [the price of] transporting the indians.

After receiving Escolan's report and assessment, the Bishop of Tahiti needed little time to make up his mind. Already on 4 April 1871 he wrote to Father Roussel:

My Reverend Father,
You are herewith authorized to remove the post at Rapanui, having those persons transported to Gambier [Mangareva] who will wish to go there; carrying away locks, casements, furniture, etc.; burning down of our churches what one will be unable to take away so that they do not become stables; betaking yourself with the Brother [Escolan] to Tahiti for a new assignment.
A sincere good day and benediction.
Tepano Jaussen, Bishop of Axiéri

But both chapels stood unfinished, because the necessary materials for their completion had never arrived from Pape'ete. Hence, they had never been consecrated. For this reason Roussel decided that they did not have to be burnt. (Instead they simply rotted away.) All for the want of a signature – Roussel's to the captain's 'sales receipts' – the Rapa Nui Mission had been lost.

THE EXODUS

The sixth of June 1871: it was one of the saddest days in Rapa Nui history. On this day more people left the island than remained. Appreciating the immediate danger – that with John Brander's sanction Dutrou-Bornier was now free to do what he wanted there – Bishop Jaussen had importuned the Maison Brander to transport to Mangareva, on the next vessel that would be sent to Rapa Nui to fetch indentured labourers, Father Roussel, Brother Escolan and all those Rapanui who wished to join them there.[61] John Brander, recognizing victory, had immediately consented.

Captain Schaffer of the *Sir John Burgoyne* was taken aback to see Rapa Nui's entire population crowding the shore in order to leave the island on his vessel. But he could take only 275 aboard, meaning that some 230 had to be left behind ... who were now weeping and wailing for their departing loved ones, most of whom they would never see again. The subsequent voyage to Mangareva was a nightmare. Scores took ill. Two Rapanui died.

At Rikitea, Mangareva, 168 Rapanui disembarked with Roussel, who defied his bishop's orders and remained there to oversee Father Laval's recently abandoned sscc Mission. (Maligned by trumped-up charges of 'murder' by the antagonistic French government, that had just declared dominion over Mangareva, Laval had been recalled to Tahiti after 37 years of dedicated service there; despite Bishop Jaussen's pique, Roussel was soon afterwards appointed Head of the Mangarevan Mission, where he remained until his death in 1898.) At Rikitea, Roussel and his exiles established a local Rapanui community that supported itself financially through the sscc's local copra and pearl-shell industries. Only 936 Mangarevans were still alive in the Gambiers at the time, and it was envisaged that this influx of neighbours should revive the archipelago's society as it also saved the Rapanui from certain doom. (Twelve years later it was reported: 'the Rapanui people transported to Mangareva are meanwhile said to be used more for the Mission's pearl-fishing than to live for Christian tenets'.)[62]

Brother Escolan carried on to Tahiti, as ordered, where he disembarked on 4 July with 109 Rapanui 'immigrants' who were indentured to work on the coconut plantations at Ha'apape and Mahina. A small number followed him to the Ha'apape Apostolic Vicariate, where they became Bishop Jaussen's personal house servants (illus. 7).

By the end of 1872 a total of 247 Rapanui had arrived at Pape'ete as indentured labourers or residential servants. 'Sadly, the unfamiliarly hot and humid climate, poor conditions and contact with unfamiliar disease claimed the lives of 95 (38 per cent) in the first year and even the arch rivals Roma and Torometi, who had decided to depart their homeland, perished in the sickly overseas Rapanui colony.'[63] Throughout the 1870s there would continue to be a measured drift of Easter Islanders to Pape'ete, then to Ha'apape and Mahina mainly to labour in the sscc's and Brander's plantations there. Most suffered from 'nostalgia' (clinical depression), which weakened their immune system and rendered them even more vulnerable to the simplest contagions. Almost immediately, they began speaking a Rapanui-Tahitian Pidgin among themselves and their Tahitian neighbours. This new hybrid tongue, which, in the late 1870s and throughout the 1880s, a few returnees to Easter Island began using among Rapa Nui's skeleton population, quickly replaced Old Rapanui. (It eventually became Modern Rapanui.)

Rapa Nui itself was like a ghost isle. The missionaries had played a major role in the conversion of the Rapanui to a more European mode of living and thinking.[64] Now there was no society left to enjoy the benefits. The depopulation had its consolation – for the first time in the island's history there were no wars; never again would Rapanui be slaying Rapanui for food, land, women or power. But it was the peace of the toppled *mo'ai*. Only one Rapa Nui 'society' remained, and its name was Te Pitopito. Henceforth the French captain would 'tailor' the island according to his commercial arrangements with the Maison Brander in Tahiti. This would never have happened had there been no labour raids, no pandemics, no missionaries and no Tahitian

7 The earliest known photograph of ethnic Rapanui: Bishop Jaussen's house staff at Ha'apepe, Tahiti, with Father Georges Eich (left, holding a *rongorongo* tablet) and Brother Théodule Escolan (centre), 28 August 1873.

market for wool and mutton. The end product of a unique series of cosmopolitan consumptions and digestions, Rapa Nui was finally market dung.

On 24 June 1871, only a little more than a fortnight after the exodus, Captain Nazimov of the Imperial Russian corvette *Vityaz* called at Easter Island for two hours, not to 'sniff out' the island for the Tsar but to enquire about the recently discovered *rongorongo* inscriptions. The Russians, however, encountered only the German Schmidt and the American, who informed them that the island population was now 230, only 30 of them being females. (A higher percentage of females than males had left with the missionaries.) Whereupon the Russians sailed off to Mangareva to interview the Rapanui there instead. There is no evidence that the few remaining Rapanui on Easter Island were forced, by Dutrou-Bornier or another, to stay there. Although subsequent vessels took more Rapanui away to Tahiti, there were always those who seemingly refused to abandon their homeland. It was they who looked after the possessions and lands of their kin abroad in Mangareva, Tahiti and soon also the Marquesas, Tuamotus and Cooks. They were the voluntary custodians of old Easter Island culture – what little of it remained.

After the abandonment of the Rapa Nui Mission, Bishop Jaussen's prime concern – now that most of his Rapanui flock were, in his opinion, 'rescued' – was restitution to the sscc for the loss of thousands of francs because of Dutrou-Bornier (in active collusion with John Brander), and the sale of all

SSCC property there. The Monseigneur flatly refused the Maison Brander's insulting offer, prompting Brander himself to reply to Jaussen on 9 August 1871: 'If you do not wish to accept my offer of ten thousand francs, I am left no alternative but to write to Mr Bornier to no longer trouble himself with looking after the property of the Mission and to abandon it entirely.'[65]

This prompted Jaussen to petition his new Vice-Provincial at the SSCC's regional headquarters at Valparaíso, Father Auguste Jamet, requesting that he personally undertake the sale of the SSCC's Rapa Nui property to the Government of Chile: 'It seems to me', wrote Jaussen, 'that the Republic [of Chile] cannot let this chance escape of appropriating for itself quite legally an important site off its coasts.'[66] The Bishop of Tahiti suggested Rapa Nui as a potential penal colony, but more importantly as a naval bastion as well, to prevent a foreign nation from installing a steamship there to halt the commercial vessels plying the coast between Valparaíso and Peru. Jaussen added that John Brander owned 'little on Rapanui and he has only a regular contract and as the acquisitions of Mr Dutrou-Bornier were completely illegal, the missionaries refused to sign them and this refusal has been one of the causes of the difficulties'. He insisted 'Mr Dutrou-Bornier or Brander has no valid title but for one or two places', and lists these legal possessions by name: He Ki'i, Nonga Teatea, Vinapū, Hanga Piko, Apina, Vai Kapua and Oro Manga. 'We can later negotiate a sale between the Republic and the transported natives there for the ceding of their lands, but the essential thing for us is to see what belongs to us.' Yet, for the moment, nothing was done.

THE 'GOVERNOR'

One thing was clear: with the missionaries gone Dutrou-Bornier, who was calling himself *Tāvana* (English-Tahitian for 'Governor'), was free to realize his dream (illus. 8), especially now that he held the Mission's sheep and buildings in the palm of his hand. On 6 October 1871 the captain arrived at Pape'ete with Captain Dunn on the *Sir John Burgoyne*, bringing 67 more indentured Rapanui and a request for John Brander: that the Maison Brander's finances be made available to allow both parties the unemcumbered commercial exploitation of Rapa Nui. Brander agreed.

One month later and Dutrou-Bornier was off in Captain McLean's *Ionia* to Sydney, where he acquired for his personal fiefdom in the South Pacific 458 merino sheep (51 would die during the voyage), 84 bundles of hay, 100 boxes of soap, 37 bundle bags, 12 tanks, 8 bags of biscuits, 420 gallons of beef, 10,500 bricks and 2 packages of hardware and sundries.[67] On the day that Dutrou-Bornier was leaving Sydney Harbour, 30 December 1871, he also took on board two cases of firearms. No enemy was to disturb his demesne.

8 Rapa Nui's French 'Governor': Jean-Baptiste Onésime Dutrou-Bornier.

After the 'Governor's' return, Mataveri became the hub of all activity on Rapa Nui, with Vaihū abandoned and Hanga Roa all but deserted. Dutrou-Bornier was the island's sole remaining *matato'a* now. Only a small group of Christians still gathered in the Sainte-Marie de Rapanui church to pray and sing, but without mass, since there was no priest. Dutrou-Bornier applied to the French administration in Pape'ete to have them declare Rapa Nui a French protectorate. But France remained non-committal: not refusing, but also not agreeing. Otherwise, the *Tāvana* concentrated all his efforts on growing rich through exporting wool and mutton to the Maison Brander in Tahiti, all the while treating the few Rapanui left on the island as if they were his personal serfs.

Genuinely intrigued by Dutrou-Bornier's proposal, France ordered their Commander-in-Chief of the Pacific Fleet, Admiral de Lapelin, to the island in the imposing man-of-war *La Flore*. From 3 to 8 January 1872, De Lapelin gathered valuable information on Easter Island for Pape'ete and Paris, questioning the only remaining European resident during Dutrou-Bornier's temporary absence: the German Schmidt, who was now also using the alias 'Adam Smith' and claiming he was a Dane. (The recent Franco-Prussian War had made Germans unwelcome in this French-dominated region of the South Pacific.) At the time, Schmidt was occupying one of the abandoned missionary houses at Hanga Roa and keeping an extensive journal about Rapa Nui, in the English language. Aboard *La Flore* were also the Surgeon-Major Dr A. Fournier (a keen anthropologist) and the young Midshipman First Class Julien Viaud, who was later to win fame as the novelist and travel writer Pierre Loti, one of France's most celebrated authors. Once back at Pape'ete, Admiral de Lapelin conducted extensive interviews with the Rapanui labouring at the Ha'apape and Mahina plantations as well, in order to achieve a full impression of Rapa Nui and its culture, past and present. He was soon agreeing with Bishop Jaussen's assessment of the situation: 'the principal aim of Mr Dutrou-Bornier's behaviour had been to recruit labourers for Mr Brander'.[68] The admiral promised the bishop that he would inform the French Government of their joint opinion.

During January 1872, Bishop Jaussen himself had sailed to Mangareva to speak with the Rapanui there. 'They have authorized me to sell their lands', he later wrote to Father Jamet in Valparaíso. 'I would probably have the same authorization from those who are at Tahiti, and Father Gaspard [Zumbohm] or another, from those who are still at Rapanui on the condition of bringing them to Tahiti. It would be useless for us to return to Rapanui . . . We would be acting as grave-diggers.'[69]

Three months after *La Flore*'s visit, Captain Karström of the *Diamen*, a Swedish ship coming from Melbourne, wrecked on Easter Island, perhaps again because of foul play by Dutrou-Bornier. The captain, crew and passengers were stranded here until the end of April, when Captain McMillan of the *Mahina* transported them safely to Pape'ete.

Sometime during 1872 Koreto gave birth to Dutrou-Bornier's second Rapanui daughter, Harriette. It was also in 1872 that the Commissaire de l'Océanie in Pape'ete recognized Dutrou-Bornier as France's 'official representative' on Rapa Nui. This at once invested the island with the status of a 'pseudo-protectorate', Dutrou-Bornier felt; he soon hoped to see Easter Island becoming wholly French – it would not merely safeguard his authority but also increase his profits.

Other 'fortuitous' shipwrecks occurred the following year, which provided the first wooden shacks for Rapa Nui's tiny population. Chile's economic boom meant increased construction in the Republic. But timber, not readily available in Chile, had to come from the US's Pacific North-west (the later Washington State). Often the routes of the timber vessels brought them 'close' to Easter Island, the upshot of this being the island's transformation where housing was concerned. On 18 March 1873 the American timber ship *William and Thomas* left the Pacific North-west bound for Valparaíso, but later took on water and so made for Easter Island, where it foundered, losing most of the timber. The *Elizabeth Kimball*, also transporting timber from the same place, but to Iquique (later within Chile's borders), was wrecked on Easter Island on 6 May 1873, both ship and cargo lost. The two crews stayed for months on Rapa Nui. Several men built a small schooner from the remains of the *Elizabeth Kimball*, and on 29 July sailed off for Tahiti. Patrick Calligan, first mate of the *Elizabeth Kimball*, constructed his own schooner and sailed alone to Tahiti, arriving there at the end of September. In the meantime, Captain Bowles of the *Tawera*, coming from Valparaíso, picked up 23 of the remaining castaways whom he brought safely to Pape'ete in August 1873, arriving just before Calligan.

By this time Dutrou-Bornier, still purchasing land from the Rapanui, was describing in his sales receipts Koreto – his 'legal guarantor' – as 'Reine de l'île de Pâques' ('Queen of Easter Island'), in imitation of the reigning queen of Tahiti. Outraged at the insolence of the man, Bishop Jaussen openly accused Dutrou-Bornier of having dealt in slave-trading in France's protectorate islands of eastern Polynesia, a serious criminal offence. He even collected damning testimonies from the captain's former crewmen. On Rapa Nui itself, however, the self-styled 'Governor' reigned supreme. Seemingly in order to keep the few remaining locals content, the 'Orongo Birdman competition – or a risible re-enactment of it – was allowed to take place annually again.

Monseigneur Jaussen's several appeals to the Government of Chile to annex Rapa Nui and to purchase the sscc's properties there had not necessarily fallen on deaf ears. Chile was in doubt whether the Bishop of Tahiti's charges – that Dutrou-Bornier's and the Maison Brander's 'ownership' of most of Rapa Nui had been obtained through fraudulent means – would hold up in a court of law. Although Chile did not officially respond to the sscc's repeated offers, in 1875 it again sent the *O'Higgins* to gather more information about Rapa Nui's present circumstances. Commander López arrived on 17 March and anchored there for three days.

Dutrou-Bornier, who resented any interference by Chile, since he wanted a French protectorate, welcomed the Chilean naval officers to his Mataveri residence, where, flying the French tricolour at his 'capital' to which nearly all of the island's population had moved, he proudly introduced to them 'Queen Koreto' and the two 'princesses' – who happened to be his own daughters, both French citizens. Dutrou-Bornier's personal holdings, he duly informed them, included 4,000 sheep, 70 cattle, 20 horses, 300 pigs and many fowl. The Chileans left with the impression of a Gallic fait accompli.

Mercedes Salas or 'Madame Smith', the Chilean wife of the German Schmidt, left Easter Island on the *Indiaman* together with her small daughter Cecilia, and Dutrou-Bornier with his two small daughters, Caroline and Harriette, arriving at Pape'ete on 8 June 1875. Before returning to the island, Dutrou-Bornier and 'Queen Koreto' again vigorously petitioned the Commissaire de l'Océanie to establish an official protectorate at Rapa Nui, as France had done earlier at the Marquesas, Tahiti, Tuamotus, Australs and elsewhere in the Pacific. But the local French government still remained non-committal, although Paris was growing interested. Either in July or September, 'Christian Schmidt' himself left Rapa Nui, too; he joined his wife and daughter at Pape'ete, then travelled with them through the Tuamotus before finally settling on Mangareva. It appears none ever returned to Easter Island.

After Dutrou-Bornier's return, Rapa Nui was apparently not visited again for 19 months, from September 1875 until April 1877. There was no trade; there were no shipments of wool or mutton going to Pape'ete. All contact with the outside world was seemingly broken. During this interval, on 3 January 1876, Bishop Jaussen annulled an earlier promise to sell the sscc's 635 hectares in Hanga Roa to Dutrou-Bornier. Yet it was not only in appearance that the *Tāvana*'s reign was nearing its dramatic climax.

Dutrou-Bornier had already ruled as 'Governor' of Easter Island for five years with impunity, beyond all law – and now all decency. The final straw came when he began kidnapping pubescent girls for his personal pleasure, demonstrating an arrogance that exceeded even that of the worst *matato'a* of legend. But it was Koreto, overweening in her own insolence, who set the final spear flying. For of the several versions of the Frenchman's death, the following seems to be the most reliable.[70] On 6 August 1876 Koreto, familiar with Pape'ete's European fashion, complained to the captain that a dress he had had made for her was unbecoming for a 'queen'. Piqued, Dutrou-Bornier picked up his rifle and went to teach the delinquent seamstress a lesson. But, forewarned of Te Pitopito's intention, three angrier Rapanui who had suffered too many indignities were waiting for him. When the Frenchman stepped into the seamstress's small wooden shack they struck, and in the ensuing struggle Dutrou-Bornier was killed. (It was the third known instance of Rapanui killing an outsider. It was not the last.) His murderers then left to kill little Caroline and Harriette, too, wanting to rid the island of Te Pitopito's blood. But other Rapanui, horrified, hid Koreto and the girls in caves until the danger had passed.

Dutrou-Bornier had been a historic personality, the stuff of legends, books and films. But he was far from what France would have wished as their 'representative' on Easter Island: violent, arrogant, immoral, he operated neither for France nor for the Rapanui nor for the Maison Brander, but only for Dutrou-Bornier. If the swashbuckling entrepreneur had had even a modicum of character, perhaps Rapa Nui would be French today. But history is not made of 'ifs'.

THE PACIFIC ORPHAN

With Dutrou-Bornier's death, peace descended on Rapa Nui at last, but virtually no one was left to enjoy it. The island's population was the same as that only one generation after the initial settlement some 1,300 years before. And they were 'old' – half of them more than 40 years of age. For the rest of 1876, there was no island leader. The Rapanui continued to look after the livestock, plantations and buildings belonging to the sscc and the Maison Brander / Dutrou-Bornier. But along with the captain all vision was gone. Ahead lay only uncertainty. More Rapanui still lived off the island than on it.

Concerned about Easter Island's situation under Dutrou-Bornier, whose death was still unknown, France sent yet another expedition. On Easter Sunday, 1 April 1877, Commander Lafontaine and Captain Aube of the *Seignelay* arrived and began trekking about the La Pérouse region. Among their company was the eminent French philologist Alphonse Pinart, and the photographer E. Bayard took the first known photographs of the island. (These photographs have never been found, though sketches made from them were published in various weeklies.)[71] On the fourth day of their visit, the French were welcomed at Mataveri, where Koreto was flying the tricolour. The island's 'reigning queen' was then presented to the party: not Koreto herself but Dutrou-Bornier's little daughter Caroline, as Koreto carefully informed them in fluent French. She herself was now only performing the duties of regent.[72] She offered the Mataveri residence as their accommodation, which the Frenchmen gratefully accepted. They dined in wholly European fashion at Dutrou-Bornier's dining table, served by knowledgeable, properly dressed Rapanui. The visitors were informed that only 110 people were now left on the island, 26 of them women. 'She let us know how much she and her people desired French protection', wrote Pinart later, 'hiding from us not at all her little sympathy for the Chileans, Americans, Germans and others, an aversion shared moreover by the island's notables present at our conversation.'[73]

The next day, Koreto led her visitors up to Dutrou-Bornier's grave on the hill between Mataveri and the volcano Rano Kau. Once arrived at the spot, she requested that they plant a Christian cross. (Today, the site is lost in thick bush.) The *Seignelay* sailed the following day. Having played her last role in the island's greater drama, Koreto retired to obscurity; she died in 1917.

Shortly after this, the *Black Eagle* foundered off Easter Island, stranding her crew there for several months.

In June 1877 the Maison Brander sent the Chilean Chavez as their new Rapa Nui agent. Not only did he assume the management of Dutrou-Bornier's stock but, like his predecessor, also included in this the sscc's sheep and buildings. Chavez and his wife took over the Mataveri residence, apparently forcing out Koreto and the girls. Afraid of the Rapanui, the new manager kept himself armed at all times. No problems occurred, however, and, by the end of 1877, ships were again calling to pick up the Maison Brander's wool-clip and mutton for the Pape'ete market. In the meantime, Chavez had learnt of the death there of John Brander: the company's interests had been thrown into disarray as a result. Brander's sons and his business partner Alexander Salmon Jr were at first uncertain what to do about their Rapa Nui investment, since Dutrou-Bornier's own legacy remained unclear. Still, every few months the wool-clip and mutton left on the *Tawera* or *Marama* that familiarly anchored off the Hanga Roa roadstead.

John Brander's widow, *née* Tetuanuireiaiteraiatea Salmon, became the legal provisional administrator of the company in January 1878, just after having remarried. Her new husband, the local wealthy Scots merchant George Darsie, was now entitled to share a claim in the Brander legacy. The faction representing the Maison Brander was represented in the Pape'ete courts by Auguste Goupil, who also happened to be the Chilean consul in Tahiti. The claimants for the deceased Dutrou-Bornier's share of Easter Island included the Frenchman's mother and widow, and also a local creditor, the Pape'ete merchant Van der Veene.

On 4 May 1878 a court in Tahiti decreed that if Dutrou-Bornier's legal heirs – three-quarters of his legacy was designated for his legitimate wife and son in France, one-quarter for his notary – did not claim their inheritance, then the Maison Brander reserved the right to exploit Easter Island commercially alone. (The following year the Pape'ete tribunal would decide against all those with legal rights in the Dutrou-Bornier case, since no one had come forward to claim the inheritance.)

With the announcement of this ruling, the sscc was concerned about its own property on Rapa Nui. On 10 June 1878 Captain Lepoumelec brought Father Roussel back to the island. He performed marriages and baptisms and, more importantly, took account of the lay of the land – Chavez was still at Mataveri – and the condition of the sscc's livestock and buildings there. His main task was to compile an exact inventory of effects in order to allow transport, sale and / or compensation. What Roussel saw shocked him: 'It is a ruin.'[74] Perhaps most alarming of all, the Maison Brander had simply appropriated everything. 'We had half an acre of vines, seven species of figs, peach trees, orange trees, acacias, pines, aniseed trees, etc., in a land where there are no trees. All this has passed to the terrain of the associates.' Roussel summarily installed Peteriko Vaka Pito and Paoa 'a Hitaki (who was later to marry Dutrou-Bornier's younger daughter) as overseers of all the sscc's livestock, mostly sheep.

At this point Roussel made important changes among the small Christian community. He appointed 'Tomenika' (French 'Dominique') Vaka Tuku Onge to lead the Christian services during the absence of an ordained priest. Perhaps most importantly, Roussel established his good friend, the practising Christian and *tangata hōnui* or 'chief' Mati, as leader of the small community, ostensibly to deflate Chavez's importance there now that Dutrou-Bornier was gone. On the question of depopulating the entire island in order to save their lives, as Roussel wrote to Bishop Jaussen once he was back at Mangareva a month later: 'the Pascuans [Rapanui] prefer to stay among themselves, at Easter Island, for white people only took them for a ride'.[75]

It was shortly thereafter, in September 1878, that the 'Orongo Birdman competition was held for the last time. All earlier significance and purpose had long been lost. The only one who could still recall the old chants was 'Daniel' Ure Va'e Iko, now a devout Christian. And the winner was neither a Birdman nor a *paoa*. Rapanui 'society', itself an empty egg, had nothing to gain from the meaningless ritual – which now ceased to the sounds of the relentless surf breaking below 'Orongo.

At this moment, with neat historic irony, the island's flesh-and-blood Birdman alighted. For, having successfully completed a difficult undertaking, Chavez and his wife now left the island for good, sailing to Pape'ete, whereupon Alexander Salmon Jr – the late John Brander's commercial partner who was still co-owner of the Maison Brander – arrived, around October 1878, with 20 Tahitian labourers and several Rapanui whose indentures had expired. Moving into the vacated Mataveri residence, Salmon became the true 'King of Easter Island' almost overnight – by virtue of his stature, status, ethnicity and charisma. The Pacific orphan had found its adoptive father.

THE CONVALESCENT YEARS

Alexander Salmon Jr – whom the Rapanui, inveterate nicknamers, dubbed 'Pa'ea', Mangarevan for 'hobble' – was the son of the Jewish Englishman Alexander Salmon, or Solomon, who had been Secretary to Tahiti's Queen Pomare IV. (She, too, had died in that eventful year of 1877.) His was a rich and influential Tahitian family. His mother, the *ari'i* Taimai, was a historic personality in her own right. His sister Marau was the current queen of Tahiti, wife of their cousin King Pomare V, from 1877 puppet monarch of the French colonial administrators. Another sister was Tetua Salmon Brander Darsie, recent widow of the magnate John Brander. A niece, Maria, was married to Herr Schlubach, the German consul-general at Valparaíso, Chile. Alexander Salmon Jr had learnt rudimentary Rapanui in 1871 among the indentured labourers at the Mahina coconut plantation of which he was a co-owner. By all accounts he was sincere, dedicated, honest and keenly interested in the Rapanui people – although his main concern, as a businessman, was always turning a profit for the Maison Brander. His informant material, however linguistically and culturally contaminated, is among the most important that survives from Rapa Nui's early historical period. (Because of his native English and Tahitian, as well as his rudimentary Rapanui, he himself would serve as principal informant for the British and Germans in 1882 and for the Americans in 1886.)

'Pa'ea' Salmon would remain on Rapa Nui for a full decade, with inter-ruptions, much longer than any other outsider until then. If the 1860s had meant the death of the 'ancient' culture and the 1870s the island's depopula-tion and ruthless exploitation, then the 1880s, solely because of Salmon's dynamic presence, heralded a new era of recuperation and radical accultur-ation. To be sure, now sheep, and not people, roamed everywhere; *ahu* were cannibalized to build stone walls; cattle trampled formerly *tapu* ceremonial centres, rubbing against prostrate *mo'ai*; 'Orongo began crumbling in the rains for want of attention. But there were new priorities and new rewards. One gesture was symbolic of the larger transformation: Salmon reintro-duced the *niu* – the Polynesian coconut tree (*Cocos nucifera*) – to Rapa Nui.

Father Roussel returned again from Mangareva, now aboard the *Marion Godeffroy*, on 23 October 1879 to monitor the Christian community and per-form marriages and baptisms. In his eight days there, he found Alexander Salmon Jr an imposing figure – and chose not to like him. Apparently it was because of Salmon's Jewish ancestry; Roussel claimed that Salmon could neither understand nor respect Christian needs.[76] Despite Tomenika's loyal service in leading the Christian liturgy and instruction, during most of the 1880s it became the labour-raid returnee Pakomio who, while he continued to oversee the sscc's livestock, led the tiny clutch of Christian faithful.[77]

Already by the 1880s the island population was slowly recovering, what with a rising birth rate and a trickle of returnees from Pape'ete and Mangareva. During this decade, Salmon was very much the avuncular auto-crat, paying his workers with sheep, cattle and chickens and encouraging them to carve traditional figures to sell to the crews and passengers of pass-ing vessels. Such was the Rapanui's enthusiasm to learn and adapt that visi-tors were often surprised to find, as did the Germans in 1882, that the locals not only accurately knew currency exchange rates, but also displayed their carvings on European-style shelves with attached price tags.

Rapa Nui was not the only isle in rapid change. On 29 June 1880 the Protectorate of Tahiti officially became the Etablissements français de l'Océanie, an annex of the French state.[78] King Pomare v, Salmon's brother-in-law and cousin, had yielded to the French Government all royal claims, ending the Kingdom of Tahiti as a public entity. But France's ineffectual for-eign policy lacked vision and continuity. (Between 1882 and 1914 no fewer than 24 governors would come and go.) Throughout the 1880s France con-tinued to consolidate its claims in eastern Polynesia. Most of the Australs became French protectorates (annexation 1900). The Tuamotus, a protec-torate since 1844, were annexed in 1881. Mangareva, which had been made a protectorate in 1871 (the year the Rapanui arrived there), was also annexed in 1881. East 'Uvea became a protectorate in 1886, Futuna in 1887. The Leeward Islands (western Society Islands), whose independence France had promised Queen Pomare IV it would honour – a promise guaranteed by Great Britain – were annexed in 1887. France was preparing to annex the Cook Islands in 1888, but Britain finally intervened and declared its own protectorate there.

One would think that Rapa Nui was France's next logical stepping stone, having already been administered by a Tahitian company for so long. But for France the island held no strategic importance. Nor was its trade that lucrative: during the 1870s and '80s only 780 sheep were brought from there to Tahiti. Certainly there was a larger market for its wool. In 1884, for example, the British rear-admiral Doughty reported that between 25 and 30 tonnes of Rapa Nui wool-clip landed each year at Pape'ete.[79] But this was insufficient to justify a French protectorate: the island was simply too far away and underpopulated, meaning insufficient labour for any projected enterprise.

In 1880 moves were made to liquidate the Brander / Dutrou-Bornier partnership once and for all. It was also at this time that Dutrou-Bornier's many land purchases on Easter Island were legally registered at Pape'ete. A local court decreed that the partnership's property on the island was indivisible; it could be transferred only as a single lot. Once she heard this in France, Dutrou-Bornier's widow objected: many of the tracts of land had nothing to do with Brander, but had been her late husband's private purchases, she maintained. At the same time, Monseigneur Jaussen asserted the sscc's stake in the Brander enterprise on Easter Island, meaning that one-third of the livestock there belonged to the Roman Catholic Church. On top of this, seven Rapanui who were now residing in Tahiti and Mo'orea, represented by the sscc's lawyer, declared before a French judge that the local Rapanui place names in the Maison Brander's land claims were erroneous. But the Maison Brander's lawyer, Auguste Goupil, convinced the judge that to effect an exact survey of the purchased lands now would cause too long a delay in the litigation concerning the partnership's precise property. The judge agreed, and in so doing failed to clarify European ownership of Easter Island's lands. It was to confuse all land issues well into the twentieth century.

Doubtless prompted by Alexander Salmon Jr, who would profit from clarification of clear entitlement only under French dominion, a small delegation of some twenty Rapanui, led by a 'chief', sailed to Pape'ete in 1881 to request of the Etablissements' current governor that France make Easter Island its protectorate and that it send them a French *gendarme*.[80] The governor, however, was as unresponsive as the Commissaire de l'Océanie had been towards Dutrou-Bornier first nine, then six, years earlier. After having visited the 88 Rapanui still alive at Pape'ete exactly one decade after their unforgettable arrival in 1871, the delegation returned empty-handed.

Certainly the Admiralty in London had not forgotten Easter Island. They now ordered Commander Clark in the man-of-war HMS *Sappho* to gather information there on his way from Coquimbo to Pitcairn Island. The *Sappho* arrived off Cook's Bay on the evening of 16 June 1882, where it anchored for only two days.[81] Flying the Union Jack in the Britons' honour at his Mataveri residence, Salmon, himself a British subject, came on board on that first evening and did everything in his power to convince the British to consider extending a protectorate over Rapa Nui. He did not shy from falsehoods. Salmon claimed, for example, as Commander Clark reported shortly afterwards, that the Maison Brander had

> bought from the Bishop of Tahiti the property of the missionaries ... There was also a Frenchman, named Bornier, who was murdered about two years ago by the natives for intriguing with their women. His property has also come into their hands, and they have bought more since, so that they own the greater part of the island.

Already Salmon had 'about 10,000 sheep and about 400 head of cattle'. With this, he was able to ship 'about 18 tons of wool a year'. In other words, it was a dynamic enterprise in which Britain could share.

Salmon described even more for his welcome visitors. 'There is also no trace left of the missionaries' work'. (No mention was made of Roussel's repeated visits, the practising Rapanui Catholics or the sscc's buildings and livestock.) 'The remaining natives have no religion at all ... They have no religious ceremonies or observances'. Salmon told what little he knew of the defunct Birdman competition. (Commander Clark wrongly assumed that this was still annually observed.) As he was clearly meant to be, the British commander was highly impressed by the Easter Island that Salmon laid out before him: 'I was immensely struck with the fertility of the soil, if it was only cultivated I believe it would produce magnificent crops, and it seemed to me to be specially adapted for the culture of vines, of which as yet there are none on the island.' At the conclusion of his official report to Rear-Admiral Algernon Lyons, Commander-in-Chief at the Admiralty, Commander Clark was anything but ambiguous: 'I beg to suggest for your consideration the advisability, seeing that the island is almost entirely owned by an English subject, of her Majesty's Government now extending some sort of protectorate over it.'[82] But, like the Elysée palace, Westminster did nothing.

Shortly after this, the Germans arrived. Germany's entry into the Pacific occurred after the unification of the German state under Bismarck in the 1870s.[83] Especially after 1881, Germany embarked on an aggressive campaign to 'collect' large parts of the Pacific Islands for the Kaiser, obliging Britain and France – then Spain, the us and Chile – to conceive and enact their own Pacific designs, sometimes despite themselves. Germany's visit to Rapa Nui must be seen in the light of the country's Pacific expansion. Kapitänleutnant

Wilhelm Geiseler of His Imperial Majesty's two-masted gunboat *Hyäne* had superficial instructions to collect ethnographic information and artefacts for Berlin's Ethnographic Museum. (Indeed, Geiseler collected more than 250 pieces and provided invaluable historical and even archæological information.) But Geiseler's main duty was to assess the island's situation, and potential, in view of Germany's changing role in the Pacific.

The *Hyäne* arrived off Hanga Roa on 19 September 1882 and anchored for eleven days. (This was a major expedition.) Paymaster Candidate J. Weisser was encharged with effecting the first German scientific survey of the island, a task he performed with impressive diligence: the later printed report, issued under Geiseler's name but mostly written by Weisser, was doubtless the nineteenth century's best.[84] Geiseler concerned himself primarily with the island's present situation, profiting from Alexander Salmon Jr's status and local knowledge. Salmon now reported that there were 12,000 sheep (lambing season had occurred), 700 cattle (calving) and 70 horses. Now 100 Rapanui were living at Mataveri and 50 at Hanga Roa: 67 men, 39 women and 44 children. As he did with each visiting vessel, Salmon had called everyone to the Mataveri residence so that they could sell their carvings. He personally oversaw each sale of an 'ethnographical object', helping to determine a fair market value. The carving of such artefacts had already become an important cottage industry, and would only grow in future. (It is thriving today.)

Kapitänleutnant Geiseler was surprised how 'Europeanized' the Rapanui were:

one could be amazed at the change that intercourse with the relatively small number of Europeans in several years has been capable of bringing about. One encounters only persons who come forth as self-possessed and adroit, demonstrating great cleverness, finding amazement in nothing any longer, knowing exactly the value of money and clothing and laughing afterwards when they believe they have somehow got the best of a European. In brief, one believes, apart from the colour of skin, to be dealing rather with Europeans than with Polynesians, at the very least with the Rapanui people considered to be so isolated.[85]

The wool production, Salmon informed the German officer, was now running at 20 tonnes a year.

In particular Geiseler noticed how Salmon 'stands in good stead with the natives; those he employs are paid in cash, but have to buy from him their requirements of cloth, tobacco etc., as is customary in the entire South Seas'.[86] Like the British commander before him, the German Kapitänleutnant was also told that 'with all of the surviving population, who had already been converted to Christianity, hardly a memory of this has remained'.[87] (Salmon, a Jew, always chose to ignore the small Roman Catholic community at Hanga Roa.) Whatever Geiseler's secret recommendation might have been to the Admiralty in Berlin, the Kaiser chose not to concern himself thereafter with Easter Island – until the First World War.

Father Roussel, for one, would have been more than surprised to learn that 'hardly a memory' of Christianity remained on his very own Rapa Nui. Arriving on 31 December 1882, now aboard Captain Piltz's *Lillian* and staying for a week this time, Roussel counted 167 residents, monitored Tomenika's performance and performed 15 marriages and nearly 20 baptisms. The Rapanui, he later alleged, now told him they wished a Catholic government to replace the previous 'pagan' one, and so Roussel installed a 'Tahitian-style monarchy'. Declaring Atamu te Kena ('Adam the Gannet') to be the new 'king' of Easter Island, Roussel appointed two counsellors and two judges who would govern with Te Kena in French-Tahitian fashion. Later, Bishop Jaussen endorsed Atamu te Kena's 'kingship', since he felt that such a local authority was necessary to protect the sscc's Rapa Nui property from the rapacious Maison Brander. Alexander Salmon Jr held the new 'monarchy' to be a farce, however, and, once Roussel had sailed away again, quickly saw to it that everything returned to normal.

Salmon was absent from Rapa Nui for most of 1883 and 1884, tending to important Maison Brander business in Tahiti. He left the German August Länder in charge, a pious Roman Catholic who assumed a very active role in the Hanga Roa church, even leading services there personally from this time until 1886, long after Salmon's return to the island. When Rear-Admiral Doughty of HMS *Constance* visited Easter Island from 6 to 7 March 1884, evidently assessing the island in light of Commander Clark's positive recommendation to the Admiralty in London, he dealt only with the German Länder. (But Westminster still failed to act on the Easter Island question.)

Two months later, on 5 May 1884, Bishop Jaussen, in failing health, ceded his apostolic vicariate at Ha'apape, Tahiti, to his co-adjudicator Monseigneur Verdier. (Jaussen would die in Tahiti seven years later.) And only a month after this, Alexander Salmon Jr and his nephew John Brander Jr succeeded in purchasing all outstanding lands and chattels on Easter Island (except for the sscc's 635 hectares) for the impressive sum of 38,100 francs. Whereupon the Darsies transferred their ownership of the Easter Island property, improvements and livestock to Mrs Darsie's son, John Brander Jr. (On 20 June 1893, after many years of appeals, depositions, judgements and counter-appeals, a French tribunal in Bordeaux would finally grant Dutrou-Bornier's widow Valentine 53,655 francs in compensation; but these monies were never paid, since by then Easter Island lay within Chile's legal jurisdiction.)[88] Now armed with legal deeds instead of rifles, Salmon and his sister's son Brander returned to Rapa Nui in 1884, intent on creating their own new Easter Island.

The Mataveri residence was now abandoned. For Salmon and young Brander had decided to build up Father Zumbohm's old Vaihū residence instead (illus. 9). Situated on the south coast, it was much closer to their sheep and cattle in Hotu'iti (formerly 'Otu 'Iti) territory. A horse-buggy was brought from Pape'ete, too, in which they could now travel the old *mo'ai* roads more speedily to attend on the herds and make deliveries, the island's first vehicle. Salmon had his labourers scour the island's caves in search of original artefacts to be sold to passing vessels. He also encouraged them more than before to make imitation pieces with imitation inscriptions copying the old *rongorongo* (but of far inferior quality). There was no deception in this, because Salmon never claimed these were originals. (Today's largest collection of Salmon-inspired artefacts graces the Museo de la Basílica de la Merced in Santiago, Chile.) For these and other reasons, Vaihū now became the 'capital' of an island that lay wholly in the hands of the Maison Brander.

In early November 1884 Father Roussel returned yet again to monitor the sscc's property, perform marriages and baptisms and admit several young Rapanui to Holy Communion. His sudden reappearance was clearly meant to reinforce the message to the Rapanui people that, despite 'Tepano' Jaussen's retirement, their church had not abandoned them – and to Salmon Jr and Brander Jr that the sscc had not given up the fight. Accompanying Roussel about this time was the Rapanui Angata, who in 1871 had left the island for Mangareva with her husband Manu Heu Roroa. At Mangareva, her husband had severely beaten her for not having collected coconuts as he had ordered: the beating had left her permanently hunchbacked. In revenge, Angata's cousins in Mangareva had killed the husband. For many years Angata, very devout, had served as Roussel's catechist, having learnt the liturgy by heart and displaying exceptional fervour. Once back on Rapa Nui, she naturally became co-catechist with Pakomio Mā'ori Ure Kino, who was still overseeing the sscc's livestock, as Roussel had first encharged him, as

9 Alexander Salmon Jr (right) at his Vaihū residence in 1886.

well as leading the small Christian community in divine services. Angata soon married Pakomio, and the two of them served as the island's principal spiritual leaders, in the absence of a permanent priest, until 1888.

In 1885, 19-year-old Vincent 'Varta' Pont of Brest, France, chanced upon the island after having cruised the Pacific as a deckhand on several schooners. A trained carpenter, he chose first to settle at 'Anakena – away from the Catholic church at Hanga Roa and away from the Maison Brander at Vaihū – to lead his own Rapanui life, marrying Maria Heremeta. Later he would move to a wooden shack in Hanga Roa, guard sheep for the Company and plant large numbers of eucalyptus and fig trees, as well as the *miro tahiti* ('bead tree' or *Melia azederach*) so prized by local carvers. The first European to spend his entire adult life on Easter Island (he left only once, to visit Tahiti), he became the patriarch of the island's large Pont family.

In February 1886 Father Albert Montiton, the sscc priest who had led the initial mission to Easter Island in 1863 before its cancellation, stopped for ten days aboard Captain Vini Brander's schooner on his way from Tahiti to Valparaíso to print a Tahitian hymnal. While ashore, Montiton performed six weddings, one of which was that of 15-year-old Caroline Dutrou-Bornier to 'Jean' (later Juan) Araki Aro Purunga. Salmon was kind enough to take the father 'sightseeing': just like modern tourists, the pair drove in Salmon's buggy out to Rano Raraku to admire the standing *mo'ai* there,[89] following the route that would still be called 'Brander's Road' in the 1920s.

Montiton also became involved with the Rapanui who were still living in Tahiti. For Monseigneur Verdier, the new bishop of Tahiti, had just ceded a considerable tract of land in the Pamata'i Valley south-west of Pape'ete (now opposite the international airport) for the Rapanui to own freehold once they reimbursed the sscc for the purchase price through selling the land's agricultural produce.[90] The sale finally came into effect in October 1887 when the sscc's title passed to 25 family heads for the sum of 22,000 francs, with 3,000 francs still outstanding.[91] Pamata'i now became Easter Island's largest exile community. But it was not to thrive. About 1900 a visitor counted only 44 survivors. (Some Rapanui have successfully regained ownership rights to their family's Pamata'i land, but most claims, despite being freehold, have since 'expired'.)

Alexander Salmon Jr's and John Brander Jr's 'new' Rapa Nui was not to be, either. The sheep ranch simply did not return the profits they had hoped for. And so they reacted favourably when a small group of Chilean entrepreneurs approached with a purchase proposal. Towards this end Salmon compiled the first Rapa Nui census, entitled *Te Ingoa* ('The Names'), which he proudly signed on its completion on 8 February 1886.[92] Although the Chilean purchase failed to materialize, Alexander Salmon Jr's census had historic repercussions: it fossilized 'official' surnames on Easter Island.[93]

(Until then, personal names were usually plastic and ephemeral, a universal Polynesian phenomenon.) *Te Ingoa* lists 157 persons, giving their baptismal and 'pagan' names. The first became the personal name, the second the island-wide surname. So Rapu, who was baptized 'Arone' (Aaron), became Arone Rapu; Ure Vaʻe Iko, baptized 'Daniel', became Daniel Vaʻe (Ure, meaning 'penis', was now avoided by Christians); Haoa, baptized 'Andrés', became Andrés Haoa; and so forth. Salmon's *Te Ingoa* established most surnames that survive on Easter Island today. Perhaps most tellingly, today's 'Rapanui, for some purposes, particularly the sharing of land and labor, regard these surname groups as functionally equivalent to the corporate kin groups of their past'.[94] That is, new descent lines had been created, bridging the Polynesian past to a European future.

Still some years away from their Hawaiian and Samoan annexations and, as booty from the Spanish–American War (1898), the acquisition of Guam and the Philippines, the us was growing interested in Rapa Nui as well, although, like the Germans, chiefly for scientific reasons. Just before his death, the eminent American zoologist and ornithologist Spencer F. Baird induced the Navy Department to dispatch one of its vessels to explore Easter Island and to forward specimens of its 'ancient culture' to the National Museum – the Smithsonian – in Washington, DC. The uss *Mohican*, commanded by Benjamin F. Day, was anchored at the time at Papeʻete, so it was randomly detailed for this historic undertaking.[95] Ship's Surgeon George H. Cooke described the *Mohican*'s instructions: 'on her return passage to the South American coast, to call at Easter Island, make certain investigations desired by the Smithsonian Institution, and especially to bring away one of the colossal stone images to be found upon the island'.[96] Cooke further noted that he, Paymaster William J. Thomson and the navigator were all assigned specific tasks 'predicated upon the information desired by the Smithsonian Institution'. There is no evidence to suggest that the first official American visit had political motivation.

The Americans arrived on 18 December 1886 and remained until New Year's Eve. A wealth of ethnographic and archæological information, also involving the *rongorongo* script and inscribed artefacts, was gathered during thirteen hectic days and nights ashore. Paymaster Thomson carried out Vinapū's first archæological excavation – using dynamite. Salmon's Vaihū residence served as headquarters for the American shore parties. Surgeon Cooke was much taken with the English-Jewish Tahitian *ariʻi*:

Mr Salmon, who is guide, philosopher, and friend to these people, unites in his person (and being a giant in stature, he can well contain them) the duties of referee, arbiter, judge. They entertain the greatest respect for him; evince the utmost affection; look up to him as their master; go to him with all their troubles; refer to him all their disputes and grievances. His word is law, and his decisions final and undisputed.[97]

Evidently the sscc's 'king' Atamu te Kena had nothing to say on the island; Alexander Salmon Jr alone ruled here. Paymaster Thomson put it succinctly: 'Pa'ea' Salmon was "king of the island"'.[98] Although relying heavily on Geiseler's (actually Weisser's) report from the German visit of 1882, Thomson's own report, eventually published by the Smithsonian in 1891,[99] would become one of the most important documents about early Easter Island, a classic in the field. After this, however, the Americans demonstrated no interest in the island, and did not return in any official capacity until the 1940s.

Meanwhile, Monseigneur Verdier of Tahiti maintained the former Bishop Jaussen's campaign for Chile's acquisition of Rapa Nui. Despite nearly a decade's exploitation of the island by British subjects (Alexander Salmon Jr and John Brander Jr), whose firm was based in French territory (Tahiti), neither Great Britain nor France appeared inclined to make the island a protectorate, much less to annex it.[100] In 1887 France annexed the Leeward Islands (western Society Islands), but seemed willing to leave Rapa Nui to Chile. Only Chile was ostensibly ready to accept international responsibility for the isolated Rapanui people. On 30 September 1887 Monseigneur Verdier, who was the current bishop of Tahiti, reported to Father Jamet, the Vice-Provincial at Valparaíso, that Captain Policarpo Toro of the Chilean Navy had written to the Archbishop of Santiago informing him that the Bishop of Tahiti was 'totally disposed' to ceding, with the accord of the Holy See, his apostolic rights of jurisdiction over Easter Island. 'The Government of Chile', wrote Verdier further, 'may take possession of that island and colonize it, transporting there from Chilean lands entire families'.[101]

In Valparaíso, Father Montiton, whose idea it had been in the first place to establish a Roman Catholic Mission on Easter Island and who had visited it recently in 1886, was justifiably troubled. Could the Rapanui people even cope with a sudden annexation by Chile? he wondered. Mightn't they need better preparation? He convinced his Vice-Provincial, Father Jamet, that such was the case. And so it happened that Montiton at last was to fulfil his lifelong dream of evangelizing on Easter Island, his immediate instructions being to prepare the Rapanui people for their handover to Chile. Bishop Jaussen as well, still passionately committed to his Rapanui converts despite his retirement, had announced a first visit to the island, planned for February 1888.

On 19 October 1887 Father Montiton arrived at Rapa Nui from Valparaíso on the German schooner *Paloma*. (On board was Captain Policarpo Toro, who was continuing on to Tahiti on behalf of the Government of Chile in order to conclude with the Etablissements and with Monseigneur Verdier the business of transference of rights over Rapa Nui.) Montiton, whom the Rapanui called 'Apereto' (Albert), stayed for six months, performing four weddings and ten baptisms, conducting other sscc business and restoring the church buildings and the cemetery where his old friend Brother Eugène Eyraud lay buried. During this time, back in Tahiti, about a dozen marriage-able Rapanui were planning to abandon their impoverished settlement at Pamata'i to return to Easter Island: they had heard the rumour about an imminent Chilean annexation and were hoping this might bring them a better future.

Prevented by worsening health, Bishop Jaussen never made it to the island. But on 15 April 1888, after France had given Chile the green light to annex Rapa Nui, Monseigneur Verdier, Tahiti's bishop, who had arrived at the island eight days earlier, personally conducted in the restored Catholic church at Hanga Roa the sacrament of confirmation for no fewer than 124 Rapanui,[102] a majority of the island population. Before quitting Easter Island, Verdier asked the Rapanui people to accept Chile's sovereignty. He also gave them his assurance – as Captain Toro had promised him in turn, on behalf of the Republic of Chile – that in all religious matters they would be attended with even greater regularity than before. On the day of Verdier and Montiton's departure:

All Christendom accompanied us down to the seashore, and there even-tually were made the final adieus among tears and sobs, while Monseigneur, from above the dinghy that was taking us to the ship, gave a last benediction to the population kneeling on the beach or on the rocks of the bay.[103]

They arrived back at Tahiti in early May. On 8 August 1888 Monseigneur Verdier sold the sscc's 635 hectares at Hanga Roa to the Republic of Chile – whereupon the Rapanui parishioners lacked sacerdotal care for 23 years.

So ended Easter Island's brief colonial period, which was 'reluctantly French', only to herald the *rancho* Isla de Pascua's protracted neo-colonial period – at first defiantly, but later only indifferently, Chilean. (The 'barbwire siesta' would not end until the mid-1960s.) Compared with most Polynesian islands, Easter Island had come very late to a continuous European presence. Only in 1862 did the island start to suffer a 'relentless process of moderniza-tion by Western agencies', which, as a result, transformed its culture and bioscape profoundly and fundamentally.[104] The 'Great Death' of the 1860s had been only the final gasp of that living corpse that Easter Island's ancient culture had already become. The following quarter of a century, that of missioning and sheep farming, then informed the new 'Rapa Nui': the Church imparting the alien creed by which the Rapanui people, as they were now calling themselves, would come to measure their behaviour, the ranch providing the social framework in which they could survive. In the later stage of this exclusively Tahitian-funded development 'Pa'ea' Salmon was indeed a Solomon to the Rapanui people. Under his Western tutelage a new Polynesian folk, with new names and new occupations, earned their alien majority, learning at last to trust outsiders again, appreciating what to borrow, what to reject.

In consequence, the 1880s in particular saw the reweaving of the island's social fabric. The remnant Roman Catholic faith, with its foreign ideology, institutionalized the borrowed belief (although traditional superstitions would forever remain strong). Alexander Salmon Jr brought a Western economy, civil law and social order. This hybrid superimposition – Western credo and cash – was negotiated and reinforced daily in all personal interactions. It generated the island's Polynesian-European progeny, who were a community wholly new, ever uncertain, yet full of grit and native genius. The borrowing and testing of everything foreign by this perennially 'jury-rigged society' would continue, eagerly embracing, if merely for a spell, all that helped and profited, and readily rejecting all that was harmful and false.

But first the nightmare of pirates and priests would yield to a Chilean dream.

four

Rancho Isla de Pascua

By the end of the nineteenth century, as feeble colonialism was crumbling before mighty neo-colonialism throughout the Pacific Islands, even tiny isolates like Easter Island were not spared. Sovereign Rapa Nui went from a 'French pseudo-colony' to a politico-commercial pawn – of both the Republic of Chile and minor Chile-based entrepreneurs. After this the island became virtually a fiefdom of a multinational corporation, 'the Company', which dominated the island and its economy, the missionary-founded sheep ranch, for half a century.[1]

For most of this time, Rapa Nui *was* the Company. Chile's interest in its Pacific possession would emerge only during periods of Church, or press, protest, or when it was renegotiating the 20-year lease: during the First World War, in the mid-1930s and in the early 1950s. Yawning interims saw the Company handling Rapa Nui as its own sovereign state, although the Republic's restrictions grew as the decades of *aburrimiento* or ennui trundled by.

It was an era of disparate forces: a steadily recovering Rapanui population experiencing ever fewer personal rights.[2] The devolution of the personal prerogative began slowly. For the first eleven years following Easter Island's annexation by the Republic of Chile in 1888, commercial failure and internal resistance kept the island's canoe luffing before two legitimate courses. But then the potential for self-rule was lost forever in 1899 when Rapa Nui's first democratically elected *'ariki*, Riro, was apparently murdered in Chile. In turn, in 1903 the commercial sheep ranch was devoured by the powerful multinational Williamson, Balfour and Co. This fossilized island life – Rapanui householders were not only excluded from all local governance but also from most pan-Polynesian developments as well. As subsequent visitors would invariably remark, it was as if time had stood still on Easter Island, which, by then, had become a 'company island' – an island Polynesians ostensibly no longer deserved.

It began when Chile claimed a last slice of the 'Pacific pie' before France swallowed up Rapa Nui too.[3] Great Britain's rivalry with France had prompted British commercial interests in Chile to urge the Republic to consider annexing this tiny speck of land in the Pacific. At the same time, Britons in the Cook Islands were appealing to Whitehall to halt France there as well. Once France lost both Easter Island and the Cooks in 1888, a series of articles in the French press soon led to the resignations of both a leading minister and the Under-Secretary for Foreign Affairs.[4] Chile's annexation of Easter Island at once halted foreign powers' 'sniffing out' of the island, and all future expeditions there were either Chilean, institutional or private. The Republic had become 'the only South American country to have an inhabited overseas colony, today still a point of pride for Chileans.'[5]

But why Chile? It was indeed extraordinary that, just when the world's greatest powers were seizing nearly every inhabited island in the Pacific for themselves, a Latin American nation that had won its independence from Spain only in 1818 should manage to secure the last piece of Polynesia, and the one nearest its shores.

But for decades Chile had been aggressively expanding its borders, subjugating its native peoples then exploiting the mineral and agricultural wealth of their lands. In particular, with Chile's defeat of Bolivia and Peru in the so-called War of the Pacific (1879–83), the Republic not only acquired large territories with great wealth in natural resources, but inaugurated 'an era of exuberant confidence'.[6] Indeed, Chile's powerbrokers regarded such aggressive growth – the same imperialism being demonstrated at the time by the US, Britain, France and Germany – as a natural and necessary course of action to promote and secure the young Republic's survival. 'Because of these successes Chileans came to regard themselves as a Latin American master race. Bismarck considered them the "Prussians of Latin America" . . . Chile enjoyed . . . the highest per capita income of any nation south of the Rio Grande.'[7] By the 1880s Chile was also Latin America's most European-like country, owing to robust immigration by Spaniards, English, Irish, Scots, Germans and others. A popular will was urging the nation to compete as an equal on the international stage.

And Chile was also a sea power, exerting a conspicuous naval presence throughout the Pacific ports. Growing wealthier from frequent commercial traffic, its location along the major trade and passenger route from Cape Horn – between the east and west coasts of the USA and between Europe and Asia – made it a central player in international commerce. For many decades before the opening of the Panama Canal, Valparaíso and Chile's several nitrate ports were among South America's richest and most active centres of trade.

All this had political repercussions. The expansion of mining brought an economic boom and created nouveaux riches and a new middle class, both of whom began challenging the 'traditional' oligarchy of landowners. Until then, wealth and power had been poorly distributed in Chile. But that era was at an end – at least temporarily. In 1886 the new 'reformist' president José Manuel Balmaceda undertook – not unlike President Salvador Allende many decades later – major social schemes designed to improve Chile's infrastructure and welfare, including schools, hospitals and agrarian reforms. Chile's Congress was still conservative, however, controlled by rich powerful landowners and their Scots, English, US and German investors, many of whom were long-time residents of Chile. In part to appease these latter interests, Balmaceda also endorsed an aggressive policy of expansion, heeding such patriotic Chilean writers as the renowned historian Benjamin Vicuña MacKenna, who was arguing that Chile needed to have a stake in the Pacific as well in order to augment the Republic's international image.

> Combined with pride in past attainments was an unbounded confidence in the future, and a conviction that Chile was well on the way to becoming one of the world's great powers. This attitude was in the 1880s as much a part of the national outlook as was ever Manifest Destiny in the United States.[8]

Such expansion was also of commercial interest, and here British entrepreneurs played an important, if not the leading, role. For to all intents and purposes Chile, like several other Latin American countries, was part of the British Empire, at least where commerce was concerned. South America's principal port, Valparaíso, was dominated by British interests. Chilean vessels were welcome in Australia and New Zealand – both then still British – and at Britain's rich Asian ports. At the time, any market in south-east Polynesia, for example, had to address the British-controlled commercial interests in Tahiti, which is where any meat or wool from Easter Island would be sent.

For already two decades strategic and commercial considerations had made Easter Island, the nearest inhabited place to Chile west of the Juan Fernández group, a serious proposal for the Republic. Although Easter Island lacked a natural port, its position could provide Chile with a naval beachhead for further expansion. As Bishop Jaussen had pointed out to Santiago, the island could also guard Chile's coastal commerce, preventing belligerent neighbours from disrupting the Republic's trade routes. Of strongest appeal, however, was Easter Island's commercial potential. Its wool-clip could swell the Republic's coffers, as the missionaries and Maison Brander had shown. Its cattle could fetch high prices in Pape'ete, too. Perhaps most enticingly, the entire island could be turned into Chile's market garden, as scientists aboard the *O'Higgins* had already suggested as early as 1870. The founder of Chile's National Museum of Natural History, the German Rudolph Philippi, had declared that 'with the exception of some very small areas, the whole island is susceptible to cultivation'.[9] Perhaps more importantly, to prevent Chile becoming a backwater should a canal through Panama open one day – which seemed a real possibility in the 1880s – a Chilean Easter Island, an 'Isla de Pascua', could be the main provisioner between Panama and Australia, preserving Valparaíso's international importance. At the very least, the Isla de Pascua could be the Pacific's most significant coaling tender.

But transcending the tangible were the intangible advantages. To Chile's contemporary statesmen – those victors of the 'War of the Pacific' – making Easter Island their Isla de Pascua would be declaring Chile an equal among giants in the Pacific. Its annexation would immediately raise Chile's international status. For although Chile possessed a navy, it still lacked sea colonies. The acquisition of Easter Island would make up for this deficit. Indeed, it would be an international coup.

Of late, Britain had been displaying a greater interest there, ostensibly to halt France's expansion in the region. For it was only a matter of time before a new French government would seize the island, where French nationals (the missionaries and Dutrou-Bornier) had already dedicated so many years and so much capital. Then Chile would forever lose this last foothold in the Pacific Islands. Jacobo Eden, in an article in Santiago's newspaper *La Unión*, best expressed the Republic's general attitude: even if no other advantages were to be had, the annexation of the Isla de Pascua would be repaid many times over by keeping such possible future enemies as Great Britain, the US and Peru out of 'Chilean waters'.[10]

The Chilean Navy's captain Policarpo Toro Hurtado, who had visited Easter Island several times, was perhaps the most convinced of all enthusiasts that here lay Chile's Pacific destiny. In the 1880s he conferred often with the French authorities and the Roman Catholic Church at Tahiti, and with Alexander Salmon Jr on Rapa Nui.[11] (He did not confer with the Rapanui people themselves, however, who for him were not part of the island's commercialization, or of sufficient 'cultural sophistication' to deserve regard.) Realistically assessing the disadvantages, several Chilean journalists, academics and statesmen opposed Toro's venture. But the expansionists, among them also President Balmaceda, relied on the expert opinion of the Navy – many of whose officers did not even know where Easter Island lay – that Chile's Pacific destiny rested here on 'the fertile shores of that Oasis of the Ocean', as Toro vaunted.[12]

Such an annexation would be difficult to legitimize, however, in the international arena – especially since other countries, particularly Spain (because of the visit in 1770) and France, but also Britain, could assert more substantial claims to the island. (It was universally held that the Rapanui people themselves – then called 'natives' or 'Indians' – had no rights.) Chile had two recourses. There was canonical jurisdiction: from 1888 Easter Island, as a sphere of Roman Catholic missioning, had already passed from the Apostolic Vicariate of Tahiti to the Archbishopric of Santiago. And there was simple 'right of cession' – the way in which Britain and France had grabbed most of the Pacific Islands for themselves.

It is telling that, in 1939, the Chilean scholar Victor M. Vergara attempted to justify Chile's annexation of the Isla de Pascua by citing the Berlin Conference of 1885, which had listed the three criteria deemed necessary for legitimizing the partitioning of Africa.[13] The land must be *res nullius* – that is, uninhabited or 'uncivilized'. (If abandoned, the land could be re-colonized as a *res derelictus*.) The annexor must show *animus domini*, the intent to establish full permanent sovereignty. And the annexor must celebrate the *apprehensio* with symbolic pomp. It might well be argued, as the Chilean Vergara then attempted to do, that Easter Island was perceived at the time to be a *res derelictus*. But only if the Rapanui people were ignored.

In any event, Chile gave no justification. And none was demanded by the international community. Chile simply 'took' the island and its people, while the world looked on. Within only 70 years, the colonized themselves had become colonizers.

It all came about, almost single-handedly, through Policarpo Toro, whose plans had developed only fully from the time of his visit to Rapa Nui aboard the Chilean corvette *Abtao* in 1886. In November of that year he argued to the Republic his case for annexation. This was his report 'Memoria sobre la Isla de Pascua' – which bore the telling subtitle (in translation), 'The Importance of Easter Island and the Need for the Chilean Government to Take Immediate Possession Thereof'. Already in 1887 the Republic had authorized Captain Toro to begin negotiations with the French administrators and the sscc in Tahiti: he was to determine the legal landowners in order to enable a possible land purchase. (A legal deed would mean certain sovereignty.) So it was that Toro made several voyages to Tahiti and Rapa Nui in this capacity, and soon learnt of the legal maze that thwarted any clear entitlement. Meanwhile, Chile sent its warships to Easter Island to display a presence.

Toro was 'successful' insofar as he could report that France had no immediate intention to annex the island. And the sscc? The Roman Catholics fully supported Chile's plans: in fact, they would sell their 635 hectares at Hanga Roa directly to the Republic. But the land titles could not be clarified so easily. To cut the Gordion knot, already early in 1887 Toro began to negotiate openly and intensively with the Maison Brander, of all the 'legal landowners' the one with the largest, and perhaps most cogent, claim, Toro felt. He secured the Republic's authorization to purchase land on Rapa Nui, then sailed on the *Paloma* to the island itself, arriving in October 1887. There he bought Alexander Salmon Jr's holdings (the Vaihū lands) and livestock (mostly sheep), although Salmon had still to compensate the sscc for their livestock.

The land sale between the Republic and Alexander Salmon Jr was ratified, and the final purchase of all the island's livestock (5,600 sheep, 209 cattle, 40 horses) was concluded, at Pape'ete, on 2 January 1888.[14] It cost Chile £2,000 sterling for Salmon's share. But the Maison Brander's title, locked up in French court battles, was *sub judice*, and, since this involved most of Easter Island, a clear title to this would not be forthcoming. So the Brander family promised Toro to sell their holdings for £4,000 sterling as soon as the case was settled, with a *terminus ad quem* of 1 January 1890.

But in early 1888 the Republic of Chile had still not conclusively decided on annexation. It only proposed land purchases, to increase the Chilean presence on, and investment in, the island. In April two Chilean authorities, Osvaldo Rengifo and Jorge Hunneus, submitted an official *informe* or report to Chile's Naval Sub-Secretariate recommending that France be formally informed of the Republic's agenda with regard to the Isla de Pascua and that the Republic maintain a 'permanent representation' on the island: merely owning lands there was not enough to control 'an important port which dominates the coast of South America and which, in the not too distant future, will become an obligatory way-station for traffic between Europe and Oceania'.[15] Largely as a result of the Rengifo-Hunneus Report, the Republic finally chose to endorse Toro's plan of annexation. Only after a series of frustrating postponements, however, did Toro manage to leave Valparaíso on the cruiser *Angamos* on 12 July 1888 for Tahiti to inform the French governor of the Etablissements français de l'Océanie of Chile's decision and to conclude the final land purchases.

Toro was not the only Chilean aboard the *Angamos*. Chile had implemented a robust agricultural colonization of Araucanía and Chile's southern reaches, and the Republic was convinced a similar scheme on the Isla de Pascua would render the place a white Chilean cornucopia. (Quite ignored were the many reports, for years now, of the island's lack of water and general desolation.) The army captain Pedro Pablo Toro Hurtado, Policarpo's brother, had already been appointed Chile's *agente de colonización* for the Isla de Pascua, encharged to compile an inventory, submit regular reports, initiate primary Spanish-language instruction among the 'natives' and undertake relevant industries. So it was that the *Angamos* arrived at Rapa Nui on 21 July 1888 with the island's first agrarian colonists – three families of some twelve persons and their livestock, seedlings, seeds and materials.[16] Pedro Pablo Toro disembarked with them. His brother Policarpo continued on his way to Tahiti, however, joined by Alexander

Salmon Jr and John Brander Jr, who now left the American Frank Allen in charge of the Vaihū property during their absence.[17]

Policarpo Toro arrived at Papeʻete on the eve of Chile's annexation, fully expecting to complete the land purchase with the Branders and Darsies. Salmon Jr and Brander Jr had even accompanied Toro from Easter Island specifically to ratify the final sales contract. And on 7 August, Salmon's lawyer Auguste Goupil did confirm the deposit of £2,000 for Salmon's share, which thus made the Vaihū lands, at least, official Chilean territory. The next day, Monseigneur Verdier, Bishop of Tahiti and Jaussen's successor, also sold all the sscc's lands, livestocks, effects and rights on Rapa Nui to Chile and to Monseñor Casanova, Archbishop of Santiago, for 5,000 francs. However, the court case regarding the Brander / Dutrou-Bornier lands – most of Easter Island – had not progressed. And so Toro had the Brander family extend their contract with Chile to 1 January 1899. As a result, Toro was compelled to sign a rental agreement for the Branders' and Darsies' lands on the island for 1,200 Chilean pesos per year, starting on 1 January 1889 and remaining in effect for ten years.[18]

Apparently, all that was left for Toro to complete the formal annexation was to celebrate the official *apprehensio* on Easter Island itself.[19] Returning with him on the *Angamos* for the ceremony were not only Salmon Jr and Brander Jr, but fifteen Rapanui who were quitting the Pamataʻi settlement on Tahiti to return home for good. It was the last substantial contact the Rapanui would have with Tahiti for nearly 40 years. And after this Easter Islanders would forever look towards South America alone – above all to Valparaíso and Santiago – for all culture, language, governance and economy.

Prominent among the passengers was the sscc catechist 'Nicolas Pakarati' (French *Pancrace*) Ure Pō Tahi of Rapa Nui's eastern Tūpa, then about 37 years of age. His father had been Te Pihi, his grandfather Ure ʻa Toro, his great-grandfather Pō Revareva.[20] Born at Mataveri, he had grown up at Hanga Piko, where he had lived with his mother and grandmother. In the exodus of 1871 he had remained with Brother Escolan and had first joined Bishop Jaussen's house staff at Haʻapape (see illus. 7), then left in 1873 to become cook and catechist-trainee at Father Georges Eich's sscc mission school on neighbouring Moʻorea. At the beginning of 1888 he had been sent to the Tuamotus to find a wife, and there had married 18-year-old Elizabeth Rangi Taki, whom he had just brought back to Papeʻete in time to sail, as the sscc's new catechist for Rapa Nui, to the annexation ceremony. (The newly-weds Nicolas and Elizabeth soon founded what eventually became Easter Island's large and influential Pakarati clan.)

On 8 September 1888 the 178 Rapanui who lived on Easter Island sighted the *Angamos* arriving off Vaihū. The non-Rapanui spent the night at Salmon's and Brander's Vaihū residence, then the next day, 9 September, they proceeded to Hanga Roa to conduct the ceremony at the Catholic church, the focal point of the small island community. Everyone gathered outside, around the flagpole. Policarpo Toro delivered a speech, then had the young Elizabeth Pakarati hoist the Chilean flag. But suddenly a Rapanui *korohua*, an elder, protested that 'the Rapanui flag' should be flown too.[21] This was a cloth of orange *mahute* or barkcloth, with traditional Rapanui designs, surrounded by white feathers. (It is now in the Museum of Natural History, Valparaíso.) The flag was inspired by Monseigneur Verdier (apparently to demonstrate the Rapanui prerogative, which also accommodated the sscc's), who, it was alleged, had had it manufactured in Tahiti.[22] Caught between wind and water, Toro diplomatically had this hoisted alongside the Republic's flag.

Two formal documents sealed the ceremony.[23] A 'proclamation' announced the island's cession. (This still awaited the Republic's ratification. The Republic, however, never did ratify it; although some scholars maintain that the omission has jeopardized Chile's formal claim, such a ratification is actually irrelevant under current international law.) A further 'deed of cession' bore the signatures or marks of twelve Rapanui, who, according to the Spanish text, were ceding the island's political authority to the Republic while retaining traditional titles. In this Spanish-language version, the 'full and entire sovereignty' of Easter Island was ceded 'for ever and without reservation' to Chile. However, the Tahitian-Rapanui version of the bilingual 'deed of cession' stated only that Chile would be Rapa Nui's protector and 'friend of the land'. Also signing as witnesses were Alexander Salmon Jr (who was interpreting for Toro), John Brander Jr, George Frederick and A. Plotmer.

In his official report about the ceremony, Toro described how the assembled Rapanui had displayed a great enthusiasm. This certainly may have been Toro's own reaction, for, from this day, what had been Rapa Nui was now Chile's Isla de Pascua, its people now and for evermore Chilean *pascuenses*, as he had long dreamed. But Toro did not describe in his report how, in the middle of the ceremony, the sscc-appointed 'King of Easter Island', Atamu te Kena, yanked out a fistful of grass and thrust it at Toro, saying in a loud voice: 'This is for your animals!', then grabbed a handful of earth, put it in the pocket of his own European jacket and said: 'This is for us!'[24]

It is something more than instructive to realize that Atamu te Kena had never been told that he was no longer to be the island's *'ariki*, although earlier in the year Monseigneur Verdier had made clear that the local government, the one that Father Roussel had established, was to be superseded by a new Chilean one. Yet if one reads the Spanish-language version of the 'deed of cession' carefully, one cannot misunderstand how 'the chiefs signing keep their titles and benefits'.[25] The inherent ambiguity would lead to later conflict.

Some Rapanui were then still living at Vaihū, at Alexander Salmon Jr's residence. But Salmon Jr and Brander Jr now quit the island, leaving on the *Paloma* on 14 December 1888; neither ever returned to Easter Island. Whereupon the Rapanui moved to Hanga Roa, to be closer to the church. The three agrarian colonist families had already, for many months, established themselves at Vaihū, under Pedro Pablo Toro's supervision as *agente*; he now oversaw the sheep and cattle and administered while his brother Policarpo Toro promoted their project back in Valparaíso. The two Toro brothers had the Maison Brander's vessel *Gironde* pick up their wool-clip for the Pape'ete market. Fully acknowledging the indigenous privilege, Pedro Pablo Toro negotiated harmoniously with Atamu te Kena in all island affairs. Already in this year of 1888, Pedro Pablo was promising to open a small school for Spanish-language instruction.

At the Hanga Roa church, Pakomio now surrendered all duties to Nicolas Pakarati. Pakomio's wife Angata, however, would continue for many years to assist Pakarati in all aspects of daily worship and grounds maintenance. As it happened, Pakarati proceeded together with Angata to appropriate the liturgy and rituals of Catholicism as an ever stronger defence against the new Chilean colonization. Every morning at the church, Pakarati recited the prayers of the Minor Mass; on Sundays and holy days, attendance was greater. Every evening, with boys and some interested adults, he recited the rosary. He taught the catechism both at church and in family shacks, performed infant baptisms and marriages, monitored moral behaviour, attended the infirm and dying with prayers and assistance. For 39 years Nicolas Pakarati was Rapa Nui's 'parish priest' in all but name.[26] In time, Rapa Nui's pious Catholic community, more than any other group, became the nucleus for local leadership, helping to forge a new Islander identity – one quite apart from Chile's (and, later, from the Company's).[27]

Policarpo Toro was flying Chile's flag – but from his own flagpole. The visionary was foremost a practical entrepreneur. But if he was hoping for great wealth and national recognition for his historic achievement, particularly since it enjoyed the patronage of President José Manuel Balmaceda, then he was to be sorely disappointed. In Chile, criticism was immediately forthcoming. On 30 September 1888 the newspaper *La Unión* criticized Toro for 'having burdened Chile with an arid, uncultivable island lacking adequate water supplies'.[28] Then *El Mercurio de Valparaíso* followed suit. (Of course, both were right.) In reply, Toro reiterated the Isla de Pascua's strategic and commercial advantages, and added that the island was eminently suitable for Chilean agricultural settlement. Yet both sides of the argument failed to recognize the greater dilemma: that lack of clear title to most of Easter Island meant lack of clear sovereignty for either Chile or entrepreneur. Ultimately this would condemn Rapa Nui to become what one scholar has called 'a company island'.[29]

Within a year the colonization scheme had failed. On 20 June 1889 two of the three colonist families left Rapa Nui for Valparaíso on the Chilean warship *O'Higgins*. A month later, the last colonist family died.[30] When Britain's HMS *Cormorant* visited Easter Island on 20 July 1889 in order to assess the effects of Chile's annexation and colonization, its commander found no colonists – only the *agente* Pedro Pablo Toro and a few continental shepherds who still resided at Vaihū. The Rapanui were scattered at various locales, but mainly at Hanga Roa. Within a month the Chilean press began describing Easter Island in realistic terms – its poor climate, dearth of food, general 'worthlessness' – and hinted that the Republic would soon be abandoning the island altogether.

Policarpo Toro struck back. Writing in *La Unión* of 21 August 1889, he opined that a successful colony would need at least ten families, a medical facility with a trained practitioner, and a vessel calling every four to six months. Once the colonists had gone, Toro still continued to develop the island. Breadfruit was introduced from Tahiti for sustenance for future colonists; but the plantings failed.[31] Bird-life was reintroduced, importing foreign species; several of these even thrived, but at the expense of some native species. To ensure more regular contact with the island the two brothers bought their own vessel, the *Clorinda*. And in December 1891 it carried as much as 13,000 kilograms of wool to Pape'ete.

Around 1891 a handful of Rapanui left to join the Chilean military in Valparaíso. Among them was young Tepano Rano 'a Veriamo, born one year after the exodus of 1871. Named 'Tepano' (Tahitian for English 'Stephan') after Tahiti's beloved bishop, and reared by his grandmother Veriamo (English 'William', via Whalers' Pidgin) of the Ure 'o Hei, he was to spend seven years in Chile, then return to play a historic role in island affairs.

In April 1892 the Maison Brander's own *Gironde* brought no less than 23,000 kilograms of wool to Pape'ete from the Toro brothers' sheep ranch. A cash economy was emerging at this time on the Isla de Pascua, as the Republic's *agente* Pedro Pablo Toro dutifully reported to the Chilean Ministry of Culture and Colonization:

> They [the Rapanui] are particularly fond of money, and by work, they obtain it from the whites established on the island or by selling their articles to sailors, with whom they also exchange for clothes and other objects. Recently on Easter there has been circulating between 600 to 700 pesos in silver coin from various countries, principally from Peru

and Chile. There were besides some pounds sterling, valued because they fetch seven silver pesos for each one of them.[32]

The Toro brothers, however, could not escape history's larger reckoning.

Already in 1890, two years after the Isla de Pascua's annexation, Chile's Congress had rejected President Balmaceda's budget, voted to depose their president, then created a 'provisional government' led by the naval commander Jorge Montt (much like the Pinochet coup of 1973). The civil war that immediately resulted cost some 10,000 Chilean lives. The army had supported Balmaceda. But Montt's navy had defeated the legal government by controlling the ports, hence the nation's economy. Granted political asylum, Balmaceda had spent several months of 1891 in the Argentine embassy; then, when all was lost, he had shot himself. (The historic upshot of this was that Chile would not again enjoy major social and economic reforms until after the Second World War.)

Policarpo Toro had always refused to admit defeat. After immediately countering the press attacks, he had first planned a major recolonization of the Isla de Pascua by Chilean farmers.[33] In November 1890 he had contracted with the Republic a 20-year lease of the 635 hectares at Hanga Roa (the former sscc land), with the authority to represent Chile at Tahiti as well as at Easter Island, and to purchase, at his own cost, all outstanding Brander / Darsie lands. All this, including all improvements, would then revert, at no cost, to Chile in 1910. Toro also had to keep at least three settler families on the island and maintain an annual vessel. On its part, the Republic would dispatch an annual naval supply vessel. If Toro failed to acquire the Brander / Darsie lands within two years, however, the contract would be null and void. 'This was the first instance in which the Chilean government sought to develop Easter Island through a private intermediary who was given almost total control. It was not to be the last, for this mode of disinvolvement remained effective Chilean policy for another 60 years.'[34]

Disturbing news arrived at Rapa Nui with the return of the *Clorinda* in January 1892: Bishop Jaussen had died. The Rapanui people were devastated. For all Rapanui, their Bishop 'Tepano' had always represented the Church, external protection, the ultimate French 'haven'. At the same time, Pedro Pablo Toro learnt that his brother Policarpo had been expelled from the Chilean Navy in the revolution of 1891. This left the Toro brothers without governmental support for their scheme. Shortly afterwards, on 23 June 1892, their ship, the *Clorinda*, foundered in a storm off Easter Island. (The Rapanui then plundered it.) The Toros tried to get funding for a new ship, but, as a result of the revolution, all doors were closed to them. No more wool shipments to Pape'ete were possible. Their income was frozen.

Comandante L. A. Castillo of the *Abtao* came to the Isla de Pascua in September 1892 to assess the island's situation for the Republic.[35] (Due to Chile's civil upheaval there had not been an official visit for several years.) He found the church to be solidly in the hands of Nicolas Pakarati. Because the Rapanui felt that Chile had turned its back on them, 181 of them now organized an independence movement, hoisting their own flag – a red *rei miro* pectoral on a white field – while their 'Declaration of Independence' was read aloud. Naturally, Castillo put paid to all such 'nonsense' and, to demonstrate Chile's concern, held court to settle immediate disputes. (The spontaneous procedure established a precedence of traditional, semi-regular, naval arbitration that would continue until 1953.) When the *Abtao* departed on 23 September with 21 adults and four children from the wreck of the *Clorinda*, it also took along the *agente* Pedro Pablo Toro and his foreman: for the sheep ranch itself was finally being abandoned. Only a small number of Chilean settlers remained behind. The *Clorinda*'s former pilot, Charles Higgins, was now left 'in charge' of the island for the Republic.

The Isla de Pascua might have been a Chilean dream. But it was not Chile's dream. Easter Island had proved to be of equivocal value as a strategic naval station. Too few vessels called. It was simply too isolated. And so Policarpo Toro failed. As per contract, in November 1892 Toro was forced to relinquish his right in the Isla de Pascua to the Republic. The end was ironic. Had Toro's contract been for three instead of two years, he might have succeeded: the Brander / Darsie land dispute was finally settled in 1893, leaving clear title. But Chile was simply too beset with its own internal problems to take up where Toro had left off – which still included loud dissent about Easter Island's true value to the Republic.

Already in 1888 Chilean-based investors 'had explicitly warned that legal ownership of the total land surface by the government would be necessary to obviate future difficulties with private landowners. The penalty for failing to heed this advice was a long series of bitter company–government wrangles which dominated the Easter Island sovereignty question throughout the first half of the twentieth century'.[36] In 1895, alarmed that his monies had not arrived, John Brander Jr finally travelled to Chile to see Policarpo Toro in person and get his £4,000 sterling. But Toro, very much a *persona non grata* there, had had his plans thwarted at every step. His letters and petitions to the Republic had found no response; he had run out of capital and his colony had utterly failed.[37] It appears the Republic had done nothing expressly *because* it had postponed any decision relating personally to Toro. Toro seriously considered buying the Brander / Darsie lands himself, but his purse just wasn't that deep. The Republic never reimbursed the Toro brothers for their colonization expenses.[38] Even a quarter of a century later, Policarpo

Toro's anger about the Government's broken promises was profound. He died – 'bitter and destitute'[39] – in 1921.

RESPITE

Father Roussel, at Bishop Jaussen's instigation,[40] had appointed Atamu te Kena 'king' of Rapa Nui because the sscc had needed someone on the island to represent their interests. But Atamu te Kena died in August 1892, just when the Toro brothers' sheep ranch was failing. Despite the absence of Church officials who might otherwise have supervised the procedure, to replace Atamu te Kena the Rapanui decided to use a Western process for the first time – a democratic vote. The historic event coincided with Comandante Castillo's visit in September, who observed and described what was involved. Apparently there were only two real contenders. Enrique Ika was closer in bloodline to the last *'ariki mau* Kerekorio, the traditional criterion for suitability to leadership. Timeone (French *Siméon*) Riro, the son of Ngure who had been one of Torometi's henchmen, was about 20 and also of the royal Miru; he was advanced by Angata, his first cousin, who also led the women at the church. Comandante Castillo was of the opinion that Riro was subsequently elected as a result of the women's vote, mainly for his 'good looks'. More likely, however, his victory reflected Angata's considerable political weight on the island.

Soon after the election, Angata also arranged for Riro to marry the Tahitian-born Véronique Mahute, adopted daughter of a Rapanui couple who had returned to the island in 1888. Because 'King' Riro had been democratically elected – and not installed by the sscc, like Atamu te Kena – his office gained credibility, which perhaps explains his subsequent success in promoting the indigenous privilege among non-Rapanui. To his name Riro now added the epithet Rokoroko He Tau, which had been one of the names earlier attributed to young Kerekorio. (In time, the derivative name 'Riroroko' would grace that of another large Rapanui clan.)

For four years – from 1892 until 1896 – apparently no vessels called at Rapa Nui, whose jurisdiction Chile had seemingly abandoned. To all appearances the island was again a *res derelictus*. The neglect boded well. The number of sheep, which had sunk to only 400, now soared to 5,600, this through conscientious management. Riro acted towards the few resident outsiders with a firmness that Atamu te Kena had always lacked, standing up to Charles Higgins, who now had little to say on the island. It was a brief moment of Rapa Nui autonomy. Peace and harmony actually ruled the island, something the Rapanui had not experienced for many decades.

In this rare climate of reconstitution, reinvigoration and renewal, the Rapanui began to reinvent their traditional history. Pua Ara Hoa, Nicolas Pakarati, Tori, Pakomio Ure Kino, Daniel Ure Va'e Iko and Tomenika Vake Tuku Onge combined old and recently borrowed or expanded tales – such as the 'Hotu Matu'a Cycle' of stories – to create a new 'traditional' corpus of settlement and other legends. Out of this evolved the 'ancient literature' of the island that survives today. It was first written down in the 1890s, in the Rapanui language, in family ledgers and then hidden away (until the 1950s) from all non-Rapanui as 'sacred lore'. These stories were usually adorned with pseudo-'texts' of *rongorongo* signs to form a collection that eventually came to be known as the '*rongorongo* books' or the 'Rapanui manuscripts'.[41] The mastermind behind this process was Pua Ara Hoa, who, mainly for his leading role in compiling the 'Rapanui manuscripts', personified Rapa Nui's most important source of oral tradition.[42] One cannot stress too strongly the reverence with which the Rapanui people today still regard these recent 'holy books', one on a par with the Holy Bible. (Shortly before his death in 1994, Nicolas Pakaraki's grandson Leonardo was completing a handwritten copy of one such family manuscript.)

The Rapanui were also sustained by their strong Catholic faith. When Father Albert Montiton of the sscc had restored the Hanga Roa church in the years 1887–8, he had erected near Brother Eyraud's grave a stone cross, telling the gathered Rapanui: 'When you see this cross fall, know for certain that Father Albert will have died.' On 25 February 1894 a storm felled the cross and so Nicolas Pakarati, understanding the omen, assembled the congregation in the church to pray for Father Montiton's departed soul. (Visiting three years later, Father Eich of the sscc informed the Rapanui congregation that Father Montiton had indeed died: at Miranda de Ebro, Spain – and on 25 February 1894.)[43] Yet even their faith could not save them, once the respite ended.

MERLET'S ISLAND

The Isla de Pascua had not been forgotten. Until 1895, with little or no interest in the sheep farm or fledgling colony, Chile had indeed largely regarded the island as Policarpo Toro's affair. For the Republic had had other, far more important concerns: torn by civil strife, the nation was unable to maintain effective control over those borders so recently established through conquest. It was now clear to most Chilean politicians that – despite what earlier strategists had argued – the Isla de Pascua could only poorly serve as a naval port, military garrison or even commercial waystation.[44] But at the same time the Republic could not simply abandon its recent annexation and so tarnish its international reputation. Yet there was a way out – one that had prominent precedents in Pacific Islands.

Once John Brander Jr had grasped that Policarpo Toro was in no financial position to make good his earlier agreement, he turned to the Valparaíso merchant Enrique Merlet. Since 1892 Merlet had been pressuring Toro to relinquish the Brander / Darsie lease of the Isla de Pascua. Now 'E. Merlet and Co.' concluded with Brander a written agreement to purchase the lands on Easter Island – but only on condition that clear title would be proved by full documentation. In June 1895 Brander returned to Tahiti, where he informed the Chilean consul there, Auguste Goupil, what had happened in Valparaíso, saying that everything with Chile had ended. Unperturbed, Goupil told Brander that the Bordeaux decree of 1893 had changed everything; he asked Brander to wait. Then Goupil hurriedly wrote to Toro that Chile would be entitled to retain ownership after all: Toro merely had to pay his £4,000 sterling before 22 February 1896.

But Policarpo Toro would have nothing more to do with the Isla de Pascua. And so, already in September 1895, Brander drew up a final comprehensive agreement with Enrique Merlet: for 1,200 pesos a year, Merlet would acquire a 20-year lease to the Republic's Rapa Nui lands, while Brander promised to sell Merlet all the Brander / Darsie lands. For this, E. Merlet and Co. were obligated to run an annual vessel from Chile, maintain a minimum of three settler families at Merlet's own cost, and return the leased lands to the Republic in 1915. For its part, the Republic could not guarantee an annual naval vessel, but it would freely transport Merlet's colonists and materials when the Chilean Navy did sail there.

E. Merlet and Co. were encumbered with other obligations, too. These involved the Republic's moribund plans to turn the Isla de Pascua into a naval base. All Chilean sailors were to receive free medical care there. Each naval vessel would get fresh meat. E. Merlet and Co. were to construct an office and house for a government official, and a pier to facilitate cargo handling. Most importantly, in the event that the Republic resolved to establish a community there, E. Merlet and Co. were to furnish an appropriate terrain.[45]

By purchasing the Brander / Darsie lands and leasing the Hanga Roa area (the former holdings of the sscc), a single non-resident had, for the first time, brought nearly the entire island under his legal control.[46] By January 1896 Enrique Merlet had taken physical possession of the Brander / Darsie lands, although the full documentation of these was still incomplete. Later in the year, as they had been instructed by their son / stepson in Pape'ete, the Darsies (John Brander Jr's widowed Tahitian mother Tetua and new Scots stepfather George), who had moved to Fife, Scotland, dispatched a legal document to Enrique Merlet in Valparaíso confirming that full legal title to the Brander / Dutrou-Bornier legacy now lay solely with John Brander Jr. The way was now clear for Brander to sell everything to Merlet, which process finally took place on 31 August 1897. (Merlet's investment had similarly been guaranteed, if only in part, by the stabilization of Chile's political situation with the democratic election of 1896.) E. Merlet and Co. were then the sole legal owner of what had been the Brander-Bornier domain – 'then believed to comprise almost the entire island'.[47]

A single company now 'owned' Easter Island, whose solitary concern was to generate profit from only one enterprise: ranching.

Now it was the Rapanui who were the intruders. Without warning, in March 1896 they were rudely awakened from their four-year respite when the *Maria Luisa* arrived from Valparaíso. Aboard were Merlet's new manager, Alberto Sánchez Manterola, with family. Accompanying them were several Chilean and European 'cowboys' and a shipload of supplies meant to establish the new *rancho* Isla de Pascua. The Republic had also created a new post there – that of *subdelegado marítimo de Isla de Pascua* – in order to bring Easter Island into Chilean naval jurisdiction, despite the permanent presence of E. Merlet and Co., who were in effective 'ownership'.[48] (It was the Republic's second official position on the island, now that that of the *agente de colonización* was defunct.) And the first *subdelegado* was also aboard: Sánchez himself, who, like Pedro Pablo Toro before him, wore two hats – Republic and Company. Sánchez established himself in Dutrou-Bornier's old residence at Mataveri. After this, Mataveri would remain the hub of foreign control.

The island's elected 'king', young Timeone Riro 'a Kāinga Rokoroko He Tau, was, of course, wholly ignorant of Enrique Merlet's plan to render a nullity all legitimate Rapanui claims to the island.[49] Riro welcomed Sánchez and his family, and all the foreign labourers too. Of the approximately 214 Rapanui, Sánchez was soon employing about 50. (A higher employment rate than this was reached only at the end of the twentieth century.) Although neither the *'ariki* Riro nor *subdelegado* Sánchez understood the other's culture or status, initially they got along together, showing mutual respect and taking pains not to offend.[50]

On 15 July 1896, while bringing cargo from E. Merlet and Co. in Valparaíso for Sánchez and his cowboys, the French vessel *Apolline Emilie* foundered at Easter Island.[51] Ten crew members, including the German captain and the pilot, drowned. But fourteen miraculously survived: three Germans, ten Chileans and one Italian. A few months later the *Maria Luisa* transported back to Valparaíso all the survivors – except for the 23-year-old Italian, Rafael Cardinali, who chose to settle permanently on Rapa Nui. Like the Frenchman Vincent 'Varta' Pont before him, Cardinali was to spend the rest of his long life here.

Beginning with Sánchez in 1896, company managers on Easter Island were like captains of a ship: some despotic, all of them firm, none paternal. Allegiance lay solely with the company. Rapanui and their culture meant little or nothing at all. A profitable wool-clip was everything, and how to achieve and maintain steady growth. By 1897 it was still unclear who really did 'own' the Isla de Pascua. In the Brander-Merlet purchase agreement of that year, the property being conveyed was described only as the property that had been designated in the French court decisions of 1884 and 1893 – 'whatever its extent or area'.[52] But these lands had never been surveyed, and even in the various filed *certificats de vente* at Pape'ete their boundaries were but vague tribal and topographical approximations.[53]

Perhaps Enrique Merlet was expecting challenges to a perceived 'illegal' seizure when, in 1897, he dispatched three armed Chilean guards to the Isla de Pascua, one of whom was supposed to replace Sánchez. For Merlet was unhappy with his manager – he judged him too deferential towards the Rapanui. When the guards arrived, they insisted that the Rapanui lower their Rapa Nui flag, still flying from the Hanga Roa flagpole. Although under no legal obligation to do this, 'King' Riro complied. The guards then replaced it with the Chilean flag.[54] In the charged atmosphere this created, Sánchez chose not to quit the island but resolved instead, despite personal inclination, to exercise that sterner hand his boss Merlet was demanding.

Arriving from Tahiti, Father Georges Eich of the sscc's mission school at Mo'orea visited Rapa Nui from 6 to 10 January 1898 in order to bid his former catechist Nicolas Pakarati and all sscc converts a sad farewell – 'adieu pour toujours', he wrote[55] – on behalf of the island's patron order now that the Archbishopric of Santiago had finally assumed full ecclesiastical responsibility. Eich was alarmed at the Rapanui people's state, something he had not expected to encounter. He judged their working conditions to be even worse than those on Tahiti, and rightfully found Sánchez too harsh a taskmaster. Not only were 30 to 40 Chileans now living on the island – three Rapanui were actually suffering from leprosy.

It appears the disease had arrived a decade earlier, brought from Tahiti by a returnee who had accompanied Nicolas and Elizabeth Pakarati back to the island for the annexation in 1888: 'Tepano' (later Estebán) Ruti Rangi, who had lived for many years on Tahiti.[56] Once he had infected other Rapanui, the Hanga Roa community isolated all lepers at Tara Heu, close to Tahai. (A few years later, they were relocated even further away – to two small shacks 3 kilometres north of Hanga Roa.)

Undaunted, Father Eich heard confession, gave extreme unction and offered the eucharist. He also baptized 65 infants and young people and administered the sacraments of confession and communion to nearly all the island's adults, including non-Rapanui. Eich had nothing but the highest praise for the work of Pakarati and his wife Elizabeth. 'All [Rapanui] know the catechism by heart', he wrote. 'On Wednesdays, Fridays and Sundays they recite all together three chapters of the catechism, supplementing in this way the lack of a sermon.'[57]

Not only leprosy afflicted the island. Because of its great isolation and fewer visits – only once or twice a year now – after each foreign visit a catarrhal fever, a type of influenza called *kokongo* in the Rapanui language, would rage throughout the tiny community. Sometimes it killed many young, infirm and elderly; at other times the symptoms were mild. (Well into the 1960s the *kokongo* would continue to strike; it disappeared only with the introduction of regular air travel.)

Throughout 1898 conditions on the island worsened as Enrique Merlet's demands to Sánchez were put into action. All Rapanui were ordered to live at Hanga Roa and Moeroa (on the way to Mataveri); all other locales were cleared for livestock, every head of which was impounded as Merlet's own personal property. For the livestock, the Rapanui were ordered to erect fences and dry-stone walls, what the Chileans call *pircas*. The Rapanui themselves were forbidden to enter these walled-off areas. The Rapanui world shrank, as the 'company world' grew. Threat of force became more common; plantations disappeared as *pircas* expanded; the Rapa Nui flag remained banned. Perhaps most ominously, Sánchez finally commanded the Rapanui to stay put in Hanga Roa and Moeroa – unless they were on company business.

To emphasize this latest, and most obscene, outrage, Sánchez had his labourers begin building a 3-metre-high *pirca* around Hanga Roa and Moeroa – eventually to enclose 1,000 hectares. Ostensibly it was to parcel out family areas for private plantations. But in reality it was to keep the Rapanui, like human livestock, confined within the Wall. And erecting this were the Rapanui themselves, grateful at the time to be earning hard cash. For this enabled them to purchase, in the company's primitive store, the imported cloth, tobacco and sugar they didn't need, at prices they couldn't afford. No one knew they were constructing a confinement camp. And no one would have believed that only their grandchildren would experience the Wall's toppling – more than half a century later.

Sometime during 1898 a delegation of Rapanui, led by Riro (who by now had three sons and a daughter), marched to Mataveri to complain to Sánchez about the low pay and poor conditions working for this new Chilean 'company' – by now a tangible concept to them. Merlet had already written to Riro, personally ordering him to cease claiming he was 'king' of the Isla de Pascua:[58] Merlet owned the island, not Riro. Now the Rapanui began shouting at Sánchez that this was untrue. The Rapanui alone were the *tangata henua*; this was their island; they were not slaves of any foreigners. A loud argument ensued and Sánchez had them evicted.[59] The Rapanui immediately agreed among themselves that they would not work again until the next Chilean naval vessel arrived: its Comandante would arbitrate the issue, just as Comandante Castillo of the *Abtao* had done six years earlier. Furious once he learnt of this, Sánchez took two of his armed guards and descended into Hanga Roa from Mataveri – just like Dutrou-Bornier back in the 1870s – to force the Rapanui to return to work. They refused. When one guard started threatening with his rifle, Riro and his men disarmed him at once.

Back in Valparaíso, Merlet was livid once he read his manager's report of the incident. Riro had subsequently appealed to Sánchez to be allowed to travel to Valparaíso on the company vessel, Sánchez had added, and so he had assured Riro that there, in Chile, Riro would be allowed to voice his grievances personally before the country's president. Perhaps too obligingly, with the next vessel Merlet sent Sánchez his written permission to this effect.[60]

At the end of 1898 or early 1899 a small delegation of Rapanui, about to depart on the company vessel, was entertained by friends and relations with a specially composed song: a hardly disguised warning *not* to go to Valparaíso. For by then no one on the island trusted either Sánchez or this invisible Merlet who claimed he 'owned' them and their island. Accompanying Riro on the voyage were three young Rapanui soldiers, the country's first. One was Tepano Rano, whom his Chilean superiors were calling 'Juan', using his baptismal name Tepano as his surname: Juan Tepano. (It would become yet another important clan name on Rapa Nui.) Caroline Dutrou-Bornier's son Juan Araki Ti'a was the second, and José Pirivato, or 'Private José', the third. The trio were completing their military service with the 'Maipo' Regiment at Valparaíso.[61] Once arrived at Chile's most important port, they were met by Enrique Merlet's man Jeffries.

What then happened is unclear. It appears that the *intendente de la provincia* did send a message expressing a wish to speak with 'King' Riro of Easter Island. But Riro insisted on talking only with an 'equal' – the President of Chile himself – as he had been promised. The four Rapanui then accompanied Jeffries and another Merlet employee, Alfredo Rodríguez, to several taverns. Once all were well into their cups, Rodríguez invited Riro to dine with him and spend the night at his house, at which point the three Rapanui soldiers left for their barracks. The following day, Rodríguez, not Jeffries, informed the trio at the 'Maipo' Regiment, either personally or by messenger, that they should pay a visit to their friend Riro, who apparently lay ill in the Van Buren Hospital: he had imbibed so much alcohol the previous evening that his condition had warranted hospitalization, they were told. Alarmed, they rushed off immediately. But once at the hospital they were informed that their friend had since succumbed to 'poisoning'. Rapanui accounts traditionally allege that Merlet had ordered Riro's poisoning. But for this there is no proof. The hospital's explanation, however, does appear to confirm that Riro had indeed died of poisoning – alcohol poisoning, almost certainly induced. 'King' Riro was then buried in a pauper's grave in Valparaíso.[62]

Enrique Merlet immediately let it be known that the young Rapanui had plainly 'drunk himself to death'. At the same time, Merlet was also spreading the fable that these Islanders were in fact *mestizos* or mulattos who were only distantly related to the Isla de Pascua's original inhabitants (and thus illegitimate heirs to the island).[63] Once the news of Riro's death reached Rapa Nui, his Miru relative María Veri Tahi 'a Pengo Hare Kohou nominally assumed leadership. In fact, she agitated for many years against Merlet's (and later the Company's) hegemony, though without Riro's success: for the fulcrum of power now lay elsewhere. Riro's widow Véronique, doubtless fearing for her life and those of her four children, already on 29 January 1900 married one of Sánchez's Chilean shepherds.[64]

She was married by Father Isidore Butaye of the sscc, who, sailing from Mangareva, visited the island from 24 January to 2 February 1900, counting 231 people there: 213 Rapanui (64 men, 64 women, 44 boys and 41 girls), a dozen Chileans, two Britons, one Frenchman (Pont) and one Italian (Cardinali). Butaye related how the Rapanui Enrique Ika had organized a strike against the company after Sánchez, on purpose, had set fire to the Rapanui's plantations. The entire local community had then revolted against the manager, who had had to barricade himself and his family inside the Mataveri residence, fearing for their lives. Sánchez managed to suppress the revolt only by threatening the Rapanui with a show of rifles.[65]

Arriving from Valparaíso on the company ship in 1900, Enrique Merlet visited his Isla de Pascua for the first time, finally replacing Sánchez – who by now was relieved to be escaping the hazardous island – with a new manager, the Englishman Horatio ('Horace') Cooper. When the anti-company demonstrations persisted as the Rapanui, frequently at rifle point, were cruelly forced to complete the Wall surrounding Hanga Roa and Moeroa, Cooper had the dissidents seized and 'exiled to Chile'. Many never arrived there at all, it appears, but instead were thrown overboard at sea.[66] Whereupon a reign of terror descended as had not been seen since the days of Dutrou-Bornier. In many ways it was worse. For the Rapanui were virtual prisoners on an island penal colony. Insufficiently fed, deprived of all social and medical attention, they were forced each day, at poor or even no pay, to build *pircas*, wooden fences, and various outbuildings and perform any number of other tasks for Merlet's ranch. Never before, or since, had the entire island population been reduced to such servitude.

The French naval gunboat *La Durance* visited for several days in July and August 1901, ostensibly to assess the situation for the French Government.[67] The vessel's chief surgeon, Dr Delabaude, conducted a superficial archæological survey, bringing away artefacts, skulls and obsidian points and photographing a variety of culturally significant sites (illus. 10). By this time, the traditional reed-thatched 'upturned-boat' huts, still so common in the 1870s,

10 Hanga Roa in 1901, photographed by Dr Delabaude during the visit of the French gunboat *La Durance*.

had been replaced almost entirely by European-style shacks of thatch, timber and galvanized metal – commonly cannibalized from foundered vessels.

Juan Araki, Juan Tepano and José Pirivato had all returned to the island from Chile, their three subsequent fates epitomizing the three recourses left the Rapanui in the following half-century. Juan Araki displayed total submission to the company, working for it for the rest of his days as one of those rarest of employees who enjoyed a regular income. Juan Tepano's role evolved over the years. He was Hanga Roa's undisputed *jefe* in 1901, living in a large stone house near the church in which he cared for his grandmother Veriamo and for several elderly men whose families had died.[68] In 1902 Tepano was officially appointed the island's first *cacique* or local headman, with corresponding police power that also allowed him special access to the entire island. Tepano mediated between the Rapanui and the company, but appreciated the realities of survival: he knew which way the wind blew on Rapa Nui (always from Mataveri). In time he would be the island's master statesman, forever tempering integrity with *Realpolitik*. José Pirivato, on the other hand, sided with Enrique Ika and María Veri Tahi and actively resisted the company at every turn.

The latter stance was invariably disadvantagous, if not fatal. Yet another revolt in 1902 resulted in Horace Cooper's taking six Rapanui into custody, including José Pirivato.[69] The Chilean Navy's training ship *General Baquedano*, under Comandante Basílio Rojas, arrived soon after. Once Rojas had learnt what had happened, in his capacity as the island's chief military official he issued a *reglamento* or edict – effectively the first Chilean regulation restricting the autonomy of the Rapanui people. The Navy now confirmed that each successive company manager was also to be the *subdelegado maritimo* and therefore the representative of Chile as well. Hence, any protest against the company would be a protest against the Republic. 'Any reason for not working was considered a revolt and those who encouraged not going to work would be accused of leading a revolt and sent to jail on the continent.'[70] Instead of having a 'king' or *'ariki* – whom the Rapanui might have regarded as their mediator, but whom the company branded as an opposition leader (such as María Veri Tahi) – Rojas established the new position of *cacique*, which would represent company policy with the Rapanui. So it was that Juan Tepano was appointed to this position. Whereupon Rojas provided Cooper with rifles and ammunition, took the six prisoners aboard for 'deportation', then sailed off again.

In 1903 the Chilean Navy returned and deemed that the previous year's measures had succeeded in establishing 'peace' on Easter Island. José Pirivato and the five other Rapanui prisoners? There is no record of their ever having disembarked in Chile. Their families never heard from them again.[71] It was the peace of the concentration camp. And it would continue for another eleven years.

THE COMPANY

After the sscc's missionaries, then Dutrou-Bornier, then Salmon Jr and then the Toro brothers, it was now Enrique Merlet's turn to defer – if indeed this had not been his secret mission all along. For it was the era's pan-Pacific phenomenon. By this time cosmopolitan companies were dominating nearly all forms of economic activity in the Pacific Islands. The company scheme developing on Easter Island was very similar to what the Kaiser had been doing in New Guinea and Samoa, the Americans in Hawai'i, the British in the Solomons, the French in New Caledonia and so forth. Even in such developed nations as Chile, European and us companies had come to wield social and political control over large segments of the population, providing social services, housing and transportation networks to create in certain regions a 'company state'.[72] In these, 'the citizens of the company state look to the company, rather than their legal government, for the benefits normally supplied by government agencies'.[73] In Chile's far south, for example, huge sheep ranches, frequently the demesnes of British companies, dominated the region until Chile developed there its oil and mineral production. The nationalistic expansion of the 1880s had created a Chile too large for its own capital and human resources to manage independently. This had resulted in political chaos, culminating in the vicious civil war of 1891.

After having tried to claim that he legally 'owned' all of the Isla de Pascua, yet having demonstrated only that his 'E. Merlet and Co.' was incapable of developing the island's wool and cattle trade without additional financial backing, Enrique Merlet, somewhat discredited, had already turned in 1897 to Williamson, Balfour and Co. for support. It is not impossible that Merlet had himself been a straw man for Williamson, Balfour all along.[74] For on 13 February 1897 Arthur Brander had written to his brother John Brander Jr that 'Williamson's people had told Mr [George] Darsie, that they had bought a lot of Easter Island wool' from Merlet.[75] The Branders, Darsies and Williamsons – Scots, or of immediate Scots parentage – all knew each other personally. All had a strong stake in Polynesia and Chile. Stephen Anstruther Williamson – his middle name from his father's birthplace, that small village in Fife to where the Darsies had retired from Tahiti – was a leading executive in Chile, what we would today call the CEO of a multinational corporation. And Williamson was actively seeking his company's Pacific expansion.

The British trading firm Williamson, Balfour and Co. (now the multinational Balfour, Williamson) had begun in 1851 as 'S. Williamson and Company', a Liverpool enterprise founded by three Scots from Fife who had wished to profit from goods to South America's west coast, then a growing arena.[76] Locating their branch headquarters at Valparaíso, in 1863 this became 'Williamson, Balfour and Co.', which focused on shipments of wool and nitrate to Liverpool. But by the 1890s a triangular trade had developed between Britain, Chile and the US's west coast, with two offices in Britain, five in Chile and six in the US. The Chilean company soon transcended simple export–import, diversifying into banking, railways, oil, minerals, cement, coffee and other things. Its activities came to involve expansion into many other South American countries, and into the US, Canada, West Africa and the Philippines.

In 1898 Stephen Williamson of Williamson, Balfour loaned Enrique Merlet, with whom he had had trade dealings for at least the two previous years relating to Easter Island, a substantial sum to underpin financially his *rancho* Isla de Pascua. When Merlet appeared unable to repay this loan on time in 1903, seemingly placing the entire Easter Island venture in jeopardy, Williamson, Balfour – rather than bankrupting Merlet, which would have been the customary recourse for such a large corporation – instead formed the Compañía Explotadora de la Isla de Pascua or 'Exploitation Company of Easter Island' (hereinafter simply called 'the Company'), with a sizable capital of £20,000 consisting of 500 shares.[77] The Merlet family's total rights to the Isla de Pascua were bought by Williamson, Balfour for 375 shares. This left 120 shares for Williamson, Balfour and five for Stephen Williamson and his associates.

The Board comprised Williamson (as President), the associates and Enrique Merlet. Merlet served as local Company manager in Valparaíso.

All the Company's associates were Chilean-based Scots from eastern or southern Scotland. Essentially, for most of its post-missionary history Easter Island's exploitation was a Scots exploitation, albeit through Chile.[78] These became the true 'kings' of Rapa Nui. Unlike their short-lived predecessors Dutrou-Bornier and Alexander Salmon Jr, the Chilean Scots ruled there for nearly 50 years.

The Company was registered on 30 July 1903 for a term of 25 years. In its official statutes, dated 20 July 1903, its objective was to 'acquire the privately owned land on Easter Island, acquire or rent the state-owned land on the said island, to exploit them both, to obtain new boats and acquire any other materials necessary for the furthering of [island] development'.[79] Of course, Williamson, Balfour dominated its majority shareholders and virtually ran the Company as a Williamson, Balfour corporate 'daughter', then an emergent strategy, enabling extensive financial resources otherwise unavailable. So the Merlet family actually had little to say. Williamson, Balfour even became the Company's banker – which meant that it could 'squeeze out' all internal competition. (As a result, the Company increasingly endebted itself to Williamson, Balfour. The Merlets placed their shares as security for a further loan in 1908 and, when their family business collapsed in 1926, all Company stock then became the Williamson family's.)

On the Isla de Pascua itself nothing changed. All real power lay with the *subdelegado marítimo*, who represented both Chile and the Company. In 1905 this was still Horace Cooper, who was pontificating: 'the administration of Merlet and Company and the natives of the island live in complete harmony'.[80] But self-promotion was ever a manager's prerogative. The Rapanui were anything but happy. Their Rapa Nui had turned into an Isla de Pascua owned and dominated by *tangata hiva*, by foreigners. The *tangata henua*, the people of the land, the Rapanui, ceased to have a traditional identity as members of the local community, but were ranked instead according to their relationship to the Company. (An exception was Nicolas Pakarati, who, as the island's catechist, defined his rank through the Church.) This ended the egalitarianism of the post-exodus depopulation and pre-Company days. Rapanui became 'haves' and 'have-nots', ranked according to what connections they enjoyed to permanent, semi-permanent or seasonal incomes and payments in kind. Instead of blood lineage, kinship or an egg competition to bestow status, it was one's favour in the eyes of the respective manager / *subdelegado* at Mataveri that achieved this. A 'community identity' no longer existed on the island. One's relationship to the Company defined one's humanity.

Although Williamson, Balfour had lordship, and the Company had nominal oversight, Enrique Merlet remained for many years in full control of the island, ruling through his on-site manager. He was secure in this position so long as his financial figures remained in the black. Easter Island was only a minor investment for Williamson, Balfour, a mere speck on its enormous corporate map. Merlet did show an interest in developing the island. Like the Toro brothers, he reintroduced terrestrial bird life, bringing in several species. Partridges thrived in the island's tussock, but ducks stocked on Rano Kau's crater lake failed to breed. The European rats from the whaling days – which had long replaced the original, much smaller Polynesian *kiore* – were kept in check by the *toketoke*, a small hawk, which, however, seemed far more interested in the introduced partridges. This soon became a problem, since partridge eggs had since assumed the importance to the Rapanui that seabird eggs once held. Sparrows and other small birds also thrived, but were preyed on by feral cats. Introduced in the 1880s, dogs were almost exclusively working dogs, requisite for sheep herding.

The environment around the Mataveri residence had also changed. Experimental plantings of carob, various acacias, a variety of eucalyptus, pines, araucarias, cypresses and coconut palms were meant to find those species best suited to the island's biosphere to provide shade, food and fodder.[81] Dutrou-Bornier's tentative gardens inside Rano Kau's caldera were replaced at this time by bananas, acacias, figs, vines, ti and similar tree crops, which were carefully tended well into the 1950s. But the Company's efforts to plant introductions elsewhere were restricted to several species of eucalyptus from Australia – which then proceeded to, and still do, desiccate the island's already dry soil. Major stands of eucalyptus were planted, many by Vincent Pont, along the southern coast, on Rano Kau's slopes above Mataveri, and, from the 1920s, at the Company's large sub-station at Vaitea (in the middle of the island). Smaller stands rose on Terevaka and atop Pōike as well. In such plantings, as in everything else, the Company treated the island as its private garden.[82]

Island life was ruled by each manager at Mataveri. Only from the 1920s was this a manager and a foreman, working together as a pair. Most of these were of lowland Scots provenance, as was the Company's associates and even Williamson, Balfour themselves. Some of the managers and foremen lived with Rapanui women and founded families, which they then customarily abandoned once their contracts ended and they returned to Chile or even Scotland. The Company's European and Chilean employees – shepherds, cowboys and farmhands – resided at Mataveri, too, while the Rapanui remained confined to Hanga Roa and Moeroa, behind the Wall. But there were other Company buildings scattered about the island, for the use of the shepherds. These often had adjacent paddocks and corrals, as at 'Anakena (where the Frenchman Pont first lived), Vaihū (Salmon Jr's old residence from the 1880s, adapted from Zumbohm's), Tongariki and Vaitea (from the 1920s the annual shearing centre).

Shearing fortnight – *la esquila* – became what 'Orongo had been: celebration and feast, but now also mutton and beef, hard cash and temporary freedom from behind the Wall. Once the Company vessel arrived and loading began, the Rapanui could trade carvings for cigarettes, clothing, soap and other 'luxury' items. (Barter fully disappeared only in the 1990s, when a cash economy finally triumphed because of rocketing tourist numbers.) Before the 1920s, all shearing was done at Mataveri, for most of the twentieth century the nominal 'capital' of Easter Island.

CONSOLIDATION

Rapanui perceptions of the outside world were still frustratingly vague. And too often superstition proxied for reason. What most Rapanui knew came from hearsay, second-hand accounts and only infrequent dealings with the manager, foreign labourers, naval visitors, the odd vessel and, later, foremen who were commonly of Scots origin and hardly spoke Spanish, much less Rapanui. (Most Rapanui did not speak Spanish either.) Thus of great interest to everyone were visits by scientific investigators, such as the eminent American marine zoologist Alexander Agassiz of Boston, who briefly stopped at the end of 1904. Some very old people – like Miguel Keremuti Hea (Timikore Keremuti) – still recalled years abroad during the exciting whaling era. Only very few Rapanui, such as Juan Tepano and Juan Araki, had served in the Chilean military and had come to know, first-hand, modern continental ways. Much information was gleaned from the fascinating stories of the two longest foreign residents on the island: the Frenchman Pont and Italian Cardinali, who were the only ones able to converse with the manager in English, with the Chilean shepherds in Spanish and with the Rapanui in the new hybrid Rapanui-Tahitian tongue nearly everyone was now using.

In 1908 the harsh Horace Cooper finally left. Replacing him as new manager of the *rancho* Isla de Pascua was Henry Percy Edmunds – equally severe, but more just and humane. Born in Hampton in 1879, Edmunds was actually an amateur photographer, traveller and artefact dealer.[83] (His grandfather had founded the Midland Bank, now HSBC, today one of Britain's most prominent.) He arrived at Rapa Nui after many years in Argentina, and stayed for a quarter of a century – longer than any manager before or after. 'He was a strong man of regular habits, who received from the annual company ship his year's supply of English periodicals with cases of whisky for himself and his workers, in return for which he dispatched a carefully selected wool clip for distant bosses.'[84]

Inveterate nicknamers, the Rapanui dubbed Edmunds 'Reherehe' ('Lanky'), because of his being tall, thin and loose-limbed.[85] But in truth they both respected and feared the man who actually controlled their lives. Having

11 The *cacique* Juan Tepano with Hanga Roa residents in their finest attire, *c.* 1910.

been a dealer of artefacts in Europe, Edmunds was very keen on collecting island curios for commercial profit to supplement his meagre income. Communicating with leading British collectors, such as A.W.F. Fuller, he would have Rapanui searching caves for originals while others carved reproductions that Edmunds's mother in England would then sell for him. At first Edmunds communicated with his handful of Rapanui employees in Spanish, which he spoke fluently; but over the years he also came to learn the new Modern Rapanui hybrid tongue, and used this more frequently.

Soon after he had arrived and got to know who was who on the island, Edmunds appointed Hanga Roa's *cacique*, Juan Tepano, to be his personal foreman (illus. 11). This, of course, placed Juan Tepano in a most difficult position: at once representing the Rapanui, the Republic and the Company.

On 13 April 1911 Comandante Arturo Swett of the *General Baquedano* arrived at the Isla de Pascua with a prominent passenger list. The German meteorologist and geophysicist Walter Knoche, director of Chile's Central Meteorological and Geophysical Institute in Santiago, was leading the Chilean Scientific Expedition to Easter Island.[86] Participants were the assistant observer at the Institute, Edgardo Martínez, who would eventually compile a short Rapanui dictionary; the technician of the Seismological Service, Ignacio Calderón; and the botanist of the Liceo de La Serena, Francisco Fuentes. The Scientific Expedition spent twelve days on the island, establishing a meteorological station and a seismic register and gathering important data.

Although Knoche rejected any idea of Easter Island's being of strategic importance for Chile, he waxed enthusiastic about its agrarian potential:

If there existed a better connection with Chile, then this island with its rich soil consisting of the products of volcanic decomposition could, with some conscientiousness in the planting and care of the cultures, become Chile's garden and the producer of all those fruits which today are imported from tropical Peru into the Republic's harbours.[87]

But the Republic was apparently not interested.

It was at this time that the Chilean officers of the *Baquedano* attempted to crown Juan Tepano 'king' of Easter Island. There was even a public investiture in the centre of Hanga Roa to mark the 'historic event'. But since no one on the island any longer took the idea of an island 'king' seriously, least of all Juan Tepano himself, the would-be 'coronation' was soon forgotten. For the spirit of Riro had vanished for good behind the ominous Wall.

Of more immediate concern to the 228 Rapanui incarcerated within Hanga Roa and Moeroa was the priest Zósimo Valenzuela, the *Baquedano*'s naval chaplain, who had accompanied Knoche's expedition on behalf of Chile's Roman Catholics – the first non-sscc clergyman to minister on Rapa Nui.[88] The Castrense Vicariate, under Monseñor Rafael Edwards (who would become bishop in 1915), had sent Valenzuela specifically to attend to the Rapa Nui church. Father Zósimo spent eleven days on the island: administering, teaching, performing the holy office and organizing the local community. Unable to pronounce Zósimo, the Rapanui called him 'Padre Totimo'. One of the priest's accomplishments was particularly poignant. Two 15-year-old girls had run off with their lovers after both their fathers had refused them permission to marry. But Juan Tepano successfully intervened and so 'Padre Totimo' married both pairs of elopers, as well as eleven more at the same time.

Once the island's general destitution was recognized, food from the *Baquedano* was also distributed among the community: flour, bread, sugar, rice and continental vegetables – most of these items still foreign to the local diet. Chilean officers and sailors, who were, nearly to a man, moved by the Islanders' perceived 'poverty' (actually, the Rapanui had never known anything else), donated personal clothing as well. On 24 April, as the *Baquedano* was preparing to sail, several Rapanui boarded to implore Comandante Swett to leave 'Padre Totimo' behind with them. But the vessel departed with its naval chaplain and full complement of expedition members – except for Edgardo Martínez, who for more than a year would remain at the Hanga Roa Meteorological Station as resident observer.

After this, the *Baquedano* would return to the Isla de Pascua annually, always bringing a naval chaplain to administer for several days during the Republic of Chile's official visitation. If on their own island the Rapanui could not walk, at least in their own church they could soar. The very edifice itself, holding a profound significance in the Rapanui psyche, assumed at this time fundamental importance. It transcended religion and approached ethnic identity. For the Church was *not* Company. It never could be. The Church alone now guarded the Rapanui soul. As it happened, the contrived perception was soon to have solemn consequences.

Meanwhile, the lonely remnants of Old Rapanui society were expiring at the would-be leprosery, 3 kilometres north of Hanga Roa. About a dozen lepers, most of them old men like the aficionado of traditional lore Tomenika Vake Tuku Onge, were now occupying two filthy, broken-down shacks. Another dozen family members and old friends had joined them there. The healthy Rapanui *korohua* or elders had voluntarily chosen to live there, too, because they felt that no one else on the island wished to hear their stories. They also felt homeless in 'foreign' Hanga Roa, behind the Wall.[89]

Ancient Easter Island society had continued, if somewhat altered, well into the nineteenth century. It was finally felled in the 1860s, with the labour raids and pandemics, then blown away with the exodus of 1871. Now only a handful of Rapanui recalled that earlier world. Even fewer could understand when the old people spoke of it, in the old language. So it came about that, in the second decade of the twentieth century, old Rapa Nui society silently passed away at two ramshackle shacks for lepers in the quiet countryside.

At the end of 1912 and the beginning of 1913, the captain and crew of the British vessel *Knight of the Garter*, en route from Valparaíso to Australia, were similarly shocked when, calling at Easter Island, they witnessed the Rapanui people's destitution and the Company's seeming lack of sympathy. An account of their negative impressions soon appeared in the British press, underscoring 'the extreme poverty of the inhabitants' of Easter Island.[90] When reports of this filtered back to Chile, many among the educated citizenry there also began to grow concerned.

In June 1913 Captain N. P. Benson and ten crewmen of the Oregon timber schooner *El Dorado* had to abandon ship at high sea, leaving their vessel adrift as they sailed in a 7-metre skiff some 300 kilometres north, then 1,000 kilometres east – to arrive finally at Easter Island after eleven harrowing days at sea. Arriving on land in a weakened state, the officers lodged with Percy Edmunds at Mataveri, while the crew camped in the deserted Mission House in Hanga Roa. 'Every sailor had a wife.'[91] After 105 days, Benson and two others sailed in the refitted skiff first to Mangareva (sixteen days), then on to Pape'ete (eleven days). Among the eight who had stayed behind were two Swedes and a Japanese cook (who had won the heart of Hanga Roa's beauty). A British steamer picked up all remaining crew members several months later – but only after its captain had paid a severance fee to their abandoned Rapanui 'wives': each girl received a bar of 'cheap, castile soap with red streaks in it – the kind they use in the second cabins'. Evidently inspired by this event, shortly afterwards a young Rapanui father stole a small skiff with rigged sail – just like Captain Benson's – and set off, too, for Tahiti. No one ever heard from him again.[92]

For the first time, Chileans appeared to appreciate that their Isla de Pascua had an indigenous population, and that these *pascuenses* were apparently suffering in some horrible way. It was even rumoured that their living conditions were so wretched that they had petitioned the Republic to emigrate en masse to Tahiti.[93] Everyone in Chile, especially the Navy who had experienced the situation first-hand, gave the Company blame. All ignored the greater issue: that the Republic had given Williamson, Balfour carte blanche on the island. The Santiago newspaper *La Unión* publicized in its issue of 13 June 1914 that the Company had taken all the Isla de Pascua's land and fresh water for its own livestock; that the Rapanui people could not leave Hanga Roa without permission; and that stealing a sheep to feed a starving family led to deportation to the continent and death there, through unaccustomed climate and 'nostalgia'.[94] Unmentioned, however, remained the Republic's part in these wrongs.

Both exaggeration and cultural disparity skewed this and similar reports. Most Rapanui families were not enslaved by debt. Nor was 'a man's entire yearly salary . . . just enough to buy a simple cotton dress for his wife'.[95] Rapanui women could easily forego a cotton dress, a foreign fashion on an island without fashion. Western value judgements were invalid for a subsistence economy that used cash only for foreign luxuries (mostly unhealthy alien foodstuffs, such as processed flour, refined sugar and coffee). What the Rapanui people truly needed was civil rights: an indigenous entitlement with equality before the law. Much more noteworthy in 1914 were the first calls by continental Chileans for their Pacific colony to be included politically in the *intendencia* or administration of Valparaíso, giving Chilean rights to all *pascuenses*. The Catholic Church, too, was paying close attention to the matter.

THE 'MANA EXPEDITION' ARRIVES

In the 1800s scientific expeditions to Easter Island had lasted only several days. But in the twentieth century most expeditions would become veritable occupations lasting several months, or even a year or more. Such visits impacted greatly. For, in return for labour, guide work, transportation and food, expeditions provided not only hard cash and goods, but also general information, about the world as well as about Rapa Nui's own history – from published European accounts of the 1700s and 1800s – which the oral tradition had long forgotten. The first such expedition was the extraordinary 'Mana Expedition', a milestone in Easter Island ethnography and an event of historic magnitude.[96]

It was conceived in 1910 when Sir Hercules Read, Keeper of Ethnography at the British Museum and President of the Royal Anthropological Institute of Great Britain and Ireland, together with the Assistant Keeper, Thomas Athol Joyce, suggested to the wealthy husband-and-wife team of adventurer-anthropologists William Scoresby Routledge and Katherine Pease that they should set sail for Easter Island, then still largely anthropological *terra incognita*. Scoresby Routlege agreed with the two Keepers that the chief goal on Easter Island should be the discovery and decipherment of *rongorongo* inscriptions in order perhaps to explain the island's ancient human origins. Katherine Routledge was more inter-ested, however, in its general archæology and ethnography.

When the Routledges realized that no ship would be available to take them there, they had one built for them at tremendous expense: a 90-foot, 126-tonne wooden schooner they named *Mana*. Then they hired a British crew. Even for wealthy Britons, 'it was an incredible stretch for them, a daunting and even dangerous, impractical proposition'.[97] Sailing out of Falmouth harbour on 25 March 1913, they would take exactly a year to reach Rapa Nui. Little did they imagine that theirs would become one of the most extraordinary anthropological endeavours of the early twentieth century.

Enrique Merlet could have refused *Mana* access to the island, but the Routledges were too wealthy, too well connected and too British for him to dare. By January 1914 the vessel had arrived at the Chilean port of Talcahuano that served Concepción, the country's largest city south of Valparaíso. This was just when many in Chile were distressed by the report-ed hardship of the *pascuenses*, and Lady Grogan, wife of the British military attaché, and the naval captain Enrique Larenas were actively fronting an organization collecting food, clothes, shoes and equipment for the poor Rapanui people. At first Katherine Routledge offered to transport these donations to the island in the *Mana*. But then she withdrew the offer, possibly fearing that Williamson, Balfour would take the gesture to be a critique and retract their permission to land. (The donations would follow on the next annual visit of the *Baquedano*.)

The *Mana* finally sighted Easter Island on 29 March 1914. (Katherine Routledge would not leave the island until 18 August 1915, after nearly seventeen months ashore.) Immediately the Routledges moved into Percy Edmunds's residence at Mataveri; later they would occupy tents outside the house, and often camp below Rano Raraku as well. At this time Edmunds was co-habiting with Nicolas Pakarati's niece, Sofía Hey Rapu, who had borne him children. But in Hanga Roa he was also beginning a relationship with the 15-year-old beauty Victoria Rapahango Tepuku, for whom he would soon abandon Sofía and the children. Katherine employed as maid

Parapina, Dutrou-Bornier's teenage granddaughter. Although the *Mana*'s crew would also sometimes assist ashore, their main responsibility was to bring supplies from Chile: over seventeen months the vessel completed seven trips, logging nearly 20,000 kilometres. (It was the only expedition in the island's history to enjoy such regular provisioning by sea.)

Unhappily, the Routledges were their own worst patrons, it seems. If anything, the expedition was famed foremost for its foibles. The crew could not stomach either's upper-class airs; there was frequent conflict; resignations occurred; mutinies were threatened. When Scoresby failed to find the *rongorongo* tablets he had come all this way to discover – as nothing ever emerged from the caves – he refused to pay his Rapanui guides, accusing them of deception. 'They turned away in disgust.'[98]

Katherine Routledge, concentrating instead on the island's archæology and ethnography, had a better time of it. She was even able to establish a certain rapport with the Rapanui – something Scoresby could never do, who declared he did not like them. Katherine was the last 'properly trained' observer to gather first-hand knowledge from those Rapanui who had been adults at the time of the Peruvian labour raids. Her register of informants reads like a 'Who's Who' of now-legendary *korohua*, whom Katherine loftily called 'my grown-up children'.[99] It included Kapiera Reva Hiva, 'the most intelligent informant' on Easter Island; the old catechist Pakomio Ure Kino (Román Hei); Eutimio Rangi Topa; Miguel Keremuti Hea, who had lived in Tahiti back in the whaling days; Pua Ara Hoa, who might once have been a Birdman and who was the island's 'living library' of oral traditions; Jotefa Mahe Renga; Te Haha, who had once trained in writing *rongorongo*; Fati Rongo Pua Tea, whose grandfather Kekepu had been one of *rongorongo*'s innovators; Porotu (Hongi 'Atua 'a Ure Au Viri); Papiano Renga Maengo; Nicolas Pakarati, the island's current catechist; Tomenika Vake Tuku Onge 'a Teatea 'a Hiva, at the leprosery; and Juan Tepano's grandmother Veriamo, who had been born about 1830. Katherine was often helped in her informant sessions by the Frenchman Pont, who was now living with his wife María in a wooden house in Hanga Roa.

Beyond their power and despite their best intentions, however, the Routledges' very presence soon 'sparked the dry tinder of Rapa Nui discontent and inflamed the community to rebellion'.[100]

ANGATA'S REVOLT[101]

It all began shortly after Scoresby Routledge fired his week-long helper in the field, 'Charlie' (Carlos) Teao Tori, for suspected theft of a large tin of biscuits, on 17 June 1914. After a series of grievances against him, this had been the last straw. The *Mana* had gone, fetching more supplies from Chile.

On 30 June Angata, who had been Nicolas Pakarati's assistant at the church for so many years (and, as one will recall, Father Roussel's on Mangareva back in the 1870s and '80s), arrived at Mataveri with a small delegation to announce to Percy Edmunds that she had had a 'dream from God'. Angata was still, if nothing else, the most pious woman on Rapa Nui. Enrique Merlet, she now declared, was 'no more'. Rapa Nui belonged to the Rapanui people. The possessions of the members of the *Mana* expedition were to be given to the Rapanui. And they were now going to seize the cattle and have a feast on the morrow. Whereupon the delegation returned promptly to Hanga Roa. Percy Edmunds didn't know what to make of it.

Later in the day someone returned to Mataveri with a manifesto, written in Spanish and Rapanui by Daniera Teave Korohua, Angata's only son from her first marriage, whom she had urged to write (here in translation):

June 30th, 1914

Senior Ema [Edmunds], Mataveri,

Now I declare to you, by-and-by we declare to you, which is the word we speak to-day, but we desire to take all the animals in the camp and all our possessions in your hands, now, for you know that all the animals and farm in the camp belong to us, our Bishop Tepano [Jaussen] gave to us originally. He gave it to us in truth and justice. There is another thing, the few animals which are in front of you [the milch-cows], are for you to eat. There is also another thing, to-morrow we are going out into the camp to fetch some animals for a banquet. God for us, His truth and justice. There is also another business, but we did not receive who gave the animals to Merlet also who gave the earth to Merlet because it is a big robbery. They took this possession of ours, and they gave nothing for the earth, money or goods or anything else. They were never given to them. Now you know all that is necessary.

Your friend,
Daniel Antonio,
Hangaroa[102]

Katherine Routledge, there at Mataveri at the time, understood the larger picture. 'If some of the arguments', she later wrote, 'are probably without foundation, as, for example, that regarding native rights in the cattle, they were at least . . . of the same kind which have inspired risings in many lands and all ages.'[103] On the same day, Charlie Teao predicted 'great winds coming'. That night, a fierce gale pounded the island.

The next day, Percy Edmunds, Scoresby Routledge and some crew members armed themselves, anticipating an attack on Mataveri. At the

Hanga Roa church, Angata instructed Daniera to ride his horse around the building then blessed him before the assembled crowd. Then those joining him in the cattle raid were blessed with holy water as well, with Nicolas Pakarati's participation. With each raider clutching a rosary for protection, his assurance of God's approval absolute, off the party rode, out through the Wall, to begin rustling. At this instant a thick fog bank rolled in, obscuring them from those at Mataveri and those at Mataveri from them. Only because of this was no rifle discharged on either side. That night the bonfire of the joyous feasting, on the flesh of ten slaughtered cattle, illuminated the Hanga Roa church.

By 3 July, Angata had had another 'dream from God', which she related at yet another church meeting: God was pleased with what the Rapanui had done, and had told her that they were to kill even more cattle. Whereupon 50 Rapanui hurriedly saddled up and rode out to collect more head.

After this, many more such 'dreams' followed, nearly each trailed by one of Angata's improvised edicts and by Daniera and his men's ever more audacious deeds of theft and vandalism. Hoisting the Rapa Nui tricolour on the Mataveri flagpole to emphasize the island's historical links to Tahiti and France, the Rapanui subsequently broke into the Company buildings and warehouses there, killed and ate its penned cattle and sheep, then freely wandered over the entire island for the first time in years. Several Rapanui assumed new identities, believing the Kingdom of God was imminent. But when Daniera told Angata he should become Rapa Nui's new 'king', finally succeeding Riro at last, she declared that only God was king on Rapa Nui – the highest station for a mortal could only be that of judge.

Military marching was regularly practised before the church, to the sound of bugles. Angata communed often with her spirits. Christ had been on Rapa Nui, they now told her; it had been Christ who had moved the *mo'ai* onto their *ahu*. The spirits instructed all Rapanui, through Angata, to wear their hair differently, to partition and occupy the island as in olden times, and to sleep on Western mattresses. In order to raise Hanga Roa's moral standing everyone was to marry, Angata told them. Chile had suffered an earthquake, and now lay beneath the sea. The *Baquedano* had sunk too. Thus the Isla de Pascua was loosed from all external bonds. It was their Rapa Nui again. Fasting during the day and working at night, carpenters at the church were building a 'Holy Ark' to hold island secrets. Angata declared that they were to stop all fishing and gardening as well: God would provide. More crucially, Edmunds was now told to quit the Mataveri residence and to surrender himself to the island's new order. Such was God's desire.

The non-Rapanui at Mataveri – only five men, Katherine and a boy – were powerless to stop what was happening. Edmunds, waving a document signed by the President of Chile appointing him Easter Island's *subdelegado marítimo*, as well as written authorization from the captain of the *Baquedano* to wield all administrative power on the island, presented these, together with an official written request, to Scoresby Routledge and the *Mana*'s shore party. He demanded their 'armed assistance' to quell the revolt. For his part, Scoresby penned a directive to his three men: 'No member is to take part in any killing of natives with the object of protecting livestock, if however the personal safety of Mr Edmunds is in danger they shall give him armed assistance'.[104]

By now, nearly every Rapanui in Hanga Roa, Moeroa and even Mataveri was involved in rustling in some way. Even the Frenchman Pont was butchering rustled sheep carcasses in his Hanga Roa kitchen. Katherine Routledge would later, with hindsight, call the affair 'a Gilbertian opera',[105] but at the time she was terrified. Free to move about, she remained under Juan Tepano's protection, who kept a middle course between kith and Company. On 18 July Angata sent Katherine a symbolic gift – two chickens and some *kumara* – evidently as an appeal, perhaps enticing Katherine, as she herself construed, to side with the Rapanui faction. Over the next two days the Rapanui indiscriminately killed more cattle – but now, ominously, left them to rot.

Scoresby wrote the Rapanui a declarative offer – he would pay for two bullocks a month until the *Baquedano* arrived – which he had someone read aloud just east of the church. But then Nicolas Pakarati had someone read aloud his open letter to the *Baquedano*'s captain at the same gathering: Angata's visions were God-inspired, Pakarati had written; thus they were for all God-fearing Rapanui to follow. When Scoresby then verbally threatened an armed response, Pakarati countered that God would never let his Rapanui people come to any harm.

Katherine tried mediating with Angata, moved in turn by the old woman's mixture of extreme piety and mysticism, which Katherine in part shared. But the rapprochement went badly and Katherine again feared for her life. She and Scoresby immediately moved from Mataveri to their tent encampment at Rano Raraku. This abrupt decision effectively split the expedition in two, as it also weakened Edmunds's protective reinforcement. The expedition never recovered from this – and Edmunds never forgave Katherine Routledge.

Angata sent a mounted 'posse' out to Rano Raraku after the Routledges, led by the catechist Pakarati. Seeing the 20 to 30 Rapanui arrive, once more Katherine was terrified. But suddenly the courteous visitors were honouring her with a Bible reading, cheers and gifts of food. (Scoresby, rifle in hand, was simply ignored.) From that moment, Katherine understood the revolt to be actually 'a war of independence' – and she appreciated that Angata would probably do her no harm.

After this, for various reasons, the expedition's land members fell out entirely; one was now fired. Three weeks of continuous rain had hampered any more overt actions by the Rapanui. Angata, who had been predicting danger for them, then envisioned during the night of 2 August the arrival of the *Baquedano* (which earlier she had declared sunk). From Katherine, Angata also requested material for a new Rapa Nui flag. Katherine provided this from her stores, and within two days the white, blue and red tricolour (imitating France's, the Rapanui's preferred country) was flying from Hanga Roa's flagstaff. Encouraged by the display, a handful of Rapanui began making preparations to attack Edmunds and the *Mana*'s three crew members at Mataveri.

Yet within hours the *Baquedano* did arrive, on 5 August. Unsurprised, the Rapanui were actually pleased to see it. For the *Baquedano*'s assorted captains had usually taken their side against the Company, which the Chilean Navy had always detested. Moreover, the captains had been fair arbitrators of island grievances. When the Rapanui now boarded the vessel, they expected the customary equity, bearing as they did a letter from Angata in which she declared her friendship to Chile and listed what had to occur on the Rapanui's – not the Chileans' – island. Comandante Almanzor Hernández calmly listened to what the Rapanui had to say. Then he questioned Percy Edmunds, who was the Company manager and Chile's *subdelegado*.

The next morning four of the ringleaders lay in the brig, in irons. Whereupon Comandante Almanzor ruled, on behalf of Chile, that the Rapanui had been fully justified in doing everything they had done, and then he released three of the perpetrators. The fourth – Daniera Teave Korohua, who had written the initial manifesto – was to be deported to Chile. No corporal punishment had been inflicted on anyone.

The Routledges had also come on board to see the Comandante. The ship happened to be bringing 'large gifts of clothes for the natives from well-wishers in Chile',[106] the same collection that Katherine had earlier refused to transport from the continent. Now she requested that these donations be given to her to distribute as she saw fit. Well aware that she would now use this to increase her status among the Rapanui, Almanzor nevertheless consented. A man of frankness, the Comandante now bluntly told the Routledges that he considered that, prior to the *Baquedano*'s arrival, the Rapanui had 'behaved very well not to murder Mr Edmunds'.[107] Confessing he could not guarantee safety to the *Mana*'s shore party, Almanzor offered to take them all back to Chile. They declined.

There were, of course, political repercussions. Aboard the *Baquedano* were one or two Europeans coming to work for the Company, and 'a German to plant tobacco'.[108] (He would stay until shortly before the Routledges left in August 1915, after having done little tobacco planting.)

Also on board was Chile's first appointed schoolmaster, José Ignacio Vives Solar, a former journalist who was bringing an expensive school building – the consequence of one of Knoche's earlier recommendations. Comandante Almanzor now dismissed Percy Edmunds as *subdelegado marítimo*, appointing Vives Solar to replace him. (Edmunds still remained Company manager, however.) In doing this, Almanzor was purposely placing Chilean authority above Company authority.[109] Never again would the *subdelegado* be a Company man. Comandante Almanzor also ruled that no other flag would fly on the Isla de Pascua but the flag of the Republic of Chile.

The Republic's response to Rapanui's first independence movement had been the outright rejection of autonomy. The sole authority on the island, indeed the Rapanui's sole representative in relations with the Company, was to be Chile's *subdelegado*, at least on paper. As per the Rojas *reglamento* of 1902, Hanga Roa's local authority would remain the *cacique*. Almost all that earlier edict remained in force, in fact, but with the difference that the island was now declared to be an 'officially' administered colony of Chile. Yet the Isla de Pascua still did not comprise a part of the Chilean state, as an incorporated territory. It remained a leased-out colony, where only the leaseholder, the Company, ruled.

Once it became known in Chile, the revolt ignited a protracted disagreement between the Republic and the Company that would lead to more significant changes, but only after four years had passed. All the same, something fundamental had occurred. Chile's eyes were now on its Isla de Pascua. The island would never again be entirely forgotten.

In the smaller picture, Angata's revolt showed how strongly 'missionization became instrumental in the reëstablishment of Rapanui leadership and Rapanui identity, in their struggle to overcome the cultural deadlock' of what had happened in the nineteenth century.[110] Remarkably, Roman Catholicism had here been appropriated as a tool of civil resistance, the revolt clearly being the product of a 'millenarian cult'. This was, of course, similar to Melanesia's cargo cults, but here on Rapa Nui the ideological, rather than the material, obtained.[111] On Easter Island the cult synthesized imported Catholic dogma with indigenous Rapanui social beliefs in order to create a strategem to cope with perceived oppression. It had taken only the presence of the *Mana* to ignite the social tinder.

The millenarians did not replace the status quo, they complemented it: Angata complemented Nicolas Pakarati as spiritual leader; Daniera complemented the *cacique* Juan Tepano as community leader. A new indigenous hybrid religion was being created to supersede the foreign borrowing, a sacred Rapanui religion handed to them directly by God – or so the Rapanui were being told by those they trusted. 'Angata created a world that was neither local nor foreign, but was constructed as a buffer between her

Rapanui and the outside world . . . Her cult became a negotiating group for power relations.'[112] But it could never be, since its *mana* lay only in dreams.

Angata's revolt was the last attempt (until 1964) by the Rapanui to challenge the imposed order. It had failed. Their only resort was total submission. Six months later Angata was dead.

THE KAISER'S NAVY

Things quickly returned to normal again. Indeed, attention focused immediately on this newcomer, Vives Solar, whom everyone appreciated was now representing the *Baquedano*'s captain on the island. Vives Solar hurriedly constructed the schoolhouse, which was done by September. It was the island's first civil school. The children came for their lessons, held in Spanish – but 'after a few days the children ceased to appear, the master declared he was "not an attendance officer", and from then till we left', wrote Katherine Routledge, 'nearly a year later [in August 1915], no school was held'.[113]

But within weeks of the school's closure, far more portentous events took place. On 12 October 1914 the Imperial German East Asian Cruiser Squadron's *Gneisenau* and *Scharnhorst*, under the command of Admiral Maximilian Reichsgraf von Spee, anchored in Cook's Bay. (Just before this, on 22 September, both warships had shelled Pape'ete and destroyed its marketplace, Tahiti's only incident of the First World War.) In addition, from Mazatlán in Mexico had come the small cruisers *Nürnberg* and *Leipzig* with several escort vessels, while from the South Atlantic coast had come the *Dresden*, with transport ships. Twelve vessels in all crowded the Hanga Roa roadstead, and the sight of such a fleet must surely have disturbed the oldest Rapanui, who had last witnessed such a spectacle when the blackbirders had descended in 1862–3 to kidnap and murder. Wireless communication had been used at sea by the Germans to designate Easter Island as their rendezvous – one of the first times in history that wireless was used in naval warfare. Yet the irony lay in no one on Easter Island being even remotely aware that, from the end of July and beginning of August, Europe was at war.

The fleet stopped from 12 to 18 October, during which time the escort vessels provided the cruisers with coal and provisions. From the island the Germans acquired fresh fruit and living livestock. Edmunds was delighted to sell them £1,000 worth of cattle and sheep; but, refusing to accept their cash offer as this would have been ungentlemanly, he insisted he be paid by order instead – and so, in the end, the Company never received payment. Coaling was made difficult by large ocean swells; merely to complete the task, the vessels had to move from Cook's Bay to the south coast. The Routledges even posted letters home with the Germans. (They arrived.) Within four days rumours became rife, however, after everyone noticed that the German officers and crew rarely disembarked, nor did they give any food or clothes to the Rapanui, the customary courtesy. After the German 'tobacco planter' had spent time aboard the ships, he returned to Mataveri with news of war in Europe and fantastically exaggerated details. No one at Mataveri believed a word.

Meanwhile, Graf von Spee determined how many non-Rapanui there were on the island and duly warned the Rapanui, through Juan Tepano and Vives Solar, that he would hold them all responsible for the safety of each foreigner. Katherine Routledge wrote much later that,

> The reason given for keeping us in the dark so long was, that hearing there were foreigners on the island, they thought that we might fight amongst ourselves . . . The real reason of the silence maintained was most probably to prevent any question being raised of their use of the island as a naval base . . . The reality of the war was brought home by the concrete fact that the ships were reliably reported to be in fighting trim, with no woodwork visible.[114]

It was here at Easter Island that Graf von Spee learnt over the wireless of the sudden appearance of British warships off South America's western coast. The German fleet left Easter Island promptly on 18 October, with Graf von Spee's flagship leading, to wage the First World War's first open sea battle, near Coronel – just south of Concepción, Chile – where the British armoured cruisers HMS *Good Hope* and HMS *Monmouth* were sunk, a tremendous loss for Britain. 'They [the Germans] had said that they would come again', wrote Katherine, 'but they never did.'

Although 1,000 Tahitian volunteers would eventually fight in Europe's trenches for France – nearly one out of three becoming a war casualty – no Rapanui was involved in warfare of any kind in the First World War. Chile itself remained officially neutral during the entire conflict.

Then, in October and November 1914, all Easter Island came under attack – by dysentery. Eight Rapanui died. People suspected contamination from the *Baquedano*'s donation of clothes, then stored at the new *subdelegado* Vives Solar's. A small ship under Chilean flag, but with an English captain, arrived to enquire how all non-Rapanui were faring on Easter Island, informing them that Europe was indeed at war, and to offer British citizens passage back to the mainland. Scoresby Routledge and another crew member left with him, in order to see after the *Mana*, then detained at Talcahuano. This left only Katherine and one other crew member on the island.

On 23 December 1914 the armed Imperial German cruiser *Prinz Eitel Friedrich* anchored in Cook's Bay. Everyone was now fearing the worst. The next day it left again, but then immediately returned with the French barque *Jean* in tow, laden with coal (then an essential steamer fuel), which the Germans had earlier towed almost to Rapa Nui. As everyone watched from shore, the Germans now removed the coal there in Cook's Bay. On board the German cruiser was the captured crew of the British ship *Kildalton* as well; but when the Britons on shore tried to shout to them, the captive sailors were ordered below decks.

'The German officers and crew then landed daily', Katherine would write later, 'rode over the island, came up to the Manager's house, and generally behaved as if the whole place belonged to them. The officers were courteous and always saluted when we met, an attention with which one would have preferred to dispense'.[115] Since Chile was a neutral country, everyone ashore was a non-combatant. 'It must be remembered', she further wrote, 'that there was no reason to suppose that it was otherwise than civilised warfare, the idea that anyone could or would injure non-combatants on neutral soil never seriously occurred to me: the story of Belgium was unknown.'

Again abusing Chile's neutrality, the Germans stopped longer than the permitted 24 hours, to have one officer and several men erect a signal station atop Rano Aroi (Terevaka). Katherine and Juan rode up there on horseback to inspect it, then Katherine, using her official title of Acting Head of the British Scientific Expedition, penned a formal letter of protest to the Republic of Chile, which she presented to Chile's *subdelegado*, Vives Solar – but only once he had returned from the German cruiser's Christmas theatrical performance!

The sole act of foreign warfare ever recorded at Easter Island occurred on the last day of 1914, when the *Prinz Eitel Friedrich* towed the *Jean* slowly out to sea while her French crew, under German guard, watched from the cliff at Hanga Roa. Still within Chile's 3-mile limit, the German vessel set the *Jean* loose, whereupon the *Prinz Eitel Friedrich* circled and fired repeated broadsides, four times, missing once. Slowly the French boat sank beneath the waves. Then the *Prinz Eitel Friedrich* returned towards shore, took on stores and landed all prisoners of war – no fewer than 48 Britons and Frenchmen. All had been impeccably treated, and they were now presented with the French stores in order to sustain themselves adequately on poorly provisioned Easter Island.

The stranded crews made camp in a Hanga Piko wool shed. The British captain, Sharp, lodged with Percy Edmunds, walking out daily 'to try to catch sight of a sail'. Dysentery struck the crews as well. One British sailor – the young Scot Campbell, 'the only son of his mother, and she was a widow' – died of the disease: Easter Island's only First World War victim. Two months later, in March 1915, a Swedish steamer arrived 'to visit the island's antiquities', it claimed. It was then that Katherine Routledge and others learnt of the annihilation of Admiral Reichsgraf von Spee's fleet by the British Navy off the Falklands on 8 December 1914. (In the great Allied victory, Graf von Spee himself had been killed.) The *Dresden* had escaped, only to be sunk a couple of months later at the Islas Juan Fernández off Chile. The Swedish captain now invited the British and French sailors to leave with him, and most accepted the invitation. A few Frenchmen remained behind, however, in order to await the express directions of their French consul at Valparaíso. 'One of them', wrote Katherine, 'who hailed from the French West Indies, subsequently married his hostess, a lady in the village.'[116]

Yet this did not conclude Easter Island's attraction for the Kaiser's navy. At the end of 1917, some 50 of Commander Felix Graf von Luckner's crew from the infamous three-masted auxiliary cruiser *Seeadler* arrived from French Polynesia in the small sailing ship *Fortuna*, which foundered in stormy weather off the island's coast. For four months the men, under the command of Leutnant Klink, lived among the Rapanui at Hanga Roa, evidently on the very best of terms.[117] At last, the Chilean schooner *Falcon* – the annual Company ship – picked up the Germans and transported them to Concepción's port of Talcahuano.

'TO SETTLE THE NATIVES'

Meanwhile, after the second German visit to the island – during the more than four months that Scoresby Routledge was detained in Chile, his British Scientific Expedition now in shambles because of war and crew problems – Juan Tepano had begun working almost daily with Katherine Routledge. In Tepano's earlier, infrequent dealings with her they had communicated in broken Spanish and English: Hanga Roa's *cacique* spoke 'a little pidgin English'. But from 1915 they began speaking more often in Modern Rapanui, which Katherine rather rudely called 'Kanaka' – Whalers' Pidgin: 'native'. (Even then, for a reputable anthropologist it was a denigrating term.) Alone with Tepano, Katherine now roamed the island for months, conducting serious archæological surveys that also included several excavations. Over time, Tepano became 'her companion in the field, chief collaborator, and friend'.[118] He had strict instructions, however, always to call her 'Ma'am' – which Tepano pronounced 'Mam-ma' – in proper aristocratic fashion, which maintained (at least for her) their appropriate social stations. At the end of their collaboration, as Katherine was particularly careful to point out later to her readers, 'He took a real interest in the work, learning through the conversations much about the island which was new to him, and at the end of the time triumphantly stated that "Mam-ma now knows everything there is to know about the island".'[119]

On 18 August 1915 the *Mana* sailed from Easter Island for the last time. Scoresby Routledge had already given up on the island early on. But

Katherine Routledge, for her part, had amassed a wealth of field notes detailing informant interviews, on-site inspections and excavations, as well as maps and sketches, so as to bequeath to future generations source material of incalculable value relating to the island's earlier society. In strictly scientific terms, however, the *Mana* expedition was a failure: the Routledges never published their findings. Yet Katherine's popular book, which was privately published in London in 1919 – *The Mystery of Easter Island*, whose author was given as 'Mrs Scoresby Routledge' in the mode of the times – proved a grand success, both commercially and critically, and awarded Easter Island an international profile it had not enjoyed before. The tome has since become a classic of Pacific literature.

The Routledges had come to Easter Island to find history, and yet within months of their arrival themselves had made history – it was their presence that had ignited Angata's revolt. Perhaps their most enduring legacy, despite everything, was to have convinced the world at last that Easter Island's spectacular *ahu* and *mo'ai* had indeed been the work of the present-day Rapanui's Polynesian forebears who, Katherine believed, had probably come from Mangareva.

Only eleven days after the *Mana*'s departure, on 29 August 1915, the Company's lease on Easter Island expired. Yet nothing happened. Only in April 1916 did Chile's President Sanfuentes finally make the Isla de Pascua a *subdelegación* of the Department of Valparaíso, placing the Rapanui people directly under the Republic's administrative and judicial authority. Enrique Merlet, doubtless under pressure from his bosses at Williamson, Balfour, pressured in turn the Ministry of External Affairs to effect a new lease of those lands on the Isla de Pascua clearly owned by the Republic. And so, in June 1916, the *Temperamento Provisorio*, which 'treated the island as a single unit for the first time',[120] provided Merlet with an extension of his lease under identical conditions, but permitting the Republic to terminate the contract whenever it so wished. That is, although Chile now established a 'legal' precedence of comprehensive sovereignty, the Company still retained actual control over Easter Island.

At this point, in September 1916, Merlet moved to legalize the opinion that the former Brander / Dutrou-Bornier lands comprised nearly the entire island. But at this the Republic balked. It challenged the claim's legality, alleging that the rulings of foreign courts (Tahiti and France) and arbitrators (Scotland) were invalid for Chile. The Republic countered that by 'right of annexation' in 1888, all Isla de Pascua lands leased to the Company were those of the Republic of Chile alone.

The new lease brought changes, mostly positive ones. Its official wording directed the Company to regulate land use, conserve the stock, prevent any further loss of statues or other artifacts [this was Easter Island's first-ever archæological protection], provide land for a leprosarium, give help to the local fishery, provide the *subdelegado* with meat for Rapanui use, provide provisions for naval vessels, and support a Chilean administrator and his family.[121]

A Civil Registry Office was established, to register marriages, births and deaths; until then, these had never been deemed important enough to acknowledge legally. Perhaps most significantly, 3,000 hectares around Hanga Roa were designated as *parcelas* or land parcels, to be distributed among Rapanui families. Missing from the new lease, however, was any mention of a new pier, coaling station, Chilean settlers, medical assistance for naval crews or similar long-standing obligations – the Republic had evidently shelved (or abandoned) its plans to settle, militarize or network its Pacific foothold. In effect, Chile was washing its hands of the dream.

Canonically, Easter Island came under the Archbishopric of Santiago, whose prelate was Monseñor Rafael Edwards, scion of one of Chile's first families, Bishop (from 1915) of Dodona and Castrense Vicar of Chile.[122] Bishop Edwards, too, had been alarmed by the reports of the Rapanui people's appalling conditions. Most Chileans had been horrified to learn that Islanders were now suffering from leprosy. And so Chilean newspapers were speculating on the horrors that the bishop might find there when he made his first trip to the Isla de Pascua at the end of 1916 on the *Baquedano* – together with the proselyte Zósimo Valenzuela, the 'Padre Totimo' who had been on the island in 1911. Stopping for three weeks and taking an active part in all Church sacraments and responsibilities, both churchmen again had only the highest praise for Nicolas Pakarati and his faithful leadership.

Once back in Chile, however, Bishop Edwards described how Easter Island's lepers had been exiled to two shacks north of Hanga Roa, where they had nothing: no food, clothing, beds or medicines. 'The lepers appear to be walking corpses', he claimed, 'brutally mutilated'.[123] After this, Bishop Edwards became a vociferous agent for Rapanui rights, undertaking an active campaign in their defence before the Republic. Most Chileans were aghast at the bishop's first-hand account of conditions on the island, and turned their revulsion into political censure. As a precaution, the Republic immediately appointed Bishop Edwards the leprosery's administrator. An investigative commission, led by the University of Chile, would also 'study' leprosy there. As for the Rapanui's actual poverty, much of the critique was perhaps 'the projection of Chilean bourgeois standards upon a Polynesian people whose needs were very few'.[124] Apart from oppression, in many ways the Rapanui were actually no worse off than before colonization, although certainly far below what Europeans and modern Chileans regarded as tolerable.

Unquestionably the Rapanui themselves were anything but happy – with the Company, that is. The resident *subdelegado* was no protection from cruel Company taskmasters, which left the Rapanui no recourse, when pushed beyond the limit, but to take justice into their own hands. In 1915 they murdered one of Percy Edmunds's continentals, Bautista Cousin, and threw his corpse into the sea.[125] After this, a succession of Republic-appointed *subdelegados* themselves meted out a severe military justice in return. 'A frequent crime was "to insult a Chilean", the penalty for which could be short term imprisonment, a public flogging or being shaved bald in front of the church, depending on the whim of the commandant.'[126]

Easter Island was infamous as Pacific Islands' worst administered colony. As a result, an unrelenting campaign for the Rapanui's emancipation from Company tyranny impassioned the Chilean middle classes throughout most of 1916 and well into 1917. Most opposed the Company on three issues: its treatment of the Rapanui people; its claim that it owned the Isla de Pascua; and its failure to develop the island beyond a mere sheep ranch.[127] Anti-Company publications heightened their tone at the end of 1916, one even claiming that the Company was, for example, 'exploiting its island as absolute lord and exercising over the unfortunate [Rapanui people] a mediæval despotism'.[128] The Catholic Church in this loud polemic – for the Company had its defenders, too – was held up as a worthy proponent of Rapanui rights and welfare. A controversial exchange of letters between Bishop Edwards and Henry Williamson in November 1916 followed just days after the Colonization Section of Chile's Ministry of External Affairs had concluded in a report that Enrique Merlet and the Company had failed to fulfil their obligations under the lease of 1895.

Bishop Edwards complained in *La Unión* of 18 November 1916 that the Rapanui's former diet, heavily shrunk, was being replaced by a 'manufactured desire' – as we would call it today – for imported foodstuffs that the Rapanui could buy only at the Company store at exorbitant prices: a sack of flour costing 100 pesos, for example. Few had such a sum, so want was widespread. (As ever, however, the Rapanui relied on *kumara*, yams, bananas, sugar cane, shellfish, eels, crayfish and some fish; no one was starving.) Meat was rationed to shearers in season, but this was not to be shared with family members. Lockouts occurred when Rapanui balked at forced labour; then no one had wages, the store was closed and all products went unsold. The Rapanui, Bishop Edwards was alleging, had become Company slaves.

In defence of Company policy, Henry Williamson replied in *La Unión* of 20 November that the Company was neither the Republic nor the Church, and that it had done quite enough in procuring houses for the natives, in inducing them to formalize their marriages, in preventing them from fighting and killing each other, in clothing the nearly naked females, in giving them land which they can cultivate if they so desire, and offering them ploughs and oxen, in providing cows for milk, in paying them a daily wage when they feel like working, and respecting their desires when they do not.[129]

In consequence of this public debate, a general collection in Chile materially aided the Rapanui people, especially with clothing. On 27 November 1916 the Catholic Vicariate announced that everyone who contributed to the Isla de Pascua appeal would be guaranteed 100 days' worth of indulgences. And the following month the Christians of Valparaíso – just as in 1869 – started a charity commission to collect donations: but for the Rapanui people directly this time, not for any Catholic Mission there (which no longer existed).

As a result of the Ministry's report – and of the overwhelming public sentiment – the Republic revoked the new lease that had just been granted to the Company. More significantly, the Republic directed its Inspector General of Colonization and Immigration to distribute the Republic's lands on the Isla de Pascua for public use by the Rapanui people.[130] Bishop Edwards was appointed to a special commission established to review the Easter Island situation. Joining him on this were Policarpo Toro, who again had been calling for agrarian colonization of the island; the captain of the *Baquedano*; and a number of government officials.

But it appears higher powers than those of the Republic intervened. The court case against Enrique Merlet first stalled, then died. Bishop Edwards was called to administer elsewhere. The commission folded. Over subsequent years, however, the Company did make more concessions, and this policy slowly eroded its absolutism on Easter Island.

A new Provisional Constitution was declared on 29 February 1917, which reconfirmed Comandante Almanzor Hernández's edict of 1914 in every part.[131] The Isla de Pascua would remain subject to naval authorities, laws and rules. The Company, however, would remain the holder of the island and its livestock, and would continue to perform general administration. Two hundred hectares were appointed 'for public service and to settle the natives' (Article 2). The Rapanui people were forbidden to leave the island, ostensibly for fear of spreading leprosy. (In reality, the Company needed their labour, especially during shearing and embarking, and the local population remained perilously small.)

After this, all visitors to the island were instructed by naval officers and Company personnel not to tell the Rapanui people about the outside world. The Republic conceded to Bishop Edwards's demands to improve the Rapanui's health and education; yet it didn't spend a peso. Instead, it encharged the Company with these responsibilities, and the Company, of course, kept this outlay at a minimum. 'The Chilean government benefitted from lease payments and meat supplies for its ships, but returned none of this to the Rapanui or the island.'[132]

In 1916 Bishop Edwards had found the lepers' shacks to be too small, and had demanded that the Company build a better and larger facility. The materials for this new complex arrived on the *Baquedano* in June 1917, bringing Bishop Edwards himself on his second visit to the island, this time together with two Capuchins: Father Bienvenido de Estella and Lay Brother Modesto de Adios. Work started immediately on the new leprosery, and new roofing was completed as well on the Hanga Roa church. Juan Tepano led Bishop Edwards around the island, who later wrote that if Nicolas Pakarati was Easter Island's spiritual head, then Juan Tepano was its 'political tail': 'A man who is moderate, prudent, possessing what one can call a sensibleness towards life, he would have been an opportunist on a more adequate political stage.'[133]

Father Estella felt particularly drawn to the Rapanui people after his short stay there, and so in April 1918 he returned on the *Baquedano* with Father Domingo de Beire.[134] Both then stayed eight months on the island – the longest sacerdotal visit since Father Montiton's in 1887–8 – while Chile's training ship completed a return voyage to Australia. They not only missioned and taught, but established plantations, hired labourers to lay out roads at Hanga Roa and generally beautified the village. Father Estella counted 46 houses on the island: 34 of them of timber, 11 of stone and 1 of stone and cement. Most were overcrowded and unhygienic. Father Estella collected stories and compiled a short lexicon of the Rapanui language. After his return to Chile he published two books about the island.

Indeed, between 1918 and 1921 Bishop Edwards and his priests published many books about Easter Island. Most were of dubious sobriety, written with 'a crusading spirit, amounting at times almost to hysterical zealotry'.[135] Father Estella and Father Domingo had tried to curb the Rapanui's singing and dancing (traditional *hiva*) and feasting during wakes, and when Percy Edmunds, the island's true leader, countered that this was traditional and should be supported (our view today), Father Estella accused the Company and Edmunds of being 'egotistical, monopolistic entrepreneurs' who failed to uphold their Christian duty to elevate primitives to superior morality. It was the ancient conflict of foreign Europe's Christian values being imposed on remote Easter Island, with either side defending inherited territory: the Company pacifying its cheap labour, the Church maintaining the moral high ground.

In fact, the Company seldom interfered in Rapanui ways, generally glad to hire and fire at will and maintain at least an adequate workforce to ensure a profitable wool-clip; otherwise, the Rapanui could go to ruin. Few did go to ruin, in fact, but most were still not 'happy' under the present situation. They coped. Bishop Edwards and his fathers, basically ignorant of Polynesian customs and standards, probably exaggerated, and overreacted to, what they perceived as the Rapanui's 'plight'. It is even possible that they may have been 'thoroughly humbugged'.[136] Easter Island was hardly the hell-hole they described. The island's population was steadily growing. Year after year, the Rapanui people were even raising their standard of living.

SCHOLARS, PADRES AND SHEEP

Yet in all these years Enrique Merlet and the Company had carried on with the same, now hopelessly antiquated, Brander / Dutrou-Bornier buildings, stock and equipment.[137] Faced with mounting demands by the Republic, the Company had purposely kept running costs to the minimum, continually deferring any upgrade of its investment. Although it had procured the services of one expert to suggest improvements that might increase yield and ensure greater profits, little had been done. With this latest lease agreement, however, the Company now appreciated its greater permanence on Easter Island.

Suddenly, in 1918, Enrique Merlet died, whereupon Henry Williamson, of Williamson, Balfour, now turned his personal attention towards his Company's Polynesian foothold, the managing of which minor subsidiary he had, until then, always delegated to Merlet. Since Williamson, Balfour held no clear land title, they could not sell the island – a recourse they actively pursued well into the 1920s – but whatever plan they chose, an immediate infusion of capital here could only be of benefit to the Company, Williamson believed. As one of his Scots partners openly stated, 'We are aiming at spending three or four thousand pounds per annum on the island and hope to get back five or six thousand pounds.'[138]

In 1920 Williamson engaged the biological engineer William A. Bryan of Hawai'i to compile a report for the Company based on a personal visit to Easter Island. His inspection successfully completed, Bryan's general assessment of the Company's Rapanui labour force, above all, was scathing: 'The available labour supply which consists of about forty adult natives is exasperatingly unsatisfactory and utterly unreliable', he wrote. 'Its efficiency is about on a par with that of an equal number of twelve year old city boys in the country on a holiday. The lack of efficient, dependable labour is the greatest present difficulty in the proper management of the existing ranch.'[139] Bryan then made a number of valuable recommendations. One resonates today: 'The beautiful bathing beach at Anakena and the prevailing agreeable temperature coupled with the extensive unique ethological [*sic*] ruins, if developed and advertized, would certainly make the Island an ideal recreation ground for the Southern Pacific, vieing in attractiveness with the famous Waikiki'.[140] But Bryan was about a century too early – getting to Rapa Nui in 1920 was like getting to Mars.

Most of William Bryan's suggestions – those, for example, concerning fences, buildings, tools, stock and watering – were taken on board, however. A further suggestion was the use of an automobile: Percy Edmunds's effectiveness, Bryan had argued, could be doubled if he could only motor about on the island. Shortly after this, the Company sent Edmunds a Model-T Ford, the island's first motor vehicle. Another suggestion was the planting of fast-growing eucalyptus and other trees to provide more wood, as well as shelter and shade for the 24,000 sheep, 4,000 cattle and 1,400 horses that Bryan had personally counted. Over the next two decades, thousands more eucalypti were planted, again mostly by the Frenchman 'Varta' Pont.

As a result of the 'Bryan Report', the Company effected a major upgrade in construction, too. When the Company ship *Falcon* foundered, its wood was now cannibalized not only to refurbish the manager's old Mataveri residence (in which Dutrou-Bornier himself would still have felt at home), but also to provide most of Hanga Roa with more substantial housing. What had been single-room shacks with earthen floors soon became two- or three-room houses with timber flooring. Warehouses, shearing sheds, stables, machine sheds and other buildings rose in both Mataveri and Hanga Roa.

Of crucial importance were the Company's improvements to the old quay at Hanga Piko. From here launches and small boats took the wool-clip, hides and other goods out to the Company vessel offshore. It was often a perilous undertaking, causing loss of time, products, boats and even lives. From the 1920s 'lighters' (flat-bottomed barges used for ferrying cargo to and from ships) were brought into action instead, with much greater success. Each was a floating rectangle of wooden poles, with empty oil drums inside for buoyancy and stability, on which rested a timber cargo platform. (They remained in service until the 1970s, when metal landing craft arrived from the continent.) The Hanga Piko cove was blasted using dynamite in order to reshape its entrance channel, resulting in a relatively protected harbour arm. Dismantling the ruins of an *ahu* there, with its *mo'ai* (probably the ones that Captain Cook had seen in 1774), helped to form a crude mole, and a stone-and-concrete quay complex led up a ramp to warehouses in which wool and machinery were now stored.[141]

In time, with improved port facilities, water supplies, roads, walls and livestock, the *rancho* Isla de Pascua 'became an efficient and profitable commercial sheep station'.[142] Between 1903 and 1931 only two Company dividends – distributions from the net profits of a company to its shareholders – had been paid. But after 1932, when the 1920s improvements truly began to take effect, substantial dividends became an annual feature, until the Company sold out.[143]

In 1920 another priest, Father Nicolás Correa of the Order of Santo Domingo, arrived to stay for eight months on the island.[144] Subsequently there were also two brief visits, in 1921 and 1923, by Chilean naval chaplains aboard the annual *Baquedano*. But after this no ordained priest visited the island for several years.

In the 1920s Modern Rapanui (Rapanui-Tahitian) was largely spoken on the island, with much English as the lingua franca among the Company's continental labourers; little Spanish was spoken yet, since there were still few Chileans on the island. Only the very old recalled their rudimentary French or Mangarevan. There was no mobility off the island and in Hanga Roa everyone had to remain this side of the Wall. Sheep rustling was still a common occurrence, incurring harsh punishment if the offender was caught.

The 76-year-old Professor of Classics and English at Canterbury College, Christchurch, New Zealand, John Macmillan Brown, arrived to spend five months on Easter Island in 1922, lodging with Percy Edmunds at Mataveri. Macmillan Brown, as he preferred to be known, collected only a small fraction of the information that Katherine Routledge had amassed – most of the island's *korohua* had died by then and Brown could hardly communicate with Juan Tepano (practically the only informant he ever approached) either in Spanish or English.[145] His later book, *The Riddle of the Pacific*, which appeared in London in 1924, was an esoteric fantasy, hypothesizing a 'Lost Continent' and 'Vanished Empire' of the Pacific.[146] (A decade later, then in his mid-eighties, Macmillan Brown was adamant that the Rapanui people had never been capable, either physically or socially, of erecting the monuments of Easter Island; these had to have been the achievements of an erstwhile great empire, he claimed, that had been destroyed by earthquake or volcanic eruption.)[147]

In the early 1920s Percy Edmunds received as official Company foreman – a newly created salaried position that released Juan Tepano from this duty in order to coordinate increasing reponsibilities in consequence of the 'Bryan Report' – Lachlan MacKinnon, a quiet, shy, dignified Scot who had immigrated to Chile with his brother. MacKinnon soon took up house with Magdalena Haoa, with whom eventually he would have five children (of whom two sons and a daughter survived to adulthood). It was MacKinnon who was the first to plant pineapples on Rapa Nui, on his own private land. Soon everyone saw that pineapples thrived in the island's soil and climate, and so cuttings from MacKinnon's crop suddenly started to appear in various *parcelas*. In time, pineapples became a major island cultivar. (Today, pineapples remain one of Easter Island's main garden crops.)

In 1923 the island's ex-*subdelegado* Vives Solar published in Chile a brief Rapanui-Spanish primer – *Te poki rapanui (El niño pascuense)* ('The Rapanui Child') – for children and adults alike, encouraging them not only to read their own language for the first time in print, but also to emulate their Polynesian neighbours, the Pitcairn Islanders and Tahitians, and plant crops that they could sell to raise their standard of living. By the mid-1920s the new *subdelegado*'s wife was the island's teacher, who taught in the small school-house that Vives Solar had built in 1914 (illus. 12). She also tried to give instruction in the Rapanui language, since so few yet understood Spanish well enough. But, as one visitor commented, 'The school-mistress does not take her duties very seriously, and the building is used as much for community dancing and feasts as for anything else.'[148]

The two most active periods of the year still came at shearing and embarkation. Before the 1920s nearly all shearing took place at Mataveri close to where the wool-clip would be loaded onto launches at Hanga Piko. But then, with better roads, larger flocks, rotating paddocks and new building complexes, Lachlan MacKinnon became responsible for overseeing the creation of a new *fundo* or ranch at Vaitea, which developed into the island's shearing centre – for a fortnight each year the hub of all island activity. It provided employment for many Rapanui who otherwise had no access to hard cash. Waggons then hauled the clip down to the warehouses at Hanga Piko for loading onto lighters to the annual Company ship.

In August 1926, when every Saturday the women of Hanga Roa were still trekking to Rano Kau to do the family's wash and when many Rapanui would, on meeting, greet one another with the English 'Morning!' in imitation of the terse Percy Edmunds and dignified Lachlan MacKinnon, a vessel arrived from Tahiti with fuel drums for a projected trans-Pacific flight (which failed to materialize). Several Rapanui sailed back to Tahiti on the vessel, working to pay their fare; there they had a historic encounter with long-lost Rapanui relations at the Pamata'i settlement. The group returned to Easter Island in January–February 1927 on the vessel, which was coming to pick up the unused fuel drums. Aboard was also a priest, the sscc missionary Father Félix Jaffuel, who spent one week on Easter Island on a pastoral visit.[149] By this time Nicolas Pakarati was old and infirm, but still the backbone of the parish. When Pakarati asked Father Jaffuel to send a missionary from Tahiti (Pakarati had had his training at the sscc's mission school on Mo'orea and still spoke fluent French), the priest told him that this was impossible: Easter Island no longer lay within Tahiti's, but Chile's ecclesiastical jurisdiction. Perhaps Chile might one day send a chaplain or missionary, he said by way of consolation. On 12 October 1927 Nicolas Pakarati – after first having encharged his son Timoteo (Timothy) with the duties of

12 Hanga Roa's school in the mid-1920s.

Rapa Nui's catechist – died, as family and friends chanted prayers and sang hymns around his bed. He was buried alongside Brother Eugène Eyraud.

Since William Bryan had, above all, faulted the island's lack of adequate fencing, the 1920s experienced a never-before rush of constructing dry-wall *pircas*. These now divided the island's terrain into manageable sectors – for pasturage, breeding control and livestock treatment. But they rose at the cost of innummerable *ahu*, of curbstones from ancient dwellings and even of wall and roof slabs from 'Orongo's ritual houses: for all of these were cannibalized for their useful stones. (Most of these *pircas* still scar Easter Island today, their erstwhile function long forgotten.)

At this time Chile also used its Isla de Pascua, still a military domain after all, as its own Devil's Island – but only infrequently, since transport was dear. Each arriving 'guest of the Republic' was a political prisoner.[150] During the dictatorship of 1928 the naval vessel *Angamos* brought eleven.[151] The Republic's political upheaval of 1931 then saw another group exiled to the Isla de Pascua on the transport ship *Huemul*; but these managed to escape on a private yacht soon after their arrival.[152] 'Many older Islanders date the clamping down on Islander travel from this escape, as a kind of punishment. In the 1930s this reached the extreme of attempting to ban all off shore fishing, which caused great hardship to a people used to seafood.'[153]

The Easter Island 'question' had resurfaced in Chile when the reformist President Ibáñez terminated the Company's *Temperamento Provisorio* on 19 April 1927. The president was planning legally to inscribe all of Easter Island as the property of the Republic alone. But Williamson, Balfour resisted this move, and so nothing was achieved. Ibáñez lost his presidency in 1931 when anarchy overwhelmed Chile once again. Partly as a result of what was happening in Chile, both Percy Edmunds and Lachlan MacKinnon left the island for good in 1933, leaving their Rapanui families behind. (MacKinnon would not see his Rapanui children again until the 1950s, for two brief reunions in Britain and Chile.)

At this period the Rapanui people's own economy still comprised subsistence agriculture. Since the best taro sites were located beyond the Wall, dry taro remained secondary to *kumara*, the island staple. Only for local consumption, not for export, were the Rapanui's delicious pineapples, melons, sugar cane, bananas, figs, grapes and other fruit crops. Fish provided most protein. Regular meat, commonly mutton, could be enjoyed only by Company permanent staff and by lepers at the leprosery, which was now endowed. Despite its severe punishment, rustling was still frequent. In just one year, 1934, the Company manager reckoned that 2,000 to 3,000 sheep had been taken out illegally.[154] Many Rapanui are still familiar today with the names of relatives who could 'gallop through a herd, grab a sheep on the run, skin it out and be off with the carcass in five minutes'.[155] Celebrated was the fisherman who, when arrested for having a sheep in his small boat, claimed in way of an alibi that he was not stealing but actually rescuing it, since he had found the sheep 'swimming away from the island'!

Despite the Company's own improvements, the sole community of Hanga Roa in the early 1930s was still 'a cluster of clapboard and sheet iron huts'.[156] On this isolated isle almost barren of trees the problem was building material, which had to be either scavenged or imported at great cost. (It is a problem that continues today.) Although the Rapanui's traditional Polynesian housing had all but disappeared, European-style housing of adequate quality was still impossible – for lack of materials. So for most of the twentieth century the Rapanui had to make do with ever-advancing compromises in this regard.

One manager would later state matter-of-factly: 'There's no law out here. This place is like the American frontier in "forty-nine".'[157] Although the Republic now maintained a prefect of police and a handful of naval personnel, the Company still ruled with 'godlike power over life and death', as one visitor attested.[158] A Catholic chaplain arrived each year with the annual naval vessel to attend to the Rapanui's spiritual needs, but he had nothing to say in face of the omnipotent manager, who also stifled all naval critique on the island.

But things began to change once more, in 1933, with the arrival of the ship that took away Percy Edmunds and Lachlan MacKinnon. And it started with death. A serious *kokongo* influenza epidemic erupted – the worst virus that had struck the island in many years. When the new catechist Timoteo Pakarati was taken ill, his brother Santiago succeeded him, but he then fell sick as well, whereupon Matías Hotus assumed the position of catechist at the church. More than 30 Rapanui died.

Back in Santiago, once political equilibrium had finally been restored in the Chilean capital, Bishop Edwards led a new commission which, at last, was successful in persuading the government to inscribe all of the Isla de Pascua as national property before the nations of the world. So it was that, on 11 November 1933, the land surface of Easter Island legally passed at last from the hands of the Compañía Explotadora de la Isla de Pascua and into those of the Republic of Chile. For two years negotiations then proceeded on how best to regulate the island economically, with the Company pressing for a 30-year lease: it declared that, in exchange, it would sign a 'final renunciation' of all its property claims on Easter Island. The government listened, but made no immediate decision on the matter.

Meanwhile, halfway around the world, in France, preparations had been going on since early 1933 for a major expedition to Easter Island. The director of the Musée d'Ethnologie (today's Musée de l'Homme) at the Trocadéro in Paris, the celebrated French ethnologist Paul Rivet, was proposing with his associate Marcel Mauss to test in this way a Hungarian scholar's 'diffusionist' claim that Easter Island's *rongorongo* script was related to the ancient Indus Valley's script, something that had caused a sensation among European scholars. The expedition leader was to be Louis Charles Watelin, known for his Kish excavations. The ethnologist Henri Lavachery, professor at the University of Brussels, and Rivet's protégé, the Swiss anthropologist Alfred Métraux, were to accompany him. They left France on the first cruise of the colonial despatch vessel *Rigault de Genouilly*.

But off Tierra del Fuego Watelin suddenly came down with pneumonia – then died. So Métraux, representing France on the expedition, was appointed the new leader: neither a Frenchman, nor a Belgian, nor a diffusionist. He also knew nothing about Easter Island, having been given only one week to prepare before departure. (In the end, what Métraux had been sent out to prove – a historical relationship between Easter Island and the ancient Indus Valley – he resoundingly disproved.)

Learning of this Franco-Belgian expedition in 1934, the University of Chile hurriedly formed a 'Study Commission on Easter Island' and began planning its own scientific expedition there for 1935. Some 30 scientists would be investigating in particular the island's history and ethnology, the university proudly announced.

Meanwhile, the Franco-Belgian expedition had been joined at Valparaíso by the Chilean physician Israel Drapkin. They arrived at Easter Island on 27 July 1934. Initial investigations – except for Drapkin's government-delegated medical and anthropomorphic research, in particular leprosy – focused exclusively on *rongorongo*. But this was soon abandoned because no tablets were to be found anywhere (as had also happened to Scoresby Routledge) and the informant information about the script was frustratingly contradictory hearsay and modern invention.

At this point Lavachery concentrated his efforts instead on the island's rock art, and completed the first survey of mainly petroglyph sites and types; he also measured and described a number of archæological sites. It was Lavachery, for example, who, in his work notes, first suggested that the coral he was finding at various *ahu* actually used to fill the eye sockets of the *mo'ai*; but his notes would remain ignored to this day (as the Rapanui archæologist Sonia Haoa has established, who, in 1978, was the one who 'rediscovered' the *mo'ai*'s eyes, at 'Anakena). For his part, Métraux gathered an enormous amount of data about the ancient culture for a projected ethnography. Drapkin subsequently collected specimens for the Muséum d'Histoire Naturelle in Paris, studied the demography and blood groups of the Rapanui, and freely offered medical assistance to everyone in Hanga Roa.[159] The new Company manager Murdoch Smith and his wife afforded the scholars every hospitality, and the island's 'administrator' W. B. Cater provided valuable information. The Chilean *subdelegado*, Señor Cornejo, liaised with the Republic to make sure all went well. The year 1934 happened to be one of the decade's busiest and most productive, as it happened, with a peak of approximately 70,000 livestock.

In 1911 the German Walter Knoche had found the Rapanui's plots 'full of weeds', but in 1934 Alfred Métraux was most impressed by the quality of their garden cultivations.[160] Such foreign products as refined sugar, processed flour, rice, coffee and tinned foods could be bought from the Company store. But because hard cash was needed for these, most Rapanui had not yet developed a dependency. Still living virtually a subsistence existence, the Rapanui had very limited sources of income: permanent Company employment (for only a small handful); temporary Company employment (only one or two weeks a year, as a rule); selling hides, wool and garden produce to the Company; or, rarest of all, selling carvings to the infrequent passing vessels.

Israel Drapkin discovered that only 159 of the 456 Rapanui were probably of 'exclusively Rapanui ancestry' (by then a dubious classification): the rest displayed admixtures of Chilean, French, Tahitian, Tuamotuan, American, British, German, Italian and even Chinese. Since the all-time population low of 110 in 1877, there had been a doubling of the population by 1911 (228), and then another doubling by 1934 (469), evidencing a reviving community. There were presently thirteen white residents on the island – Pont (nearly 40 years now), Cardinali (30 years), the Scotsman Smith with a wife and two sons, the Briton Cater and six Chileans, of whom one was the naval *subdelegado* with a wife and son, the Hanga Roa schoolmaster and two foreign women married to Rapanui husbands.

Lavachery and Drapkin got along with everyone, but Métraux was asocial and curt. The Swiss leader of the expedition often worked with the unreliable 'Charlie' Teao as his informant, although he preferred the dignified and trustworthy Juan Tepano, now 62, who had been the island's chief informant since the beginning of the century. Still, Métraux frequently challenged Tepano as well, and one evening it was one time too many: Tepano, acutely insulted by Métraux's persistent suspiciousness, physically pushed the Swiss out of his house. (Juan Tepano was to die in 1938, a great loss to all.)

On 3 January 1935 the Franco-Belgian expedition departed on the Belgian training ship *Mercator*, taking with them the large *mo'ai* that now dominates the interior of the national museum in Brussels, the Cinquantenaire. Lavachery returned to Brussels, where he soon published many articles, his account of the expedition, then later his superficial survey of the island's petroglyphs.[161] Drapkin returned to Chile, but Métraux joined the staff at the Bishop Museum in Honolulu, where, from 1936 to 1938, he compiled his Easter Island notes and researched pan-Polynesian cultures and history in order to produce, in the Bishop Museum's outstanding Bulletin series of Pacific monographs, his *Ethnology of Easter Island*, which appeared in 1940. Now a classic in the field, it was the book that finally took the 'mystery' out of Easter Island. Several popular books[162] and a large number of academic and general articles followed, both popularizing and demystifying Easter Island in the public consciousness.

The wealthy American Templeton Crocker, owner of the yacht *Zaca*, led an expedition for the American Museum of Natural History first to Pitcairn and then to Easter Island, arriving only a few days after the departure of the Franco-Belgian expedition. Among the few participants was H. L. Shapiro, a physical anthropologist with the AMNH who made a brief study of the Rapanui's 'racial' composition.

In Chile, the Franco-Belgian expedition had roused a keen interest in the island again, resulting in the appointment of the island's first naval *practicante* ('medical orderly'). For nearly two decades the leprosery had been staffed by resident nuns, and a naval doctor would call only during the semi-annual official visitation. But the new resident *practicante* was now there for everyone, all the time, attending to most needs. If a medical mission was necessary, this was still most often undertaken and funded by private societies in Chile, not by the Company or the Republic. Also, the Republic erected the first permanent government school for Spanish-language primary education, operated by the resident schoolmaster and nuns (until the end of the 1960s). At this time about half of the Rapanui had learnt to read and write Spanish, albeit in only a rudimentary fashion.[163] Both innovations helped to produce a new generation of healthier and better educated Rapanui – who also began to question their inferior status on their own island.

For two years, as the Company had continued to press for a 30-year lease, the Republic had been deliberating how best to regulate Easter Island economically. Frustrated by the delay, the Company finally approached the government with a modified proposal: for a 20-year lease, then, it would exploit the entire island except for 2,000 hectares reserved for exclusive Rapanui use. The Republic agreed, and this new lease came into effect on 19 March 1936.

In the meantime, the University of Chile's own expedition to the Isla de Pascua had been severely downscaled. In the end, only two expedition members boarded the Company ship: Humberto Fuenzalida, who would study the island's geology during the brief loading of the wool-clip; and Father Sebastian Englert, a German Capuchin missionary from Araucanía who would remain on the island to study the Rapanui language and then catch a later vessel back to Chile.[164] (Bishop Edwards himself had approached Monseñor Guido Beck to have Father Englert loan his services in this regard.) Englert sighted Easter Island on 25 November 1935. Little did he appreciate the historic significance of the moment.

Born in Dillingen, Bavaria, in 1888, the same year that Chile had annexed Easter Island, the German Sebastian Englert had been ordained a priest of the Order of Friors Minor Capuchin in 1912 and had served on the French and Belgian fronts between 1917 and 1918 as a German army chaplain.[165] There followed many years as a missionary to the Araucans in Chile, at Villa Rica and Pucón. An amateur linguist and ethnologist, Englert had long been fascinated by Easter Island's Polynesian culture, in particular by its language, which is why he had eagerly volunteered to be a member of the university's expedition. At once he dedicated himself to his 'double labour' – pastoral care and scholarship.

In that same year of 1935 the Republic had declared the Isla de Pascua a National Park and Historic Monument: no more *toromiro* trees could be cut down (it was already too late); no artefact could be removed from the island; and every expedition hereafter would require a government licence. The Republic had also begun to compile an inventory of what artefacts remained. Towards this end, the naval *subdelegado*, Hernán Cornejo, had contracted the Rapanui Pedro Atán to make a full inventory of 'all stone monuments' on the island, including painting a number, in white oil-based paint, on their right side. In all, 688 numbers were painted during three months' labour, many still visible today. Most of this had been the direct result of the Chilean public's consternation at hearing that the Franco-Belgian expedition had taken away so many artefacts, including a huge *mo'ai*. (Identifying closely with their Isla de Pascua as an expression of national pride, many Chileans had been outraged.) But despite the declaration of a National Park, the Company still ruled here, and no *ahu* restoration, *mo'ai* re-erection or park reforestation –

except for the usual windbreaks – were undertaken. The Republic's gesture was a public relations manœuvre, without result. (The National Park would remain a 'paper park' until 1968.)

When the Chilean naval vessel *Maipo* arrived in February 1936, its captain offered to return Father Englert to Chile in order to resume his mission work at Araucanía. But he also handed Englert a sealed letter from Bishop Edwards, in which the Monseñor was asking Englert to prolong his stay for two more months, for the Rapanui's sake: 'Well do our good children of Pascua merit and need it, who have lived in such great spiritual abandon.'[166] Englert, who had not yet finished his study of the local language and who was bothered that so many Rapanui boys and girls had not yet received their First Communion, agreed to stay – but only for two more months.

Although Chile had again failed – after its annexation in 1888 and its inscription of legal ownership in 1933 – to develop the island, merely leasing it again to the same Company, it tried now to make up for this with a new regulation, the *reglamento* of April 1936, that effectively ratified only Company 'sovereignty'.[167] In this *reglamento*, the Chilean Navy (for Easter Island was officially still under military jurisdiction) stipulated such things as daily rations, salary details, sickness benefits, death grants and so forth that compelled the Company to assume those social responsibilities that elsewhere fell to states. Visitors were further restricted access to the Rapanui people, not merely to protect visitors from leprosy but to shield the Rapanui from dangerous ideas. The *reglamento* also intruded into intimate domains that hitherto had concerned only the Church.[168] It delineated the 'duties and responsibilities that each member has, especially the head of the family, and the responsibilities older children have to their elderly or sick parents' (Article 14).[169] Moral instruction now lay with a foreign-born priest, or with a functionary so designated to this task by the Chilean *subdelegado*. The *reglamento*'s overall reading was that the Rapanui were now to be raised from state-perceived barbarism to Chile's civilized urban norm.

Still the Rapanui were not allowed to enter Company land – that is, to go beyond the Wall – unless getting animal fodder or going to fish, and this only with written permission from the *subdelegado* and agreement of the resident manager. All supply, employment and care lay wholly with the Company. Not only the Rapanui but also all naval personnel, too, were under effective control of the Company. Although governmentally regulated and monitored, the 'company island', even now, differed little from Merlet's island. The *rancho* Isla de Pascua had become a fossilized institution.

Little wonder, then, that in 1936 a Rapanui man should choose to hide himself in a cargo vessel and flee this island prison. Over many subsequent years the man would send his relatives postcards from Europe, Africa and the Middle East.[170] Yet only a small handful of claustrophobic Rapanui ever managed to break out in this way. (The Republic's departure ban was finally lifted in the mid-1950s.)

Yet the whole world, it appears, was now coming to the island at last: for the Chilean Navy installed a permanent wireless station, manned full-time by a trained operator. Although the navy set up, maintained and operated the station, the Company, of course, enjoyed full use. No longer did it take months for news to arrive at Easter Island. For the first time, all Islanders could share what was happening in the greater world. However, this was neither the Republic's intention nor its practice. For the most part, transmissions remained official or Company-related. And so the Rapanui themselves profited little from the new technology, which otherwise might have brought them so much.

Father Englert – already called 'Padre Sebastian' by his parishioners – had been 'stranded' on Easter Island now for a further ten months. The next ship to arrive was the annual Company ship, the *Allipén*, which finally dropped anchor in Cook's Bay on 1 January 1937. In his fourteen months on the island – the longest sacerdotal presence since the sscc's Mission – Englert had quite revived and transformed church life there. It had also changed his own life: he himself had begun to 'strike roots in the soil of Rapanui'.[171] A letter from Bishop Edwards calmly informed him that, canonically, Easter Island had been 'detached from the Archbishopric of Santiago and attached to the Apostolic Vicariate of Araucanía', and he wished him well. Bishop Edwards alone had effected this change in jurisdiction, and for one purpose only – to give the Rapanui their first permanent priest since 1871.

Padre Sebastian returned to Chile on the *Allipén*, but that same year Monseñor Beck approved a permanent missionary parish on the Isla de Pascua and, of course, announced that the German missionary was his personal appointee to the benefice, whereupon Padre Sebastian returned to the island at the end of November 1937. He would remain there shepherding the Rapa Nui parish, with few absences, for the rest of his long life.

Despite the Republic's superficial commitment to its Isla de Pascua, the current government of Chile, led by President Arturo Palma, was entertaining altogether different plans. In mid-1937 Chile was actually involved in secret negotiations with Japan – then committed to Pacific expansion – to sell them Easter Island in exchange for hard-needed cash.[172] The Chilean Defence Ministry even made a secret offer of cession, and the Japanese Navy was 'keenly interested in the island', as a former Japanese ambassador to Chile recalled. 'The Chilean Government is recorded as having offered Rapanui for sale to the highest bidder on 8 June 1937.'[173] The Japanese legation in Santiago cabled Tokyo on 10 June, quoting Chile's Under-Secretary of the Navy: 'Owing to a difficult financial situation, the government wishes to sell Easter Island and Sala y Gomez to Japan, England, the USA or

Germany, by order of the President and the Ministry of Defense. It is wished to know if Japan is interested in acquiring it'. But by August, Japan had declined, apparently deeming Easter Island of insufficient value to His Imperial Majesty at the time. The extraordinary proposal was then retracted, its proponents perhaps encountering unexpected opposition. (President Palma failed in his re-election bid of 1938 principally because of public condemnation of his government's wanting social commitment.)

Once the new Rapa Nui parish was more firmly established, more active pastoral care followed. Padre Sebastian's immediate superior, Monseñor Guido Beck, visited Easter Island from 10 to 17 December 1938. (He would return again in January and February 1952.) Although visits were rare in the 1940s, with only three naval chaplains arriving, from the 1950s more and more chaplains, priests and Church superiors would arrive, their appearance always a cause for joyous celebration and feasting among both the pious and not-so-pious Rapanui.

Over many years, Padre Sebastian would write several books about Easter Island, the most important being his *La tierra de Hotu Matu'a* (1948). If anything, he became even more impassioned about Rapa Nui's past, recording and documenting family histories, tales and legends. With the Rapanui he was strict, authoritarian and patriarchal – almost a re-embodiment of Father Roussel, who had commanded similar fear and respect.

Yet Padre Sebastian was not only the island's parish priest. He was also its resident naval chaplain, a role he took equally seriously. So he supported the authorities in restricting the Rapanui's travels. Preferring his charges to remain at home, within the Wall, he even divulged secret travel plans to the *subdelegado*. Padre Sebastian often used his sermons to chastise worshippers of those sins admitted during sacred confession. And his censure could affect job, pay and access to imported goods, although Padre Sebastian forever railed against the Company. If the Company manager was the island's 'king', then Padre Sebastian very much set himself up as opposing 'bishop'. (This would soon have serious repercussions for him.) Perhaps partly because of Padre Sebastian's Chilean orientation, too, the Rapanui never came to internalize Catholicism fully during those crucial developmental years, but still wore it lightly as a 'cultural overlay upon a diffuse belief in spirits',[174] as they had learnt from Nicolas Pakarati.

Their spiritual beliefs struggled with a new perception as well. Especially once Chilean officials and the Roman Catholic Church effected these latest improvements in the Hanga Roa community in the 1930s, for the first time the Rapanui people became conscious of their true relative poverty.[175] Increased numbers of visitors from abroad, and a small number of Rapanui returnees from Chile, only confirmed these newly perceived deprivations. As a result, an ever growing number of Rapanui began to comprehend, and suffer from, what they really were in the world's eyes. Poor, imprisoned 'natives'.

On 1 September 1939 war broke out again in Europe. Although under great pressure, Chile officially maintained strict neutrality, resisting any break in diplomatic relations with the Axis (Germany and Italy; later Japan and others) – until January 1943, that is, when Chile suddenly joined the Allies. This was the achievement, above all, of those British and American commercial interests – such as Williamson, Balfour – that still wielded great political clout in the Republic. Long before this, however, tiny Easter Island had already felt their puissance. As a Scots-Chilean 'company island', the Isla de Pascua was actually more British than Chilean. And since Padre Sebastian had failed to endorse the Company, the island's current manager, a lowland Scot, used the outbreak of war with Germany to protest at the presence on the island of a former German army chaplain. Father Sebastian Englert compromised Chile's neutrality, he managed to convince the *subdelegado*, who then had Padre Sebastian arrested as a 'suspicious alien' and deported to the mainland in December 1939. Padre Sebastian would have been confined for the duration of the war, too, had it not been for an influential friend who succeeded in convincing the Republic of Sebastian Englert's utter loyalty to Chile since 1922.

An entire year passed. In the meantime, from the Vicariate of Araucanía came the young Capuchin Father Melchor – also a German – who then served as Hanga Roa's parish priest and Mataveri's naval chaplain, cautiously accommodating the Company's wishes. Finally, in November 1940, Padre Sebastian was allowed to return. After this he would always keep a low profile, aware of his vulnerability so long as Germany remained at war. He was also closely watched by the resident naval personnel, who filed regular reports about his behaviour. (Padre Sebastian seldom left the island after this unhappy episode.)

Although Chile was then still maintaining neutrality, both sides were played to the Republic's advantage. The Republic was attempting above all to profit from its vast stores of copper. Most profit could, of course, be had from the Americans, who, from early 1942, were spending enormous sums to create a Pacific defence against the Japanese. By March of this year, US forces had gathered along a line of islands and archipelagos to form a linked southern bulwark that stretched from New Caledonia in the west to Samoa in the east.[176] Once Chile declared itself behind the Allied cause in January 1943, Easter Island became incorporated into this enormous military line of defence: indeed, the Isla de Pascua represented its eastern terminus. There was never a US 'occupation' here, however. In 1943 a task force of US Navy ships arrived off Cook's Bay. A scout plane from one of the vessels first flew over the island to determine whether it was safe – the first time the Rapanui had ever seen an æroplane. Then a launch arrived with marines. Once the island's safety had been assured, many US Navy personnel came ashore and fraternized with the locals in a most friendly fashion. The navy even set up a large portable motion-picture screen, invited the island population, and treated them to the first cinema experience of their lives. Soon after, the task force departed. Five US Navy personnel remained behind, however, to man a radio post that would monitor any German or Japanese naval activity in the region; with the cessation of armed conflict in 1945, the post was abandoned.

Of course, the war had impinged on Company production. By 1943 sheep numbers had dropped, from an all-time high of 70,000 in the mid-1930s down to 41,412 (and 775 pigs, 387 cattle and only 98 horses).[177] The Company's permanent staff were kept to a minimum: two administrators (manager and foreman, both lowland Scots), eight shepherds and guards, and only six labourers. For the wool-clip of 73 tonnes in 1943, up to 70 Rapanui were hired to assist with shearing at Vaitea and with loading down at Hanga Piko – the work of about a fortnight. Thus only one out of 25 Rapanui had any regular paid employment on the island: an unemployment rate of 96 per cent.

Rapanui's discontent and sporadic conflict with the Company continued well into the 1940s, and even beyond. They found the political climate – above all, the lack of mobility – stifling. Many now chose to take wing, and at the risk of their lives. Between 1944 and 1958 no fewer than 41 Rapanui took to sea in small boats, 'all but one heading for Tahiti'.[178] Most of the escapees were young men in their prime. And more than half died at sea.[179] One later flight was particularly poignant: two lovers, forbidden to marry by their parents, appropriated a racing shell and paddled out from the shore during the night of 16 October 1955 – and were never heard of again.

After the Second World War, because of changing markets and shifting global revenues, the multinational Williamson, Balfour and Co. (and its many subsidiaries) suffered an unaccustomed lack of liquid capital.[180] As a result, among many other divested ventures it decided in 1946 also to bail out of Easter Island, entirely, subsequently selling its Easter Island business, chattels, livestock and goodwill, as well as the Republic's lease, to an Anglo-Chilean corporation. It is more than probable that Williamson, Balfour had got wind of the Republic's new long-term plans for its far-flung Pacific outpost.

For major political changes were in the offing. Chilean public sentiment was again turning towards the Isla de Pascua. In Santiago a new Sociedad de Amigos de Isla de Pascua was announced on 9 May 1947 by its founder, Dr Roberto Gajardo, its main purpose being the improvement of the island's medical care, especially that of leprosy – then nearly erased from the island, but still of concern to Chileans.[181] More importantly, the Republic was finally resolving to implement those ideas it had first advocated back in 1888. It still envisaged an agricultural future for Easter Island, although strategic considerations and even possible tourism were now cogent factors that government officials entertained, appreciating the changed world situation. Post-war Chilean governments tended to be nationalistic and centralist, pressing for greater federal control.[182]

By 1951 Easter Island's future was being mapped by the Republic's Corporación de Fomento de Producción (CORFO), which oversaw national development. In addition to its wool, the Isla de Pascua was to be economically incorporated into Chile at last through modern industries that processed fish, maize and such semi-tropical products as sugar and bananas, things that Chile and the larger world could use. Regular transport vessels would replace the annual Company and naval ships, establishing a Chile-Isla de Pascua line. A new age seemed to be dawning for the Rapanui, similar to what had already occurred at Tahiti, the Cook Islands, Tonga, Samoa and Fiji. Easter Island would no longer be alone but comprise part of a larger Pacific network – although still via Chile.

The Republic was set to involve itself actively and dynamically in island affairs for the first time.[183] And a private Company – particularly one in foreign ownership – had little place in this process. Experts in agriculture, fishing and civil engineering now came to the island, projecting farms, processing plants, piers, wharves – even an international airport. (That Easter Island could be a stopover between South America and Australia had been proved by Chile's Captain Roberto Parragué Singer, who, with his crew, sensationally arrived at the island in an amphibious Catalina 405 on 20 January 1951, and, shortly after this, by the Australian Taylor, who arrived from Australia in another Catalina.) In 1951–2 the Sociedad de Amigos were actively promoting the general modernization of Rapa Nui, calling for Hanga Roa's electrification and canalization as well as improved medical, educational and sanitation facilities.[184] President González Videla, who was also honorary president of the Sociedad, declared: 'The Isla de Pascua is, and will eternally be, Chilean',[185] a public commitment no earlier Chilean leader had made.

Chile's move to 'nationalize' Easter Island was part of a larger dynamic that was militaristic and nationalistic (no longer merely patriotic). It was designed to integrate the Republic's hitherto largely ignored and backward peripheries and to extend the centralist hegemony. From 1951 and especially from early 1952, an active campaign was underway to convince all Chileans that the Rapanui were also fully fledged *chilenos*. In November

1953 the new Anglo-Chilean corporation's lease was revoked, leaving only the Republic in charge of the economy and society of the *rancho* Isla de Pascua – an island that still, in many ways, did not differ all that greatly from that of 1888.

And the Republic's chosen method to achieve control? – complete naval domination. It effectively rendered the 'company island' a 'Navy island'. In truth, Chile could envisage no other form of administration here than a military one. It was an externally strong, but internally weak, scheme that in the end did little to benefit Chile. Or the 788 Rapanui.

It had been a relentless course of economic evolution. The sscc's fledgling sheep ranch was taken over and supplemented first by Dutrou-Bornier (1871), then by Salmon / Brander (1877), then by the Toro brothers (1888), then by Enrique Merlet (1895), then by the Company (1903) – each greater and seemingly more rapacious than the previous – until an entire country finally finished the feeding chain. The island ranch was a golden goose, explaining why one Company stayed there for nearly half a century (1903–46). 'What fell into oblivion were the Rapanui themselves, as sheep roamed and Islanders were confined to pens.'[186]

During the Company's and its successor's '50-year incumbency' the island was transformed: its terrain largely depopulated, its earlier plantations reduced to sheepwalks, its monuments cannibalized to build hundreds of *pircas*, corrals and paddocks – overseen almost exclusively by lowland Scots. In this, the Company 'acted as if Rapanui were a tropical version of the 18th-century Scottish Highlands'.[187] The Company introduced grasses for ideal sheep grazing, rejuvenated the old livestock (and human) bloodlines, planted thousands of trees to provide windbreaks, sun shelters and building material and to halt erosion. It expanded and built roads, enlarged then modernized Hanga Piko's quay, walled in and laid out Hanga Roa, erected a complete ranch at Vaitea, and provided hereby a permanent infrastructure for the island.[188]

For all of the Company's and its successor's half-century there, however, most Rapanui lived independently of it. Very few Rapanui – mostly shepherds and wall repairmen – were ever employed in permanent Company positions. In walled-in Hanga Roa, Rapanui had their 5-hectare *parcelas* ('allotments') for traditional plantations. But over successive decades they acquired Western tastes and ultimately abandoned time-honoured and site-evolved dietary practices. The new cash economy forced them to trade with the Company, placing them in dependence where none was needed.

The question of 'Company oppression' remains ambiguous, at least in the larger time scale. Until the 1950s too few non-Rapanui lived on the island to have exerted a continuous oppression without some sort of support in this by the local population. Rapanui women and girls openly lived with Company managers, foremen and shepherds, founding families with them when the total population hovered between only 200 and 400 people. In other words, nearly each Rapanui, though independent of the Company, was intimately involved in some way with the very system ostensibly 'oppressing' him or her.[189] (Ironically, the interbreeding created the stock of many of today's Rapanui, belying the dire predictions of the 1860s and '70s that the Rapanui would 'soon' be extinct as a people.)

In fact, during the contentious Company years most Rapanui developed a successful coping strategem enabling them to switch at will between the extremes of Rapanui and non-Rapanui activity and attitude. Only exaggerated injustice might 'snap' this divide – leading to revolt, even murder. But such instances were rare. In one way or another, most Rapanui were nearly always willing or begrudging participants in island events. For there was no recourse to Company life. (The situation was infinitely better than the tyranny of a Birdman or the carnage of intertribal warfare.) Yet out of this dual psyche there also emerged the Rapanui's latent resentment towards authority of any kind, which still permeates island society and continues to worry the social web.

For more than 60 years the Chilean dream had remained just this, a dream. But after the Second World War the Republic finally awoke to the *Realpolitik* of a changed world and turned its *rancho* Isla de Pascua into a veritable naval enterprise with tens of thousands of recruits – sheep. It appears only the *rancheros* had changed.

five

Museum Island

The Grand Myth had confused post-war perceptions in the Pacific. This was the belief among most victor nations that the war in the Pacific had been fought for democracy and, once won, should automatically lead to the region's self-determination – that is, to the end of old colonialism. The reality, however, was that, first, the Pacific's development was too diverse to allow this to happen everywhere in the region, and, secondly, each colonial power had its own, usually quite different, agenda. Britain, Australia and New Zealand indeed believed in independence for their Pacific colonies, and eventually offered this alternative to their prepared Islanders. The US either tightened its Pacific bonds – the erstwhile kingdom of Hawai'i (Polynesia) was at last subsumed into the union of states – or promised eventual discussion of 'dependent independence' (Micronesia). France and Indonesia (which finally wrested Western Papua from the Netherlands in 1962, which it renamed Irian Jaya) remained nineteenth-century-style colonial masters in the Pacific who refused any mention of independence.[1]

Since the 1950s Chile has followed the example of France and Indonesia, in that the Republic has been similarly treating its Isla de Pascua as an internal colony. Hardly deliberate, however, this course was chiefly the result of the region's larger historical 'drag-chain'. One must appreciate that, in the first two decades following the Second World War, successive British governments chose to withdraw before aggressive US involvement there. At the same time that Britain was selling out and retiring from the Pacific and South America, the US was robustly expanding its commercial and military influence. The historic process also forced successive Chilean governments to reassess, in light of changing foreign relations, their relative needs. It was during this era of national reassessment that Easter Island's new identity emerged – more the collateral effect of global realignment than any focused regeneration by the Republic of Chile.

The swift, near-fatal impact brought to Easter Island in the 1860s had been followed by more than 80 years of that sluggish alien callousness that had characterized the 'company island' – as we have seen, more British-commercial than Chilean-political. But, from the 1960s, changes again arrived with the swiftness of the 1860s, creating an altogether different place. And, in turn, Easter Island of the twenty-first century bears little resemblance to that island, so eagerly have the Rapanui subsequently embraced tourism and technology as the Republic has been forced to devolve more purposefully. It was during this half-century that the *rancho* Isla de Pascua became at last 'Museum Island', only the latest of Easter Island's many convoluted identities. Its emblem – the *mo'ai* – is an international icon.

This most recent manifestation may well similarly derive from the Rapanui's own past. But it is no less a foreign obligation, too, once again the product of outsiders imposing on the Rapanui people Western science, values and goals. Symbolically, Museum Island first emerged perhaps in 1955, when the Norwegian expedition re-erected the single toppled *mo'ai* of *ahu* Ature Hiki at 'Anakena. (Already in the mid-1930s a *mo'ai* had been re-erected before Hanga Roa's *caleta* or cove when the mole was built there, but this had no consequence.) After this, particularly under the guidance and / or inspiration of the American archæologist William T. Mulloy, not only were individual statues re-erected but entire *ahu* and their terrains restored. Eventually this involved many projects over several decades – the last, from 1992 to 2002, being the reconstruction, re-erection and full restoration of the island's largest ritual complex, majestic Tongariki.

With varying degrees of expertise, all site reconstruction on Easter Island has been select, limited and closely supervised by professional archæologists and government authorities. The overall objective has been to improve the island's archæological image, preserve endangered sites, test theories of ancient construction, reawaken Rapanui pride and render the place more attractive to international tourism – all in order, it is hoped, to improve local living standards through the revenues generated by tourism. The haphazard 'scheme' has had its share of both triumphs and failures over the years.

While the *rancho* Isla de Pascua may have continued up into the 1970s, when 15,000 sheep were still grazing barren island sweeps, the 'company island' was gone forever and what had superseded it –Museum Island – was now connecting to the world at large. Those Rapanui born after the Second World War have been witness to the most sudden and comprehensive changes in Easter Island's human history. It has been an extraordinary transformation, matched in its robustness only by that of the social schism that, by the end of the twentieth century, was ripping the island apart.

Yet the social avalanche started slowly, imperceptibly. Only outwardly was this because of naval intransigence. The true cause lay, of course, in the Republic's enduring want of a larger vision for the island.

'LIKE A MEXICAN HACIENDA'

The last external authority to wield unlimited power on the Isla de Pascua was the Chilean Navy, which seized effective control in 1953 when the new Anglo-Chilean corporation's lease was not renewed. If in the past the Navy had always been a weak presence, dependent on the Company for food and supplies (and most human company), by this time Easter Island was being run as if it were the *Baquedano* itself. For Rapa Nui duty the Navy appointed 'a commander as governor, a second-in-command, a navy doctor, pay-master, three petty officers, four sergeants, three corporals, four marines, one seaman medical helper, and a naval carpenter'.[2] The naval *comandante*, replacing the former *subdelegado* as a true *gobernador* ('Governor'), effective-ly became what the Company manager used to be under Enrique Merlet: state and enterprise in one. The Navy also assumed the role that the Company had played as importer of all Western civilization.

No more annual Company ship arrived. Instead, there was the annual Navy vessel. The *comandante* ruled – as before him Dutrou-Bornier, Salmon Jr and the Company manager – from the Mataveri residence, now upgraded, and it was he who also oversaw the *fundo* or sheep ranch that was still most of the Isla de Pascua (although most direct activity in this regard was now restricted to Vaitea, with its own overseer). With this, Mataveri turned 'military' – and has remained so ever since. Here settled the Chilean Navy, Air Force, *carabineros* and their dependents (and later the Security Police). Separating Mataveri from Hanga Roa like an alien 'no man's land' since 1965 has been the airport runway. It has effectly partitioned the island's population into Rapanui and non-Rapanui – a miniature Polynesian version of Cold War Berlin or present-day Jerusalem. (Since mutual distrust and aloofness long burdened both sides, it was never a healthy arrangement.)

If anything, restrictions were even tighter under naval rule, when the island changed from nominal military control to actual military control. Like the Company, the Navy kept the Rapanui people confined within the Wall. Unlike the Company, however, it had the men and guns to make sure they stayed there. (Up to 1966 written passes were needed to venture anywhere outside Hanga Roa.) Only a few dozen Rapanui ever worked for the Navy's sheep ranch. And only a handful of Rapanui worked for the Chilean govern-ment inside the Wall, as infirmary staff or labourers. Access to Easter Island by foreigners was also strictly controlled.

A naval doctor was appointed for a short-term contract to oversee all medical concerns, both naval and civilian. The leprosery had always been staffed by resident Catholic nuns, and in earlier years the naval doctor, on his semi-annual visit, would attend to the lepers and otherwise only monitor general needs, which then comprised the island's entire 'medical care'. From the 1930s a naval *practicante* or nursing orderly was commonly resident on the island, who provided only the most basic care. If a medical mission was necessary – once wireless communication was possible from 1936 – this was undertaken and funded by private societies in Chile, not by the Company or by the Republic. From 1953 the semi-permanent doctor became a local institution. Indeed, he was a local authority, representing the Republic and its 'superior' mindset. Dr Valenzuela Davila, for one, pontificated from this lofty position that the Rapanui failed to appreciate the benefits of Chilean civilization, still dreaming as they did of voyaging to Tahiti, their perceived 'sanctuary'. He recommended that all Rapanui be relocated to northern Chile, where, given land, they might become productive farmers instead.[3]

It was a strange world, perhaps as any contemporary Chilean military post would seem to civilian observers. Lashings and head shavings were dealt out for the smallest infractions. At the same time, some freedoms were granted that the Company had always held back. The Rapanui, in general, led lives of undisturbed subsistence, approaching sufficiency. Soon the Navy became more accommodating towards outsiders, bringing to the island on the annual naval vessel, now the *Pinto*, journalists, writers, scholars, even tourists. In time, photojournalistic articles about Easter Island began to appear throughout the world in many languages, fascinating millions of readers. Until then, the Company had been the Rapanui's sole link to the outside world. These visitors, though closely monitored by the Navy, introduced new values and suggested alternative lifestyles to the Rapanui (illus. 13).

In the mid-1950s the greatest annual event was always the *Pinto*'s arrival, which brought supplies for the entire year. By the time it arrived virtually everything was in short supply, except fruit and vegetables. After the sheep shearing, offloading of supplies and loading of the wool-chip, for about eight days the whole island feasted and celebrated. No work was accomplished. Then off the *Pinto* sailed, not to be seen again for another full year.

Throughout the 1940s and '50s the Rapanui's perceptions and possibilities broadened in general, mainly because of improved religious instruction (Padre Sebastian's permanent and dedicated presence), local schooling and then stable medical care. It was above all, however, the Norwegian expedition of 1955–6 that altered local perceptions radically; it also introduced – like no expedition, book or article before it – Easter Island to the world at large.[4] The expedition was the brainchild and product of one man, Thor Heyerdahl, famous as the leader of the *Kon-Tiki* exploit of 1947, who 'conceived, planned,

13 The mid-1950s:
between a bitter past
and an unknown
future.

organized and financed' the Easter Island venture himself. Whereas the
Franco-Belgian expedition of 1934 had been concerned largely with ethnological data, including both material artefacts and legends, the Norwegian
expedition focused on archæological work, which included the first carbon
dating of Rapa Nui objects. For this, four professional archæologists were
recruited: the Norwegian Arne Skjølsvold and the Americans Edwin N.
Ferdon Jr, Carlyle S. Smith and William T. Mulloy. A Chilean student,
Gonzalo Figueroa García-Huidobro, was the professional assistant representing the Republic. Despite Heyerdahl's pet theory of South American origins
for Easter Island's archæological remains, none of the participating archæologists was specifically requested to find links with South America (then still a
hotly debated topic).

They arrived on the Norwegian ship *Christian Bjelland* on 27 October 1955
and remained until 6 April 1956. Skjølsvold concentrated his efforts on Rano
Raraku and its *mo'ai*, Ferdon on 'Orongo, Smith on several habitation and
ahu sites, including Te Peu and the Pōike 'Ditch', and Mulloy on Vinapū.
Heyerdahl's base camp was at 'Anakena, where the ship, Heyerdahl with his

family, and Smith stayed. Skjølsvold encamped at Rano Raraku, while Ferdon and Mulloy moved to the west coast. Figueroa gained an overview by visiting all the archæologists' scattered sites. From 'Anakena, a Jeep was used for supply, fresh water and official liaising. The naval governor at Mataveri, Captain Amaldo 'Gigi' Curti, was only one of about a dozen Chileans then on the island, among whom were his wife, two sons (aged 10 and 7) and one daughter (4).

Mulloy's letters home afford a rare insight not only into the expedition but also into Easter Island life at this threshold moment in its history, the closing stages of the island's protracted isolation:

> The whole place is run and looks for that matter, like a Mexican hacienda out of the 16th century. The men on the [Vinapū] dig call me patron and take off their hats when they come to speak to me. This gripes me … Pay is a little under 40 cents a day and we are paying the highest wages ever paid on the island. In addition to the money these men get 10 cigarettes and a cup of rice every day … Everybody on the island is wild to work for us. They are a good bunch and it is a shame to see such fine people in such shape. They do get enough to eat though, I have yet to see a man on the island who looks as though he is not getting enough to eat. But no clothes and little of anything else.[5]

The expedition members got along well with one another: 'Thor is about as good a man to work for as I have ever seen and there isn't a bad apple in the whole group.'[6] Mulloy was much taken by the Vaitea sheep ranch, which was then overseen by Arturo Ugarte and one of the loveliest spots on the island. 'This is the place I would like to live and if we come to the island in the future this is the place we will live.'[7] Whereas Mataveri was the naval administration, Vaitea was the island's commercial centre and was becoming heavily forested with eucalyptus.

The expedition members were, one and all, amazed by Easter Island's archæological splendour, which they quickly surveyed within a few days of their arrival: 'At present we are more or less exploring the island and from one end to the other it is a fabulous collection of archæological ruins. I never would have believed it had I not seen it.'[8] But at the same time they were equally fascinated by the Rapanui people, and their unique lifestyle:

> The people of the island who number about 8 or 9 hundred live in the village of Hanga Roa which is on the opposite side of the island from us. Each family has a farm of about 10 hectares of land so the village is spread out over several miles of territory. The nearest thing to a center is the church for there are no stores – and each family is self sufficient on

their land. The bulk of the island belongs to the Chilean government and is used for sheep, the people not being permitted to enter the government territory except with permission.[9]

After two months ashore, Mulloy, for one, had become genuinely impressed by the remarkable Rapanui people:

Here is a group of people who have very little more than plenty to eat – no shoes, not enough clothing to cover them and houses that will sometimes keep out the rain. But the most open-handed friendliness it is possible to conceive. Everybody is happy all the time.[10]

This sentiment only grew as the months passed:

I have been extremely close to these people for six months and they have taught me more about living than I have learned in all my previous life. There is a rapport among individuals – a selflessness that European culture has lost many thousands of years ago. These people live every minute of their lives.[11]

Only a month after the expedition's arrival, however, disaster struck.[12] At the beginning of December 1955, when Padre Sebastian had the idea that, for the end of the school term, the *Christian Bjelland* should take the approximately 70 schoolchildren of Hanga Roa over to 'Anakena for a picnic, Heyerdahl and the ship's captain enthusiastically agreed. Once they had arrived at 'Anakena in heavy seas, all the children, with about seven supervisors who included three nuns, happily spent the afternoon ashore eating and playing. Then they began returning to the ship in the launch. On the third trip, which included the schoolteacher Lorenzo Baeza Vega and the pilot, the launch swamped about 40 metres offshore when the children, as many as 48 in number, inexplicably rushed altogether to the bow. Suddenly all the children were in the water, swimming for their lives. (In 1955 Rapanui children were not good swimmers. Most lived inland from the shore and were never taught to swim: there was no need, since most fishing was still discouraged in the mid-1950s. Neither girls nor most women ever swam, then.) Norwegians from the *Christian Bjelland* dived in to save them; several Rapanui on shore swam out as well. The schoolteacher Baeza was also in the water, loudly calling out: 'Kau! Kau, pōki!' ('Swim! Swim, children!') Back on shore, twelve children were given artificial respiration. Two of them – the daughter of the government-appointed *alcalde* ('mayor') Juan Atán and Andrés Pakomio's son – could not be revived, however. Nor could the teacher Lorenzo Baeza Vega. A popular song, 'Kau! Kau, Pōki!', was composed after this tragedy and sung often, well into the 1960s. Hanga Roa's public school was later renamed the Escuela Publica Lorenzo Baeza Vega.

In every other regard the expedition was a great success. After Rapa Nui, the expedition members sailed on to Rapa and Ra'ivavae in the Australs and to Nuku Hiva and Hiva 'Oa in the Marquesas, for further ground-breaking surveys and excavations. The scholarly harvest of all these activities, with supplementary studies from foreign contributors, was published much later in two volumes, affording a wealth of detailed information that still engages experts today.[13] For Easter Island, the Norwegian expedition enabled the first preliminary periodification of the island's history: Early, Middle and Late, suggesting an 'observable cultural change' but avoiding the sensitive question of ethnic replacement.[14] The expedition set the scientific foundation for all future work on Easter Island. More personally, Heyerdahl revived the abiding 'myth of Easter Island' with his phenomenally successful account of the expedition, *Aku-Aku: The Secret of Easter Island* (Norwegian 1957, English 1958).[15] This book, more than any other before or since, brought the island to the world's attention.

The expedition inspired an entire generation of scholars to address Easter Island, with the upshot that it eventually became the best-known smaller island in the Pacific. There were also other far-reaching effects. Perhaps most immediately, the critique arising from Heyerdahl's writings in the international press, combined with Chile's growing liberalism, resulted in the first group of Rapanui children being allowed to voyage to Chile. From 1956 they sailed on the annual supply ship *Pinto*, in order to attend secondary school on the continent. It was a historic occasion – which nearly broke many parents' hearts. Numerous young Rapanui would have excellent *apoderados* or 'sponsors' on the mainland who cushioned their adolescence and prepared them for life in an increasingly urbane, Westernized world.[16] The current Hanga Roa church was built from contributions that Thor Heyerdahl made in the late 1950s. And members of the Norwegian expedition would continue to return to Easter Island for a variety of reasons. Carlyle Smith sailed thirteen times between 1967 and 1978 as a guest expert for Lindblad Travel cruise ships and the Norwegian-American Line. Both Heyerdahl and Skjølsvold returned to excavate in later years. Gonzalo Figueroa, too, revisited many times, to excavate, restore and advise, serving on many Chilean commissions. But it was the American archæologist William T. Mulloy who was to have the greatest immediate impact on Easter Island.[17]

It was also Mulloy who, in a letter to his family dated 1 November 1955, wrote: 'There is a good deal of evidence that the island was once covered [with trees] but that it was denuded by the prehistoric population' – certainly one of the most significant discoveries about Easter Island in the second half of the twentieth century. (The scale and timing of the island's massive

deforestation were finally determined in the late 1970s and early 1980s, mainly by the British palæobotanist John Flenley.)[18] Mulloy returned more than
twenty further times – when travel to the island was still difficult – spending
a total of five years there, in order to excavate, restore and foster research into
the island's ancient past, not only inspiring but also actively encouraging and
supporting the next generation of Easter Island archæologists (including the
Rapanui student Sergio Rapu, whom Mulloy brought to the University of
Wyoming in the 1970s to study). Perhaps most importantly, Mulloy regarded
his restoration of the monuments as a social campaign to reaffirm the
identity and dignity of the Rapanui people.[19]

Mulloy's inaugural project, together with Gonzalo Figueroa, was the
reconstruction, with financial assistance from the Fulbright Commission and
the University of Chile, of the important *ahu* 'A Kivi that included the re-erection of its seven majestic *mo'ai*. The site was officially dedicated on 12 October
1960, the first of Easter Island's ancient monuments to be restored in modern
times. (At the dedication, Luis 'Kiko' Paté sang a special song he had
composed to commemorate the restoration.) Encountering root moulds at
'A Kivi, Mulloy and Figueroa both became convinced that the 'area was once
covered with significantly more vegetation than has been reported in historic
times. Some of this vegetation must have been quite large'.[20] The Tahai complex came next, in a major project that included its ancient canoe slipways.
The statue *Ko te Riku*, with its massive red *pukao* 'topknot', finally rose again
at Tahai in 1968, through French funding. Many other projects followed,
including the rebuilding of 'Orongo and concluding with the inland *ahu* of
'O Kava in 1976 (*mo'ai* 1978). By the mid-1970s Mulloy had arrived at the crucial insight that the island's environment had been 'progressively depleted by
man since human occupation'.[21] When Mulloy was planning to take early
retirement in order to settle permanently on Easter Island in 1978, he was
diagnosed with lung cancer and died soon afterwards. Today his ashes rest
beneath a special memorial to one side of glorious Tahai.

In succeeding years, other archæologists, several of them Mulloy's former
students, carried out further excavations, restorations, reconstructions and
mo'ai re-erections with the same spirit of dedication: Sergio Rapu and Sonia
Haoa, for example, restored *ahu* Naunau at 'Anakena already in 1978. Similar
projects have continued over the past generation – the most impressive being
that of resplendent, problematical Tongariki (1992–2002). All reconstructed
sites have, after several years, also been regularly cleaned, restored, upgraded
and monitored to maintain their integrity – for both conservation and
touristic enhancement. In recent years, such projects have been particularly
robust, despite perennial under-funding.

Immediately after the Norwegian expedition's departure, however, things
returned to the status quo at the 'Mexican hacienda', with little to break the

customary stern tedium. After researching and writing his monograph on the island's *rongorongo* script from 1953 to 1956,[22] Thomas S. Barthel, then of Hamburg, Germany, between July 1957 and February 1958 joined the Chilean scholar Ruperto Vargas for a joint Chilean-German Rapa Nui expedition. On 16 September 1958 seven Rapanui from the leprosery took a boat and disappeared over the horizon; like so many before them, they were never heard of again. It was the last such escape from the *rancho* Isla de Pascua.[23] And the long-time catechist Timoteo Pakarati, Padre Sebastian's faithful support and son of legendary sscc catechist Nicolas Pakarati Ure Pō Tahi, died in June 1959, a loss mourned by the entire island population.

Perhaps the most shocking event of these tedious years of harsh neglect was Tongariki's sudden, violent destruction.[24] The great earthquake of 21 May 1960 that devastated the Chilean metropolis of Concepción – at 9.5 on the Moment-Magnitude Scale the most powerful that human history has ever experienced, sending tsunamis to Alaska, New Zealand and even Japan (where some 200 died and 50,000 lost their homes) – sent a tsunami that struck Easter Island's south-eastern coast on 22 May with a vengeance. It washed Tongariki's fifteen toppled *moʻai*, among the largest on the island, as far as 100 metres inland, whereupon the backwash obliterated the *ahu* itself. Fortunately, no one was killed.

The Navy had introduced many vehicles to the island – descendants of Salmon Jr's buggy, Edmunds's Model-T Ford and the Americans' wartime Jeeps – which Heyerdahl's expedition Jeep, bequeathed to Padre Sebastian in 1956, had also since joined. For these vehicles, by the 1960s the Navy had widened several of Hanga Roa's roads to create broad, unpaved, Latino avenues. (Thereafter, for three decades, heavy rains would invariably turn these into blood-red quagmires.) In the process the Navy also demolished the sscc's ancient row of lovely fig-trees from the 1860s, as well as many other fine old trees. In seeming compensation, however, the Navy imported palm-trees from Tahiti, which they planted throughout the village to reduce the barrenness they had created and to provide new shade. (They required two decades to mature.) In general, sheep and cattle stocks constantly declined as the Navy gradually reduced the *fundo*'s, the ranch's, productivity. The Navy also did not regularly burn the terrain as the Company had done, with the result that pasture quality was reduced and the number of flies increased. In 1961 a coconut plantation was begun at ʻAnakena, as a continuation of the Republic's commitment to diversify the island's agricultural economy. (Although the project ultimately failed, it did transform ʻAnakena into the island's loveliest palm forest, beach and picnic area – if only after two decades of growth.) Indeed, nothing on this stupored island by the middle of the 1960s – after eleven years of aimless subsistence – betrayed any hint of the imminent eruption.

Up until now, Rapa Nui had remained 'an anachronism, a semi-subsistence society where barter and payment in kind were prominent exchange mechanisms and where information regarding the outside world filtered through irregularly via occasional scientific expeditions, radio or the annual boat'.[25] An intimation of things to come, however, was provided by the now retired Chilean Air Force captain Roberto Parragué, who, in his small private aircraft 'Manutara 2' in 1961, piloted the first commercial flight to Easter Island, landing this time at an improvised airfield at Mataveri. But Chile and Chileans seemed happy with their Isla de Pascua's naval autocracy. Even Santiago's Sociedad de Amigos de Isla de Pascua, which also had been directly involved in the naval 'coup' at the highest political level back in 1952–3, though aware of the Rapanui's persistent desire for basic Chilean rights, voiced no grievance. One of the Navy's doctors on the island in the 1960s, Ramón Campbell, spoke for many when he later wrote that the Navy's paternalist and generous rule was 'the happiest moment in two centuries of Easter Island history'.[26]

The Easter Islanders themselves, however, were anything but happy – especially those who had lived and been educated on the mainland and now felt their incarceration keenly. Only now did they fully comprehend that others, outsiders, *tangata hiva*, had been imposing their will on the Rapanui people since the 1860s. In fact, not since Nga'ara – the last effective *'ariki mau*, who had died in the 1850s – had there been true Rapanui leadership. But the Western tutelage was now over. The Rapanui had reached their majority.

Many Rapanui had left the island in the late 1950s and early 1960s for education and military service. Indeed, there had been so many of these that, by the early 1960s, 'nearly as many Rapanui were censused living on the mainland as on the Island itself'.[27] It was almost a repetition of the exodus of 1871, though not to Mangareva and Tahiti but to Chile this time. While there on what had become for most Rapanui simply *el Conti* ('the Continent') – becoming true Chileans at last, intermarrying, being fully Westernized in every sense of the word – they had also followed the increased media attention about their island. Those in the military would soon be hearing Padre Sebastian's series of radio lectures about the Isla de Pascua to the Arturo Prat naval base at Suberanía Bay on the Palmer Peninsula in Antarctica. All those involved became aware of what real Chilean suffrage meant, and they communicated this new knowledge to their friends and family back on Rapa Nui.

At this time, in February 1963, the French travel writer Francis Mazière, his Tahitian wife and their British friend Robert Terry arrived from France on the ketch *Calédonien* to spend nine months on Easter Island.[28] Mazière's wife remained in Hanga Roa conducting linguistic and ethnological research, while Mazière, Terry and three Rapanui helpers spent a month at

'Anakena, then four months at Rano Raraku, carrying out 'private excavations'. (No scholarly reports were ever published.) The rest of their time they then spent mingling with the locals, wandering about and sharing ideas. Not all Rapanui approved of the trio's presence, it appears.[29] For Mazière was a forceful critic of Chile, and seems to have encouraged a 'Polynesian *rapprochement*' with Tahiti. Detractors labelled Mazière's influence 'communism' and spread the rumour that he was promoting an independence movement. This is because Mazière was pointing out to the Rapanui what their own children and friends had been reporting from the mainland: that under this naval rule the Rapanui were more restricted behind the Wall than they had been under the old Company. And they were not only physically confined; in contrast to freer Tahiti, they were not even allowed to speak their own language – only Spanish was permitted in all official contexts. Much labour remained unpaid; travel was still restricted; no one was eligible to vote; and the Navy governed with arbitrary rulings.[30] In other words, they were still a colonized people, not true citizens of a free and democratic nation – like the Tahitians of France. Mazière's subsequent account of his time on Easter Island, *Fantastique Ile de Pâques* (1965), became a runaway bestseller in French-speaking nations – weak in scholarship but strong in emotion.

It was true that the Rapanui people still had no vote. But, officially, they were nonetheless 'citizens' of the Fifth Region of Valparaíso. They also had their own 'native council', the traditional *korohua*, of which each member (a male elder) was approved by the naval *comandante*.[31] And it was precisely on this fragile basis of democratic rights that a 'bloodless revolution' could take place that, within five years, was no less transformational, indeed tumultuous, in its own way, than those events of 1862–71, but this time with positive results. For these five years brought self-governance, the Canadian medical expedition, the American military-scientific presence and, most revolutionary of all, regular air service from and to Santiago and Tahiti. That is, it brought Easter Island's internationalization. The old Easter Island culture had collapsed in the 1860s. The new Easter Island culture emerged, after a century of rugged subsistence, in the 1960s. It was the end of the island's isolation and the beginning of its modern infrastructure and communications: its reconnection to the world at large. And it all began with Alfonso Rapu.

Alfonso 'Israel' Rapu had been born in 1942 to Elias Rapu and Reina Haoa.[32] A gifted pupil, in 1957 he was sent to Chile to live with a liberal foster family and to study. Once he had received his teaching diploma he returned to Easter Island in 1963, age 21, as a third-grade teacher. Full of new ideas and, above all, an objective understanding of the Rapanui people's genuine lack of civil rights, despite his youth he greatly impressed the local *korohua*, who recognized in him a natural leader.

At this time most Rapanui were still obliged to labour for the authorities at roadworks, planting trees or cutting grass one day a week, without pay. In exchange, the Republic administered all civilian life, defended the island from foreign forces, provided all basic services and maintained military and government communications with the Chilean mainland – without levies, fees or taxes of any kind. It put Chile in the red, but the Rapanui had little sympathy for this totalitarian paternalism.[33] After a decade of naval rule, things were nearing a critical stage. The Rapanui were only too aware of the concurrent Tahitian independence movement that had already led to strikes and violence in which also resident Rapanui had been involved, while on Rapa Nui itself all talk of simple civil rights fell on deaf ears. Hanga Roa's Wall was now reinforced with barbed wire and the two gates were locked for the night at 6 pm.[34] Many Rapanui applied to travel to Chile on the annual Navy vessel *Pinto*, but two-thirds of the applicants were usually refused passage.[35] Although Rapa Nui was part of Chile and the Rapanui people indeed enjoyed certain rights through the Fifth Region of Valparaíso, the island was still very much a colony, its inhabitants mere 'natives'.

But in October 1964 Eduardo Frei Montalva, leader of the recently formed Democracia Cristiana, a reformist party based on Catholic humanism, won Chile's presidential election. Frei's Christian Democrats, radiating a mood of optimistic change as they promised improvements in the Republic's social services, were committed to social transformation: rapid reforms in many spheres were to be implemented quickly. President Frei's own executive office, acutely aware also of the shifting dynamics on Easter Island and recognizing that changes were needed there as well, had presented already in the same month of October a proposed law to the National Congress creating a separate 'Communal Sub-Delegation of Easter Island'. This new commission would consult with Frei's government on various measures that concerned the island's development.[36]

Alfonso Rapu now took public issue with the Rapanui people's forced tutelage: 'We were not Chileans', he would later explain, 'we had rights to nothing, every child in the mother's womb was another sailor'. Whereupon the *korohua*, concerned about the intolerable situation on their island, aware of events on Tahiti and elsewhere, and impressed by the young teacher's vision and dedication, told the *alcalde* or 'mayor' – which office had superseded that of *cacique* – to step down in favour of Rapu. Alfonso Rapu was to be the new *alcalde*, by popular demand, they said. And Rapu himself was pledging throughout Hanga Roa that he would help all Rapanui 'to be Chileans' at last. It was the era's rallying call: 'to be Chilean'.

At this moment word arrived that a large Canadian medical expedition was soon to land. Encouraged by the fortuitous turn of events – it promised protection against a zealous naval governor – Alfonso Rapu assisted Germán

Hotus on 5 December 1964 to draft an open protest letter to Chile's newly elected President Frei. In it the Rapanui reformers, only armchair revolutionaries at best, criticized the continued naval autocracy and its harsh and antiquated restrictions. They particularly protested against the repressive governorship of Jorge Portilla, a naval *capitán de corbeta*, but also offered suggestions as to how the local economy could be diversified in order to improve the Rapanui people's standard of living.[37]

Three days later Rapu, with a small group of followers, held independent municipal elections for the offices of *alcalde* and local councillors: the first independent democratic election on Easter Island since 1892, when Timeone Riro had been elected *'ariki*. As expected, Rapu was elected Hanga Roa's new *alcalde*. But because Governor Portilla had not been consulted in this process, as the Navy required, he nullified Rapu's election victory, stating that there was already a government-appointed *alcalde* and that the new elections were illegal and thus invalid. For espousing such radical ideas Portilla also branded the young teacher a 'communist'. But then the governor offered a compromise solution, seemingly to defuse a potentially explosive situation only days before the Canadians would land: fresh elections would be held, he proposed, but with all factions 'fairly represented'. It was into this political hotbed that the Canadians then stepped.

The Medical Expedition to Easter Island (METEI) had been the brainchild of the Canadian physician Dr Stanley Skoryna of McGill University, Montreal, who had 'persuaded the World Health Organization to provide the initial funding for a pilot project which would examine the relationship between heredity, disease, and the environment on Easter Island'.[38] By the 1960s the health situation on the island had already markedly improved, although TB continued to be a serious problem. Six lepers did still live in isolation, but others could live with their families, no longer a danger. As ever, the flu-like *kokongo* struck with a vengeance with each annual visit of the *Pinto*. The island's naval infirmary – with no modern operative or diagnostic equipment, no immunization programme, no adequate stock of drugs – left much to be desired.[39] (One of the Navy doctors, excessively obese, had been dubbed 'Killer Whale' by the Rapanui because so many of his patients had died.)[40] Aware of many of these shortcomings, the Canadians had hoped to be able also to help the local population. The Royal Canadian Navy had furnished transport to the island for the medical team of ten Canadians and one Chilean, and for their 24 prefabricated trailer units. Arriving on 13 December 1964, the physicians carried out, from then until 11 February 1965, 'the most exhaustive medical and scientific examination that has ever been conducted on a South Pacific Island population'.[41]

Unlike the Routledges' presence in 1914, METEI did not ignite the civil disturbance of December 1964 – the civil rights movement had already begun months before. But their immediate proximity lent the Rapanui confidence, since Governor Portilla could not imagine to suppress the 'insurrection' before international witnesses in true naval fashion. The Rapanui were safer to agitate because of the Canadians – and to play one 'intruder' against the other.

The Navy doctor on the island, Guido Andrade, was greatly liked by the Rapanui. He had actually supported their demand for greater autonomy. And so Governor Portilla now ordered him to stand trial before a naval Tribunal in Chile, and placed him aboard the Canadian vessel for deportation. In support of the doctor, METEI's Chilean nutritianist also left with him, and so the ten Canadian doctors, by default, had to develop a much closer relationship with the Rapanui than they had anticipated.

Because the naval ship *Pinto* had not supplied the island for more than a year, the Canadians found all Rapanui without cooking oil, flour, sugar, tea, coffee, soap, shoes, antibiotics and much more. Governor Portilla asked the Canadians to supply the Rapanui's basic needs, whereupon the Canadian commander, C. Anthony Law, in turn asked Padre Sebastian, whom all Rapanui evidently respected and followed, how best to effect such a distribution. The island's priest replied that Law should do this himself, because the Rapanui did not trust the Chileans.[42] And so, on 19 December, just six days after their arrival, the Canadians handed out approximately 200 food parcels. Their apparent generosity won the Rapanui's immediate goodwill – as the Canadians learnt, too, how deeply lay the Rapanui's antipathy towards all Chilean authority.

Alfonso Rapu skilfully exploited the Canadians' presence to attain maximal political leverage with Governor Portilla. In fact, Rapu's manœuvring almost torpedoed the METEI project. (Fortunately, Stanley Skoryna managed to negotiate ethnically sensitive arrangements that allowed the Canadians to proceed nonetheless.) When acts of sabotage occurred, Governor Portilla radioed Chile for reinforcements and Rapu went underground. The rumour quickly spread that Rapu's people were working for a Tahitian-based 'Polynesian Union' that was seeking independence from Chile. Seemingly confirming the rumour, in the first days of 1965 a French warship appeared off Cook's Bay – but then it left again, just as swiftly. Whereupon, on 5 January 1965, the Chilean arctic patrol ship *Yelcho* arrived. This was the same Chilean vessel that, in 1916, had rescued Sir Ernest Shackleton's 22 men from Elephant Island. But now it was carrying 40 marines and an investigative commissioner, ex-Governor José Martin. As one marine told a Canadian ashore, they had come to defend 'Chileans' – that is, not the Rapanui.

The *Yelcho's comandante*, Guillermo Rojas, immediately assumed naval control of Easter Island. Establishing a small encampment at Hanga Piko, he set up an investigative team, with the assistance of Martin, who was representing Santiago. Rumours were rife. On 8 January a warning shot was even fired after violence had been threatened when a crowd of women suddenly shielded Alfonso Rapu at the end of his two-day interrogation. (Apparently the marines were retreating back to their encampment as Rapu, dressed in the women's clothing a relative had smuggled to him, hurriedly escaped.)[43] Two days after this episode, Comandante Rojas and ex-Governor Martin announced that fresh elections would be held, on 12 January.[44] Even women over 21 would be allowed to vote as well for the first time, but no one could vote who could not read Spanish or not speak Rapanui. Most important of all, constitutional reforms would be forthcoming from the Republic, they declared. As Stanley Skoryna wrote many decades after the event: 'Commander Rojas made one of the best decisions a naval commander could make: he declared free elections on the island during our stay; he did more than the islanders asked and transformed an explosive situation into a "glorious revolution" with one of the best *Sau-Sau* [dance festivals] held on Rapa Nui.'[45] All Rapanui knew at once that Martin's official statement effectively condemned – and ended – Governor Portilla's excessive and ineffectual administration. Not only were the Rapanui vindicated – they were 'free' at last.

And so, on 12 January 1965, Alfonso Rapu was legally elected Hanga Roa's new *alcalde* in fresh democratic elections both approved and confirmed by the Republic. Years later, Rapu would declare that it had all been not 'so much a revolution as a misunderstanding'.[46] Soon after the election, the Chilean warship *Aquila* arrived at the island – bringing not marines this time, but a shipful of supplies and post.

When the Canadians departed in February 1965, they donated to the naval authorities the prefabricated hospital of 20 beds along with x-ray equipment, a medical laboratory, an ambulance and a generator. (All these served the island well until 1975, when the first Hanga Roa Hospital was built.) Scientifically, METEI had been a great success; a number of publications followed, but there was never a comprehensive correlation of data.[47] Socially, much as with the Routledges in 1914, the METEI's presence did have an encouraging effect on the Rapanui's behaviour. Unlike the Angata revolt, however, the ultimate result was political enfranchisement. Acting like Comandante Castillo in 1892, Comandante Rojas in 1902 and Comandante Almanzor in 1914, this Comandante Rojas of 1965 enforced the naval prerogative yet again to mediate and immediately institutionalize. He finally enabled the Rapanui people 'to be Chileans'.

Of course, the new *alcalde* Alfonso Rapu had little actual power. The naval governor still ran the island. Yet things were fundamentally different now. Chile had acted immediately because it had feared international attention might be drawn to Easter Island's embarrassing neo-colonial situation.[48] This was also why, even before the election, Santiago had granted its Isla de Pascua the status of a civil department within the province of Valparaíso.[49]

Government officials were now encharged to establish a *municipalidad* – a municipal form of governance – for the island's single community of Hanga Roa. (Mataveri would remain under naval jurisdiction.)

It was in this way that total naval control of the island effectively ended in 1966, 'when Easter Island became a civil territory fully incorporated into the Chilean state'.[50] On 22 February of that year, President Frei signed Law 16,441 – the *Ley Pascua* – which created the 'Departamento de Isla de Pascua' within the jurisdiction of Chile's Fifth Region (Valparaíso). The new *Ley Pascua* granted the Rapanui people the right to suffrage; the sole authority to own land on the island; exemption from all levies, duties and taxes; free education; scholarships for tertiary study; certain subsidies for housing and fishing boats; more lenient penalties for misdemeanours than on the mainland; and other special dispensations. The island's governor would be nominated by, and would represent on the island, no longer the Navy but the President of Chile himself. Since the *Ley Pascua* did not permit the island's *municipalidad* to collect taxes of any kind, it has kept the municipality in political thralldom ever since: because throughout Chile each *municipalidad* is almost entirely dependent on the Republic's common municipal fund. (Chronic underfunding for most necessary services is thus endemic in Chile.) On 16 March Easter Island's officially authorized *junta de vecinos* or 'neighbourhood council' sat for its inaugural session. In June Santiago declared the Rapanui to be full Chilean citizens, as the Isla de Pascua was reclassified from a military colony to a civil territory. For the first time since 1895, Easter Island was free of unrestricted domination.[51]

It would not be until 21 May 1967 that Easter Island's municipal constitution would officially come into effect.[52] However much this act would signal the Rapanui's achievement of self-governance, it was the governor who still very much controlled the island: usually military, non-Rapanui (for the next 17 years) and loyal above all to Santiago. Yet the puppet masters themselves wore strings. It would perhaps be comforting to believe that Easter Island's change in legal status was the result of Chile's maturation to a historical patronage in the Pacific – as had occurred with Britain, Australia and New Zealand. But Easter Island's 'freedom' clearly came as the result of a much larger global strategy that was mainly American and military in nature. It involved – immediately after the assassination of the US president John F. Kennedy – President Lyndon Johnson's escalation of the Cold War, of Vietnam and of aggressive expansion into Latin American governments and economies. Ironically, Easter Island's newly won 'emancipation' committed the island even more intensely to the process of Chileanization.

For it was also in 1966–7 that a secret US satellite tracking station, conceived to maintain surveillance on the USSR, came to the island (see below). The Americans had demanded, and received, a stable and secure political environment for their clandestine operations here. The facility would also serve to promote the US's surveillance of all South American telecommunications, and help to bind Chile even closer to its American partner. For Santiago, the Isla de Pascua was apparently a votive offering, with abundant patronage the promised reward. Few Rapanui would have recognized this greater game, of course. For the moment, everyone profited from the charade.

Mayor Rapu's incumbency was troubled from the beginning. Given his pro-Rapanui activism, he was manifestly more a Timeone Riro than a Juan Tepano – more champion than diplomat. The precariousness of the Republic's funding for the *municipalidad* severely handicapped his managerial competence.[53] Rapu publicly prioritized private Rapanui co-operatives over the various government co-operatives that were being established. Authorities who resented this posture accused Rapu of being anti-Chilean, even separatist.[54] Chile's Christian Democrats called Rapu a 'Marxist' for his failure to share their ideology and to cooperate with their generous government schemes. Ironically, what Alfonso Rapu did achieve in the end 'was a greater Chileanization, eventually leading to the civil status of the island in 1966, a brief flirtation as an American military colony and eventual integration into the Chilean state, accomplished not so much through the growth in the governor's office, but through the increasing bureaucratization of the Rapanui-controlled municipality'.[55]

From 1966 all Easter Islanders received the same Chilean public services as on the mainland. Also allowed was the establishment of political parties on the island. Of course, especially favoured was the Christian Democratic Party, the one then in power in Santiago. The island's economy boomed as the Rapanui-run co-operatives intentionally maintained more traditional ways of doing things. However, those who were managing these non-governmental co-operatives 'created a conflict of power'.[56] In the end, 'the combination of lack of technical consultation, planning, and credit conventions drove these organizations to failure'.[57] A local agency of Chile's Corporación de Fomento (CORFO) was also created on the island in 1966. This was responsible for domestic water supply, electricity, the Hanga Piko wharf facility and the 'Fundo Vaitea', the sheep ranch in the centre of the island.

From 1966 the *municipalidad* assumed all common functions of such an institution throughout the civilized world: sanitation, fruit and fish prices and other market matters, liquor distribution, licensing, building permits, the regulation of Hanga Roa's handful of private motor vehicles and other things. Its funding came from Chile's municipal fund, the revenues that the local fees generated, certain governmental grants and a cut from the profits of Viña del Mar's casino on the Chilean coast.[58] Perhaps most significantly, the *municipalidad* was not located at Mataveri – the island's 'foreign capital' since the days of Dutrou-Bornier – but in the centre of Hanga Roa itself. It was symbolic of the new era. The Wall was also demolished at last, and all Rapanui were free to move anywhere on their island.

The employment situation would also improve, if slowly. In 1966 few Rapanui had a permanent, salaried job: one in ten worked for CORFO, the Air Force or other agencies, and one in five farmed; the rest simply 'made do', as ever. Within seven years, however, under the subsequent regime of the new leftist coalition of the Unidad Popular (Popular Unity Party), whose leader Dr Salvador Allende was elected Chile's president in 1970, 'about two-thirds of the Rapanui males were employed by the Chilean Public Services'.[59] (Many of these also continued to pursue other pursuits as well, such as carving and fishing, a common feature of small, isolated Pacific islands.) The Parque Nacional de Turismo Isla de Pascua was also created during this formative period, with a view towards international tourism.[60] Initially this was defined, by 1968, as comprising Rano Kau (including 'Orongo) and Terevaka (including 'Anakena); but many important archæological sites, such as Rano Raraku and Tongariki, remained on CORFO land.

In 1966 Governor Portilla was replaced. But his replacement, Enrique Rogers Sotomayor, the first civilian governor of Easter Island, did everything, it seems, but please the Rapanui.[61] He consulted only fellow Christian Democrats; 'lost' important documents granting the Rapanui-run co-operatives a legal status; and widened existing streets in Hanga Roa excessively to create treeless avenues, after having coerced Rapanui into giving up their lands for these or for new public buildings there. Governor Rogers alone dictated where civil facilities and amenities were to be sited. He was, in fact, fomenting political differences on the island. One Santiago newspaper even went so far as to claim that Rogers was turning the Isla de Pascua into 'a bridge for Yankee ships on their way to Vietnam'.[62] Rapanui in particular objected to Rogers's applying mainland candidate registration practices for the elections of December 1966. These practices, while favouring the Christian Democrats, disqualified Alfonso Rapu from standing.

In his new responsibilities as Hanga Roa's *alcalde*, Rapu had been closely assisted by the Chilean civil engineer Mario Olivares. Olivares, who had been sent by the Ministry of Education in 1966 to help construct Hanga Roa's new Escuela Publica Lorenzo Baeza Vega, had actively involved himself in the burgeoning civil rights movement. He now became Rapu's campaign manager and personal political counsellor.

On 16 December 1966 Governor Rogers, when coming ashore by launch at Hanga Piko after a journey from Chile on the *Navarino*, was met by a crowd of angry Rapanui women throwing both insults and stones. Almost forty Chilean *carabineros* had to rush in to protect the president's representative. But one woman broke through their cordon, shouting: 'There is the *Navarino*. Go back!'[63] At this moment the *carabineros* started assaulting the women with their batons. Nothing like this had ever happened before on Rapa Nui. Chile's newspapers had a field day with the story.

The incident polarized the island overnight. There were those for Rogers and those for Rapu. Those for Rogers sent a letter to President Frei, claiming that Rapu's followers were 'lepers and illiterates who are disposed to turn the island over to France'.[64] Fearing imminent arrest, Rapu again went into hiding. The Republic denied that any such incident had ever occurred. But then the launch pilot was officially prosecuted: for not having informed Governor Rogers of the women's intentions beforehand. Most, but certainly not all, Rapanui supported Alfonso Rapu in the unhappy affair.

The protest highlighted the Republic's planning *for* the Rapanui and not *with* the Rapanui. Chile was ignoring local values, disregarding respected *korohua*. True, it had been Alfonso Rapu, leader of the 'revolution' of 1964–5, who now lay behind this violent protest of 1966–7. But the few Rapanui who were opposing Rapu were mostly those who still irrationally alleged that he was a 'communist' supported by the French in order to establish a 'Polynesian Union'. Confirmation of most Rapanui's true feelings for Alfonso Rapu, and strong sentiments against President Frei's hypocritical Easter Island policy, came with Rapu's re-election as Hanga Roa's *alcalde* in Easter Island's first truly municipal election, in April 1967. At this juncture, after only six months in office, Governor Rogers quit the island.

'To be Chilean' at last meant, of course, a weakening of the indigenous inheritance. And nowhere was this more apparent than in the use of the Rapanui language.[65] Until the mid-1960s Rapanui had still been the island's dominant tongue. But Chilean civil administration promoted assimilation – not integration – and thus bilingualism. And so Spanish soon became necessary in nearly every public act. All Rapanui now used Spanish not only with the *continentales* but increasingly among themselves. With this the Rapanui language changed, too, becoming more Spanish-influenced. Many Rapanui parents no longer spoke Rapanui at all to their children, believing that Spanish would better their chances in life. It was understood that 'to be Chilean' meant, above all, being Spanish-speaking. The extremely popular volunteer radio station (there was still no television) transmitted only in Spanish to nearly every household. Within two decades the Rapanui language would be approaching extinction. That is, with 'emancipation' the Rapanui were losing an essential part of what it meant to be Rapanui.

THE NEW BIRDMEN

After the foreign onslaught of the 1860s and the Chilean annexation of 1888, the third greatest transformational event was, in fact, neither the historic establishment of the Rapanui's own *municipalidad* nor their attainment of full Chilean citizenship. Rather it was the inauguration of regular passenger flights to and from the island – 'which thrust Rapanui abruptly into the "global village"'.[66] With this, modern tourism – bringing benefits and blights – began at last. Already in 1951 Parragué had flown to the island from Chile, and Taylor from Australia. Ten years later, after the opening of Tahiti's Faaʻa International Airport on 5 May 1961, Parragué piloted the first commercial flight to Easter Island, landing at Mataveri's hurriedly improvised airstrip. In November 1961 an air link between Paris and Santiago was inaugurated, putting pressure on governments to open the south-eastern Pacific to air travel as well, similar to what already existed between California, Hawaiʻi, American Samoa, Western Samoa, Fiji and New Zealand. By 1965 six personnel of the Chilean Air Force were assigned permanently to the Mataveri facility – which still comprised only grass and wire matting – when Parragué now flew successfully from Easter Island to Tahiti for the first time.

On this occasion, the Republic appreciated the importance of commandeering a strategic role – that is, before any other South American nation – in the growing trans-Pacific aviation network, routing most flights, and revenues, through Santiago. At first, 'Anakena had been selected as the site for Easter Island's new airport; but this was soon rejected, being too costly.[67] Instead, in 1965 work began on simply upgrading the primitive Mataveri airstrip. By early 1967 C-118s and DC-6s were testing the new tarmac runway that stretched from Hanga Piko towards Vinapū – now extended by the US Air Force.

The Republic had indeed been anything but alone in this abrupt enterprise. Although it is true that Easter Island's final incarnation was enabled ultimately by modern technology, by aviation, this happened only because of the Americans. From 1964 the aggressive expansionist policy of the new US president, Lyndon Johnson, indirectly made possible the connection of this remotest of Pacific settlements to the rest of humankind, seemingly in spite of the Republic of Chile's own lack of vision in this regard.

The US was intimately involved with President Frei's government. The latter had agreed to allow the US Air Force to install a top-secret satellite tracking station on the island. This would not only gather weather information – the public role of the nearly 100-man installation – but also monitor Soviet naval movements, as well as South American telecommunications. For such a massive base, a proper airport – not a primitive airstrip – was required. It would be jointly run with the Chilean Air Force. Indeed, as we have seen, it was this base that actually allowed the Rapanui people to become Chilean 'by default': the Republic wanted to avoid its secret arrangement with the US being disturbed by local troublemakers. In January 1967 some 80 American Air Force personnel and civilians finally arrived to occupy what their landsmen had constructed, and they and later replacements would remain for four years. From their base camp at Mataveri they would drive up each day to their sophisticated facility atop Rano Kau, which was soon in full operation.

It was the Rapanui's first long-term encounter with a large number of non-Chileans, and nearly all of them enjoyed the Americans' forceful presence. (This, and the influence of William Mulloy over so many years, explains why Americans in particular are so welcome on the island today.) The Americans appeared to integrate much more freely and readily in Rapanui society than the *continentales*, the mainland Chileans. As the Rapanui came to think ever more highly of the *yanquis*, who handed out cigarettes, alcohol and other desirables, their opinion towards the *contis*, who seemed arrogant and aloof in comparison, collapsed. Rather ungraciously, the Americans were also disparaging of their Chilean colleagues, as frequently witnessed by Rapanui.[68] Within the first year, American-Rapanui marriages had resulted, bars had opened up, and cash and goods were flowing more freely than ever before.[69]

So it happened that the airport was not built to serve tourism, the Rapanui or even Chile. 'The main purpose of the airport was to fly in military supplies for the American base which, officially at least, was under the command of the Chilean Air Force. In reality, the area was strictly out of bounds for all but American personnel and the few Rapanui in their employ.'[70] In their four years there, however, the Americans' contributions were considerable: an enormous surge of *matériel* and money, a tarmac runway and upgraded roads to some archæological sites and beaches – where the Americans even set up litter bins, the island's first.[71] US Air Force personnel also regularly attended Padre Sebastian's masses. It is little wonder that, by the time that the Americans departed in 1970, all prices on the island were being quoted in US dollars. (The custom continues today, alongside Chilean pesos.)

The American presence also prompted a robust campaign of municipal projects. From 1967 Mataveri and central Hanga Roa were reticulated with piped water from aquifers. Supplementary roof tanks for rainwater were still retained for drinking water, since Easter Island's water can be, as Captain Cook had found in 1774, 'so bad as not to be worth carrying on board'.[72] Because those Rapanui with permanent government employment could improve their housing through access to government stores of imported timber, cement and island stone, modern-style houses began to appear for the first time in the late 1960s, surrounded by tended gardens of flowering plants and fruit trees. Also in the late 1960s the state-owned shipping agency EMPREMAR superseded the annual naval supply ship, to deliver goods now twice a year from Valparaíso and pick up the wool-clip – from the mid-1970s via military-like landing craft – at the Hanga Piko wharf facility.

Despite the military secrecy of Mataveri airport during its American occupation, international tourism was also kindled here, if haltingly at first. A New York-based firm that specialized in tailored holidays acquired the rights to fly in foreign tourists to Mataveri on an old LAN-Chile DC-6B that had room for 40 passengers on the nearly nine-hour flight from the continent.[73] So it was that on 3 April 1967 the first commercial tourists arrived at Easter Island. They encamped in a 'tent hotel' serviced by Rapanui who also drove them in two (later three) firm-owned Dodge pick-ups to the various archæological sites, always the goal of the enterprise. In 1967 the monthly flights brought 444 passengers to the island. From 1970, when Boeing 707s were introduced, flight times were halved. And after 1971 flights were arriving twice a week. Their impact on Easter Island was enormous, making tourism a viable economic mainstay for the first time. LAN-Chile then also flew weekly Santiago–Easter Island–Tahiti runs, competing with Air France's Lima–Easter Island–Tahiti route. (Air France pulled out in January 1977, however, because the route had incurred financial losses.)[74]

At first the local tourist 'industry' remained small, because of limited accommodation and food supplies: all the tourists' food had to be flown in from Chile. The Republic's hotel corporation, HONSA, actively promoted this tourism, because the government 'hoped that tourism, in conjunction with the new South Pacific air route, would not only revive the island's economy but would also reaffirm Chile's geopolitical position in Oceania'.[75] Ironically, the US Air Force welcomed and assisted the foreign tourists far more than local Chilean authorities did, even giving them guided tours of their 'top-secret' satellite tracking station while offering, in true American fashion, free doughnuts and coffee.

In 1968 the Republic divided Easter Island into five sectors: Hanga Roa's urban area; the agricultural terrain just beyond; the two National Parks of Rano Kau and Ma'unga Terevaka, including 'Anakena; and CORFO's sheep ranch, comprising most of the island's south and east. Government offices were being constructed along Hanga Roa's widened central avenue – newly named Policarpo Toro after Chile's 'hero of annexation'. (It was a signal of the Rapanui's pride to be full citizens of the Republic.) Over subsequent years a bank, fire station, magistracy, land office, telegraph office, municipal office and governor's office all rose here, as a true island 'main street' gradually took shape that eventually also welcomed commercial shops, tourist and airline offices, later also cafés and restaurants. Within several years all Rapanui were being drawn daily to 'downtown' Hanga Roa, a cosmopolitan capital that had not existed earlier.

In the late 1960s and early 1970s it was common for the governor to be a retired *general de carabineros* or even an active *mayor de carabineros*. No Rapanui was yet allowed to be governor. The Republic did, however, begin large-scale employment of Rapanui in municipal and government positions, particularly from 1966 to 1975. This raised, through permanent wages sent from the mainland, the island's standard of living hugely. Education also improved with the construction of the new primary school – the re-estab-lished Escuela Publica Lorenzo Baeza Vega, the island's only school – in 1966–7 at the corner of Policarpo Toro and Te Pito te Henua (the road leading down from the church to the *caleta* or cove). The building of the new school was prompted in part by the great influx of *contis*, whose children required a 'proper' Chilean education. The nuns who had been running the primary school since the 1930s were replaced at this time by certified Chilean teachers, appointed by the Republic. If Rapanui children were deemed bright enough to profit from a secondary education, they were still sent at state expense to Valparaíso. (By the 1970s several Rapanui were studying at Chilean and US universities as well. From 1978 a secondary education was finally offered at the upgraded Liceo Lorenzo Baeza Vega, and an even larger number of graduates went on to tertiary education and training in Chile and other countries.)

For many years, the indefatigable Padre Sebastian Englert had been try-ing, among his many projects, to get support for the conservation and restoration of Easter Island's *ahu* and *mo'ai*. Indeed, he had 'pointed out to anyone who would listen that Easter Island was potentially the most signif-icant museum of art and architecture to be found anywhere in the Pacific', as his good friend William Mulloy later recalled.[76] Consequently Padre Sebastian had agreed to be honorary chairman of the International Fund for Monuments, Inc., of New York. In the 1960s he spoke and wrote widely about Easter Island, and he even made two trips to the US and Canada, delivering public lectures and supporting fund-raising campaigns for the island. During his return from the second trip, however, Padre Sebastian fell ill in New Orleans and died there on 8 January 1969. His body was returned to Easter Island and buried next to the church, alongside Brother Eugène Eyraud, with the participation of the entire island's population. After this, the German-born Father Melchor returned from South America to lead the parish he had run from 1939 to 1940 (during Padre Sebastian's exile). A gen-tle, caring man much loved by all, like Padre Sebastian, he, too, was dedi-cated to the Rapanui and understood their unique needs.

On a lighter note, Easter Island's first 'Semana de Rapa Nui' or summer festival – later to be called 'Tāpati' (Tahitian for 'Sunday', from the English 'sabbath') – was held in 1969 after Florencia Atamu, one of Hanga Roa's new Rapanui councillors, had witnessed the 'Tiura'i Festival' at Pape'ete and had suggested something similar for Hanga Roa. The 'Semana' began small, but enthusiastically (illus. 14). Over the years Easter Island's 'Tāpati Festival' was to become one of the Pacific's most fascinating annual cultural events, attracting tourists from around the world.

An increase in population of 50 per cent had occurred between 1960 and 1970. By 1971, with a regular air service that not only boosted the Rapanui's income but also amplified their mobility, change was coming even more

14 Selecting the new 'Miss Rapa Nui' at the annual 'Semana de Rapa Nui', early 1970s.

rapidly. Ever since the early 1970s, the island's modernization has continued with increasing momentum.

Because of the Norwegian expedition, Heyerdahl's books, Mulloy's and Figueroa's frequent visits and restoration projects, and Padre Sebastian's own international cultural efforts, more and more archæologists, sociologists, physical anthropologists, palæobotanists and other scientists and graduate students were inspired to visit the island. Some, like the American-born Australian sociologist Grant McCall, stayed for years. It was not only 'Museum Island' that was attracting these visitors from 1967 – although, admittedly, nearly all tourists have targeted the island's archæology foremost – but also increasingly the contemporary island and its unique Polynesian population as well.

Also beginning in the early 1970s, with Dr Salvador Allende's election as President of Chile, was the Republic's announced modernization of Easter Island's infrastructure – one quite equal in impact to the Company's massive upgrades of the 1920s and '30s. The new scheme called specifically for the establishment of touristic, agricultural and fishery co-operatives, its overall objective being 'the incorporation of the islander into the mainstream of national life'.[77] A universal improvement of the island's utilities, housing, transport, communications and social services was also planned and shortly to be implemented, the government revealed. Such plans were nothing new. Already in 1967, under President Frei, a similar scheme had been heralded. 'Infrastructual improvements were motivated on the one hand by the need to provide basic standards for a nascent tourist industry, and on the other by feelings of guilt regarding Chile's neglect of the island during the previous 80 years', as Chile's press had pointed out even then, in 1967.[78]

The government of America's rightist Republican president Richard Nixon recalled all US military and civilian personnel from Easter Island in 1970, as soon as Dr Allende's leftist Unidad Popular party came to power, which resented any American presence on Chilean national territory. When still a parliamentarian, Dr Allende had flown to Easter Island in the late 1960s in order to pay an official visit to the American satellite tracking station. But whereas foreign tourists had often been welcomed with doughnuts and coffee, Dr Allende had been refused entry. Once Dr Allende was president, the Americans 'summarily departed, leaving equipment and a few dozen illigitimate children'.[79]

In fact, an enormous amount of American equipment was left behind at this time, of significant value to the Rapanui people. There was building material, office supplies, vehicles, even complete buildings that now went to various governmental and municipal agencies. Throughout the 1950s and '60s a small naval generator had provided limited electricity, for basic provision and street lighting; the large generator that the Americans now abandoned enabled a much greater expansion of services. The Chilean Air Force took over the American's Mataveri camp as its own airbase. When the New York-based tourist firm also chose to quit the island at the same time, the Rapanui drivers purchased the three Dodge pick-ups in order to start their own tourist transport businesses.

With this the Rapanui-owned tourist industry was born. For the growing number of tourists, more vehicles were then imported from Chile. In 1971 HONSA imported a 120-bed prefabricated hotel from Miami in Florida (today's Hotel Hanga Roa, the only one on the island to be in Chilean, not Rapanui, ownership). But many Rapanui themselves began opening up, in their private homes, bed and breakfasts called *residenciales*. Soon tourism was booming. A few co-operatives were also set up during Dr Allende's tenure.

The National Economic Plan of 1972 envisaged a unique status for Easter Island within the Republic, recommending that local government agencies restrict afforestation, zone rural land and preserve the uniqueness of the terrain. In 1973 Chile's Corporación Nacional Forestal (CONAF) was created under the Ministry of Agriculture, as a semi-private institution. Although specializing in forestry, it was also given the 'administration, custody and control' of the country's entire National System of Protected Areas, which included the new Parque Nacional de Turismo Isla de Pascua.[80] Within three years of Dr Allende's coming to power, almost everybody in Hanga Roa and Mataveri had electricity, because most houses, offices and Policarpo Toro's few shops had been connected to the new central power station. But because of high local usage – mainly for lighting at night – a general power tariff was charged for the first time in 1973.[81] Small canning factories were being planned for the island, benefitting from President Allende's development scheme, which would provide all necessary financial assistance. Towards this end canning machines even arrived from the mainland.

By this time the Rapanui people had learnt self-governance through their local *municipalidad*. As with Western Samoa (1962), the Cook Islands (1965), Tonga (1970) and Fiji (1970), the lesson might indeed have been the all-important step towards Easter Island's own independence – had history itself not rudely intervened.

THE JUNTA, 1973–90

General Augusto Pinochet Ugarte's brutal military *golpe de estado* of 11 September 1973 killed President Allende, overthrew his Unidad Popular government and terminated all civilian rule everywhere in Chile. This included the Isla de Pascua, where the clock was suddenly turned back to 1953.

Sheer terror marked the debut of the junta. On the day of the *golpe*, a military vehicle pulled up outside a house in a quiet Santiago suburb in which Rapanui high-school and university students were boarding. Whereupon a group of

> armed soldiers bundled the youngsters inside, battering to the ground a Rapanui university student who was the chaperone for the house. With abuse and taunts, the soldiers herded the frightened teenagers into a room, ordering both the girls and the boys to remove their clothing. One of the young girls, an intelligent, attractive girl whose parents did not go to Tahiti so that she could continue her studies, was taken to another room, where her naked cousins and kin could hear her screams as she was raped by each of the small band of soldiers.[82]

Within a few weeks, an unscheduled LAN-Chile jet brought new government officials to Easter Island, then flew out with ex-President Allende's men. Most of their dependents followed on the next flight.

In contrast to nearly everywhere on mainland Chile, however, daily life changed very little on Rapa Nui after the coup – apart from the unimpeded modernization, that is. Such a harsh military dictatorship was already only too familiar to most Rapanui. And many Rapanui had not supported Dr Allende's leftist regime, because it had always thwarted private entrepreneurial plans. Some even took advantage of the situation, siding with the junta and its henchmen for personal gain. Others made effective use of the junta's generous schemes to modernize – though at the price of civil rights and municipal autonomy. No criticism was tolerated. The slightest infringement would incur the harshest penalty. The Isla de Pascua became the outpost of an internationally censured police state.

As Chile's economy weakened, education on the mainland became too expensive for most Rapanui families. Tourism fell. Rising prices meant that, from the middle of the 1970s, the cost of living on the island suddenly soared. Because of Pinochet's rationist policies – funds were diverted above all to the military and police – Chile's public sector was greatly reduced. Many government jobs – on which up to two-thirds of Rapanui families now depended – ceased to exist. If merely to survive, most Rapanui families began recultivating their *parcelas*, their inherited plots of land. More started accommodating tourists in their private homes, just to make ends meet.

Acutely aware of what was happening on the island – and truly concerned for their international image because of Easter Island's newly acquired global profile – the junta in Santiago reassessed the island's strategic position, but, incredibly, along the lines of Chile's expansionist vision of the 1870s.[83] On 5 June 1974, only nine months into its dictatorship, the junta leaders renamed the Pacific Ocean between Chile and its Isla de Pascua the official 'Sea of Chile' – once again raising Policarpo Toro's symbolic fist in the Pacific Islands. Although President Allende's leftist government had promised the island a new hospital, in 1975 'it was the Junta who actually produced the prefabricated buildings and new equipment. A more intensive health service came with the new hospital, though the same economic restrictions still require relatives to supply the daily meals of patients'.[84] The first street was paved during the Pinochet years, and over time the number of tourists began again to rise.

Those on the island who suffered particularly during the junta years were the *continentales*, the continental Chileans, by this time a sizable proportion of the population. Historians often forget that Easter Island's history is not just that of the Rapanui people, but also that of its foreign residents, who have contributed greatly to the island.[85] Especially in the last half of the twentieth century, the *contis* began to shape the island and its society in a significant way, participating in all spheres of activity. These urban dwellers had no 'Pacific paradise' here. The cost of living was high for them too, freight services were exorbitant and irregular, and the isolation they suffered was crushing. In 1965 the Frei government had granted a 200-per-cent salary adjustment as compensation for Chileans relocating to the island – just like Russians in Siberia at the time – but the military junta in 1974 reduced this to 50 per cent. For this the *contis* had their new hospital, though, and in 1976 a television relay station for local recorded Spanish-language broadcasting. (Only few could afford a television set, however.) Nevertheless it was not until two decades later that the *contis* began to feel 'at home' on their own Isla de Pascua, when the word *pascuense* was coming to define both *rapanui* and *chileno*. A significant factor in this socio-evolutionary process was the growing number of mixed marriages, with an ever larger number of schoolchildren being of Rapanui-Chilean parentage. (Now, in the twenty-first century, these children are becoming parents in turn, and regard both heritages with equal pride.)

Even to General Pinochet himself, Chile's Isla de Pascua was something special. In 1974 he became the first president of Chile to visit the island, and he returned again in the early 1980s and yet again in 1987. Many of his ministers and police officials, too, came to the island – since it was one of the few places 'abroad' where they were allowed entry. In consequence of the junta's special regard, public funding for Easter Island increased and the island's infrastructure generally improved. Ironically, it was General Pinochet's repressive dictatorship that displayed the Republic's first real commitment to the island. For the first time in Easter Island's history, Chile became a 'friend' of the Rapanui – the near-universal sentiment at the time.

It was also during the junta years that Easter Island became the focus of the scholarly world's attention. Seminal studies were now appearing that continued the elite tradition of Métraux, Lavachery, Englert, the Norwegian Expedition, Barthel and others. Most notably, these began with American archæologist William Mulloy and his students; the Australian sociologist Grant McCall and the York-born Canadian geographer J. Douglas Porteous; and the British palæobotanist John Flenley. They were then followed, in the 1980s and '90s, by dozens of scientists and scholars from many countries – but chiefly Chile and the USA – each specializing in aspects of mainly the island's ancient culture. Soon thick dissertations and monographs were appearing on Easter Island's rock art, *ahu*, *mo'ai*, habitation sites, osteology, woodcarving, *rongorongo*, flora, fauna and many other important subjects. Easter Island had not only assumed centre stage in international scholarship: it was possible for the first time to provide tentative panoramas of the island's complete story (which includes the present book). Two generations ago, this story was still largely unknown. Only in the last half of the twentieth century was its depiction enabled, by many scholars from many countries.

Also in the 1970s the Republic offered to subsidize Rapanui (not *conti*) housing – so long as the Rapanui agreed to register formally Rapanui-held plots of land. Opponents to the scheme objected: this placed the Republic in a donor status, they claimed; yet most Rapanui still regarded themselves as the sole possessors of Easter Island's land. Many Rapanui, needing housing desperately, did agree all the same and signed. And so it was that, beginning in the late 1970s in a project that has continued to the present day, Hanga Roa saw prefabricated, asbestos-sheet (from the early 1980s), *subsidio* houses rising everywhere: subsidized residences on plots registered to individual, nuclear, Rapanui families as household units (in Chilean, not Polynesian, fashion). After this, the Rapanui also began to exchange, for cash or goods, individual parcels of these officially registered plots among themselves. As a result, one's property on the island has since come to be defined by formal title – that is, bestowed by an 'authorized' grantor – rather than by tradition-al kin relation.[86] (By the twenty-first century, relations built on kinship had mostly been replaced by those based on contract.) A much more serious con-cern, however, involves the health effects of living in such asbestos-sheet housing: it has possibly damned an entire generation of Rapanui to the risk of death by one of several lethal diseases.

The manipulative use of housing subsidies on Easter Island by General Pinochet's junta, and by all subsequent Chilean governments, has caused a succession of land-related disputes that have since overwhelmed and divided Rapanui society. 'The legal code of Chile says that only the state has title over land, but many islanders do not accept it.'[87] (In fact, it is the island's most con-tentious issue in the early twenty-first century.) Ironically, the *subsidios* that had ignited the conflict often stood empty for years at a time in the 1970s and '80s – their owners absent, working on the mainland. Many of these houses remained unfinished, because imported materials were unavailable for years on end.

Aware that only tourism could provide the island with the revenues nec-essary for improvements, the junta robustly invested here in order to secure the island's future. Annual tourist arrivals had finally exceeded 5,000. 'On this slender base a complete tourist infrastructure was built up, including a state-run hotel and a wide array of Rapanui guesthouses. French, American, and German tourists predominated, with almost half of all arrivals occurring in the 4 months December to March.'[88] By the mid-1970s hundreds of beds were available for tourist stopovers, including those in a newly constructed (not prefabricated) 20-bed hotel in Hanga Roa.

Cultural tourism appeared indeed to be the key, for – unlike agriculture, fishing and light industry – it was only here that Easter Island offered 'a unique product, the landscape itself, which no other place can duplicate.'[89] The Rapanui possess no natural resources to exchange for those consumer goods on which they had come to depend. Their sole resource would always be their island. And this just happened to contain the greatest archæology in the Pacific Islands. 'Museum Island' was actually the lifeblood of all who had to earn their living here, as everyone was now beginning to appreciate for the first time. That is, the past was Easter Island's future.

Tourism, as opposed to labour-intensive resource industries, also enables local personal advancement. Driver to vehicle owner to office manager to tour operator to hotelier and entrepreneur: many Rapanui of the 'junta gen-eration' experienced just such a career. Young Rapanui are among the most fortunate in Pacific Islands – generally a region of high unemployment and limited local career opportunities – because they need not leave their home island to prosper.

The arrival of ever more tourists also meant greater international atten-tion. Hundreds of newspaper and magazine articles, and a good number of journalistic books, in many of the world's languages, were now appearing as well, most of them generally inaccurate, superficial and invariably stressing the 'mysteries of Easter Island'. The New Age had also discovered the island, lauding its 'supernatural emanations'. UFO afficionados began identifying here those notorious vestiges of alien intrusion. Television documentary makers descended to exaggerate dark mysteries and generally ignore signifi-cant scientific discoveries.

Such attention also prompted increased cultural activity and archæologi-cal restoration, however. The underlying purpose was to enhance tourism and generate more revenue, of course. But at the same time the Rapanui were also rediscovering their own forgotten history. The cultural dedication of such local personalities as the brothers Rafael and Niko Haoa (Lachlan MacKinnon's sons), Juan Haoa, Leonardo Pakarati, Emilia Pakarati, Victoria Rapahango, Luis 'Kiko' Paté and many others – often in tandem with a strong Roman Catholic faith – helped to inspire the younger generation to take greater interest in their Rapanui heritage. In 1974 the mainly Tuki and Huke families founded the performance group 'Tu'u Hotu 'Iti', one dedicated to reviving and performing, in costume, 'traditional' Rapanui songs and dances. (Three decades later the group is still going strong.) Archæological restora-tion in the 1970s focused mainly on 'Orongo, which was in danger of ruin because of animals, tourists, quarrying and natural erosion. An interest group comprising members of the Chilean Air Force and government agencies, LAN-Chile, a large US tour operator and US private individuals funded 'Orongo's restoration, which began in July 1974. (Ever more enthusiastic support was coming from US private citizens, above all, whose financial and scholarly contributions to Easter Island would increase exponentially in the 1980s and '90s.)

In 1978 the Rapanui archæologist Sergio Rapu, who had trained under William Mulloy at the University of Wyoming, together with the Rapanui archæologist Sonia Haoa, led the restoration of *ahu* Naunau at 'Anakena, which included the re-erection of its seven *mo'ai*, four with *pukao* or 'top-knots'. (Haoa then rediscovered the *mo'ai*'s coral 'eyes', correctly identified on the spot by Leonardo Pakarati, who exclaimed: *"Aringa ora!"*) During the restoration, one of the island's leading carvers, the *korohua* Juan Haoa, effect-ed a 'face-lift' of the site's five statues that retain their heads; although it gave them a special grace and beauty, it forever altered the original features. With the 1980s, as the annual 'Semana de Rapa Nui' continued to enthrall, and especially from the 1990s when this turned into the Tāpati Festival, increasing ethnic pride has inspired the founding of several more Rapanui cultural groups, and has also fostered the revival of 'traditional' tattooing, body art and sporting activities (such as *hakape'i*, 'banana-stem sledding', and canoe racing) – all the purview of a growing number of enthusiastic young Rapanui.

Already in 1975 the junta had permitted two American military specialists to 'reactivate' the US satellite tracking station on Rano Kau. The following year, the junta had then released its own *Plan de Manejo* or 'Management Plan' to control the island's two National Parks, as well as a greater scheme to develop agriculture and local fishing in order to reduce food imports and feed more tourists. From this came the new Parque Nacional Rapa Nui. In addition, the three south-western islets were declared a nature sanctuary. But despite expert planning with this project (a second elaborate CONAF plan followed in 1997), which included various regulations, activities, programmes and particularized zones, in truth political exigency and insufficient funding have thwarted most good intentions.[90] (Ever since, the Park area has constantly altered in size, depending on 'direct relevant need'.) And all large-scale agrarian undertakings eventually halted because of the apparent advantages of cultural tourism: for a relatively modest investment here, returns have been immediate and large. As a result, since the 1980s nearly all Easter Island development plans have either served, or have been peripherally involved with, 'Museum Island's' tourist industry.

With the incursion of hundreds of *continentales* following the establishment of regular passenger flights from the mainland, there also came modern postal, radiotelephone and telegraph services. Telephones were now common in private households. (Not only were local Spanish-language radio and TV transmitters broadcasting programmes and pre-recorded videotapes to local homes, but by the late 1980s videotape players were also in common use in private households. Favourites included American action movies – the violent scenes of which were then immediately copied at the Hanga Roa school, much to the teachers' consternation.)

Resident foreigners were also making a difference on the island. Among those most dedicated to the Rapanui language and culture have been the American linguists Robert and Nancy Weber of the church-funded Summer Institute of Linguistics. Since their arrival in 1977, they have worked to translate Scripture into Modern Rapanui and to revitalize the language in various educational and publishing projects; indeed, they have selflessly dedicated their professional lives towards this end. The celebrated French oceanographer Jacques Cousteau arrived in 1978 with his son Phillipe and a film crew to make a documentary about Easter Island; it was eventually broadcast throughout the world, fascinating millions. (Phillipe Cousteau flew a gyrocopter here for the first time, and nearly died when a sudden gust of wind caused a crash; he was flown immediately to a Santiago hospital.) It was also in 1978–9 that the Rapanui had to wait eight months for a supply ship to arrive. And in 1979, in Paris, André Valenta founded a society dedicated to the study of Easter Island; in 1982 this was renamed the Cercle d'Etudes sur l'Ile de Pâques et la Polynésie, and included several highly respected French and Belgian scientists and scholars.

By 1980 the island population had finally surpassed 2,000, which included approximately 500 non-Rapanui – almost all of these *contis*. For the first time, the Rapanui people were becoming aware of the massive, permanent, foreign presence on their island. In this year the local agency of CORFO ceded its responsibilities to its filial agency, the Sociedad Agrícola y de Servicios Isla de Pascua (SASIPA). The Fundo Vaitea, the Company's old ranch in the centre of the island, was now only raising cattle and planting eucalyptus: SASIPA was proposing to generate electricity for the island by burning eucalyptus wood, but the project eventually failed. (Still today, SASIPA lands include the island's central terrain and the Pōike Peninsula.) In Valparaíso, a *hogar* or 'boarding home' was opened for Rapanui students; most were attending secondary schools there, although a small number attended university or a training college.

During General Pinochet's seventeen-year dictatorship, more criticism was permitted on Rapa Nui than elsewhere in Chile, especially from the 1980s. 'Te Mau Hatu' – the *Consejo de Ancianos* or 'Council of Elders' – was formed in the early 1980s by Alberto Hotus, who had returned to the island, after retiring from the Navy, to begin dedicating his life to advancing Rapanui civil and cultural rights. Such a group had existed on the island since the post-exodus days of the 1870s, as the *korohua* or 'elders'. But Hotus now reformed and reinvigorated the venerable institution, and has led it with passion ever since. Although not at first officially recognized by the junta authorities, Te Mau Hatu was tolerated nonetheless and, at times, even consulted. In 1983 Hotus and his fellow *korohua* wrote an open letter to the United Nations – copies of which were dispatched to President Ronald Reagan in Washington, to Pope John Paul II in Rome and to other world leaders – accusing Chile of treating the Rapanui people poorly. Although the wider world might have taken scant notice, the junta leaders were disturbed once Chile's press seized upon the story as a vehicle to criticize the regime indirectly.

Shortly after this embarrassment, in 1984 General Pinochet appointed the Chile- and US-educated archæologist Sergio Rapu as the first ethnic Rapanui governor of Easter Island. Rapu was an open supporter of the junta, which – perhaps ironically, given the circumstances – had been the only Chilean government thus far to act as the Rapanui people's 'friend'. Although Rapu openly declared himself to be 'first a Chilean, then a Rapanui',[91] he did much to further the Rapanui privilege, despite the difficult political situation. By this time a permanent cement structure fronting Policarpo Toro Avenue was serving as the *municipalidad* ('town hall') – already known simply as the 'Muni'. Horses had given way to motorbikes and more cars, and shops had started lining Hanga Roa's emerging 'high street'.

Sergio Rapu's appointment was possibly a cleverly calculated manœuvre. Underlying this superficial response to Te Mau Hatu's politically embarrassing action was perhaps the desire to satisfy further American demands. In 1984 the space agency NASA was proposing Easter Island as an emergency landing site for America's new space shuttles; the site would host a space tracking facility that could also serve military goals. 'Many people internationally were suspicious of NASA's Cold War motives and actions and saw the Chilean government's . . . eager acquiescence [as] a sign that the country was willing to trade part of their control of Rapanui for American money.'[92] Negotiations followed. In August 1985, although many on the continent were against the plan, General Pinochet finally approved it. (The Rapanui, of course, had no say in the matter.) Construction then began on extending the Mataveri runway, making it Chile's longest. But in 1986 the *Challenger* disaster abruptly disrupted NASA's elaborate design, especially in what pertained to the equipping of the site.

It was not the first ethnic Rapanui governor but another community leader who established the bureaucratic tradition that still obtains on the island today. Alfonso Rapu's brother-in-law, the Air Force-trained Samuel Cardinali (grandson of Rafael Cardinali), was appointed by the authorities – not elected – as Hanga Roa's *alcalde* in the 1980s. He went on to reorganize the municipal government as a series of distinct but interdependent offices whose overall control lay with the *alcalde* himself. The design of Hanga Roa's new Muni, architecturally enabling this distinction, reinforced physically the inspired managerial style that clearly had derived from Cardinali's Air Force experience on the mainland.

The 1980s also brought a new upsurge of ethnic pride. It was a phenomenon that was taking place not only among all Chile's native peoples, but also among most Polynesians as well – Tahitians, Hawaiians, Māori and others. The new appreciation of one's Pacific heritage and a desire to express the indigenous patrimony also raised questions of local autonomy, land ownership and reparation of past injustices nearly everywhere in the region. Such issues were enthusiastically exchanged at the quadrennial Festival of Pacific Arts held at rotating venues in the Pacific Islands, which Rapanui performance groups also began attending in the 1980s. They were heartily welcomed by their Pacific cousins. And the same indigenous pride continued to fire Te Mau Hatu, which, in 1988, published a monograph describing genealogical relationships on Easter Island and criticizing, yet again, Chile's century of neglectful rule.[93] No Rapanui had published anything of the kind before and, if anything, the action at once transformed Te Mau Hatu into a serious political contender.

In the early 1980s the Republic had instituted a 'Sons of Rapa Nui Award' for deserving Rapanui personalities in order to encourage public commitment towards common Chilean goals. Te Mau Hatu soon adopted a similar scheme. But it honoured foreigners: that is, those who might be able to herald for the Rapanui people, not for Chile, and on a much larger stage. Its award in 1986, for example, went to Thor Heyerdahl – despite the fact that Heyerdahl was still alleging that the Rapanui people had not been the creators, but the destroyers, of the island's archæological heritage. (It appears that the Rapanui never understood Heyerdahl's orientation.) Heyerdahl had first returned to the island in 1984. Later he spent three seasons carrying out excavations that were still meant to prove that the Rapanui had arrived from Polynesia to annihilate the island's indigenous South American *ahu*- and *mo'ai*-makers. By the 1980s, however, modern science had disproved the old theory to (nearly) everyone's satisfaction.[94]

Fortunately, sound scholarship continued apace. Heyerdahl had first returned to the island to attend the First International Conference on Easter Island, sponsored by the University of Chile. Since then, many such International Conferences have followed at varying venues: Frankfurt, Germany (1989, Senckenberg Museum, Deutsch-Ibero-Amerikanische Gesellschaft); Laramie, Wyoming (1993, University of Wyoming); Albuquerque, New Mexico (1997, Easter Island Foundation); Kamuela, Hawai'i (2000, Easter Island Foundation); and Reñaca, Chile (2004, Easter Island Foundation, Universidad de Valparaíso, Centro de Estudios Rapa Nui). A couple of dozen scholars came to the first. Now more than 200 attend regularly, and the Easter Island Foundation subsequently publishes the Conference papers as an encyclopædic tome that helps to chronicle and circulate the current state of knowledge about Easter Island and the Pacific.

During these years Rapa Nui's religious life also altered. Until recently, the island remained a mission parish of the southern German Capuchin Order. Since Padre Sebastian's death in 1969, however, a succession of parish priests sent from Chile – including German and US citizens – have failed to engage the Rapanui with the same passion and dedication. Many of these priests kept aloof from the Rapanui community, dedicating themselves exclusively to religious duties, and this only for an interim. The situation has not affected the Rapanui people's faith, since the Roman Catholic Church still very much comprises the community heart, helping to define the Rapanui identity by maintaining ancestral tradition. A respective parish priest's attitude does, however, affect individual commitment. The authoritative censure of a Padre Sebastian has gone forever. Still, following the international mode, younger Easter Islanders in particular are now more indifferent towards personal faith.

Also, since a more regular air service began in the early 1970s, a number of Christian and other denominations have arrived: Pentecostals, Baha'i,

Mormons (who entice with scholarships to their Hawai'i campus), Assembly of God, Jehovah's Witnesses, Seventh Day Adventists and 'Interdenominationals'. But these groups have always remained small and peripheral. Most Rapanui still perceive their Roman Catholicism as a defining feature of Rapanui ethnicity. And it is still a devout and sincere faith, too, as one finds in many parts of the Pacific Islands, especially among the elderly: very much the Western cloak on a Rapanui 'spiritual body' that, to this day, has survived fairly intact – although ancestral deities may no longer be invoked by name.

There were still some 12,000 to 14,000 sheep in the 1970s, but in November 1985 the last sheep was butchered at the Fundo Vaitea.[95] Beef production alone remained, although almost all beef and pork consumed on Easter Island would continue to come from Chile and elsewhere – shipped or flown in as frozen freight. By 1986 out of 3,009 Rapanui no fewer than 1,070 – or 37 per cent – were living either in Chile (the majority) or in fifteen other countries.[96] In seeming reciprocation of this human outflow, there was a concentrated effort to reintroduce Easter Island's unique shrub-like *Sophora toromiro* tree, which, because of human depredations and animal grazing, by the 1950s had disappeared from the island. Seed collected from the last specimen had germinated and thrived in Göteborg, Sweden, and in Bonn, Germany, and despite initial setbacks the reintroduction of the *toromiro* to the island by CONAF, in a protracted project that was keenly followed by scientists and lay persons alike, has recently shown signs of possible success.[97]

Towards the end of the 1980s foreign dedication to the island was accelerating. The archæologist Georgia Lee, who for her UCLA doctoral dissertation had already successfully completed the largest survey of Easter Island's rock art (later documented in a definitive monograph),[98] began publishing *Rapa Nui Notes* in California in 1986, a modest quarterly newsletter of only four pages. By 1987 this was eight pages and professionally printed; in 1988 it became the *Rapa Nui Journal*, now of twelve pages and with a decidedly more scholarly tone. By 2004 the 76-page biannual *Rapa Nui Journal* had become the world's leading serial publication in Easter Island scholarship and related Pacific topics. In 1987 in Belgium, the engineer François Dederen began publishing his French-language periodical *L'Echo de Rapa Nui*, which, though mostly collating photocopied articles about the island from magazines and newspapers, also offered general island news for its Francophone audience. (*L'Echo* closed with number 40 in October 1997.)

In 1986 the Republic announced that approximately 2,000 hectares of *parcelas* were to be distributed, just outside Hanga Roa, to Rapanui who would agree to farm the land. If the scheme worked, then a further 2,000 hectares would be distributed. At the same time, construction of the new Sebastian Englert Museum began just north of Tahai, as plans were also finally underway to pave all the island's major roads.

Within a year, large cruise ships were beginning to include Easter Island in their itinerary, bringing up to 2,000 visitors in a single day. Hanga Roa's school was remodelled in 1987, as was the church, and palms were being planted around the airport and village in order to enhance the island's 'Polynesian image' for the steadily growing number of tourists. In July a Japanese television documentary crew filmed on the island and, when the archæologist Toru Hayashi and the governor Sergio Rapu mentioned in their interviews that a crane would be needed to re-erect more of the island's *mo'ai*, many Japanese enthusiastically called for Japan to send a crane to the island. Although not wholly finished, the Sebastian Englert Museum was opened. In November 1987 a BBC crew arrived, led by the eminent British television producer John Lynch, to film a major documentary: it proved to be one of the finest ever made about Easter Island, viewed by millions worldwide the following year. At the end of 1987 a street market opened on Policarpo Toro, thereafter held every Saturday and Tuesday morning, and a new cement quay enabled fishermen to tie up safely at Vaihū, below where Alexander Salmon Jr's old residence had once stood.

Further changes followed in 1988. Various major projects engaged the Muni: the sewage system, improvements at the Hanga Piko wharf, rainwater drainage and continuing work on the Englert Museum. In May the World Monuments Fund declared its support to raise money for a 'William Mulloy Memorial Research Library' on the island, forming an International Executive Board of mostly American academics to pursue the project; it was led by the American art historian Joan T. Seaver, who had just completed a UCLA doctoral dissertation on Easter Island's woodcarving. By December the supply ship had still not arrived, meaning that the island had run out of butane for cooking, flour, sugar and powdered milk: restaurants and bakeries had to close as a result. (The ship finally arrived in February 1989.) The paving of Hanga Roa's streets finally began, the first project being upper Te Pito te Henua by the church, with deep rain gutters of cement being constructed on either side of the street as well.

In early 1989 the new school library was under construction, as final touches were being put to the new Englert Museum. The Mulloy Library was planned to rise alongside the museum, once sufficient funding and governmental permissions were obtained. Near the end of the year, when some 450 vehicles (150 of them motorcycles) were now registered on the island, Te Mau Hatu proposed foundations of a different sort altogether: a new legislation for the Rapanui. 'Our proposal is inspired by the recognition and the protection of the autonomy of the Rapanui people, and especially the fact that the territory of Rapa Nui is the private property of the ancestral tribes and of the present-day successors of the Rapanui people.'[99] The issue would dominate the 1990s.

In December 1989 the Easter Island Foundation (EIF) was created in California, in part out of the World Monuments Fund's William Mulloy Library Executive Board.[100] The Easter Island Committee of the World Monuments Fund had just reorganized itself as the Planning Committee for the Mulloy Library. At the same time, the EIF was established as a separate legal entity, an independent not-for-profit organization, incorporated in California, whose first president was Joan T. Seaver. The EIF's immediate purpose was to raise funds for the construction and equipping of the Mulloy Library. (As the years passed, other worthwhile projects – especially educational scholarships for deserving Rapanui students – would also occupy the EIF. In December 1991 the *Rapa Nui Journal* would become the EIF's official vehicle.) Whereupon a new decade brought new leadership, in both Chile and Rapa Nui.

THE 1990S AND BEYOND

General Pinochet's military dictatorship ended in 1990, as a result of the Christian Democrat Patricio Aylwin Azocar's victory of 1989 in multi-party elections. (In Chile's plebiscite of late 1988, voters had already rejected Pinochet's attempt to extend his presidency for another nine years.) The Isla de Pascua immediately benefitted from the new ruling Christian Democrats: President Aylwin appointed, as Governor of Easter Island, Jacobo Hey Paoa, the first Rapanui to have earned a law degree. Jacobo Hey had already been a notary at Easter Island's Court of Letters. Uncommonly mature for his young age, he would help to steer the Rapanui people through this difficult period of transition, back towards their merited majority once again.

Almost at once Alberto Hotus, President of Te Mau Hatu, was proposing to the new government in Santiago that a special district be formed for Easter Island, with proper constitutional recognition of the Rapanui people. Under such a proposal, Hotus suggested, the Isla de Pascua would be an electoral district with its own representative in Congress.[101]

The Sociedad de Amigos de Isla de Pascua that had been formed in 1948 was reactivated in Santiago in 1990, with several projects to benefit the Rapanui. Later in the year, Hanga Roa's new public library – the Biblioteca Rongorongo – was officially opened at the prominent junction of Policarpo Toro and Te Pito te Henua.

In the early 1990s it was still difficult for anyone on Easter Island to communicate with the outside world: the postal service was slow and unreliable, telephones problematic and expensive. But on 25 November 1990 hourly radio broadcasts were suddenly being sent from the island live, throughout the world, when a BBC journalist, stranded with other passengers at the Mataveri airport, had found that women and children had surrounded his

LAN-Chile jet after it had landed from Santiago, bound for Tahiti.[102] Up to 150 Rapanui 'captured' it there, blocking the runway with cars and rubble as they loudly protested against LAN-Chile's having discarded the Rapanui people's special airfare reductions, doubled their charges, curtailed their seats and limited Easter Island-bound freight. A weekend of negotiations in a picnic-like atmosphere then followed, after which the Republic offered a temporary settlement. Only one hour before a military transport plane filled with armed troops was to land, the Rapanui protestors simply melted back into Hanga Roa again. It had been the island's first major civil demonstration since emancipation 25 years earlier. (This would never have happened during the junta years.) It reflected a swelling local confidence. Tens of millions worldwide had followed the humorous story, and TV broadcasts had mentioned it in most developed nations. Having lost international prestige as a result, the Aylwin government learnt from the episode to exercise more caution and diplomacy with the Rapanui people in future. The days of callous Republic pontifications were over.

By 1991 there were 6,449 tourists visiting the island annually, many of these being cruise-ship passengers ashore for only one day. By this time, the annual Tāpati Festival, commonly held in the first week of February, was a week-long celebration of folklore dances, choral groups, costumes, body painting, sporting events (*hakape'i* sledding at Ma'unga Pu'i; a triathlon within Rano Raraku; canoe races; and more), re-enactments, a parade, a beauty contest for a 'Miss Rapa Nui', arts and crafts and much more – at times highly professional and always exciting. During the 1990s it became the highlight of Easter Island's cultural calendar, the island's annual Mardi Gras and more.

The Chilean Navy demonstrably began strengthening its presence on the island at this time, as a consequence of agitation for independence and renewed questions about the island's sovereignty. President Aylwin himself visited on 9 September 1991 to celebrate the anniversary of Chile's annexation, and announced plans to modernize the island, upgrade its infrastructure and promote greater tourism. There were new ceremonies at the Englert Museum for the Biblioteca William Mulloy on 13 October, with distinguished guests from the US in attendance, most of them from the Easter Island Foundation that was supporting the project.[103] Actual construction of the library could now begin; it would take over a decade to complete. By the end of the year, Te Pito te Henua street was still only partially paved, up by the church.

The reactivated Sociedad de Amigos was relocated in 1992 to the Fonck Museum at Viña del Mar on Chile's coast; the Fonck's dynamic young director, José Miguel Ramírez Aliaga, was now making this the main Chilean centre for Easter Island studies. The Japanese crane company Tadano agreed in this year to finance the restoration of the archæological site of Tongariki, after continuing public pressure in Japan to do something for Easter Island. Yet there was concern among international archæologists and conservationists about Tadano's plans simply to re-erect Tongariki's *mo'ai* – using one of Tadano's cranes for publicity purposes – without proper preliminary work.[104] By December the project had started, however, and many Rapanui were employed in excavation and debris-clearance. Over the following years there was an escalation of the controversy surrounding the 'unscientific' restoration at what was, after all, Polynesia's most complex archæological site. From 1992 CONAF began charging foreigners US $10 for entry into 'Orongo, valid for all other archæological locations and for multiple visits as well; the charge was (and still is) sorely needed for staff, maintenance and equipment, since the National Park, under CONAF, was desperately under-funded. These paying tourists were now arriving on 767s, LAN-Chile having finally replaced their aging 707s.

The paving of Te Pito te Henua and Policarpo Toro was progressing. Policarpo Toro Avenue in particular was now becoming the 'commercial centre' of Hanga Roa: boasting grocery stores, shops, a launderette, restaurants, snack bars and commercial offices, in addition to the twice-weekly *feria* or street market. Te Mau Hatu's president, Alberto Hotus, became Hanga Roa's first elected *alcalde* after the collapse of General Pinochet's junta (who had always appointed the island's mayor), which result at once empowered this faction of Rapanui traditionalists.

Portentously, a new Chilean naval base was rising at Hanga Piko, with eighteen prefabricated housing modules, twelve personnel, fourteen marines and a crew of four for the rescue-patrol launch *Tokerau*. When in November 1992 the Navy announced that it would also build a 12-metre-high lighthouse on the cusp of Rano Kau – just opposite 'Orongo – and then immediately began construction, street marches in Hanga Roa resulted, which attracted once more the mainland press. The media attention forced the Aylwin government to halt construction at once and to reconsider the ill-advised project. (Construction never resumed.) At the end of December 1992 Chile's Office of Customs began operations on Easter Island – up to this time the *carabineros* had handled customs – with the Rapanui Anastasia Teao, who had been professionally trained at Valparaíso, as the island's first customs official.

In 1962, 90 per cent of live births on the island had been ethnic Rapanui; in 1992, only 35 per cent.[105] That is, Rapanui ethnicity was being rapidly diluted. In response, the Rapanui people simply redefined what it meant to be a Rapanui: an overt pedigree no longer determined ethnic affiliation. For example, by this time the many descendants of the former Company manager Henry Percy Edmunds – from both his Rapanui 'wives' – were regarding themselves, and were regarded by all others in the Hanga Roa community, as full Rapanui.

One of Alberto Hotus's first, and proudest, accomplishments as new *alcalde* was the formal opening of Hanga Roa's Cultural Centre – a protracted project of Te Mau Hatu – on 8 February 1993. The Centre was envisioned as a permanent venue for traditional arts, crafts, performances and classes in Rapanui language and culture. (Within a decade it had turned into rented-out offices, however.) Especially from 1993, José Miguel Ramírez, late of the Fonck Museum and now CONAF's provincial director on the Isla de Pascua, had many of the island's archæological sites upgraded, in order both to make them more accessible and attractive to tourists, and to preserve their material integrity: with new signs and barriers, minor restorations, ornamental trees, trails, picnic areas with tables and lavatories, ranger stations, booklets and an attractive CONAF map. Special lectures helped to train local Rapanui tour guides. Still, the dearth of funding and staff was keenly felt by many.

In 1993, when some 500 vehicles were now cluttering the island's many dusty roads, Alberto Hotus proposed the founding of a new village that would accommodate the growing population and provide young people with their own land: 200 houses and a church could rise on the south coast near *ahu* Te Tenga, he declared.[106] Early in the year Chile's Minister of Housing visited the island and announced a plan to pave all the island's roads in order to reduce dust and erosion. A new market was being constructed on Policarpo Toro. The entire length of Policarpo Toro was being paved with cement bricks (far too slowly, however, because of the lack of willing labourers); Te Pito te Henua was being repaved, because the brick paving of the previous year had already started to disintegrate.

But most Rapanui were too busy to care about such ephemera. Even the annual Tāpati Festival was forgotten in 1993. For Hollywood had come to Easter Island. Although the Tongariki restoration was providing ready cash, this was less than one-tenth of what the Americans were doling out, who were involved with producing a major historical film about ancient Rapa Nui filmed entirely on the island. And so, for the movie, hundreds of Rapanui were now frantically sewing costumes, raising a traditional village south of Rano Raraku, browning bare breasts or fulfilling any number of even more questionable tasks for the American film producers and their large crew, who, not unlike the US Air Force in the late 1960s, were flooding the island with *yanqui* dollars.

During the first half of 1993 the *película* or movie – later titled *Rapa Nui*, which was produced by the actor Kevin Costner, who flew to the island in his private jet – would motivate, enthuse or enrage all those affected. Hundreds of locals were employed, though none had a speaking part. (The Americans had paid large sums to CORFO for site filming; but Santiago did not return these monies to Rapa Nui.) A carnival atmosphere intoxicated the island. The stars of the film were welcomed as if international royalty. But overall the phenomenon was a disappointment. There had been benefits: the sudden income enabled many to bring even more cars to the island or to travel overseas; old people who had been employed as extras could buy their first washing machine, cooker or television; and many young people felt a new pride in their indigenous past once they understood Rapa Nui's international marketability. Yet not only was the film later panned by critics and failed at the box office, it was withdrawn from distribution after only a few days. For Rapa Nui it had meant too much loose cash, drugs, site depredation and toxic waste. A house at 'Orongo had collapsed as a result of too much weight having been placed on its roof during filming; at Rano Raraku, a piece of statue had been broken off. (The local judge had been asked to investigate both incidents.) Many of the island's rare palm-trees had been felled – several from Hanga Roa residences – to serve as rollers and levers for scenes involving *mo'ai* transport. And, not only to the parish priest's chagrin, most young men had immediately spent their wages on alcohol.

Just as the *película* had caused general mayhem, the *ahu* restoration and *mo'ai* re-erections at Tongariki were progressing with similar controversy. A visiting Chilean professor, climbing down into a trench to view nine skulls left in situ to dry out, slipped and stepped on the cache: only one ancient Rapanui escaped pulverization.[107] Yet landmarks distinguished 1993 as well. On 17 April, for example, the Franciscan friar Francisco 'Pancho' Nahoe, OFM Conv., grandson of William T. Mulloy, was ordained a deacon in the Roman Catholic Church in a special ceremony in Rome. Father Nahoe was the first – and hitherto only – Catholic priest of ethnic Rapanui descent.

An activist group of younger Rapanui agitating for more land, local funding, cultural recognition and 'political freedom' formed in 1993 the Consejo de Ancianos 2 ('Council of Elders 2') in provocative opposition to the *alcalde* Alberto Hotus's and the *korohua*'s Te Mau Hatu (which now became Consejo de Ancianos 1). The young firebrands were also against the faction represented by the Rapanui governor, Jacobo Hey. These younger Rapanui had perceived in their elders' Te Mau Hatu a bias towards the Republic, and they took a conflicting position regarding the government's restitution of land: they wanted the land to go to individual families, not to the Rapanui community at large. Ever since, their stance has remained both anti-government and anti-Chilean and they continue to promulgate a fictional and exaggerated 'pseudo-Polynesian' privilege. Their at times aggressive and irrational actions most disturb elderly and educated Rapanui, as well as those with a respect for the island's factual past. Dismissing Te Mau Hatu's cultural priority, Consejo 2 has always focused on direct political engagement.

In this same eventful year of 1993 the Republic passed a new *Ley Indígena* ('Indigenous Peoples Law'), one that gave legal recognition to six distinct ethnic groups within Chile, including the Rapanui people of Easter Island. A

Development Fund would assist development and living conditions of these groups, and 'native' lands would be legally recognized and protected, with all indigenous cultures and languages equitably respected and supported. The Biblioteca William Mulloy opened at the Fonck Museum, Viña del Mar, too, through the auspices of the Easter Island Foundation (whose vice-president for Chile, a retired Harvard professor of astronomy, William Liller, was spearheading, directing and helping to finance the project) and the Fonck Museum (whose former director, José Miguel Ramírez, had enabled the successful negotiations). This was intended to serve not only as a holding facility until the Biblioteca moved to its permanent site at the Englert Museum on Rapa Nui, but also as a permanent Easter Island research centre in its own right.

Increasingly throughout the 1990s, scientific expeditions and projects, by many nations, intruded on the island to such a degree that many Rapanui began voicing misgivings about what they perceived – and not without certain justification – as an exploitation of their patrimony. Few scientists shared their findings, or their time, with the Rapanui people. (The infrastructure for such a sharing was missing.) Consequently, the Rapanui had little idea of the foreigners' research or of its importance for them and their place in the Pacific. Yet the very label 'Rapanui' was beginning to fade. By 1994 more than half of the residents of Easter Island had originated from mainland Chile.[108] There were now also 1,200 cars on the island, excluding motorcycles and motorbikes. A Rotary Club was established, with thirty associates, five of them women; these new Rotarians liaised with Chilean Rotarians in various community projects, such as the distribution of textbooks and videos for the Hanga Roa school.

Just as in Company days, some 200 Rapanui went on strike in June 1994 – but this time to regain ownership of their 'ancestral' lands and to have a Senator and a Congressman to represent the Rapanui people in the Chilean Parliament. For many of the younger Rapanui in particular, the Republic's incessant delays at implementation of public policy, as well as its many broken promises, had become intolerable. And the result this time, too, was yet another commission to be formed in order 'to study the land problem'.[109] Two peaceful protest marches in July, however, now organized by Te Mau Hatu and conducted with Governor Hey's permission, reinforced the message of all Rapanui: that there was general dissatisfaction with the present state of affairs on the island. The Rapanui flag – a modest red *rei miro* pectoral on a white field – was distributed and waved, and later flown proudly in the front garden of many houses.

Just before stepping down as *alcalde*, Alberto Hotus requested of the Republic a modification of Chile's new *Ley Indígena* in order to prevent foreigners who marry Rapanui from purchasing 'ancestral' lands, since there was concern about a sudden influx of *tangata hiva* or non-Rapanui on the island.[110] In consequence, the Republic did alter the *Ley Indígena* to accommodate the *Ley Pascua*, thereby creating a new law that would recognize the Rapanui people's special cultural heritage and economic needs.

By December 1994 LAN-Chile was scheduling four flights a week. Some 8,000 tourists visited the island that year, many of them still cruise-ship passengers visiting for only a few hours. The island's greatest social problems continued to be high unemployment and alcoholism, with the general impression of isolation 'caused by the lack of a promised deep water port and the monopolistic policies of the now-privatized national airline [LAN-Chile] and the Chilean government'.[111] Throughout the first half of the 1990s there had been serious supply difficulties – including running out of flour for bread and propane gas for cooking – when the supply ship failed to arrive at up to six-month intervals. *Alcalde* Alberto Hotus had put the blame for this on the *Intendente* of the Fifth Region (Valparaíso), who, he alleged, appeared to be favouring prejudicial contracts with Easter Island's official suppliers. The criticism had led to considerable tension between Hanga Roa and Valparaíso.

By 1995 LAN-Chile was 100 per cent privately owned – no longer the Republic's national airline but an entirely private firm. This had implications for Easter Island, which was again seemingly at the mercy of 'a company'. No other airline was allowed regular air service to the island; LAN-Chile held a monopoly and could do as it wished. (This still obtains today.) Everyone by this time understood that the air link had become the island's lifeblood. And so all were fearful that they could easily be victimized again, by arbitrary fare and freight-charge increases. The threat was not imagined.

The Consejo 2 now became even more politically active. Taking an extreme stand against the Republic and calling for more autonomy, indeed for a statute similar to French Polynesia's, it even opened its own private FM radio station – 'Te Re'o Rapa Nui' – which broadcast six hours a day in the Rapanui language. In its programmes, apart from island news, music and history, 'Te Re'o Rapa Nui' was demanding that the Republic suspend the *Ley Indígena* altogether on Rapa Nui. When Alberto Hotus of Te Mau Hatu (Consejo 1) tried to have the station closed down, Consejo 2 attacked Hotus verbally, alleging his election to the presidency of Te Mau Hatu had been 'illegal'. Even Hanga Roa's new *alcalde*, Petero Edmunds Paoa, entered the fray at this juncture, proposing that 'Rapa Nui be made a separate region of Chile' and suggesting that the first move should be completed towards political autonomy under the Republic.[112] A local newsletter began circulation at this time, but soon folded.

For most Rapanui, ideology always has been secondary to personal *mana* in civil politics. A candidate will commonly run for three different, and ideologically contrary, political parties in the same election, just to win a voice in local affairs. One leading island politician began as a Socialist, became a

Christian Democrat, and has subsequently turned into an Independent. For on Easter Island individual presence is paramount. A Rapanui does not 'stand for an idea' or represent a particular political orientation. A Rapanui *acts*. Politics is here not a passive posture but an active engagement.

In 1995 the Park (not SASIPA, the Republic's cattle company) lost 500 hectares of land, finally ceded in 1999, to private use. But for this, it gained other terrains – which, for lack of resources, were never incorporated into the Park, as it happened. This was the immediate result of the local authorities having initiated an action to return 'ancestral' land to the Rapanui people.[113] Although enjoying wide political support, the initiative did not have sound management. Nor did it consider the Law of National Monuments that protected the island's archæological heritage.

By this time, 10 hotels and 28 *residenciales* served Hanga Roa. Two supermarkets adorned Policarpo Toro; another had opened on a side street. There were new stores and restaurants. Charge cards were accepted by some carvers at the *mercado*, and Visa and Mastercard signs brightened store windows. The 'Tumu Kai' mall, built by the former archæologist Sergio Rapu, was a true *hipermercado* with trolleys and self-service. The ex-governor had stated that his aim in this venture was to help Easter Island become more self-sufficient in meat, eggs and other foodstuffs, because up to US $500,000 annually was leaving the island for food alone.[114] (In the 1950s the island had been almost wholly self-sufficient.)

Whereas the first commercial tourists to Easter Island in 1967 had encountered a barren, near-treeless wasteland filled with volcanic debris, by 1995 they were greeted with the sight of flowering shrubs and imported tropical trees – including many palms – that were still being planted the length of Policarpo Toro. This was increasingly giving Hanga Roa a Polynesian aspect. The paving programme within the town was still continuing, and work had begun on asphalting the road out to 'Anakena. Improvements to the Mataveri runway had also begun. Some inner streets now had proper pavements and even litter bins. Hanga Roa looked even neater and cleaner than Pape'ete, Tahiti – which it had come to resemble.

Tempers still flared at Rapanui-attended meetings about long-term plans for the island. At one of these, a fist-fight broke out and riot police charged in to evacuate the hall. Many Rapanui then went on strike again. When Chile's visiting under-secretary of the Ministry of the Interior opened another meeting, he would not allow tape recording, he cried loudly, pounding his fist on the table – and so the Rapanui shouted back at him, pounding their fists too. The meeting lasted only five minutes and the under-secretary fled back to Santiago. The strike then became protracted, just as in the old Company days, with some Rapanui now calling for all Chileans to leave the island – and within 30 days.[115] On 16 August 1995 approximately 500 Rapanui and others were suddenly marching in protest through Hanga Roa – this time not against Chile, but against France's resumed nuclear testing at Mururoa. Transcending local grievances, the Rapanui people could now equally rise to Polynesian comity.

Also in 1995, Chile's Senate Commission on Indigenous Peoples in general approved a law ensuring that ownership of Easter Island lands would remain within 'defined ethnic limits' in order to prevent non-Rapanui from obtaining ownership. This legislation was meant to deter, as Alberto Hotus and other *korohua* had feared, a sudden influx of mainlanders, and to avoid the injustices of foreign ownership, such as that, for example, that had always encumbered land transactions in Tahiti.

In 1996 many mainland workers on the island – accepting less pay than Rapanui – were still occupied with the runway project and with asphalting the 'Anakena road. Indeed, so many *contis* were now resident that it was estimated that the Rapanui people themselves made up only 30 per cent of all Easter Islanders.[116] The 16-kilometre road to 'Anakena, passing through Vaitea (the sole route through the centre of the island), was fully paved within the year. A television tower, with a satellite dish 13 metres in diameter for direct mainland transmission (to replace flown-in recorded programming), also rose near the CONAF office at the base of Rano Kau; in August, it inaugurated direct transmissions from the Chilean mainland. A new kindergarten was built, separate from the Liceo Lorenzo Baeza Vega, which itself was now being enlarged and remodelled.

At its 28th General Conference in Paris the year before, UNESCO had announced that Easter Island had been nominated for its 'List of World Heritage Sites'. Many Rapanui had been pleased by the news. Others had not, for they were reluctant to share with the rest of the world an island whose land claims had yet to be equitably settled. The new *alcalde* Petero Edmunds had seen the nomination as an attack against the island's necessary development 'by a group of people claiming to be experts'. Te Mau Hatu's Alberto Hotus had even declared that he would try to prevent UNESCO's vote from succeeding. But on 22 March 1996 Easter Island's 'World Heritage Site' designation was approved by UNESCO. (Rapa Nui was the first of Chile's possessions to receive the prestigious designation.) This obliged Chile to monitor the island's archæology, which now came under the greater supervision of 148 signatory nations. Many Rapanui immediately complained that the designation, only at first blush an honour, would restrict progress on the island: necessary construction or other works that could modify the local environment might now be prohibited.[117] UNESCO countered that the new status would enable the Rapanui to secure funds and experts for essential conservation and restoration. It ignored, however, the Rapanui's chief complaint: that the Rapanui people themselves, yet again, had not been consulted in the matter.

This led to even greater Rapanui resentment of foreign experts. In consequence, many Rapanui have begun instead to listen to alternative 'scholars',
who, though not qualified professionals, at least share their time with the
Rapanui. Exotic and factually erroneous publications, ostensibly with the
'native' imprimatur, have since proliferated. As in ethnically charged Hawai'i
and New Zealand, many Rapanui have started to claim as well that only they
have a right to tell their story – as passed down by their ancestors 'in time-
honoured tradition'. Unhappily, it is the interface of two mutually exclusive
worlds. Once modernity has been embraced there can be no compromise.
The Rapanui's 'progressive step backwards' is not irrational. For the indigenous position antecedes rationality itself. A separate 'Rapanui reality' is being
championed here, for better or worse. (The chasm between mainstream
academia and mostly younger, politically motivated Rapanui has not yet
been bridged.)

Easter Island exhibitions were now being opened at museums and galleries
across the world. Internationally celebrated Rapanui carvers such as Benedicto
Tuki Tepano and Bene Aukara Tuki were being invited to fashion *mo'ai* of
stone or wood before government buildings, institutions, private firms and art
centres from Tahiti to Washington, DC. The governor, *alcalde* and president of
Te Mau Hatu were frequently invited, in trio, to participate at international
conferences, cultural festivals and other special events featuring Easter Island.
Rapanui performance groups, among Polynesia's finest, were being flown to
New York and Tokyo. In fact, Rapanui were being invited more than any other
Polynesians: because of the 'mysterious' Easter Island, which was rapidly
becoming an international phenomenon. For the first time since the collapse
of the south-eastern Voyaging Sphere some 500 years earlier, not only were
Polynesians returning to Easter Island but Easter Islanders themselves were
experiencing the world. The interaction has since become synergistic, resulting in even more greatly accelerating cultural change on the island.

The number of tourists spending a minimum of one night had doubled
between 1990 (4,961) and 1996 (10,568). Chileans comprised the most enthusiastic visitors, during this time their numbers increasing five-fold (502 to
2,418). All Rapanui were now profiting from tourism. Some were even
becoming moderately 'wealthy': the entrepreneurs, hotel owners and travel
agents. This trend also eroded the egalitarianism that had always characterized the Hanga Roa community. Before, everyone was dirt poor. By the mid-
1990s, however, a veritable abyss separated the handful of affluent from those
still only 'making do'. Actually, far too many Rapanui were eking out an
existence, lacking regular employment. And almost everyone continued to
moonlight and / or multi-task in some way, just to get by.

Sea tragedies still occurred. The 32-metre cargo ship *Praga*, carrying goods
to Easter Island, sank just 90 kilometres west of Valparaíso on 13 September

1996. Only five of the crew of eight were rescued.[118] And monuments continued to suffer, too. A serious fire that started within Rano Raraku's crater and slightly damaged 46 *mo'ai* there in December 1996 led to immediate calls for increased funding to protect, above all, the vulnerable *mo'ai*. (The single ranger who had been on duty there that day had had to walk to Hanga Roa to fetch help, since he had no vehicle, much less a walkie-talkie or telephone.) By now all fifteen of Tongariki's huge *mo'ai* were standing again atop the *ahu*, the largest salvage and reconstruction project carried out anywhere in Polynesia. But work was still continuing on both wings, and the *pukao* or 'topknots' had yet to be placed on the giant statues' heads.[119] In November 1996 King Juan Carlos and Queen Sofía of Spain, travelling together with President and Mrs Frei of Chile, visited Easter Island briefly. In the same month, the Czech president Václav Havel also came to the island, fulfilling a childhood dream.

In late 1996 the Frei government agreed to return approximately 1,500 hectares of land to the Rapanui people from CORFO (the former Brander / Bornier holdings). It was to be the beginning of the island's return to rural farms – a process that, once started, could not be halted. And it led to immediate conflict, as does anything relating to land on Easter Island. Contrary to Chilean law, no environmental impact study had preceded this action, as one official pointed out. (No study had preceded the redefinition of the Rapa Nui National Park, or the road-paving project within Park lands, either.) In 1997 the provincial governor in Valparaíso at last created an *ad hoc* commission to collaborate with the Office of Lands to determine distributable parcels on Rapa Nui: out of 500 Rapanui applicants, only 267 were to be given lands because of the insufficient amount of terrain made available.[120] But a conflict of interest arose between the general manager of SASIPA and CONAF's provincial director, who was also the administrator of the National Park. Distribution was then further delayed by Rapanui critics and by the aggressive intercession of Consejo 2.

So some disgruntled Rapanui simply started to seize land for themselves, not even waiting for an official distribution they felt would be inherently 'unfair' anyway. Alejandro Rapu, for one, claimed that the popular archæological site Ahu Huri 'a Ū Renga ('The Toppled *Ahu* of Ū Renga') – restored by William Mulloy and Sergio Rapu in 1972 with one re-erected *mo'ai* – was 'traditional' family land, and he closed off access to the site. He even frightened away visitors with a speargun. Rapu alleged that his family was 'supposed' to have received another parcel as compensation for this land. The matter was never properly settled.

In September 1997 Japan's Imperial Prince Naruhito and Princess Masako visited the island for three days as part of an official tour of Chile. (Over many years the Japanese, who have always been particularly fascinated by Easter Island, have contributed generously to cultural and restoration projects there.) And in November, the New Zealander Sir Edmund Hillary also came to the island for a brief visit. Even Concorde came roaring in with an around-the-world 'boutique tour', spending 24 hours on Easter Island. By this time, about a third of the ethnic Rapanui population was living off the island permanently: most of them in Chile, the rest in Tahiti, the US and various other countries.[121]

In November and December 1997 things came to a head between Te Mau Hatu and Consejo 2, who now numbered about 60, when the latter began illegally occupying land and charging foreign archæologists and filmmakers their own designated 'culture tax'.[122] When two members of Consejo 2 even blocked 'Orongo's entrance to charge tourists a fee there as well, they were arrested. Governor Hey denied that any 'subversive organization' existed, as many were alleging, but conceded that family divisions on the island had created groups with conflicting interests. Like Te Mau Hatu, the Muni also denounced the actions of Consejo 2.

Actually, more Rapanui were following Chile's national television station TVN. This was producing a soap opera on the island, starting in November 1997 and continuing into 1998. For many, '*Iorana*, Bienvenido al Amor' ("*Iorana*, Welcome to Love') was *the* event of 1998: the heart-wrenching saga of a female archæologist from the mainland who comes to the Isla de Pascua and, while excavating there, meets the love of her life. Typically, few Rapanui had any part in the production. Chilean contract actors were used, and much of the soap was filmed in a Santiago studio.

In January 1998 filming on the island was disturbed yet again by Consejo 2, which had resumed demanding payment of its 'culture tax'.[123] Alberto Hotus of Te Mau Hatu called them a 'terrorist group' and challenged their right to call themselves a 'Consejo de Ancianos' at all. Valparaíso's Court of Appeals eventually ruled against Consejo 2, ordering detention for its six leaders. About 100 Rapanui then protested outside Governor Hey's office at the Muni, and after complicated negotiations bail was granted to Consejo 2's leaders on 5 February, but only after an arsonist had set fire to the SASIPA offices the night before. The protestors were a small minority, mostly young Rapanui from families not linked to Te Mau Hatu, which still comprised the island's *korohua* or traditional elders. The regional councillor José Letelier of Valparaíso, who represented Easter Island, brusquely criticized Governor Hey's 'negligence' and pointed out that on Easter Island one segment of the population wished land distribution to proceed according to community farming requirements, whereas another was demanding rapid distribution of land plots to effect a sharing of economic power: the issue was seemingly tearing the island apart. In July a group of Rapanui, including ex-Governor Sergio Rapu and other directors and members of Consejo 2, announced that they would formally ask President Frei to create an autonomous region for the Isla de Pascua, one that would be politically separate from the Fifth Region of Valparaíso.[124]

By this time, the approximately 1,300 cars on the island could navigate most of Hanga Roa's streets on cement brick and asphalt, while plans were being made to asphalt the south-coast route all the way to Rano Raraku. No restrictions had encumbered car imports, and so traffic jams had become a part of everyday life in Hanga Roa. The Internet was made accessible to Easter Island residents in 1998, meaning that e-mail could instantly link each computerized household to the rest of the world. Rapa Nui had joined the global *barrio*.

In October 1998 the name of Hanga Roa's main street, Policarpo Toro, was changed to 'Atamu Tekena' after that nineteenth-century Rapanui hero, the sscc-appointed *'ariki* Atamu te Kena ('Adam the Gannet'), who was now portentously recast as the island's first 'freedom fighter'. Significantly, it was the *municipalidad* itself that had instigated the change, in order better to reflect the island's preferred cultural orientation, away from Chile and towards Polynesia. By this time, the three local FM radio stations had ceased transmission, including the one in the Rapanui language. The Navy was considering, however, the revival of its Spanish-language Radio Vaikava.

Throughout the 1980s and '90s there had been an active campaign to reintroduce Easter Island's extinct *toromiro* tree, with mixed results. In 1998 the Chilean Air Force brought 400 Chilean wine palms (the *Jubæa chilensis*, at up to 20 metres one of the world's largest, and perhaps Easter Island's original, palms), which agricultural experts began to plant at a new botanic garden at Vaitea. No Rapanui had been informed of the project, and the trees were planted on the island's best grazing land – while cattle still grazed among the *ahu*, petroglyph sites and toppled *mo'ai*. Many Rapanui were angered by the unilateral action.

In 1999 Consejo 2 (now enjoying increasing popular support) and CONAF were working together to re-raise *pircas* or stone walls in many areas: not to control livestock, as in Company days, but to protect vulnerable archæological sites from vehicular intrusion. It was announced that a new high school would be built on the site of the old leprosery north of Hanga Roa; the present high school would then be vacating its premises at the 'Liceo Lorenzo Baeza Vega', leaving this a primary and middle school only.

On 26 March 1999, 20 members of Consejo 2 occupied the offices of the Muni, protesting against an election organized by the National Commission of Indigenous Development: they were demanding a 'more democratic election' for the presidency of Te Mau Hatu, by secret ballot.[125] Six days later, ten protestors burnt the electoral registry; there were no arrests. On 7 April Alberto Hotus was ratified in the election as continuing president of Te Mau Hatu, and he would also serve in this capacity on the new Development Commission of Isla de Pascua. This is a unit of the Island

Assembly, as provided by Chile's *Ley Indígena*. It has fourteen members: the governor, *alcalde*, six representatives of government institutions and six ethnic Rapanui (one of whom must be the president of Te Mau Hatu). The Commission's brief is land development and economic, social and cultural programming, in collaboration with CONAF (Rapa Nui National Park) and the National Council of Monuments.

During this year municipal funds were not being made available by the Republic in sufficient amounts – only a little over half of what was needed was forthcoming. Since municipal workers in Chile are legally obliged to work whether their salary is paid or not, many felt as if they were working for the old Company and they voiced their displeasure. The *alcalde* Petero Edmunds even threatened to 'quit being a gentleman' and to take direct action against the Republic, closing down the Muni. Whereupon Santiago promised to make emergency funds available, since Rapa Nui had no local resources of its own.[126]

Also in this year, another 1,000 hectares of Park were lost to the parcelling out of land to Rapanui families. Private land ownership was expanding rural settlement onto protected sites, at the expense of Park territory (not the government's SASIPA cattle farm). In all, 267 Rapanui would finally receive their 1,500 hectares of Park land, since the earlier 500 hectares were also transferred at last in August 1999. One month later, new lands were announced for inscription. And two months after this, 250 hectares of Park were formally separated by the Office of Lands for distribution to more than 800 applicants. Since 1998, more than 10 hectares had been bulldozed flat for development – without an archæological survey or environmental impact report.[127]

All Rapanui celebrated the arrival of the traditional Hawaiian double-hulled voyaging canoe *Hōkūle'a* that landed at Easter Island on 9 October 1999 after a voyage of nearly 6,000 nautical miles (covering a distance of some 4,200 nautical miles). For the first time in many centuries, the Rapanui were now 'reconnected' to their ancestral Polynesian roots physically, and the reality of this affected all Rapanui profoundly, despite their greatly diluted pedigree. The *Hōkūle'a* arrived off Cook's Bay via the Marquesas, Mangareva and Pitcairn – that is, intentionally tracing the ancient route of the original South-east Polynesian settlers of Easter Island.

The *Hōkūle'a* called at a time when the Rapanui's main concern was land distribution and its cumulative impact on the environment, cultural heritage and the National Park's sustainable management. A resolution to this effect, calling upon the aid and support of the visiting Hawaiians of the *Hōkūle'a* 'to protect the island, and to restore its forests, marine wildlife and seabird colonies', was duly signed by various representatives of local institutions. It even resulted in considerable coverage in the mainland press. When José Miguel Ramírez, CONAF's provincial director since 1993, used this unique opportunity to protest against the Republic's taking National Park lands –

rather than SASIPA cattle lands or other terrains – to distribute to Rapanui families, he was immediately relieved of his duties.[128] Soon, the Development Commission of Isla de Pascua was requesting a further 1,000 hectares for private farming – to be taken again from the Rapa Nui National Park.

In 1999 the American-Rapanui Franciscan priest Francisco Nahoe and the Australian sociologist Grant McCall estimated that there were now more than 4,000 ethnic Rapanui in the world: 3,000 on the island, 700 in continental Chile, 300 in French Polynesia, 50 in the USA and a few more in Europe, New Zealand and elsewhere. (One Rapanui had been living in Israel for more than 25 years.)[129] On the island itself, there had been no fewer than 21,434 tourists (up from 4,961 in 1990): 8,517 from Europe (mostly Germans and French), 7,352 from South America (6,248 Chileans), 2,460 North Americans (mostly US), 1,588 from Oceania (mostly Australians, New Zealanders and Tahitians) and 1,513 from Asia.[130] By this time, the island could 'boast' 1,400 cars, 60 taxis, and 46 hotels and *residenciales*. Easter Island also enjoyed the highest proportion of tourists to residents in all of Polynesia. As to per capita income from tourism, in all the Pacific Islands it ranked second. By now, four planes a week were arriving from Santiago, with two additional planes a week in summer months. Three came each week from Tahiti. Nonetheless, the tallest structure on the island still remained Mataveri International Airport's control tower.

For the millennium celebration on 31 December 1999, Tahai's row of giant floodlit *mo'ai* featured prominently on Chile's TVN. This was then sourced by the BBC in London for global broadcasting. It was the first live television broadcast from Easter Island to be seen throughout the world: costumed Rapanui dancers performing in front of their ancestors' 'living faces'. America's *Time* magazine also included a Rapa Nui page in its special millennium issue of 1 January 2000.[131]

Despite the auspicious inauguration of a new millennium, the troubles continued. Anti-Chilean sentiment on the island climaxed in 2000 – with some Rapanui threatening to 'seize back the island from Chile' – when the Republic hesitated in explaining the fraudulent transfer of land titles to non-Rapanui entrepreneurs.[132] It appears that, for a fee, certain unscrupulous Rapanui had allowed their names to be used on titles. The *alcalde* Petero Edmunds featured in a headline quote in *El Mercurio de Valparaíso*: 'We Want the Island to Pass into the Hands of the Islanders'. The article detailed Edmunds's wish for autonomy for the Isla de Pascua; the Rapanui people simply wanted rights over their own land, which, he explained, they should be administering for themselves.[133] The *intendente* for the Fifth Region, Josefina Bilbao, responded publicly to this the next day, labelling Edmunds's position 'infantile' and suggesting that electoral motives lay behind his declaration. Easter Island's newly appointed governor, Enrique Pakarati Ika (great-grandson of the nineteenth-century French-trained catechist Nicolas

Pakarati Ure Pō Tahi), stated: 'I do not share [Edmunds's] opinions at all. He tends to magnify things'.[134] But the regional councillor representing Easter Island, José Letelier, declared that he supported the *alcalde*'s remarks totally. 'However, the island has the autonomy that it needs, and the municipality is autonomous by definition. Another matter is that the mayor does not know how to use that autonomy.'[135]

From 2000 up to the writing of this book in 2003 and 2004, Park lands have continued to be distributed to ethnic Rapanui for farming. Park land is, however, virtually useless for farming; the cattle land is farmland, but cattle land is still monopolized by the Republic's SASIPA, which sends the few cattle to the mainland (local beef is not consumed on Rapa Nui). The Republic promises protection of the island's archæological heritage, as it is obligated to do with Easter Island now a World Heritage Site; but the Rapa Nui National Park, within which many, but not all, archæological sites are located, is still not protected. Numerous Rapanui, local Chileans, mainland Chileans and other interested parties find this an unacceptable situation.

In 2000 in the corner park where Te Pito te Henua and Atamu Tekena (formerly Policarpo Toro) cross, a second bust atop a high white pedestal now stood alongside Policarpo Toro's: that of Atamu te Kena, who had become the new symbol of Rapa Nui autonomy (or, for some, independence). Inland areas south of Vaitea and north of Vaihū were being bulldozed clear, still without archæological surveys or environmental impact reports. Unpaved roads divided the new tracts into square parcels, each enclosed with barbed-wire fences – ostensibly for planting as private farms. Many locals were alarmed by this sudden exploitation of their limited natural resources. Speaking for many, Nicolás Haoa Cardinali pointed out: 'Tourists do not travel here to see cattle, high-rise buildings, or shacks on the sites. Having a plan for the future will create a better future for all . . . Such measures will ensure that this island remains a destination of value and importance as a World Heritage site, unique in the world.'[136]

From the Catholic Church's electronic campanile to the new computer shop, Easter Island already stood firmly in the twenty-first century. Hanga Roa was becoming increasingly indistinguishable from most mainland towns in Chile. There were more than 1,500 houses on the island now, most of them inhabited by a single couple or even a single person.[137] (Large Rapanui households are now a thing of the past.) Perhaps as many as 800 asbestos-sheet subsidized prefabs were standing by this time, with some 40 still being constructed each year. More and more *pa'epa'e* or 'little houses', private shacks without electricity or plumbing, were being raised within the National Park and also on archæological sites. In 2001 most of these shacks were bulldozed by the Development Commission, after Governor Pakarati, denouncing as illegal such constructions on the lands of others, had resolved to take a firm stand.

Hardly any Rapanui yet earns wages from another Rapanui, although tourism has been slowly creating this new relationship. Wage labour is still government labour on Easter Island, making almost three-quarters of everyone on the island – Rapanui and *conti* alike – dependent on the Republic, or on someone who works for the Republic, for their existence: paving roads, maintaining government vehicles, managing small offices or herding cattle at Pōike. The barter economy, traces of which still existed in the early 1990s, was wholly gone by the early 2000s, with the money economy dictating all daily life. As nearly all Rapanui families have a regular income now, the traditional Polynesian extended family has disintegrated and the Western-style nuclear family has taken its place. Nevertheless, as the geographer J. Douglas Porteous already pointed out in the 1980s, 'the island's small population, meaning most are related to one another in some fashion, has braked this trend and encouraged more egalitarianism and sharing than elsewhere would be the case'.[138] All the same, the Chilean middle-class ideal – which mirrors European and North American models – is targeted by nearly all Rapanui and *conti* on the island: who seek to maintain regular employment, send their children to higher education, own at least one car, travel regularly abroad and furnish their growing premises with colour television, computer, microwave, lounge suite, tiled floors, hot-water unit, telephone and so forth – just like any other family in the First World. Rafael Hereveri's current bilingual (Spanish and Rapanui) morning FM radio programme entertains with Rapanui songs, Tahitian tunes, US country-and-western fare, together with public announcements and humorous comments and anecdotes reinforcing the new foreign ideal. The Wall is not merely down. It is wholly forgotten.

Physical and social erosion has been the price. When sand was extracted from the beaches to mix with cement in construction, entire lengths of shoreline were washed away. Bulldozing tracks of land for farming has razed irreplaceable archæological sites, the island's economic lifeblood. In search of further education, training and employment, and to fulfil those new demands that the local economy cannot always satisfy, like Polynesians throughout the Pacific Islands many young Rapanui have left their island for good, cutting off its human lifeblood. Chile's modern infrastructure has brought in an entire generation of *contis* to maintain public sector operations,[139] diluting the Polynesian heritage even further.

Yet life continues, and at a giddy rate of change. Despite relative tourist numbers, due to the island's isolation tourism still remains small: it costs too much for most tourists to travel to Easter Island. Tourist growth is actually still slower here than on mainland Chile. Apart from those visitors from cruise ships, all tourists have to fly to Easter Island, and LAN-Chile maintains its monopoly. Now, fewer than 10 per cent of visitors originate from Europe or North America. Most are Chileans, but ever larger numbers are coming from other South American countries as well, and Tahiti, Hawai'i, Japan, Australia and New Zealand.[140] Accommodation on the island (with the exception of the Hotel Hanga Roa) is still owned exclusively by Rapanui; the *Ley Pascua* prevents potential development by foreign investors. Yet everything for tourism – except for eggs, vegetables and most fruit – must be imported, including all building materials and vehicles. Although supply ships now arrive off Hanga Roa approximately five times a year (there has been no lengthy interruption of supplies for years now), there is still no deep-water port, meaning that all goods have to be offloaded onto launches that then land at the Hanga Piko wharf complex. Importation makes everything expensive on Easter Island, which in turn discourages many tourists from coming.

On 23 April 2002 the official result of the first census to be taken in ten years revealed Easter Island's population to be 3,837 (a 38.8 per cent increase since the 2,764 of 1992).[141] And on 19 October of that year the Biblioteca William Mulloy was officially opened at last, alongside the Museo Antropológico P. Sebastian Englert (MAPSE). Attending the ceremony, hosted by the gifted director of MAPSE, Francisco Torres, was Mulloy's widow Emily Ross Mulloy – herself a recognized scholar of Rapanui culture – together with family members. An ongoing project since the late 1980s, the Biblioteca was supported by a founding grant from the Easter Island Foundation and the Fundación Andes, and by Chile's National Administration of Libraries, Archives and Museums. A state-of-the-art research facility with full electronic support systems, it is the island's new centre for Easter Island studies.

By the end of 2002 both of *ahu* Tongariki's wings had been fully restored. The site now appears very much as it would have done back in the fifteenth century. Comprising one of the most splendid archæological centres – a museum of monolithic magnificence – anywhere in Pacific Islands, Tongariki alone would justify a visit to Easter Island.

By 2004 all of the island's major roads except that of the eastern coast had been asphalted, and the project was continuing apace for the remaining touristic, secondary and Hanga Roa roads. (A new road that would include the northern route – from Te Peu around the coast behind Terevaka all the way to 'Anakena – is still in discussion.) The Muni now runs its own 'Educational, Radio and Television Corporation', which administers the television station Te Mata o Rapanui, the Liceo, the Tāpati Festival and the FM Manukena Radio. Two other FM stations are the Navy's Vaikava and the private Chilean Polynesia Radio (entirely in Spanish). Local cultural groups – such as Kari-Kari, Ngā Pōki, Polinesia, Matato'a and Topatangi – are not only performing at the annual Tāpati and even overseas, but are now recording CDs that earn tourist dollars and feature prominently in local radio programming. (All the above-named groups are among Polynesia's best.) Other culturally oriented organizations that are currently active are the Junta de

Vecimos (established in 1959), the tourism operators' own AGET (1990) and Amanecer el Rapanui (2001). The influential Kahukahu o Hera organization concerns itself with the Rapanui language, traditional sports and culturally significant plants. The international not-for-profit Easter Island Foundation, based in Los Osos, California, continues to publish the biannual *Rapa Nui Journal* and scholarly books about Easter Island and Polynesia, to award educational scholarships and support professional research about Easter Island and other isles of the Pacific, among several further worthwhile programmes.

One of the *municipalidad*'s more recent innovative schemes includes the possible construction, north of Hanga Roa near where the new Hanga Roa high school is currently rising, of an entire Educational Village 'to include and coordinate existing activities and promote local identity and development' in education, science and culture.[142] At the time of writing, the European Community had just approved the installation at Easter Island of a centre for biological sciences – similar to UNESCO's programme on Tahiti – with a recurrent annual investment of more than US $1 million.[143]

And so it goes on. In early 2004, visiting the island once more before completing this book, I found the Muni complex being entirely rebuilt in cement, with an attractive red-scoria cladding. The Tāpati Festival was a great success, again held by the Rapanui for the Rapanui at what has become its 'traditional' site only recently: a temporarily erected stage and booth complex at Hanga Varevare between the *caleta* and the cemetery. One of the world's foremost experts on conserving the stone of the *mo'ai*, Professor Masaaki Sawada, financed by Japan and encharged by UNESCO, was leading a team that was busy conserving Tongariki's statues with a special chemical to halt their rapid deterioration. Suddenly, aggressive members of Consejo 2 threatened him and his workers. When the *alcalde* Petero Edmunds sided with Consejo 2 in the matter and ordered that all work at Tongariki be halted, a frantic correspondence ensued between Tokyo and Santiago. (Significantly, Santiago told Tokyo that this was wholly a Rapanui affair: a devolution of competences that would have been unimaginable only a decade ago.) Two weeks later, however, the *alcalde* decided to allow UNESCO's conservation work to resume. The new governor, Enrique Pakarati, was, as ever, still trying to cope with the challenge of balancing the fragile inheritance of the past with the robust demands of the future. Rivalry and patronage continue to burden especially the ethnic Rapanui, who now comprise only half the resident population – but who wield nearly all immediate authority.

AN EGG IN THE HAND

In olden days the *tangata hōnui*'s champion struggled up 'Orongo's sheer cliff to hand his leader the first-discovered egg of the sooty tern from Motu Nui.

With this symbol of 'ao, of temporal power, in hand, the new Birdman could steer, for better or worse, Rapa Nui's destiny with impunity. Who holds the precious egg now?

The question is anything but romantic, but coldly obligatory at this juncture. For no history has an end. There must first be a stocktaking, to understand what has been learnt. And then another run must open, to continue the flow. At the time of writing, Easter Island is once more enacting – despite relative affluence, mobility and such personal freedoms as never before enjoyed – a particularly violent 'egg contest'. Many factions oppose one another with contrary plans, values, goals and visions. Chilean nationalists challenge Rapanui traditionalists. Rapanui traditionalists challenge Rapanui entrepreneurs. Each faction professes to be holding the egg. And the opposing demands on both the governor and *alcalde* are almost insupportable.

Who would want the 'ao? one might well ask. For among current island problems are poor health facilities, inadequate educational services, growing crime, overgrazing, soil erosion, uncontrolled and unplanned land distribution and agricultural production, lack of urban planning, poor waste and noxious-substance management, overgrowth of shrubs and grasses, noxious species and unwanted rodents and insects (rats, cockroaches, mosquitos), over-fishing, uncontrolled car importing and serious social division. The economy is linked to a single revenue – cultural tourism – that is fickle and capricious. When gross national product is considered, French Polynesians are three times richer than Rapanui.[144] There is no local press, no local newspapers or magazines. Most local knowledge comes by word of mouth, by gossip and rumour. And the general feeling of the Rapanui people today is that the Republic of Chile still does not really care about them or their island.

In the 1980s and '90s successive Chilean commissions on Easter Island were created, which then, one and all, promised to do this and that, often announced by visiting dignitaries from Santiago or Valparaíso. In the end, little, if anything, was done at all; and what was implemented was invariably under-resourced and under-staffed. Many knowledgeable individuals share the belief that Chile 'will continue to be troubled by its "uncertain sovereignty" over Rapanui until it changes the way that it has related to the place since 1888'.[145] Chileans are dissatisfied with their Isla de Pascua. Rapanui are dissatisfied with Chile. Both peoples need, and want, a solution that is satisfactory to both sides. It is the single greatest issue hanging over the island at the beginning of the twenty-first century.

'The Chilean government did not know what to do with Rapanui at the end of the 19th century and scarcely has come to any conclusion about what to do with it at the close of this one', wrote the sociologist Grant McCall back in 1995.[146] That vision for the island is still missing a decade later. One problem is Easter Island's 'novelty'. It is only since 1967 that Rapa Nui has been 'opened up to the world through the activities of tourists, scholars, filmmakers, expeditionaries, and the efforts of the islanders themselves'.[147] Viewing the island from Santiago's eyes, it has largely lost all value as a productive asset – a viable cattle ranch – and can only assume status 'as a modest tourist destination and a strategic base for communications and defense'. The Rapanui still pay no taxes. All improvements on the island are either private, municipal or state. Thus everything is highly subsidized, which imposes a financial strain on the Republic, with few visible returns for its investment. Chile spends millions of dollars a year on Easter Island; still, there is never enough funding to accomplish what is needed. The island remains chronically under-resourced and under-staffed.

The single most important investment for the island in the twenty-first century will be the building of a deep-water port to supersede the current Hanga Piko wharf complex. The main potential site that has been in discussion for the past decade – Hanga Ho'onu (formerly Hanga 'o Honu or 'Bay of Turtles', La Pérouse Bay) – is, as everyone agrees, culturally and ecologically too sensitive. But two reasonable alternatives remain. The Republic could improve and enlarge the Hanga Piko cove, rendering it a true port. Or it could construct a wholly new port at Papa Haoa in southern Cook's Bay, which would be an expensive undertaking (estimates range between US $70 and $90 million, if begun now). The decision must be made by someone – and it must be made soon.

For Easter Island's population is exploding. Continuing an earlier trend, there was a doubling of the island's population from 1960 (1,134) to 1980 (c.2,000), and another doubling of the population from 1980 to 2004 (c.4,000, with great mobility). If this trend continues, then some 8,000 Rapanui, contis and foreigners will be living on Easter Island by 2024. It reflects a healthy natural increase, as well as accelerating immigration. Higher growth rates are checked by frequent emigration and by increased mobility, with the concept of a 'permanent resident' slowly becoming an anachronism. One thing is certain: in coming years mainland Chilean immigration will increase even more.

Of course, this raises the issue of 'identity'. For that is what the egg – the 'ao, that temporal power that drives and defines the island – is all about. On present-day Easter Island there are four relevant identities that make up what it means to be an 'Easter Islander': *cultural* identity, *economic* identity, *proprietary* identity and *political* identity.

Cultural identity immediately comes to the fore when one hears of vandalism and site desecrations. Human bones are stolen. Ancient artefacts are sold to tourists. Tourists themselves trample on fragile sites that remain without fences or ropes. (Only four sites presently enjoy 'permanent' Park Rangers, with limited hours: 'Orongo, Rano Raraku, Tahai and 'Anakena.) Land development is destroying many archæological sites, and there is continued erosion. Funds are too limited even to maintain the status quo – while the Rapanui try to entice even more tourists to come to see what is rapidly disappearing. The modern Tāpati Festival is now an electronically amplified and illuminated disco-like extravaganza, regretted by some who perceive here a loss of dignity, but embraced by others as a dynamic reinvention of the Rapanui future. At the same time, individual avarice and virulent consumerism are undermining social cohesion. The Church no longer maintains its earlier role of community regulator in the island's increasingly modern, materialistic society. Nuclear families chiefly seek enrichment, and so communal dedication erodes as steadily as the *campo*'s topsoil.

Although it is impossible that there is a single Islander alive today of exclusively Rapanui ancestry, the Rapanui people still hold on to a perceived 'cultural identity'. In the face of the accelerating foreign-inspired changes, many Rapanui have responded by seeking out, and flaunting, what they understand to be their true cultural selves, emphasizing language, cultural revival and 'traditional' Rapanui values. Language is particularly important in this regard. From the 1980s the reassertion of the Rapanui prerogative weakened the value of Spanish and enhanced the value of Rapanui, even in formal contexts (where Rapanui had not been allowed). 'The situation has raised awareness of the value of their language as a symbol of distinctive group identity, and therefore as a tool of resistance against the Chilean state's political, economic, and cultural control.'[148] It has also linked the Rapanui to ancestral origins, particularly to Tahitians, Hawaiians and Māori. Tourists acknowledge, and appreciate, the Rapanui-language orientation: after all, they come to the island to see Polynesia, not Chile. This, in turn, reinforces the cultural identity, and is a source of great local pride. The Rapanui language has taken on a new significance in island society. 'The increased symbolic importance is reflected in an emerging practice among the Rapanui of speaking only Rapanui, making efforts to avoid mixing Spanish in their Rapanui speech, especially among the cultural and political leaders in the community.'[149]

Yet what is 'Rapanui' ethnicity? By the twenty-first century the massive foreign presence – at any given time, nearly half the people on the island are non-Rapanui – is no longer perceived as 'foreign' at all, but a commonplace. The island is gravitating towards shared indigenousness, a normal transition within the colonialization process witnessed throughout Pacific Islands, but especially in Hawai'i and New Zealand. Both ethnicities mutually assimilate: here, the Chileans become more Rapanui as the Rapanui become more Chilean. Perhaps the greatest socio-psychological change of the last two decades has been the near-total assimilation of the *contis*, the Chilean mainlanders. Earlier envied, suspected, even resented, they are now more commonly colleague, friend, even spouse. For the first time, many *contis* are finally learning to speak Rapanui, to enjoy 'traditional' island customs, even to join some of the Rapanui performance troupes.

Some might argue, in the light of the above, that today's Rapanui do not belong to the same cultural continuity as the carvers and movers of the *mo'ai*: that that culture and people disappeared forever in the 1860s and '70s. But they do share the same genes, physical traits, language (albeit greatly altered) and sense of 'belonging'. As we have seen, Easter Island's was always a culture of change. Even those who perished in the labour raids of 1862–3 had little in common superficially with the *mo'ai*-carving Rapanui of 400 years earlier. The 'cultural continuity' binding all Rapanui is the indigenous transformation itself. Easter Island's small population in extreme isolation has always maintained a distinct ethnic identity, no matter how much dilution and intrusion have occurred over the centuries. Whether the Rapanui will be able to preserve a distinct cultural identity within the accelerating process of globalization is another matter. It is to be wished that something 'identifiably Rapanui' – perhaps multicultural, mobile, affluent, yet distinctly Polynesian – will prevail in the course of this century.

Old Rapanui society still continues today traditionally – if by 'tradition' we mean 'the contemporary interpretation of the past'.[150] Little has been passed along directly, of course, but a great ethnic revival has occurred from paintings, sketches, Western transcriptions of old chants and songs, travellers' and scholars' accounts and studies – and with much recent borrowing, in particular from Tahiti, Hawai'i and New Zealand. Many younger Rapanui consider the issue of the 'authenticity' of their cultural activities to be superfluous: if a Rapanui does it, it is 'Rapanui tradition'.[151] This is a valid stance, for the act or product itself is a symbol of the collective Rapanui identity, perceived to be the same by all who share local pride. It is the vision that once empowered the erectors of the colossus *Ko te Riku* at Tahai. It still defines what it means to be an Easter Islander.

In view of the rapidly diluting Rapanui pedigree, such an attitude is, in fact, essential. Perhaps the most dramatic change in Rapanui life has been the increase of foreign spouses: most Rapanui now opt for non-Rapanui as their partners (mostly Chileans, but also North Americans and Europeans).[152] This has never happened before, and it spells the end of 'Rapanui' as an ethnic label. All are Easter Islanders, *pascuenses*, which is a geographical distinction – just as one sees with the ethnic displacements of Hawai'i and New Zealand, the two other vertices of the Polynesian Triangle. Many island children are growing up bicultural and bilingual (some even trilingual, as English is now common). This is slowly creating the 'New Easter Islander' – someone who lives on the island, despite her or his background, and shares the locale's special experience for a protracted length of time, usually involving marriage and children. Many Rapanui, however, resent this term and what it stands for, insisting on a blood pedigree that is contradicted by their own genes.

All the same, 'true' ethnicity is now a questionable classification basis nearly everywhere in the Pacific.[153] The brown, indigenous, uni-insular Pacific Islander is an anachronism. Demographic heterogeneity now characterizes much of the Pacific Islands, with multiple ethnicities defying traditional categorizations. The islands are currently uniting all indigenous (and acculturated) Islanders in a way not seen in the Pacific since the great voyaging spheres of the Middle Ages. Indeed, the phenomenon is so widespread that it has been labelled 'contemporary voyaging'.[154] The indigenous and non-indigenous Islander, and the mixture of both, are being recognized everywhere in the Pacific Islands as 'New Islanders' – an emergent label embracing the region's resultant variety and mobility.

Economic identity, regardless of ethnic orientation, comes to the fore when one regards all Easter Islanders' limited resources for generating revenue. Irian Jaya and Papua New Guinea have gold and copper; New Caledonia nickel; Western Samoa timber; Nauru phosphate (what little remains);Tuvalu and Kiribati fish; Fiji sugar; and much of eastern Polynesia copra and cultured pearls. Rapa Nui has only 'Museum Island', and at least for the foreseeable future there is no indication that this will change. Although there is still high unemployment, most Easter Islanders can scrape together an income through multiple activities. Wood and stone carving is still the most common and profitable independent employment, although tour guiding with one's own vehicle has greatly increased in recent years. A steadily growing occupation, especially following the recent distribution of *campo* farms, is crop gardening, which, once properly organized, will perhaps within a few years be supplying all local needs and end the reliance on costly Chilean imports. (Rapa Nui will never be Chile's fruit garden.) The three major sources of income for all Islanders, however, remain SASIPA (the old cattle ranch and the water and electricity supplier), Chilean government positions (administration, services, police, military, health and education) and tourism. The only real 'mystery' of Easter Island is why SASIPA continues to raise cattle here: almost all the meat consumed on the island is still flown in from Chile. SASIPA is the last descendant of the Company. The island's largest employer, it is a quasi-non-governmental organization still managed by a non-Rapanui, invariably a mainland Chilean. The cattle ranch – there are no sheep – occupies 40 per cent of the island (*c.*6,500 hectares) as the largest landholder, and it has continually run at a loss, although its economy has brought financial benefits to individual Rapanui families and its supply of water and electricity enables modern life here. SASIPA also periodically researches in animal husbandry, agriculture and fisheries.

The only truly productive industry on the island is cultural tourism.[155] The extreme poverty still visible on the island two decades ago has almost entirely disappeared. This is because cultural tourism – above all, through its 'trickle-down' effect – has caused the local standard of living to rise, together with introducing a run-away materialism. Although tourist assessments from the late 1960s to the mid-1990s frequently criticized poor accommodation, prices, services, pollution, pests and uninformed guides, most such complaints disappeared by the twenty-first century. A major investment in tourism, amenities, education and infrastructure by the Republic and by the Muni, as well as the new international awareness of the globetrotting Rapanui themselves, have meant that Easter Island is a fully level member of the comity of Pacific Islands, no longer a poor, substandard waif – but finally that beautiful, exciting, unique locale that every tourist would enthusiastically recommend. It has, however, been a long and difficult path.

Problems still remain with this only development option that is open to all Easter Islanders, regardless of pedigree. Demand is not being stimulated by effective marketing. Tourism is still constrained by air transport supply.[156] (A deep-water port is crucially needed to eliminate persisting supply difficulties.) That long-stay, beach-oriented mass tourism envisaged by the Honolulu biological engineer William A. Bryan in 1920 has effectively been prevented because of the cost of getting to isolated Rapa Nui, the natural deficiencies of the physical environment, and the persistent high costs of food and accommodation.[157] Fortunately, a mainlander-organized system of package tourism never became a dominant feature in the local economy, because tourism on Rapa Nui has always remained, by law, in Rapanui hands. Mass tourism will never be an economic recourse for the island anyway, because of its isolation. Instead, above all in the past decade, a trend towards 'boutique tourism' for the discerning, wealthier tourist – apart from increasing numbers of visiting Chileans – has become apparent, and will perhaps long be a substantial source for island revenues.

Tourism is hardly Pacific Island's panacea. In most other places of the Pacific, only about 40 per cent of the net earnings from tourism remains in the host country; the other 60 per cent is lost to foreign wages, repatriated profits, commissions, imported goods and other things. The maintenance of the infrastructure that modern competitive tourism demands burdens host governments. And the environmental and social effects of tourism generally impact negatively on small island nations. Rapa Nui is different in this regard, however, and not only because of its isolation. Here, the Rapanui have only import costs to worry about. Tourists come to the island chiefly because of its archæological patrimony – not because of present-day Polynesians and their culture, or because of tropical, palm-fringed beaches. Rapa Nui offers cultural tourism, a class in its own, as it possesses the Pacific's most spectacular

15 The tourist destination Hanga Roa in 2004, as viewed from Puna Pau.

'open-air museum' (illus. 15). Preservation and conservation of the archæological heritage are currently among the Rapanui people's highest priorities,
also because of reawakened ethnic pride. But these are costly and difficult,
involving a sophistication of methods and planning beyond most Rapanui's
purse and secondary-education training. It finds locals all too often dependent yet again on foreign agencies and experts.

But Easter Island's archæology is gold in the hand. When a cruise ship
lands 1,000 tourists, it is Tahai, 'Orongo, Rano Raraku, Tongariki and
'Anakena most will visit. Visitors staying for a week will also seek out 'Ana Kai
Tangata, Puna Pau, 'A Kiwi, Te Pahu, Te Peu, Vinapū, Vaihū, Akahanga, Te Pito
te Kura and other such famous sites. Few will stand atop Terevaka or Pū 'a
Katiki or take a boat out to Motu Nui. (And even fewer will ever visit a
Rapanui household.)

For this living treasury, there must be a management plan. This still does
not exist. 'Nor is there a plan for the fragile and complex ecosystems . . . There
is neither a consistent plan for conservation nor for archæological investigations.'[158] This must be remedied if Easter Island's economy is to grow. The
current problem is real, and it is serious: 'as long as it is not solved, the future
of the Fundo Vaitea [cattle ranch] and the effective protection of the Park
clearly threaten the sustainable development of the island as well as the
preservation of its archæological and natural heritage.'[159] What it means to be
an Easter Islander in the twenty-first century is shaped and defined by this
economic identity as well.

Proprietary identity has made itself heard, above all, in the call for the
return of 'ancestral' lands, since the end of the twentieth century one of the

island's most contentious issues. All Rapanui – but not all Easter Islanders – want their land 'back'. Most educated Rapanui, the traditionalists, wish returned lands to be held by the local Rapanui-run government in steward-ship. Others, the entrepreneurs, want it for themselves, in order to increase personal wealth. And many Easter Islanders, particularly the non-Rapanui nationalists, would like to keep Chile in control of the lands, in order not to weaken their own privilege. The Republic is continuing to return Rapa Nui land, but on an individual basis, preventing the creation of a strong, empow-ered, local, Rapanui-run government. Land – how to distribute, manage and work it – is the greatest dilemma on the island today, alienating traditionalist, entrepreneur and nationalist. Its eventual solution will perhaps determine the 'true' Easter Island identity.

At present many agencies are competing with one another on the island, often with opposite goals: the Republic's CONAF, CORFO and SASIPA, the Rapanui's own Muni, the governor (a Republic-appointed ethnic Rapanui), the *alcalde*, Te Mau Hatu (Consejo 1), Consejo 2, the Chamber of Tourism and the recently formed Rapa Nui Parliament (a local-interest group seeking com-plete political independence from Chile). The Republic wants to dominate. Nearly all ethnic Rapanui want to control their own destiny. Mainlanders wish to invest in the island for a profit. And foreign-born Easter Islanders with eth-nic Rapanui spouses seek to acquire land and its inheritance rights.

Although the Republic has directed all development strategies in the past, focusing on local political control and its geopolitical influence in the Pacific and ignoring Rapanui development visions and concerns,[160] Chilean nation-alists of late have been ceding more *mana* to both traditionalists and entre-preneurs. Albeit with differing purposes, appointed and elected Rapanui leaders, as well as many other community representatives, are coming togeth-er in this one cause – land restitution – in order to weaken the Chilean nation-alists' base and to strengthen, above all, the indigenous privilege. Most ethnic Rapanui are united at least in this one thing: forging a stronger indigenous role in the decision-making process as regards local development plans.[161]

The *alcalde* Petero Edmunds, for one, has again raised the issue of internal autonomy for Rapa Nui – an island that would still be Chilean, but with self-determination. He sides with those who believe that returned lands should be owned and stewarded by local Rapanui-run government, not by private indi-viduals. Perhaps Chile is prepared for this new tack. The Republic has recent-ly taken a course in the Pacific that resembles what Great Britain, Australia and New Zealand were adopting shortly after the Second World War: that is, moving away from internal colonialism and towards autonomy, shifting from commercial exploitation to political patronage.

Some would say that it was time. In 1964 'to be Chilean' meant emancipa-tion. In 2004 to many it means domination. 'Some are still greatly bitter toward Chile', the sociologist Grant McCall once observed, 'not because the government maltreated them but because those authorities who had promised to protect them in the "cession" and "proclamation" [of 1888] allowed others to abuse both the land and the people'.[162] Finally, after 100 years of dependence, Easter Island may anticipate administrative autonomy at last. A Republic-appointed commission studying this possibility, which included an ex-President of Chile, agreed unanimously in July 2003 to convert the island into Chile's first Special Territory.[163] This would entail two types of authorities: one with executive power and the other functioning as a type of cabinet, the holders of these offices to be elected by popular mandate. The *alcalde* Petero Edmunds, who also serves on the commission, has stated that the one with executive power should be the 'President of the Special Territory'. If the plan is adopted, Rapa Nui would have its own president, then, whereas the cabinet would be like an elected Assembly.

The future status of Easter Island will probably comprise one of three scenarios: a Rapa Nui decentralized from Santiago, with greater administrative powers than at present; an autonomous Rapa Nui, within the Chilean state, as the government commission is presently recommending; or a fully independent Rapa Nui.[164] Chile would actually prefer the first recourse; many Rapanui wish the second; a small, but very vociferous, group of young Rapanui are calling for the third. At the Tāpati Festival of 2004, the Rapa Nui flag – that modest red *rei miro* pectoral on a white field – was flying prominently everywhere, even from many car aerials. Something will occur, and soon. Decentralization would not solve the many problems on the island. Independence would be anathema to Chile, and without a wealthy and powerful protector as guarantor Rapa Nui could simply never afford to stand on its own.

The answer? 'Autonomy is the only viable solution for Rapa Nui.'[165] Chile's primary role will still include justice, defence and international representation. But most other functions would devolve to the Rapanui people (that is, to all legal Easter Islanders, regardless of pedigree): taxation, land use, health, education, immigration, economic and cultural development, as well as other things. Chile will still be a visible presence on Easter Island, but all Easter Islanders themselves – the Rapanui and their non-Rapanui spouses, friends and neighbours – will be in daily charge of their lives and their island.

Easter Island's political status would then very much resemble that of the tiny Polynesian nation of Niue. Located halfway between Tonga and the Cook Islands, Niue has been internally self-governing since 1974, in free association with New Zealand. Each Niuean is a citizen of both Niue and New Zealand. There are fewer than 30,000 Niueans, all but about 1,500 of them living not on Niue but in New Zealand. Despite its tiny resident population, Niue has a seat at the United Nations. Its National Assembly has 20 members, 14 from village constituencies and 6 elected in an island-wide vote. The premier of Niue is then elected by the 20 assemblymen and assemblywomen (by a simple show of hands). Three cabinet ministers are then chosen by the premier from among the Assembly. Easter Island might well soon emulate such an eminently successful scheme – that is, the self-governing Republic of Rapa Nui would be in free association with the Republic of Chile. Each Easter Islander would then be a citizen of both Rapa Nui and Chile. And a Rapanui, too, would occupy a seat at the United Nations.

Some level of economic self-sufficiency, almost exclusively through tourism, would be possible for this new Republic of Rapa Nui. Dedicated support from Chile, however, would have to be forthcoming – and this for decades – in order to ensure Rapa Nui's economic survival.

The fragile egg now rests with these newest Birdmen: the present-day leaders, Rapanui and non-Rapanui alike, who cradle this precious symbol of the *'ao*, the island's temporal power. Will it pass unbroken to the next generation, or will other champions have to go in search of further, perhaps less desirable, solutions? Although Easter Island's history has always been one of autocracy,[166] perhaps this, too, will change. Perhaps democracy will finally have its chance at Earth's inimitable terminus.

Museum Island is, after all, only another episode. Today's Rapanui and their fellow Easter Islanders of many nations, creeds and hues are actively renegotiating their relationship to, and roles within, the modern Chilean state. At least the Rapanui themselves, whom no Polynesian population can equal for their subjection 'to such a succession of disintegrating influences',[167] no longer need to validate their narrative. For their long and tortuous history, as we have seen, is no longer their burden, but their asset. The Rapanui, all Easter Islanders, are themselves the future: renewed, reconstituted and autonomous in partnership with Chile. As the first *'ariki mau* Hotu Matu'a – at least in early twentieth-century myth – prophesied to his heir Tu'u mā Heke on his deathbed: 'your descendants shall multiply like the shells of the sea, and the reeds of the crater, and the pebbles of the beach'.[168]

References

INTRODUCTION

1   K. M. Hasse, P. Stoffers and C. D. Garbe-Schonberg, 'The Petrogenetic Evolution of Lavas from
    Easter Island and Neighbouring Seamounts, Near-ridge Hotspot Volcanoes in the SE Pacific',
    Journal of Petrology, XXXVIII (1997), pp. 785–813. See also P. E. Baker, 'Petrological Factors
    Influencing the Utilization of Stone on Easter Island', in *Easter Island in Pacific Context.
    Proceedings of the Fourth International Conference on Easter Island and East Polynesia: University
    of New Mexico, Albuquerque, 5–10 August 1997*, ed. Christopher M. Stevenson, Georgia Lee and
    Frank J. Morin (Los Osos, CA, 1998), pp. 279–83.
2   J. M. O'Connor, P. Stoffers and M. O. McWilliams, 'Time-space Mapping of Easter Chain
    Volcanism', *Earth and Planetary Science Letters*, CXXXVI (1995), pp. 197–212.
3   L. L. Henry, 'The Area of Rapa Nui', *Rapa Nui Journal*, VIII/3 (1994), pp. 71–3.
4   Steven Roger Fischer and Charles M. Love, 'Rapanui: The Geological Parameters', in *Easter Island
    Studies: Contributions to the History of Rapanui in Memory of William T. Mulloy*, ed. Steven Roger
    Fischer (Oxford, 1993), pp. 1–6.
5   John R. Flenley, 'The Present Flora of Easter Island and Its Origins', in *Easter Island Studies*, ed.
    Fischer, pp. 7–15.
6   Kevin Butler and John Flenley, 'Further Pollen Evidence from Easter Island', in *Pacific 2000.
    Proceedings of the Fifth International Conference on Easter Island and the Pacific: Hawai'i
    Preparatory Academy, Kamuela, Hawai'i, 7–12 August 2000*, ed. Christopher M. Stevenson,
    Georgia Lee and Frank J. Morin (Los Osos, 2001), pp. 79–81.
7   Hans-Rudolf Bork and Andreas Mieth, 'The Key Role of *Jubæa* Palm Trees in the History of Rapa
    Nui: A Provocative Interpretation', *Rapa Nui Journal*, XVII/2 (2003), p. 120.
8   J. Dransfield et al., 'A Recently Extinct Palm from Easter Island', *Nature*, CCCXII (1984), pp. 750–52.
9   Louis H. DiSalvo and John E. Randall, 'The Marine Fauna of Rapanui, Past and Present', in *Easter
    Island Studies*, ed. Fischer, pp. 16–23.
10 Konrad Klemmer and Georg Zizka, 'The Terrestrial Fauna of Easter Island', in *Easter Island
    Studies*, ed. Fischer, pp. 24–6.
11 D. W. Steadman, P. Vargas and C. Cristino, 'Stratigraphy, Chronology and Cultural Context of an
    Early Faunal Assemblage from Easter Island', *Asian Perspectives*, XXXIII/1 (1994), pp. 79–96.
12 John R. Flenley, 'The Palæoecology of Easter Island, and its Ecological Disaster', in *Easter Island
    Studies*, ed. Fischer, pp. 27–45.
13 Butler and Flenley, 'Further Pollen Evidence from Easter Island'.
14 Alfred Métraux, *Ethnology of Easter Island* (Honolulu, 1940), p. 3.
15 Adapted from Steven Roger Fischer, *A History of the Pacific Islands* (Basingstoke, 2002), pp. xii–xiii.
16 In regard to the ongoing debate surrounding the 'acceptable' way of writing the recent indige-
    nous name of the island, its people and their language, see Steven Roger Fischer, 'Rapanui is Rapa
    Nui is Rapa-nui', *Rapa Nui Journal*, V/3 (1991), p. 42, and the suggested compromise that estab-
    lished the current convention: Emily Ross Mulloy, 'Letter to the Editor', *Rapa Nui Journal*, V/3
    (1991), p. 43.

1 Sebastian Englert, *Tradiciones de la Isla de Pascua en idioma rapanui y castellano* (Padre Las Casas, Chile, 1939), pp. 17–18, quoted here with a corrected translation. The Capuchin priest Englert translated Old Rapanui *tuki* ('fuck') with the more socially acceptable Spanish *fecundizar* or 'fecundate'.

2 Steven Roger Fischer, *Rongorongo: The Easter Island Script. History, Traditions, Texts* (Oxford, 1997), p. 268.

3 Englert, *Tradiciones*, p. 19.

4 Edward S. Craighill Handy, *The Native Culture in the Marquesas* (Honolulu, 1923), p. 344.

5 Modern *hotu* is a doublet of Old Rapanui *hatu* ('lord'). See Steven Roger Fischer, 'Rapanui's *Tu'u ko Iho* Versus Mangareva's *'Atu Motua*: Evidence for Multiple Reanalysis and Replacement in Rapanui Settlement Traditions, Easter Island', *Journal of Pacific History*, XXIX (1994), pp. 3–18.

6 Thomas S. Barthel, *The Eighth Land: The Polynesian Discovery and Settlement of Easter Island*, trans. Anneliese Martin (Honolulu, 1978), p. 2.

7 *Ibid.*, p. 1.

8 Its most comprehensive version is 'Manuscript E', compiled by Pua Ara Hoa (born c.1840) about 1910 and published in Barthel, *The Eighth Land*. Earlier fragmentary versions can be found in William Judah Thomson, 'Te Pito te Henua, or Easter Island', Report of the United States National Museum for the Year Ending June 30, 1889, *Annual Reports of the Smithsonian Institution for 1889* (Washington, DC, 1891), pp. 526–8; Florentin Etienne ('Tepano') Jaussen, 'L'île de Pâques. Historique et écriture', posthumously edited by Ildefonse Alazard, *Bulletin de géographie historique et descriptive*, II (1893), p. 241; and Katherine Routledge (Mrs Scorseby Routledge), *The Mystery of Easter Island: The Story of an Expedition* (London, 1919), pp. 277–80. An excellent general review is in Alfred Métraux, *Ethnology of Easter Island* (Honolulu, 1940), pp. 56–68.

9 Métraux, *Ethnology of Easter Island*, p. 60.

10 Hippolyte Roussel, 'Ile de Pâques' [Valparaíso 1869], *Annales de la Congrégation des Sacrés-Cœurs de Jésus et de Marie*, n.s., XXXII/305 (1926), p. 357, trans. by Métraux in *Ethnology of Easter Island*, p. 61 (with Roussel's original spellings here standardized).

11 Te Rangi Hiroa (Peter Buck), *Ethnology of Mangareva* (Honolulu, 1938), p. 6 and figs 2 and 142.

12 Thomas S. Barthel, 'Wer waren die ersten Siedler auf der Osterinsel?', *Ethnologica*, N.F., II (1960), p. 237.

13 *Ibid.*, p. 233.

14 For the most comprehensive and rational argument against the 'South American hypothesis', see John Flenley and Paul Bahn, *The Enigmas of Easter Island* (Oxford, 2002), pp. 27–60.

15 Steven Roger Fischer, 'Homogeneity in Old Rapanui', *Oceanic Linguistics*, XXXI/2 (1992), pp. 181–90.

16 Peter Bellwood, *Prehistory of the Indo-Malaysian Archipelago*, 2nd edn (Honolulu, 1997).

17 Darrell T. Tryon, 'The Austronesian Languages', in *Comparative Austronesian Dictionary: An Introduction to Austronesian Studies, Part 1: Fascicle 1*, ed. Darrell T. Tryon et al. (Berlin and New York, 1995), pp. 5–44.

18 Geoffrey Irwin, *The Prehistoric Exploration and Colonisation of the Pacific* (Cambridge, 1992), pp. 13–16 and 53–62.

19 Steven Roger Fischer, *A History of the Pacific Islands* (Basingstoke, 2002), p. 33.

20 Flenley and Bahn, *The Enigmas of Easter Island*, p. 59.

21 Roger C. Green and Marshall I. Weisler, 'The Mangarevan Sequence and Dating of the Geographic Expansion into Southeast Polynesia', *Asian Perspectives*, XLI/2 (2002), pp. 213–41. See also Atholl Anderson et al., 'Cultural Chronology in Mangareva (Gambier Islands), French Polynesia: Evidence from Recent Radiocarbon Dating', *Journal of the Polynesian Society*, CXII/2 (2003), pp. 119–40.

22 John R. Flenley, 'Further Evidence of Vegetational Change on Easter Island', *South Pacific Study*, XVI (1996), pp. 135–41.

23 William S. Ayres, 'Radiocarbon Dates from Easter Island', *Journal of the Polynesian Society*, LXXX (1971), pp. 497–504.

24 Roger C. Green, 'Rapanui Origins Prior to European Contact: The View from Eastern Polynesia', in *Easter Island and East Polynesian Prehistory*, ed. Patricia Vargas Casanova

(Santiago, 1998), pp. 87–110.

25 H. L. Shapiro (who conducted anthropometric studies on Easter Island in 1935), in Métraux, *Ethnology of Easter Island*, p. 30; and, more recently, Vincent H. Stefan, 'Origin and Evolution of the Rapanui of Easter Island', in *Pacific 2000. Proceedings of the Fifth International Conference on Easter Island and the Pacific: Hawai'i Preparatory Academy, Kamuela, Hawai'i, 7–12 August 2000*, ed. Christopher M. Stevenson, Georgia Lee and Frank J. Morin (Los Osos, CA, 2001), pp. 495–522.

26 Steven Roger Fischer, 'Mangarevan Doublets: Preliminary Evidence for Proto-Southeastern Polynesian', *Oceanic Linguistics*, XL (2001), pp. 112–24.

27 Roger C. Green and Marshall I. Weisler, *Mangarevan Archæology: Interpretations Using New Data and 40 Year Old Excavations to Establish a Sequence from 1200 to 1900 AD* (Dunedin, NZ, 2000).

28 Ben Finney and Bernard Kilonsky, 'Closing and Opening the Polynesian Triangle: *Hōkūle'a*'s Voyage to Rapa Nui', in *Pacific 2000*, pp. 353–63.

29 Flenley and Bahn, *The Enigmas of Easter Island*, p. 87.

30 Irving Goldman, *Ancient Polynesian Society* (Chicago, IL, and London, 1970), pp. 97–8.

31 Flenley and Bahn, *The Enigmas of Easter Island*, pp. 65–6.

32 John R. Flenley, 'The Present Flora of Easter Island and its Origins', in *Easter Island Studies: Contributions to the History of Rapanui in Memory of William T. Mulloy*, ed. Steven Roger Fischer (Oxford, 1993), pp. 11–13.

33 Métraux, *Ethnology of Easter Island*, p. 155.

34 Edgardo Martínez, *Vocabulario de la lengua Rapa-Nui: Isla de Pascua* (Santiago, 1913), p. 37.

35 Patrick V. Kirch, *The Evolution of the Polynesian Chiefdoms* (Cambridge, 1984), p. 268.

36 Flenley and Bahn, *The Enigmas of Easter Island*, pp. 166–7.

37 *Ibid.*, p. 88.

38 Métraux, *Ethnology of Easter Island*, p. 128.

39 *Ibid.*

40 Roger C. Green, 'Origins for the Rapanui of Easter Island before European Contact: Solutions from Holistic Anthropology to an Issue No Longer Much of a Mystery', *Rapa Nui Journal*, XIV/3 (2000), p. 73. See also Christopher Stevenson and Sonia Haoa, 'Diminished Agricultural Productivity and the Collapse of Ranked Society on Easter Island', in *Archæology, Agriculture and Identity: No Barriers Seminar Papers* (Oslo, 1999), vol. II, pp. 4–12.

41 Green and Weisler, 'The Mangarevan Sequence', pp. 213–14.

42 *Ibid.*, p. 233.

43 Green, 'Origins for the Rapanui of Easter Island', p. 74.

44 Goldman, *Ancient Polynesian Society*, p. 116.

45 Kirch, *The Evolution of the Polynesian Chiefdoms*, pp. 264–78.

46 Métraux, *Ethnology of Easter Island*, p. 136.

47 *Ibid.*, p. 130. See also Alfred Métraux, 'The Kings of Easter Island', *Journal of the Polynesian Society*, XLVI (1937), pp. 41–62.

48 Annette Bierbach and Horst Cain, *Religion and Language of Easter Island* (Berlin, 1996), p. 134. Alfred Métraux, 'La culture sociale de l'Ile de Pâques', *Anales del Instituto de Etnografia Americana*, III (1942), p. 137, mentions Easter Island's *roi-prêtre*.

49 Goldman, *Ancient Polynesian Society*, p. 120.

50 Métraux, *Ethnology of Easter Island*, p. 121.

51 George W. Gill, 'Skeletal Remains from Ahu Nau Nau: Land of the Royal Miru', in *Eastern Island Archæology: Research on Early Rapanui Culture*, ed. Christopher M. Stevenson and William S. Ayres (Los Osos, CA, 2000), pp. 109–24.

52 Patricia Vargas Casanova, 'Rapa Nui Settlement Patterns: Types, Function and Spatial Distribution of Households' Structural Components', in *Easter Island and East Polynesian Prehistory*, ed. Patricia Vargas Casanova (Santiago, 1998), pp. 111–30.

53 Flenley and Bahn, *The Enigmas of Easter Island*, pp. 93–4.

54 *Ibid.*, p. 96.

55 Herbert von Saher, 'Some Details from the Journal of Captain Bouman on the Discovery of Easter Island', *Rapa Nui Journal*, IV/4 (1990–91), p. 51.

56 Georgia Lee, *The Rock Art of Easter Island: Symbols of Power, Prayers to the Gods* (Los Angeles, 1992), pp. 113–15.

57 Kirch, *The Evolution of the Polynesian Chiefdoms*, pp. 271–2.

58 Catherine Orliac, 'The Woody Vegetation of Easter Island Between the Early 14th and the Mid-17th Centuries AD', in *Eastern Island Archæology*, p. 216.

59 Flenley and Bahn, *The Enigmas of Easter Island*, p. 100.

60 *Ibid.*, p. 92. See also Métraux, *Ethnology of Easter Island*, pp. 151–61, and William S. Ayres, 'Easter Island Subsistence', *Journal de la Société des Océanistes*, LXXX (1985), pp. 103–24.

61 Métraux, *Ethnology of Easter Island*, p. 132.

62 Fischer, *A History of the Pacific Islands*, p. 43.

63 *Ibid.*, pp. 72–3.

64 Bierbach and Cain, *Religion and Language of Easter Island*, p. 134.

65 Fischer, *A History of the Pacific Islands*, pp. 71–2.

66 *Ibid.*

67 Bierbach and Cain, *Religion and Language of Easter Island*, pp. 135–6.

68 *Ibid.*, p. 137.

69 Fischer, *A History of the Pacific Islands*, p. 76.

70 Joan Seaver Kurze, *Ingrained Images: Wood Carvings from Easter Island* (Woodland, CA, 1997), p. 22.

71 Steven Roger Fischer, 'Hugh Cuming's Account of an Anchorage at Rapanui (Easter Island), November 27–8, 1827', *Journal of the Polynesian Society*, c/3 (1991), p. 304.

72 Joseph-Eugène Eyraud, 'Lettre du F. Eugène Eyraud, au T.R.P. Supérieur général', *Annales de la Propagation de la Foi*, XXXVIII (1866), p. 71, in an English translation by Thor Heyerdahl, 'An Introduction to Easter Island', in *Reports of the Norwegian Archaeological Expedition to Easter Island and the East Pacific*, vol. I: *Archaeology of Easter Island*, ed. Thor Heyerdahl and Edwin N. Ferdon, Jr (Stockholm, 1961), p. 68.

73 Kurze, *Ingrained Images*, p. 22.

74 Henri Lavachery, 'Foreword', in Thor Heyerdahl, *The Art of Easter Island* (London, 1976), p. 11. See (Joan T. Seaver) Kurze, *Ingrained Images*, and Joan T. Seaver, 'An Ethnography of Wood Carving: Continuity in Cultural Transformations on Rapa Nui', PhD dissertation, University of California at Los Angeles, 1988; see also Francina Forment, *Les figures moai kavakava de l'Ile de Pâques* (Ghent, 1991).

75 Mark Blackburn, *Tattoos from Paradise: Traditional Polynesian Patterns* (Atglen, PA, 1999), p. 161.

76 Cited in Friedrich Schulze-Maizier, *Die Osterinsel* (Leipzig, 1926), p. 226.

77 Cited in Blackburn, *Tattoos from Paradise*, p. 161.

78 George Forster, *A Voyage Round the World in HBM's Sloop 'Resolution' (1772–75)* (London, 1777), vol. I, p. 564.

79 Walter Knoche, *Die Osterinsel: Eine Zusammenfassung der chilenischen Osterinselexpedition des Jahres 1911* (Concepción, 1925), p. 167.

80 Lee, *The Rock Art of Easter Island*, p. 183, note 1.

81 Teuira Henry, *Ancient Tahiti* (Honolulu, 1928), p. 287.

82 Lee, *The Rock Art of Easter Island*, p. 208.

83 Flenley and Bahn, *The Enigmas of Easter Island*, p. 192.

84 William Ayres, 'The Cultural Context of Easter Island Religious Structures', PhD dissertation, Tulane University, 1973.

85 Kirch, *The Evolution of the Polynesian Chiefdoms*, pp. 268 and 269–70.

86 William T. Mulloy and Gonzalo Figueroa, *The Akivi – Vai Teka Complex* (Honolulu, 1978), p. 137.

87 *Ibid.*

88 Helene Martinsson-Wallin, *Ahu – The Ceremonial Stone Structures of Easter Island: Analyses of Variation and Interpretation of Meanings* (Uppsala, 1994), p. 106.

89 Goldman, *Ancient Polynesian Society*, p. 108.

90 Green, 'Origins for the Rapanui of Easter Island', p. 74.

91 Flenley and Bahn, *The Enigmas of Easter Island*, p. 174.

92 *Ibid.*, p. 191.

93 Sebastian Englert, *Island at the Centre of the World: New Light on Easter Island*, trans. and ed. William T. Mulloy (London, 1970), pp. 108 and 121.

94 Jacob Roggeveen, *Extracts from the Official Log of Mynheer J. Roggeveen (1721–22)* (London, 1908), p. 15.

95 James Cook, *A Voyage Towards the South Pole and Round the World (1772–75)*, 2nd edn (London,

1777), vol. I, p. 296.

96 Quoted in Flenley and Bahn, *The Enigmas of Easter Island*, p. 108.

97 Francisco Mellén Blanco, *Manuscritos y documentos españoles para la historia de la Isla de Pascua* (Madrid, 1986), p. 159.

98 [Wilhelm] Geiseler, *Die Osterinsel, eine Stätte prähistorischer Kultur in der Südsee: Bericht des Kommandanten S.M. Kbt. 'Hyäne', Kapitänleutnant Geiseler, über die ethnologische Untersuchung der Oster-Insel (Rapanui) an den Chef der Kaiserlichen Admiralität* (Berlin, 1883), p. 14.

99 Goldman, *Ancient Polynesian Society*, p. 106.

100 Flenley and Bahn, *The Enigmas of Easter Island*, p. 109.

101 See Jo Anne van Tilburg, *Power and Symbol: The Stylistic Analysis of Easter Island Monolithic Sculpture*, PhD dissertation, University of California at Los Angeles, 1986, and her book *Easter Island: Archæology, Ecology and Culture* (London, 1994), for relevant statistical information.

102 Above all, van Tilburg's works (note 101 above) and Flenley and Bahn, *The Enigmas of Easter Island*, pp. 103–46.

103 Flenley and Bahn, *The Enigmas of Easter Island*, pp. 111–12.

104 Métraux, *Ethnology of Easter Island*, p. 137.

105 Bierbach and Cain, *Religion and Language of Easter Island*, p. 136.

106 Pavel Pavel, 'Reconstruction of the Transport of the *moai* Statues and *pukao* Hats', *Rapa Nui Journal*, IX/3 (1995), pp. 69–72.

107 Routledge, *The Mystery of Easter Island*, p. 182.

108 Flenley and Bahn, *The Enigmas of Easter Island*, p. 157.

109 Edwin N. Ferdon, Jr, 'The Ceremonial Site of Orongo', in *Reports of the Norwegian Archaeological Expedition*, vol. I, p. 250.

110 Métraux, *Ethnology of Easter Island*, pp. 105–6.

111 Lee, *The Rock Art of Easter Island*, pp. 193–6.

112 Flenley and Bahn, *The Enigmas of Easter Island*, p. 77.

113 Arne Skjølsvold, 'Archeological Investigations at Anakena, Easter Island', *Occasional Papers of the Kon-Tiki Museum*, CXI (1994), pp. 5–121.

114 Green, 'Origins for the Rapanui of Easter Island', p. 73.

115 Cook, *A Voyage Towards the South Pole*, vol. I, p. 288.

116 Knoche, *Die Osterinsel*, pp. 109–14.

117 Christopher M. Stevenson, *Archæological Investigations on Easter Island. Maunga Tari: An Upland Agricultural Complex* (Los Osos, CA, 1997), pp. 141–2.

118 Andreas Mieth and Hans-Rudolf Bork, 'Diminution and Degradation of Environmental Resources by Prehistoric Land Use on Poike Peninsula, Easter Island (Rapa Nui)', *Rapa Nui Journal*, XVII/1 (2003), pp. 34–41.

119 *Ibid.*, p. 34.

120 Leslie C. Shaw, 'The Use of Caves as Burial Chambers on Easter Island', *Rapa Nui Journal*, X/4 (1996), pp. 101–3, and Flenley and Bahn, *The Enigmas of Easter Island*, p. 170.

121 Stevenson, *Archæological Investigations on Easter Island*, pp. 141–2.

122 Flenley and Bahn, *The Enigmas of Easter Island*, p. 192.

123 See in this regard, above all, Métraux, *Ethnology of Easter Island*, pp. 69–74.

124 Flenley and Bahn, *The Enigmas of Easter Island*, p. 86.

125 *Ibid.*, p. 20.

126 Roggeveen, *Extracts from the Official Log of Mynheer J. Roggeveen*, p. 21.

127 Paul Rainbird, 'A Message for Our Future? The Rapa Nui (Easter Island) Eco-disaster and the Pacific Island Environments', *World Archæology*, XXXIII (2002), pp. 436–51.

128 George W. Gill, 'Skeletal Remains from Ahu Nau Nau: Land of the Royal Miru', in *Eastern Island Archæology*, pp. 109–24.

129 David W. Steadman, Patricia Vargas and Claudio Cristino, 'Stratigraphy, Chronology and Cultural Context of an Early Faunal Assemblage from Easter Island', *Asian Perspectives*, XXXIII/1 (1994), p. 91.

130 Flenley and Bahn, *The Enigmas of Easter Island*, p. 167.

131 *Ibid.*, p. 170.

TWO: WHITE MEN AND BIRDMEN

1   Herbert von Saher, 'Some Details of the Journal of Jacob Roggeveen', *Rapa Nui Journal*, IV/3 (1990), pp. 33–5 and 45.
2   Herbert von Saher, 'The Complete Journal of Captain Cornelis Bouman, Master of the Ship *Thienhoven* Forming Part of the Fleet of Jacob Roggeveen, from 31 March to 13 April 1722 during their Stay Around Easter Island', *Rapa Nui Journal*, VIII/4 (1994), p. 96.
3   Herbert von Saher, 'Roggeveen and Bouman: An Inventory of All the Narratives', *Rapa Nui Journal*, VII/4 (1993), p. 80.
4   Andrew Sharp, ed., *The Journal of Jacob Roggeveen* (Oxford, 1970), pp. 91–2.
5   Herbert von Saher, 'Some Details from the Journal of Captain Bouman on the Discovery of Easter Island', *Rapa Nui Journal*, IV/4 (1990–91), p. 50.
6   Friedrich Schulze-Maizier, *Die Osterinsel* (Leipzig, 1926), pp. 222–3.
7   *Ibid.*, p. 223.
8   Sebastian Englert, *La tierra de Hotu Matu'a: historia, etnología y lengua de la Isla de Pascua* (Padre Las Casas, Chile, 1948), p. 480.
9   Saher, 'Some Details from the Journal of Captain Bouman' (1990–91), p. 50.
10 Schulze-Maizier, *Die Osterinsel*, p. 223.
11 Saher, 'Some Details from the Journal of Captain Bouman' (1990–91), p. 51.
12 *Ibid.*
13 Schulze-Maizier, *Die Osterinsel*, pp. 225–6.
14 Saher, 'Some Details from the Journal of Captain Bouman' (1990–91), p. 51.
15 Schulze-Maizier, *Die Osterinsel*, p. 224.
16 Paul Monin, *This Is My Place: Hauraki Contested, 1769–1875* (Wellington, NZ, 2001), p. 24.
17 Alan Moorehead, *The Fatal Impact: An Account of the Invasion of the South Pacific, 1767–1840* (Harmondsworth, 1966).
18 Patrick C. McCoy, *Easter Island Settlement Patterns in the Late Prehistoric and Proto-Historic Periods* (New York, 1976), pp. 145–6.
19 Alfred Métraux, 'The Kings of Easter Island', *Journal of the Polynesian Society*, XLVI (1937), pp. 41–62.
20 John Flenley and Paul Bahn, *The Enigmas of Easter Island* (Oxford, 2002), p. 174.
21 Alfred Métraux, *Ethnology of Easter Island* (Honolulu, 1940), p. 138.
22 Irving Goldman, *Ancient Polynesian Society* (Chicago, IL, and London, 1970), p. 99.
23 Métraux, *Ethnology of Easter Island*, pp. 69–74.
24 William Judah Thomson, 'Te Pito te Henua, or Easter Island', Report of the United States National Museum for the Year Ending June 30, 1889, *Annual Reports of the Smithsonian Institution for 1889* (Washington, DC, 1891), p. 476.
25 *Ibid.*, pp. 150–51.
26 Flenley and Bahn, *The Enigmas of Easter Island*, p. 156.
27 Te Rangi Hiroa (Peter H. Buck), *Ethnology of Mangareva* (Honolulu, 1938), p. 147.
28 Sebastian Englert, *Island at the Centre of the World: New Light on Easter Island*, trans. and ed. William Mulloy (London, 1970), pp. 137–8.
29 Cited in Flenley and Bahn, *The Enigmas of Easter Island*, p. 169.
30 Englert, *Island at the Centre of the World*, p. 138.
31 Goldman, *Ancient Polynesian Society*, p. 96.
32 Grant McCall, *Rapanui: Tradition and Survival on Easter Island* (Honolulu, 1980), pp. 38–9.
33 Thomson, 'Te Pito te Henua, or Easter Island', p. 482.
34 Patrick V. Kirch, *The Evolution of the Polynesian Chiefdoms* (Cambridge, 1984), p. 277.
35 [Wilhelm] Geiseler, *Die Osterinsel, eine Stätte prähistorischer Kultur in der Südsee: Bericht des Kommandanten S.M. Kbt. 'Hyäne', Kapitänleutnant Geiseler, über die ethnologische Untersuchung der Oster-Insel (Rapanui) an den Chef der Kaiserlichen Admiralität* (Berlin, 1883), p. 31.
36 Herbert von Saher, 'More Journals on Easter Island', *Rapa Nui Journal*, VI/2 (1992), p. 36.
37 For the most complete documentation of the cult, see Heide-Margaret Esen-Baur, *Untersuchungen über den Vogelmann-Kult auf der Osterinsel* (Wiesbaden, 1983). Excellent shorter descriptions can be found in Katherine Routledge, 'Easter Island', *Geographical Journal*, XLIX (1917), pp. 321–49, and *The Mystery of Easter Island: The Story of an Expedition* (London, 1919),

pp. 254–66, as well as in Métraux, *Ethnology of Easter Island*, pp. 331–41.
38 McCall, *Rapanui*, p. 38.
39 Francisco Mellén Blanco, *Manuscritos y documentos españoles para la historia de la isla de Pascua* (Madrid, 1986), p. 17.
40 Bolton Glanvill Corney, ed., *The Voyage of Captain Don Felipe Gonzalez . . . Preceded by an Extract from Mynheer Jacob Roggeveen's Official Log* (Cambridge, 1908), p. 122.
41 Francisco Mellén Blanco, 'Viceroy Amat and the Easter Island Expedition', in *Spanish Pacific from Magellan to Malaspina* (Madrid, 1988), p. 116.
42 *Ibid.*, p. 115.
43 Saher, 'More Journals on Easter Island', p. 35.
44 The full documentation for *rongorongo* can be found in Steven Roger Fischer, *Rongorongo: The Easter Island Script. History, Traditions, Texts* (Oxford, 1997). A popular account is available in Steven Roger Fischer, *Glyphbreaker* (New York, 1997), pp. 139–222.
45 Alfred Métraux, *Easter Island: A Stone-Age Civilization of the Pacific*, trans. Michael Bullock (London, 1957), p. 172.
46 F. T. de Lapelin, 'L'île de Pâques (Rapa-Nui)', *Revue maritime et coloniale*, XXXV (1872), p. 122, note 1.
47 Florentin Etienne (Tepano) Jaussen, 'L'île de Pâques: historique et écriture', ed. Ildefonse Alazard, *Bulletin de géographie historique et descriptive*, II (1893), p. 245.
48 William S. Ayres, 'The Cultural Context of Easter Island Religious Structures', PhD dissertation, Tulane University, New Orleans, LA, 1973, p. 132.
49 Geiseler, *Die Osterinsel*, p. 14.
50 Flenley and Bahn, *The Enigmas of Easter Island*, p. 152.
51 *Ibid.*, p. 150.
52 Aubert Dupetit-Thouars, *Voyage autour du monde sur la frégate 'La Vénus' (1836–39)* (Paris, 1841), vol. II, p. 225.
53 Saher, 'More Journals on Easter Island', p. 34.
54 *Ibid.*
55 Métraux, *Ethnology of Easter Island*, p. 38.
56 Saher, 'More Journals on Easter Island', p. 38.
57 *Ibid.*, p. 36.
58 James Cook, *A Voyage Towards the South Pole and Round the World (1772–75)*, 2nd edn (London, 1777), vol. I, p. 281.
59 Saher, 'More Journals on Easter Island', p. 39.
60 *Ibid.*, p. 37.
61 Métraux, *Ethnology of Easter Island*, p. 38.
62 Cook, *A Voyage Towards the South Pole*, p. 288.
63 Schulze-Maizier, *Die Osterinsel*, p. 228. See also John Dunmore, *The Journal of Jean-François de Galaup de la Pérouse, 1785–1788* (London, 1994), vol. I, pp. 57–69.
64 *Ibid.*, p. 229.
65 *Ibid.*, pp. 233–4.
66 The best summaries of early nineteenth-century visits are Grant McCall, 'Reaction to Disaster: Continuity and Change in Rapanui Social Organisation', PhD dissertation, Australian National University, Canberra, 1976, pp. 53–61; and Grant McCall, 'Rapanui and Outsiders: The Early Days', in *Circumpacifica: Festschrift für Thomas S. Barthel*, ed. Bruno Illius and Matthias Laubscher (Frankfurt, 1990), vol. II, pp. 165–225.
67 Steven Roger Fischer, *A History of the Pacific Islands* (Basingstoke, 2002), p. 95.
68 The facts remain unclear. See Glynn Barratt, *Russia and the South Pacific*, vol. II: *Southern and Eastern Polynesia* (Vancouver, 1988), p. 47; and McCall, 'Reaction to Disaster', pp. 59 and 369.
69 Otto von Kotzebue, *A Voyage of Discovery into the South Sea and Bering Straits* (London, 1821), vol. I, pp. 142–4.
70 McCall, 'Reaction to Disaster', p. 56.
71 Steven Roger Fischer, 'The Calling of HMS *Seringapatam* at Rapanui (Easter Island) on March 6, 1830', *Pacific Studies*, XVI/1 (1993), p. 73.
72 *Ibid.*, p. 76.
73 Jacques Antoine Moerenhout, *Voyages aux îles du Grand Océan* (Paris, 1837), vol. I, pp. 23–8.

74 Katherine Routledge (Mrs Scoresby Routledge), *The Mystery of Easter Island: The Story of an Expedition* (London, 1919), pp. 239–40; Métraux, *Ethnology of Easter Island*, p. 351.
75 McCall, 'Reaction to Disaster', p. 58.
76 See R. Gerard Ward, ed., *American Activities in the Central Pacific, 1790–1870* (Ridgewood, NJ, 1967), vol. II, p. 230; and McCall, 'Reaction to Disaster', pp. 367–8, note 34.
77 McCall, 'Reaction to Disaster', pp. 367–8, note 34.
78 Fischer, *Rongorongo*, p. 325.
79 *Ibid.*, p. 129.
80 Gaspard Zumbohm, 'Lettres du R. P. Gaspard Zumbohm au Directeur des *Annales* sur la mission de l'île de Pâques', *Annales de la Congrégation des Sacrés-Cœurs*, series A, VI (1880), pp. 120–21.
81 *Additional Supplement to the Hobart Town Gazette*, 28 July 1821.
82 McCall, 'Reaction to Disaster', p. 60.
83 Edward Dobson (?), 'Journal of the Ship *Surry* 1820–21', MLA 131, Mitchell Library, State Library of New South Wales, Sydney, Australia.
84 Moerenhout, *Voyages aux îles du Grand Océan*, vol. II, pp. 278–9.
85 Barry M. Gough, *To the Pacific and Arctic with Beechey: The Journal of Lieutenant George Peard of HMS 'Blossom', 1825–1828* (Cambridge, 1973), p. 73.
86 McCall, *Reaction to Disaster*, p. 369, note 36.
87 Albert van Hoorebeeck, *La vérité sur l'île de Pâques* (Le Havre, 1979), pp. 43–4.
88 McCall, *Reaction to Disaster*, p. 298.
89 Ward, ed., *American Activities in the Central Pacific, 1790–1870*, p. 241; and McCall, 'Reaction to Disaster', p. 299.
90 Métraux, *Ethnology of Easter Island*, p. 135.
91 Routledge, *The Mystery of Easter Island*, p. 172.
92 *Ibid.*, p. 241.
93 See the best compilation in Métraux, *Ethnology of Easter Island*, p. 90 (fold-out).
94 Routledge, *The Mystery of Easter Island*, pp. 241–3. Routledge is our best source of information about Nga'ara. All nineteenth-century sources provide only the briefest of fragments about this remarkable personality, but Routledge's informants had known Nga'ara personally.
95 *Ibid.*, p. 242.
96 *Ibid.*, p. 243.
97 William Judah Thomson, 'Te Pito te Henua, or Easter Island', Report of the United States National Museum for the Year Ending June 30, 1889, *Annual Reports of the Smithsonian Institution for 1889* (Washington, DC, 1891), pp. 523–4; and Alfred Métraux, 'The Kings of Easter Island', *Journal of the Polynesian Society*, XLVI (1937), pp. 52–4.
98 Fischer, *Rongorongo*, p. 329.
99 Routledge, *The Mystery of Easter Island*, p. 245.
100 *Ibid.*, p. 258.
101 Sebastian Englert, *Primer siglo cristiano de la Isla de Pascua, 1864–1964* (Villarrica, Chile, 1964), p. 16.

THREE: PIRATES AND PRIESTS

1 Recent literature: Corinne Raybaud, 'L'île de Pâques de 1862 à 1888', doctoral thesis, Université Paris X, Nanterre, 1993, and also *L'île de Pâques de 1862 à 1888: 26 années de diaspora pascuane en Océanie Orientale* (Pape'ete, 1996); Nelson Castro, 'Misioneros y milinaristas: Isla de Pascua, 1864–1914', thesis, Universidad de Valparaíso, 1996; S. Rochna, *La propiedad de la tierra en Isla de Pascua* (Santiago, 1996); Alejandra M. Grifferos A., 'La otra cara del paraíso: comunidad, tradición y colonialismo en Rapa Nui, 1864–1964', thesis, Universidad de Valparaíso, 1997; and Marcos Rauch G. and María E. Noel B., eds, *Manual de capacitación sobre el patrimonio cultural y natural de Rapa Nui* (Hanga Roa, 1998).
2 Steven Roger Fischer, *A History of the Pacific Islands* (Basingstoke, 2002), p. 122.
3 Grant McCall, 'Riro, Rapu and Rapanui: Refoundations in Easter Island Colonial History', *Rapa Nui Journal*, XI/3 (1997), p. 112.
4 J. Douglas Porteous, 'The Modernization of Rapanui', in *Easter Island Studies: Contributions to the History of Rapanui in Memory of William T. Mulloy*, ed. Steven Roger Fischer (Oxford, 1993), p. 225.

5 The best studies are Grant McCall, 'European Impact on Easter Island: Response, Recruitment and the Polynesian Experience in Peru', *Journal of Pacific History*, XI (1976), pp. 90–105; H. E. Maude, *Slavers in Paradise: The Peruvian Slave Trade in Polynesia, 1862–1864* (Canberra, 1981); and Raybaud, 'L'île de Pâques de 1862 à 1888', chapter 1.

6 Grant McCall, *Rapanui: Tradition and Survival on Easter Island*, 2nd edn (Honolulu, 1994), p. 56.

7 Letter from Father Clair Fouqué to Bishop Jaussen, 4 December 1862, SSCC Archives, Rome, Pq 73/7.

8 McCall, *Rapanui*, p. 370, note 40.

9 Richard Sainthill, 'Rapa-Nui, or Easter Island, in November 1868. By an Officer of HMS "Topaze"', *Macmillan's Magazine*, XXI (1870), p. 449.

10 Alfred Métraux, *Ethnology of Easter Island* (Honolulu, 1940), p. 150.

11 McCall, *Rapanui*, p. 57.

12 Grant McCall, 'Reaction to Disaster: Continuity and Change in Rapanui Social Organisation', PhD dissertation, Australian National University, Canberra, 1976, p. 371, note 42.

13 Raybaud, *L'île de Pâques de 1862 à 1888*, p. 55.

14 F. T. de Lapelin, 'L'île de Pâques (Rapa-Nui)', *Revue maritime et coloniale*, XXXV (1872), p. 109.

15 Raybaud, *L'île de Pâques de 1862 à 1888*, p. 56.

16 Emile Franceschini, 'Un animateur et un savant: Mgr Jaussen', *Encyclopédie mensuelle d'Outre-Mer*, IV/52 (1954), pp. 353–4.

17 McCall, 'European Impact on Easter Island', pp. 98–9.

18 Gaspard Zumbohm, 'Lettres du R. P. Gaspard Zumbohm au Directeur des *Annales* sur la mission de l'île de Pâques', *Annales de la Congrégation des Sacrés-Cœurs*, series A, V (1879), p. 662; Sebastian Englert, *Primer siglo cristiano de la Isla de Pascua, 1864–1964* (Villarrica, Chile, 1964), p. 13; McCall, 'Reaction to Disaster', pp. 66 and 371, note 43.

19 Zumbohm, 'Lettres du R. P. Gaspard Zumbohm', pp. 662–3.

20 Steven Roger Fischer, 'The Naming of Rapanui', in *Easter Island Studies*, pp. 63–6.

21 Zumbohm, 'Lettres du R. P. Gaspard Zumbohm', p. 663.

22 Main secondary sources about Easter Island's missionization include Julio T. Ramírez O., *El conquistador de Pascua: biografía del Hermano Eugenio Eyraud de los Sdos Corazones*, 2 vols (Santiago, 1944); Dalmas Mouly, *L'île de Pâques, Ile de mystère et d'héroïsme* (Tours, 1948); Englert, *Primer siglo cristiano de la Isla de Pascua*; François Dederen, 'L'évangélisation de l'Ile de Pâques par les frères de la Congrégation des Sacrés-Cœurs de Picpus', in *Circumpacifica: Festschrift für Thomas S. Barthel*, ed. Bruno Illius and Matthias Laubscher (Frankfurt, New York and Paris, 1990), vol. II, pp. 103–23; and Raybaud, *L'île de Pâques de 1862 à 1888*.

23 Jean Eyraud, 'Lettre de M. l'abbé Jean Eyraud (Notice biographique sur le frère Joseph-Eugène Eyraud)', *Annales de la Congrégation des Sacrés-Cœurs*, VI (1880), pp. 804–16.

24 Eugène Eyraud, 'Lettre du F. Eugène Eyraud, au T.R.P. Supérieur général', *Annales de la Propagation de la Foi*, XXXVIII (1866), pp. 52–71 and 124–38.

25 McCall, *Rapanui*, p. 59.

26 Grant McCall, 'Rapanui Wanderings: Diasporas from Easter Island', in *Easter Island in Pacific Context. South Seas Symposium: Proceedings of the Fourth International Conference on Easter Island and East Polynesia, University of New Mexico, Albuquerque, 5–10 August 1997*, ed. Christopher M. Stevenson, Georgia Lee and Frank J. Morin (Los Osos, CA, 1998), p. 372.

27 Letter from Bishop Jaussen to Captain Lauray, 16 December 1865, SSCC Archives, Rome, Pq 75/2.

28 Cited in Englert, *Primer siglo cristiano*, p. 39.

29 John Linton Palmer, 'Observations on the Inhabitants and the Antiquities of Easter Island', *Journal of the Ethnological Society*, I (1870), p. 372.

30 McCall, 'Reaction to Disaster', p. 68.

31 McCall, *Rapanui*, p. 60.

32 McCall, 'Reaction to Disaster', p. 299.

33 Letter from Father Olivier to Superior General Rouchouze, 22 December 1866, SSCC Archives, Rome, Pq 75/2.

34 Hippolyte Roussel, 'Ile de Pâques [Valparaíso 1869]', *Annales de la Congrégation des Sacrés-Cœurs de Jésus et de Marie*, n.s., XXXII/308 (1926), p. 495.

35 McCall, *Rapanui*, p. 60.

36 Letter from Bishop Jaussen to Admiral Cloué, after September 1870, SSCC Archives, Rome, Pq 75/2.

37   Letter from Olivier to Superior General Rouchouze, 22 December 1866, sscc Archives, Rome, Pq 75/2.

38   McCall, 'Reaction to Disaster', pp. 299 and 372, note 46.

39   Steven Roger Fischer, 'Rapanui's *Tu'u ko Iho* Versus Mangareva's *'Atu Motua*: Evidence for Multiple Reanalysis and Replacement in Rapanui Settlement Traditions, Easter Island', *Journal of Pacific History*, XXIX (1994), pp. 3–18.

40   Letter from Zumbohm to Superior General Rouchouze, 4 October 1868, sscc Archives, Rome, Pq 75/2.

41   *Ibid.*

42   H. Vere Barclay, 'Easter Island and its Colossal Statues', *Proceedings of the Royal Geographical Society of Australasia*, South Australian Branch (Adelaide), III (1899), p. 129.

43   Letter from Roussel to Bishop Jaussen, 29 November 1868, sscc Archives, Rome, Pq 75/1.

44   Letter from Zumbohm to Bishop Jaussen, 6 December 1868, sscc Archives, Rome, Pq 75/2.

45   Letter from Escolan to Bishop Jaussen, 16 May 1869, sscc Archives, Rome, Pq 75/2.

46   McCall, 'Reaction to Disaster', p. 70.

47   Raybaud, *L'île de Pâques de 1862 à 1888*, p. 213.

48   Zumbohm, 'Lettres du R. P. Gaspard Zumbohm', p. 777.

49   Englert, *Primer siglo cristiano*, p. 52.

50   McCall, 'Reaction to Disaster', p. 71.

51   Letter from Dutrou-Bornier to Bishop Jaussen, 25 February 1871, sscc Archives, Rome, Pq 75/3. See also Raybaud, *L'île de Pâques de 1862 à 1888*, p. 270.

52   Englert, *Primer siglo cristiano*, p. 51.

53   Letter from Zumbohm to Bishop Jaussen, 28 January 1870, sscc Archives, Rome, Pq 75/2.

54   Letter from Zumbohm to Bishop Jaussen, 14 March 1870, sscc Archives, Rome, Pq 75/2.

55   The following details are from Escolan's letter to Bishop Jaussen, *circa* July 1870, sscc Archives, Rome, Pq 75/2.

56   Letter from Zumbohm to Dutrou-Bornier, 7 July 1870, sscc Archives, Rome, Pq 75/2.

57   Letter from Escolan to Bishop Jaussen, 26 September 1870, sscc Archives, Rome, Pq 75/2.

58   Letter from Zumbohm to Bishop Jaussen, 27 September 1870, sscc Archives, Rome, Pq 75/2.

59   Letter from Bishop Jaussen to Admiral Cloué, after September 1870, sscc Archives, Rome, Pq 75/2.

60   Letter from Escolan to Bishop Jaussen, 15 February 1871, sscc Archives, Rome, Pq 75/2.

61   Patricia Anguita, 'L'insertion des rapanui à Tahiti et Moorea (1871–1920)', *Bulletin de la Société des Etudes Océaniennes*, CCXLIII (1988), pp. 21–39. For further details about this period, see Patricia Anguita, 'La migration rapanui vers Tahiti et Mangaréva (1871–1920)', MA thesis, University of Paris, 1986.

62   [Wilhelm] Geiseler, *Die Osterinsel, eine Stätte prähistorischer Kultur in der Südsee: Bericht des Kommandanten S.M. Kbt. 'Hyäne', Kapitänleutnant Geiseler, über die ethnologische Untersuchung der Oster-Insel (Rapanui) an den Chef der Kaiserlichen Admiralität* (Berlin, 1883), pp. 43–4.

63   McCall, 'Reaction to Disaster', pp. 71–2.

64   Porteous, 'The Modernization of Rapanui', p. 225.

65   Letter from John Brander to Bishop Jaussen, 9 August 1871, sscc Archives, Rome, Pq 75/2.

66   Letter from Bishop Jaussen to Father Auguste Jamet, 30 September 1871, sscc Archives, Rome, Pq 75/2.

67   McCall, 'Reaction to Disaster', p. 72, and McCall, 'Riro, Rapu and Rapanui', p. 113.

68   Letter of Admiral de Lapelin to Bishop Jaussen, 17 March 1872, sscc Archives, Rome, Pq 75/2.

69   Letter from Bishop Jaussen to Father Auguste Jamet, 16 February 1872, sscc Archives, Rome, Pq 75/2.

70   McCall, *Rapanui*, p. 63.

71   Grant McCall, 'Rapanui Images', *Pacific Studies*, XVII (1994), pp. 85–102.

72   Alphonse Pinart, 'Exploration de l'île de Pâques', *Bulletin de la Société de Géographie de Paris*, XVI (1878), p. 207.

73   *Ibid.*, p. 208.

74   Letter from Roussel to Bishop Jaussen, 2 July 1878, sscc Archives, Rome, Pq 75/1.

75   *Ibid.*

76   McCall, 'Riro, Rapu and Rapanui', p. 114.

77   Englert, *Primer siglo cristiano*, p. 57.

78 Fischer, *A History of the Pacific Islands*, pp. 134–5.
79 McCall, 'Reaction to Disaster', pp. 75.
80 A.-C. Eugène Caillot, *Histoire de la Polynésie Orientale* (Paris, 1910), p. 485.
81 Bouverie F. Clark, 'Reporting Calling at Sala-y-Gomez and Easter Islands', *Proceedings of the Royal Geographical Society of Australia*, South Australian Branch (Adelaide), III (1899), pp. 143–6.
82 *Ibid.*, p. 146.
83 Fischer, *A History of the Pacific Islands*, p. 123.
84 Geiseler, *Die Osterinsel*. A superb translation, with valuable introductory material and additional notes, is *Geiseler's Easter Island Report: An 1880s Anthropological Account*, trans. William S. Ayres and Gabriella S. Ayres (Honolulu, 1995).
85 *Ibid.*, pp. 21–2.
86 *Ibid.*, p. 6.
87 *Ibid.*, p. 44.
88 Raybaud, *L'île de Pâques de 1862 à 1888*, p. 277.
89 Letter from Father Montiton to Superior General Bousquet, 13 March 1886, SSCC Archives, Rome, Pq 75/2.
90 *Ibid.*
91 McCall, 'Rapanui Wanderings', p. 372.
92 McCall, 'Riro, Rapu and Rapanui', p. 114.
93 Grant McCall, *Las fundaciones de Rapanui* (Hanga Roa, 1986); Alberto Hotus et al., *Te Mau Hatu 'o Rapa Núi: 'Los soberamos de Rapa Nui'. Pasado, presente y futuro* (Santiago, 1988).
94 McCall, 'Riro, Rapu and Rapanui', p. 114.
95 Walter Hough, 'Notes on the Archæology and Ethnology of Easter Island', *American Naturalist*, XXIII (1889), p. 877.
96 George H. Cooke, 'Te Pito te Henua, Known as Rapa Nui; Commonly Called Easter Island, South Pacific Ocean', Annual Report of the Board of Regents of the Smithsonian Institution for the Year Ending June 30, 1897, *Report of the US National Museum, Part I* (Washington, DC, 1899), p. 691.
97 *Ibid.*, p. 719.
98 William Judah Thomson, 'Te Pito te Henua, or Easter Island', Report of the United States National Museum for the Year Ending June 30, 1889, *Annual Reports of the Smithsonian Institution for 1889* (Washington, DC, 1891), p. 473.
99 *Ibid.*, pp. 447–552.
100 Porteous, 'The Modernization of Rapanui', p. 225.
101 Letter from Bishop Verdier to Father Jamet, 30 September 1887, SSCC Archives, Rome, Pq 75/3.
102 Sebastian Englert's autographic correction from the printed '63', in Englert, *Primer siglo cristiano*, p. 60, Institute of Polynesian Languages and Literatures, Auckland, New Zealand.
103 Albert Montiton, 'Lettre du R. P. Albert Montiton . . . à son Supérieur général', *Annales de l'Association pour la Propagation de la Foi*, LXI (1889), p. 135.
104 Porteous, 'The Modernization of Rapanui', p. 225.

FOUR: *RANCHO* ISLA DE PASCUA

1 For an in-depth review of this era, see J. Douglas Porteous, *The Modernization of Easter Island* (Victoria, 1981).
2 Grant McCall, 'Reaction to Disaster: Continuity and Change in Rapanui Social Organisation', PhD dissertation, Australian National University, Canberra, 1976, p. 78.
3 For the larger contemporary picture, see Steven Roger Fischer, *A History of the Pacific Islands* (Basingstoke, 2002), p. 167.
4 Grant McCall, 'French Images of Rapanui (Easter Island)', *Journal of the Polynesian Society*, CIV/2 (1995), p. 182.
5 Grant McCall, 'Riro, Rapu and Rapanui: Refoundations in Easter Island Colonial History', *Rapa Nui Journal*, XI/3 (1997), p. 114.
6 F. B. Pike, *Chile and the United States, 1880–1962: The Emergence of Chile's Social Crisis and the Challenge to United States Diplomacy* (Notre Dame, IN, 1963), p. 31, cited in Porteous, *The Modernization of Easter Island*, p. 24.
7 Porteous, *The Modernization of Easter Island*, p. 27.

8   Pike, *Chile and the United States, 1880–1962*, p. 36, cited in Porteous, *The Modernization of Easter Island*, p. 26.

9   Rudolph (Rodulfo) A. Philippi, 'La isla de Pascua i sus habitantes', *Anales de la Universidad, Santiago de Chile*, XLIII (1873), p. 376.

10 *La Unión*, 30 September 1888, cited in Porteous, *The Modernization of Easter Island*, p. 32.

11 Grant McCall, 'Chile's Bitter Pacific Legacy', *Pacific Islands Monthly*, November 1988, pp. 43–5.

12 Policarpo Toro Hurtado, November 1886, cited in Porteous, *The Modernization of Easter Island*, p. 32.

13 Victor M. Vergara, *La Isla de Pascua: dominación y dominio* (Santiago, 1939). The present discussion is condensed from Porteous, *The Modernization of Easter Island*, p. 34.

14 Porteous, *The Modernization of Easter Island*, p. 37.

15 Cited in *ibid.*, p. 39.

16 Walter Knoche, *Die Osterinsel: Eine Zusammenfassung der chilenischen Osterinselexpedition des Jahres 1911* (Concepción, 1925), p. 36.

17 McCall, 'Reaction to Disaster', p. 305.

18 Porteous, *The Modernization of Easter Island*, pp. 37–8.

19 Relevant historical documents relating to Easter Island's annexation can be found in the appendices in Vergara, *La Isla de Pascua*; Isidoro Vázquez de Acuña et al., *Primeras jornadas territoriales: Isla de Pascua* (Santiago, 1987); and Stephan Chauvet, *La Isla de Pascua y sus misterios* (Santiago, 1965).

20 Sebastian Englert, *La tierra de Hotu Matu'a: historia, etnología y lengua de la Isla de Pascua* (Padre Las Casas, Chile, 1948), p. 53.

21 Carlos López, 'How Did Chile Acquire Easter Island?', *Rapa Nui Journal*, XII/4 (1998), pp. 120 and 121, note 16.

22 Francesco di Castri, 'Tahitian and French Influences in Easter Island, or the Zoopal Mystery Solved Thanks to Grant McCall', *Rapa Nui Journal*, XIII/4 (1999), p. 102.

23 McCall, 'Chile's Bitter Pacific Legacy', pp. 43–4.

24 *Ibid.*, p. 44.

25 McCall, 'Riro, Rapu and Rapanui', p. 114.

26 Sebastian Englert, *Primer siglo cristiano de la Isla de Pascua, 1864–1964* (Villarrica, Chile, 1964), p. 68.

27 Nelson Castro, 'Misioneros y milinaristas: Isla de Pascua, 1864–1914', thesis, Universidad de Valparaíso, 1996.

28 *La Unión*, 30 September 1888, cited in Porteous, *The Modernization of Easter Island*, p. 40.

29 Porteous, *The Modernization of Easter Island*, p. 45.

30 McCall, *Reaction to Disaster*, p. 305.

31 M. C. Bandy, 'Geology and Petrology of Easter Island', *Bulletin of the Geological Society of America*, XLVIII (1937), pp. 1591–2.

32 Pedro Pablo Toro Hurtado, *Memoria del Ministerio del Culto i Colonización presentada al Congreso Nacional en 1892* (Santiago, 1893), vol. III, pp. 205–6, cited in McCall, 'Reaction to Disaster', p. 156.

33 Porteous, *The Modernization of Easter Island*, pp. 49–50.

34 *Ibid.*, p. 50.

35 *Ibid.*

36 *Ibid.*, p. 62.

37 McCall, 'Riro, Rapu and Rapanui', p. 115.

38 Grant McCall, 'Japan, Rapanui and Chile's Uncertain Sovereignty', *Rapa Nui Journal*, IX/1 (1995), p. 2.

39 McCall, 'Chile's Bitter Pacific Legacy', p. 43.

40 Alfred Métraux, *Ethnology of Easter Island* (Honolulu, 1940), p. 92.

41 See Steven Roger Fischer, *Rongorongo: The Easter Island Script. History, Traditions, Texts* (Oxford, 1997), pp. 113–14, and Thomas S. Barthel, 'Native Documents from Easter Island', in *Reports of the Norwegian Archæological Expedition to Easter Island and the East Pacific*, vol. II: *Miscellaneous Papers*, ed. Padre Las Casas, Thor Heyerdahl and Edwin N. Ferdon, Jr (Stockholm, 1965), pp. 387–9.

42 Thomas S. Barthel, *The Eighth Land: The Polynesian Discovery and Settlement of Easter Island* (Honolulu, 1978), pp. 296–8; originally published as *Das achte Land: Die Entdeckung und*

Besiedlung der Osterinsel nach Eingeborenentraditionen übersetzt und erläutert (Munich, 1974), pp. 319–20.

43 Englert, *Primer siglo cristiano de la Isla de Pascua*, p. 70.

44 Porteous, *The Modernization of Easter Island*, p. 47.

45 *Ibid.*, p. 53.

46 J. Douglas Porteous, 'The Modernization of Rapanui', in *Easter Island Studies: Contributions to the History of Rapanui in Memory of William T. Mulloy*, ed. Steven Roger Fischer (Oxford, 1993), p. 225.

47 Porteous, *The Modernization of Easter Island*, p. 53.

48 Vázquez de Acuña et al., *Primeras jornadas territoriales*, p. 163.

49 McCall, 'Japan, Rapanui and Chile's Uncertain Sovereignty', p. 2.

50 Sánchez's side of the story can be read in Alberto Sánchez Manterola, 'Cinco años en la Isla de Pascua', unpublished typescript, Viña del Mar, March 1921, Archives of the Institute of Easter Island Studies, Santiago, Chile.

51 'Anniversary of a Shipwreck', *Rapa Nui Journal*, x/4 (1996), p. 119.

52 Cited in Porteous, *The Modernization of Easter Island*, p. 62.

53 Detailed in D. E. Rocuant, *La Isla de Pascua: estudio de los titulos de dominio, de las derechos y de los contratos de Don Enrique Merlet y de la Compañía Explotadora de la Isla de Pascua* (Valparaíso, 1916).

54 McCall, 'Riro, Rapu and Rapanui', p. 116.

55 Georges Eich, 'Lettre du R. P. Georges Eich, provincial de la mission de Tahiti . . . 1er avril 1898', *Annales des Sacrés-Cœurs*, n.s., v (1898), pp. 416–23.

56 Englert, *Primer siglo cristiano de la Isla de Pascua*, pp. 78–9.

57 *Ibid.*, p. 69.

58 Grant McCall, *Rapanui: Tradition and Survival on Easter Island*, 2nd edn (Honolulu, 1994), pp. 145–6.

59 McCall, 'Riro, Rapu and Rapanui', p. 116.

60 *Ibid.*

61 Alberto Hotus et al., *Te Mau Hatu 'o Rapa Núi: 'Los soberamos de Rapa Nui'. Pasado, presente y futuro* (Santiago, 1988), pp. 302–3.

62 McCall, *Rapanui*, p. 146.

63 McCall, 'Japan, Rapanui and Chile's Uncertain Sovereignty', p. 2.

64 McCall, 'Reaction to Disaster', p. 375, note 55.

65 Letter from Father Isidore Butaye to Father Palmace Ehrard, 18 April 1900, sscc Archives, Rome, Pq 75/2.

66 McCall, *Rapanui*, p. 146.

67 Stephen Chauvet, *L'île de Pâques et ses mystères* (Paris, 1935), p. 13.

68 Grant McCall, '37 Days That Shook the (Rapanui) World: The Angata Cult on Rapanui', in *Proceedings of the Pacific History Association*, ed. D. H. Rubinstein (Mangilao, Guam, 1992), p. 22.

69 McCall, 'Riro, Rapu and Rapanui', pp. 116–17.

70 Alejandra M. Grifferos A., 'Colonialism and Rapanui Identity', in *Easter Island in Pacific Context. Proceedings of the Fourth International Conference on Easter Island and East Polynesia: University of New Mexico, Albuquerque, 5–10 August 1997*, ed. Christopher M. Stevenson, Georgia Lee and Frank J. Morin (Los Osos, CA, 1998), p. 366.

71 McCall, 'Riro, Rapu and Rapanui', p. 117.

72 J. Douglas Porteous, 'The Company State: A Chilean Case Study', *Canadian Geographer*, xvii (1973), pp. 113–26.

73 Porteous, *The Modernization of Easter Island*, pp. 45–6.

74 *Ibid.*, p. 68.

75 *Ibid.*, p. 66.

76 W. Hunt, *Heirs of Great Adventure: The History of Balfour, Williamson and Company Limited*, 2 vols (London, 1951–60).

77 Porteous, *The Modernization of Easter Island*, p. 68.

78 *Ibid.*, p. 123.

79 *Ibid.*, p. 68.

80 *Ibid.*, p. 69.

81 *Ibid.*, pp. 140–41.
82 *Ibid.*, p. 141.
83 Jo Anne Van Tilburg, *Among Stone Giants: The Life of Katherine Routledge and her Remarkable Expedition to Easter Island* (New York, 2003), pp. 79–80.
84 McCall, '37 Days That Shook the (Rapanui) World', p. 17.
85 On the Rapanui's sophisticated nicknaming, see Grant McCall, 'Nicknames and What They Mean', *Rapa Nui Journal*, v/2 (1991), pp. 17–20. McCall was told by eyewitness informants that Edmunds was called 'Reherehe' because he 'walked with a floppy, swinging gait' (p. 20).
86 Walter Knoche, *Die Osterinsel: Eine Zusammenfassung der chilenischen Osterinselexpedition des Jahres 1911* (Concepción, 1925), p. 37.
87 *Ibid.*, p. 91. See also Walter Knoche, 'De la Isla de Pascua', *Pacífico Magazine*, vi (1913), pp. 347–51.
88 Englert, *Primer siglo cristiano de la Isla de Pascua*, pp. 75–6.
89 Sebastian Englert, *Tradiciones de la Isla de Pascua: en idioma rapanui y castellano* (Padre Las Casas, Chile, 1939), p. 7; and Barthel, *Das achte Land*, p. 321.
90 Van Tilburg, *Among Stone Giants*, p. 93.
91 [N. P. Benson], 'Captain Benson's Own Story', *Rapa Nui Journal*, xv/1 (2001), pp. 31–42.
92 Grant McCall, 'Rapanui Wanderings: Diasporas from Easter Island', in *Easter Island in Pacific Context*, p. 374.
93 Porteous, *The Modernization of Easter Island*, p. 72.
94 *Ibid.*, pp. 72–3.
95 Van Tilburg, *Among Stone Giants*, p. 118.
96 Katherine Routledge (Mrs Scoresby Routledge), *The Mystery of Easter Island: The Story of an Expedition* (London, 1919). See also Van Tilburg, *Among Stone Giants*.
97 Van Tilburg, *Among Stone Giants*, p. 82.
98 *Ibid.*, p. 125.
99 Routledge, *The Mystery of Easter Island*, p. 160.
100 Van Tilburg, *Among Stone Giants*, p. 151.
101 Literature: José Ignacio Vives Solar, 'Una revolución en la Isla de Pascua en 1914', *Pacífico Magazine*, x (1917), pp. 655–64; Routledge, *The Mystery of Easter Island*, pp. 141–9; McCall, '37 Days That Shook the (Rapanui) World', pp. 17–23; Van Tilburg, *Among Stone Giants*, pp. 148–63.
102 Routledge, *The Mystery of Easter Island*, p. 142.
103 *Ibid.*, pp. 142–3.
104 Van Tilburg, *Among Stone Giants*, pp. 151–2.
105 Routledge, *The Mystery of Easter Island*, p. 142.
106 *Ibid.*, p. 148.
107 *Ibid.*
108 *Ibid.*, p. 150.
109 Grifferos, 'Colonialism and Rapanui Identity', p. 366.
110 Nelson Castro, 'Misioneros y milinaristas: Isla de Pascua 1864–1914', thesis, Universidad de Valparaíso, 1996.
111 McCall, '37 Days That Shook the (Rapanui) World', pp. 20–21.
112 *Ibid.*, pp. 21–2.
113 Routledge, *The Mystery of Easter Island*, pp. 151–3. See also Knoche, *Die Osterinsel*, p. 38.
114 Routledge, *The Mystery of Easter Island*, pp. 153–4.
115 *Ibid.*, pp. 157–8.
116 *Ibid.*, p. 160.
117 Knoche, *Die Osterinsel*, p. 39.
118 Van Tilburg, *Among Stone Giants*, p. 119.
119 Routledge, *The Mystery of Easter Island*, p. 214.
120 Porteous, *The Modernization of Easter Island*, p. 79.
121 *Ibid.*, pp. 79–80.
122 Englert, *Primer siglo cristiano de la Isla de Pascua*, p. 77.
123 *La Unión*, 26 October 1916, cited in Porteous, *The Modernization of Easter Island*, p. 72.
124 Porteous, *The Modernization of Easter Island*, p. 218.
125 Routledge, *The Mystery of Easter Island*, p. 149, and R. J. Casey, *Easter Island: Home of the Scornful Gods* (London, 1932), p. 249.

126 McCall, 'Rapanui Wanderings', p. 374.
127 Porteous, *The Modernization of Easter Island*, p. 69.
128 *La Unión*, 8 November 1916, cited in Porteous, *The Modernization of Easter Island*, p. 78.
129 Cited in Porteous, *The Modernization of Easter Island*, p. 75.
130 *Ibid.*, p. 79.
131 Grifferos, 'Colonialism and Rapanui Identity', p. 366.
132 McCall, 'Japan, Rapanui and Chile's Uncertain Sovereignty', p. 2.
133 Rafael Edwards, 'La Isla de Pascua', *La Revista Católica*, XXXIV (1918), p. 273.
134 Englert, *Primer siglo cristiano de la Isla de Pascua*, pp. 79–80.
135 Porteous, *The Modernization of Easter Island*, p. 75.
136 *Ibid.*, p. 76.
137 *Ibid.*, p. 137.
138 Hunt, *Heirs of Great Adventure*, vol. II, p. 161, cited in Porteous, *The Modernization of Easter Island*, p. 138.
139 Cited in Porteous, *The Modernization of Easter Island*, p. 139.
140 *Ibid.*, p. 196.
141 *Ibid.*, pp. 149–50.
142 *Ibid.*, p. 151.
143 Hunt, *Heirs of Great Adventure*, vol. II, p. 224; quoted in Porteous, *The Modernization of Easter Island*, p. 151.
144 Englert, *Primer siglo cristiano de la Isla de Pascua*, p. 80.
145 John Macmillan Brown, *The Riddle of the Pacific* (London, 1924), p. 280.
146 *Ibid.*, pp. 47–56.
147 John Macmillan Brown, 'L'île de Pâques et son mystère', *La Géographie*, LX (1933), pp. 335–7.
148 J. Harland Paul, 'The Last Cruise of the Carnegie', *Rapa Nui Journal*, XVI/2 (2002), p. 107.
149 Englert, *Primer siglo cristiano de la Isla de Pascua*, p. 80.
150 McCall, 'Rapanui Wanderings', p. 374.
151 E. Lafertte, *Vida de un comunista*, 2nd edn (Santiago, 1971), p. 205, cited in McCall, 'Rapanui Wanderings', p. 374.
152 C. Vicuña, *En las prisiones políticas de Chile. Cuatro evasiones novelescas* (Santiago, 1946), pp. 141–75, cited in McCall, 'Rapanui Wanderings', p. 374.
153 McCall, 'Rapanui Wanderings', p. 374.
154 Métraux, *Ethnology of Easter Island*, p. 47.
155 A. M. Smith, 'A Look Backward . . .', *Rapa Nui Journal*, IV/3 (1990), p. 37.
156 Casey, *Easter Island*, p. 114.
157 *Ibid.*, p. 118.
158 *Ibid.*
159 Métraux, *Ethnology of Easter Island*, p. 4.
160 *Ibid.*, p. 152.
161 Henri Lavachery, *Ile de Pâques* (Paris, 1935); Lavachery, *Les pétroglyphes de l'Ile de Pâques*, 2 vols (Antwerp, 1939).
162 Alfred Métraux, *L'île de Pâques* (Paris, 1941); *Easter Island: A Stone-Age Civilization of the Pacific*, trans. Michael Bullock (London, 1957); and *L'île de Pâques*, 2nd edn (Paris, 1965), published posthumously.
163 Israel Drapkin, *Contribution to the Demographic Study of Easter Island* (Honolulu, 1935).
164 Englert, *Primer siglo cristiano de la Isla de Pascua*, pp. 81–2.
165 Matthias Buschkühl, *Missionsgeschichte der Osterinsel, Pater Sebastian Englert OFM Cap (1888–1969) zum 100. Geburtstag* (Eichstätt, 1988).
166 Cited in Englert, *Primer siglo cristiano de la Isla de Pascua*, p. 82.
167 Porteous, *The Modernization of Easter Island*, p. 81.
168 Grifferos, 'Colonialism and Rapanui Identity', p. 366.
169 Cited in *ibid.*, pp. 366–7.
170 McCall, *Rapanui*, p. 147.
171 Englert, *Primer siglo cristiano de la Isla de Pascua*, p. 83.
172 McCall, 'Japan, Rapanui and Chile's Uncertain Sovereignty', pp. 2–5.
173 *Ibid.*, p. 4.

174 McCall, 'Reaction to Disaster', p. xxvi.
175 Porteous, *The Modernization of Easter Island*, p. 218.
176 Fischer, *A History of the Pacific Islands*, p. 202.
177 Porteous, *The Modernization of Easter Island*, p. 224.
178 McCall, 'Rapanui Wanderings', p. 374. See also Porteous, *The Modernization of Easter Island*, p. 82.
179 For the most complete register of escapes, see McCall, 'Rapanui Wanderings', p. 375.
180 Porteous, *The Modernization of Easter Island*, p. 81.
181 McCall, 'Riro, Rapu and Rapanui', p. 117.
182 Porteous, *The Modernization of Easter Island*, p. 82.
183 *Ibid.*
184 *Ibid.*
185 *El Mercurio*, 13 January 1952, cited in Porteous, *The Modernization of Easter Island*, p. 82.
186 Grant McCall, 'Review of Raybaud's *L'île de Pâques de 1862 à 1888*', *Rapa Nui Journal*, xi/4 (1997), p. 167.
187 J. Douglas Porteous, 'Easter Island: The Scottish Connection', *Geographical Review*, lxviii/2 (1978), pp. 145–56.
188 Porteous, *The Modernization of Easter Island*, p. 226.
189 *Ibid.*, p. 218.

FIVE: MUSEUM ISLAND

1 Steven Roger Fischer, *A History of the Pacific Islands* (Basingstoke, 2002), p. 220.
2 Edwin N. Ferdon, Jr, *One Man's Log* (London, 1966), p. 71, cited in J. Douglas Porteous, *The Modernization of Easter Island* (Victoria, 1981), p. 168.
3 Grant McCall, 'Riro, Rapu and Rapanui: Refoundations in Easter Island Colonial History', *Rapa Nui Journal*, xi/3 (1997), p. 117.
4 Carlyle S. Smith, 'The Norwegian Expedition to Easter Island in Retrospect', in *Easter Island Studies: Contributions to the History of Rapanui in Memory of William T. Mulloy*, ed. Steven Roger Fischer (Oxford, 1993), pp. 79–81.
5 Mulloy's letter to his family, mid-November 1955, typescript photocopy, Institute of Polynesian Languages and Literatures, Auckland, New Zealand, cited with the kind permission of the Mulloy family.
6 Mulloy's letter to Marie Wormington, 19 January 1956, typescript photocopy, Institute of Polynesian Languages and Literatures, Auckland, New Zealand, cited with the kind permission of the Mulloy family.
7 Mulloy's letter to his family, 17 January 1956, typescript photocopy, Institute of Polynesian Languages and Literatures, Auckland, New Zealand, cited with the kind permission of the Mulloy family.
8 Mulloy's letter to his family, 1 November 1955, typescript photocopy, Institute of Polynesian Languages and Literatures, Auckland, New Zealand, cited with the kind permission of the Mulloy family.
9 *Ibid.*
10 Mulloy's letter to Marie Wormington, 19 January 1956, typescript photocopy, Institute of Polynesian Languages and Literatures, Auckland, New Zealand, cited with the kind permission of the Mulloy family.
11 Mulloy's letter to his family, April 1956, in Emily Ross Mulloy, 'William Mulloy: A Memoir', in *Easter Island Studies*, p. ix.
12 Mulloy's letter to his family, c. 5 December 1955, typescript photocopy, Institute of Polynesian Languages and Literatures, Auckland, New Zealand, cited with the kind permission of the Mulloy family; also Emily Ross Mulloy, 'Kau Kau Poki: A Tragedy at Anakena', *Rapa Nui Journal*, v/1 (1991), pp. 8–9.
13 Thor Heyerdahl and Edwin N. Ferdon, Jr, eds, *Reports of the Norwegian Archaeological Expedition to Easter Island and the East Pacific*, vol. 1: *Archaeology of Easter Island* (Stockholm, 1961), and vol. ii: *Miscellaneous Papers* (Stockholm, 1965).
14 Smith, 'The Norwegian Expedition', p. 80.
15 Thor Heyerdahl, *Aku-Aku: The Secret of Easter Island* (Chicago, 1958). A noteworthy contribution

to ethnography was his later *The Art of Easter Island* (London, 1976).

16 McCall, 'Riro, Rapu and Rapanui', p. 117.

17 Emily Ross Mulloy, 'William Mulloy: A Memoir', in *Easter Island Studies*, pp. ix–x; George W. Gill, 'William Mulloy and Rapanui', in *ibid.*, pp. xi–xiii; and Gonzalo Figueroa, 'William Mulloy: 1917–1978', in *William Mulloy: A Tribute*, ed. Yosihiko H. Sinoto, special edition of *Asian Perspectives*, xxii/1 (1981), pp. 101–5, and also (in Spanish) 'William Mulloy, 1917–1978', in *Estudios sobre la Isla de Pascua*, ed. Claudio Cristino Ferrando *et al.* (Santiago, 1980), pp. 11–15.

18 Among the many relevant publications, see J. Dransfield et al., 'A Recently Extinct Palm from Easter Island', *Nature*, cccxii (1984), pp. 750–52; John R. Flenley, 'The Palæoecology of Easter Island, and its Ecological Disaster', in *Easter Island Studies*, pp. 27–45; and John R. Flenley and Paul G. Bahn, *The Enigmas of Easter Island* (Oxford, 2002), pp. 80–88.

19 Compare Flenley and Bahn, *The Enigmas of Easter Island*, p. 193.

20 William T. Mulloy and Gonzalo Figueroa, *The A Kivi – Vai Teka Complex and Its Relationship to Easter Island Architectural History* (Honolulu, 1978), p. 22.

21 William T. Mulloy, 'Preliminary Culture-Historical Research Model for Easter Island', in *The Easter Island Bulletins of William Mulloy* (Houston, 1997), p. 110.

22 Published two years later: Thomas S. Barthel, *Grundlagen zur Entzifferung der Osterinselschrift* (Hamburg, 1958).

23 Grant McCall, 'Rapanui Wanderings: Diasporas from Easter Island', in *Easter Island in Pacific Context. South Seas Symposium: Proceedings of the Fourth International Conference on Easter Island and East Polynesia: University of New Mexico, Albuquerque, 5–10 August 1997*, ed. Christopher M. Stevenson, Georgia Lee and Frank J. Morin (Los Osos, CA, 1998), p. 375.

24 Emily Ross Mulloy, 'The Destruction of Tongariki', *Rapa Nui Journal*, v/3 (1991), pp. 33–4.

25 J. Douglas Porteous, 'The Modernization of Rapanui', in *Easter Island Studies*, p. 226.

26 Ramón Campbell, *El misterioso mundo de Rapanui* (Buenos Aires, 1973), p. 35.

27 Grant McCall, *Rapanui: Tradition and Survival on Easter Island* (Honolulu, 1980), p. 148.

28 Francis Mazière, *Fantastique Ile de Pâques* (Paris, 1965).

29 James A. Boutelier, 'METEI: A Canadian Medical Expedition to Easter Island, 1964–65', *Rapa Nui Journal*, vi/2 (1992), p. 30.

30 Porteous, *The Modernization of Easter Island*, pp. 226–7.

31 Ferdon Jr, *One Man's Log*, p. 72.

32 McCall, 'Riro, Rapu and Rapanui', p. 117.

33 C. Hocker, *And Christmas Day on Easter Island* (London, 1968), p. 210.

34 Porteous, *The Modernization of Easter Island*, p. 170.

35 Alejandra M. Grifferos A., 'La otra cara del paraíso: comunidad, tradición y colonialismo en Rapa Nui, 1864–1964', thesis, Universidad de Valparaíso, 1997, p. 109.

36 Alejandra M. Grifferos A., 'We Are Merely Asking for Respect: The Reformulation of Ethnicity in Rapa Nui (Easter Island 1966)', in *Pacific 2000. Proceedings of the Fifth International Conference on Easter Island and the Pacific: Hawai'i Preparatory Academy, Kamuela, Hawai'i, 7–12 August 2000*, ed. Christopher M. Stevenson, Georgia Lee and Frank J. Morin (Los Osos, 2001), p. 378.

37 H. E. Reid, *A World Away: A Canadian Adventure on Easter Island* (Toronto, 1965), p. 36.

38 Boutilier, 'METEI', p. 21.

39 Porteous, *The Modernization of Easter Island*, p. 178.

40 M. Dodds, 'Life and Times on Easter Island', *Rapa Nui Journal*, iv/4 (1990), p. 62.

41 Boutilier, 'METEI', p. 21.

42 *Ibid.*, p. 30.

43 McCall, 'Riro, Rapu and Rapanui', p. 118.

44 James A. Boutilier, 'METEI: A Canadian Medical Expedition to Easter Island, 1964–65, Part II', *Rapa Nui Journal*, vi/3 (1992), pp. 45–53.

45 Stanley C. Skoryna, 'METEI: An Epiloque', *Rapa Nui Journal*, vi/4 (1992), p. 69.

46 Interview of 7 July 1983, cited in Boutilier, 'METEI, Part II', p. 46.

47 A preliminary bibliography appears in Boutilier, 'METEI, Part II', pp. 52–3; compare the comments by J. Douglas Porteous, 'METEI: The Canadian Medical Expedition to Easter Island', *Rapa Nui Journal*, iii/3 (1989), p. 11. Only one scientific book resulted: Georges L. Nógrády, ed., *The Microbiology of Easter Island* (Montreal, 1974).

48 Porteous, *The Modernization of Easter Island*, pp. 171–2.

49 *El Mercurio*, 11 January 1965, cited in Porteous, *The Modernization of Easter Island*, p. 172.
50 Grant McCall, 'Reaction to Disaster: Continuity and Change in Rapanui Social Organisation', PhD dissertation, Australian National University, Canberra, 1976, p. 79.
51 McCall, 'Riro, Rapu and Rapanui', p. 118.
52 *Libro de Actas de la Municipalidad de Hangaroa, Isla de Pascua*, cited in Porteous, *The Modernization of Easter Island*, p. 172.
53 Grifferos A., 'We Are Merely Asking for Respect', p. 378.
54 Grant McCall, 'Sympathy and Antipathy in Easter Islander and Chilean Relations', *Journal of the Polynesian Society*, LXXXIV (1975), pp. 467–76.
55 McCall, 'Riro, Rapu and Rapanui', p. 118.
56 Grifferos A., 'We Are Merely Asking for Respect', p. 378.
57 C. Cristino et al., *Isla de Pascua: proceso, alcanses y efectos de la aculturación* (Santiago, 1984), p. 32; quoted in Grifferos A., 'We Are Merely Asking for Respect', p. 378.
58 Porteous, *The Modernization of Easter Island*, p. 172.
59 *Ibid.*, p. 224.
60 José Miguel Ramírez, 'Cultural Resource Management on Easter Island: Utopia and Reality', in *Pacific 2000*, p. 385.
61 Grifferos A., 'We Are Merely Asking for Respect', p. 378.
62 Quoted in *ibid.*
63 *Ibid.*, p. 379.
64 *Las Últimas Noticias*, 5 January 1967, cited in Grifferos A., 'We Are Merely Asking for Respect', p. 379.
65 Miki Makihara, 'Rapanui-Spanish Bilingual Language Choice and Code Switching', in *Easter Island in Pacific Context*, p. 33.
66 Porteous, 'The Modernization of Rapanui', p. 225.
67 *El Mercurio*, 20 April 1965, cited in Porteous, *The Modernization of Easter Island*, p. 174.
68 Grant McCall, *Rapanui: Tradition and Survival on Easter Island*, 2nd edn (Honolulu, 1994), pp. 159–60.
69 Porteous, *The Modernization of Easter Island*, pp. 172–3.
70 McCall, *Rapanui*, p. 136.
71 Hanns Ebensten, '24 Years of Tourism on Easter Island', *Rapa Nui Journal*, V/2 (1991), pp. 25–6.
72 James Cook, *A Voyage Towards the South Pole and Round the World (1772–75)*, 2nd edn (London, 1777), vol. 1, p. 289.
73 McCall, *Rapanui*, p. 136.
74 Porteous, *The Modernization of Easter Island*, p. 174.
75 *Ibid.*, p. 198.
76 William T. Mulloy, 'Foreword', in Sebastian Englert, *Island at the Centre of the World: New Light on Easter Island* (London, 1970), p. 12.
77 *Plan de Desarrollo del Departamento de Isla de Pascua 1971–76*, Plan de la Economía Nacional, Series 1, no. 15 (Santiago, 1972), p. 34, cited in Porteous, *The Modernization of Easter Island*, p. 176.
78 *El Mercurio*, 7 February 1967, cited in Porteous, *The Modernization of Easter Island*, p. 176.
79 Grant McCall, 'Japan, Rapanui and Chile's Uncertain Sovereignty', *Rapa Nui Journal*, IX/1 (1995), p. 1.
80 Ramírez, 'Cultural Resource Management on Easter Island', p. 385.
81 Porteous, *The Modernization of Easter Island*, p. 177.
82 McCall, *Rapanui*, p. 184.
83 Porteous, *The Modernization of Easter Island*, p. 234.
84 McCall, *Rapanui*, p. 187.
85 Porteous, *The Modernization of Easter Island*, p. 230.
86 McCall, 'Riro, Rapu and Rapanui', p. 120.
87 McCall, 'Sympathy and Antipathy in Easter Islander and Chilean Relations', p. 44.
88 J. Douglas Porteous, 'The Development of Tourism on Easter Island', *Geography*, LXV/2 (1980), pp. 137–8.
89 McCall, *Rapanui*, p. 138.
90 Ramírez, 'Cultural Resource Management on Easter Island', p. 385.
91 Sergio Rapu, lecture at the XVIIth Pacific Science Congress, 27 May–2 June 1991, Honolulu,

Hawai'i.

92 McCall, 'Japan, Rapanui and Chile's Uncertain Sovereignty', p. 2.

93 Alberto Hotus et al., *Te Mau Hatu 'o Rapa Núi: 'Los soberamos de Rapa Nui'. Pasado, presente y futuro* (Santiago, 1988).

94 This antiquated theory, revived only by Heyerdahl, has best been refuted by Paul Bahn and John Flenley, *Easter Island, Earth Island* (London, 1992), pp. 38–68.

95 McCall, *Rapanui*, p. 126.

96 McCall, 'Rapanui Wanderings', p. 376.

97 M. Maunder, 'Conservation of the Extinct Toromiro Tree, *Sophora toromiro*', *Curtiss's Botanical Magazine*, xiv/4 (1997), pp. 226–31.

98 Georgia Lee, *The Rock Art of Easter Island: Symbols of Power, Prayers to the Gods* (Los Angeles, 1992).

99 *El Mercurio*, 14 October 1989; quoted in *Rapa Nui Journal*, iii/3 (1989), p. 10.

100 *Rapa Nui Journal*, iii/4 (1989–90), p. 15.

101 *Rapa Nui Journal*, iv/2 (1990), p. 32.

102 *Rapa Nui Journal*, iv/4 (1990–91), pp. 49 and 52.

103 *Rapa Nui Journal*, v/4 (1991), pp. 56–8.

104 'On the Japanese Restoration of Tongariki', *Rapa Nui Journal*, vi/3 (1992), pp. 58–9, and A. Elena Charola, 'Algunas consideraciones sobra la restauración de un nuevo sitio arqueológico en Isla de Pascua', *Rapa Nui Journal*, vi/3 (1992), pp. 59–60.

105 Riet Delsing, 'Cultural Politics and Globalization on Rapa Nui', *Rapa Nui Journal*, xii/4 (1998), p. 104.

106 *Rapa Nui Journal*, vii/1 (1993), p. 20.

107 *Rapa Nui Journal*, vii/2 (1993), p. 37.

108 *Rapa Nui Journal*, viii/1 (1994), p. 22.

109 *El Mercurio de Valparaíso*, 23 June 1994; quoted in *Rapa Nui Journal*, viii/3 (1994), p. 81.

110 *Ibid.*, 19 September 1994; quoted in *Rapa Nui Journal*, viii/4 (1994), p. 116.

111 William Liller, 'Review of Grant McCall, *Rapanui*', *Rapa Nui Journal*, viii/4 (1994), p. 109.

112 *El Mercurio de Valparaíso*, 12 February 1995; quoted in *Rapa Nui Journal*, ix/1 (1995), p. 26.

113 Ramírez, 'Cultural Resource Management on Easter Island', p. 387.

114 *Rapa Nui Journal*, ix/3 (1995), p. 88.

115 *Ibid.*, p. 89.

116 *Rapa Nui Journal*, x/1 (1996), p. 25.

117 Myra Shackley, 'Cultural Tourism and World Heritage Designation on Easter Island', in *Easter Island in Pacific Context*, p. 390.

118 *El Mercurio de Santiago*, 15 September 1996, cited in *Rapa Nui Journal*, x/4 (1996), p. 118.

119 Claudio P. Cristino and Patricia Vargas Casanova, 'Ahu Tongariki, Easter Island: Chronological and Sociopolitical Significance', *Rapa Nui Journal*, xiii/3 (1999), p. 69.

120 Ramírez, 'Cultural Resource Management on Easter Island', p. 387.

121 McCall, 'Riro, Rapu and Rapanui', p. 119.

122 *El Mercurio de Valparaíso*, 6 December 1997, cited in *Rapa Nui Journal*, xii/1 (1998), pp. 23–4.

123 *El Mercurio de Valparaíso*, 7 February 1998, cited in *Rapa Nui Journal*, xii/1 (1998), pp. 24–5.

124 *El Mercurio de Valparaíso*, 9 July 1998, cited in *Rapa Nui Journal*, xii/3 (1998), p. 92.

125 *El Mercurio de Valparaíso*, 6 April 1999, cited in *Rapa Nui Journal*, xiii/2 (1999), p. 58.

126 *El Mercurio de Valparaíso*, 26 June 1999, cited in *Rapa Nui Journal*, xiii/3 (1999), p. 85.

127 Ramírez, 'Cultural Resource Management on Easter Island', p. 388.

128 José Miguel Ramírez, 'Rapa Nui Land Management: A Personal Chronicle', *Rapa Nui Journal*, xiv/2 (2000), pp. 47–8.

129 *Rapa Nui Journal*, xiii/3 (1999), p. 86.

130 *Rapa Nui Journal*, xiv/4 (2000), p. 121.

131 *Time*, 1 January 2000, p. 124.

132 Grifferos A., 'We Are Merely Asking for Respect', p. 377.

133 *El Mercurio de Valparaíso*, 26 October 2000, cited in *Rapa Nui Journal*, xiv/4 (2000), p. 120.

134 *Ibid.*

135 *Ibid.*

136 *Rapa Nui Journal*, xiv/4 (2000), p. 126.

137 Grant McCall, 'A Report from Rapa Nui', *Rapa Nui Journal*, xv/1 (2001), p. 5.
138 Porteous, *The Modernization of Easter Island*, p. 226.
139 Porteous, 'The Modernization of Rapanui', p. 227.
140 Shackley, 'Cultural Tourism and World Heritage Designation on Easter Island', p. 388.
141 *Rapa Nui Journal*, xvi/2 (2002), p. 119.
142 Grant McCall, 'Culture Bursting Out All Over on Rapanui, 2001–2002', *Rapa Nui Journal*, xv/2 (2001), p. 81.
143 *Rapa Nui Journal*, xvii/2 (2003), pp. 151–2.
144 Francesco di Castri, 'Toward the Autonomy of Rapa Nui?', *Rapa Nui Journal*, xvii/2 (2003), p. 126.
145 McCall, 'Japan, Rapanui and Chile's Uncertain Sovereignty', p. 6.
146 *Ibid.*
147 Porteous, 'The Modernization of Rapanui', p. 227.
148 Makihara, 'Rapanui-Spanish Bilingual Language Choice and Code Switching', p. 36.
149 *Ibid.*
150 Jocelyn Linnekin, 'The Politics of Culture in the Pacific', in *Cultural Identity and Ethnicity in the Pacific*, ed. J. Linnekin and L. Poyer (Honolulu, 1990), p. 152.
151 Delsing, 'Cultural Politics and Globalization on Rapa Nui', p. 106.
152 McCall, *Rapanui*, p. 191.
153 Fischer, *A History of the Pacific Islands*, p. 263.
154 *Ibid.*, p. 262.
155 Ramírez, 'Cultural Resource Management on Easter Island', p. 388.
156 Shackley, 'Cultural Tourism and World Heritage Designation on Easter Island', p. 391.
157 Porteous, *The Modernization of Easter Island*, p. 215.
158 Ramírez, 'Cultural Resource Management on Easter Island', p. 387.
159 *Ibid.*, p. 389.
160 Tandy Shephard-Toomey, 'The Development of Rapa Nui (Easter Island), Chile 1967–2001', *Rapa Nui Journal*, xv/2 (2001), p. 111.
161 *Ibid.*, p. 113.
162 Grant McCall, 'Chile's Bitter Pacific Legacy', *Pacific Islands Monthly*, November 1988, p. 44.
163 *Rapa Nui Journal*, xvii/2 (2003), p. 150.
164 Di Castri, 'Toward the Autonomy of Rapa Nui?', p. 128.
165 *Ibid.*, p. 129.
166 Porteous, *The Modernization of Easter Island*, p. 167.
167 Francesco di Castri, 'Tahitian and French Influences in Easter Island, or the Zoopal Mystery Solved Thanks to Grant McCall', *Rapa Nui Journal*, xiii/3 (1999), p. 101.
168 Katherine Routledge (Mrs Scoresby Routledge), *The Mystery of Easter Island: The Story of an Expedition* (London, 1919), p. 280.

Bibliography

Anguita, Patricia, 'La migration rapanui vers Tahiti et Mangaréva (1871–1920)', MA thesis, University of
    Paris, 1986
—, 'L'insertion des rapanui à Tahiti et Moorea (1871–1920)', *Bulletin de la Société des Etudes
    Océaniennes*, CCXLIII (1988), pp. 21–39
Anonymous, *Additional Supplement to the Hobart Town Gazette*, 28 July 1821
—, 'On the Japanese Restoration of Tongariki', *Rapa Nui Journal*, VI/3 (1992), pp. 58–9
Ayres, William S., 'Radiocarbon Dates from Easter Island', *Journal of the Polynesian Society*, LXXX
    (1971), pp. 497–504
—, 'The Cultural Context of Easter Island Religious Structures'. PhD dissertation, Tulane University,
    New Orleans, LA, 1973
—, 'Easter Island Subsistence', *Journal de la Société des Océanistes*, LXXX (1985), pp. 103–24
Bahn, Paul, and John Flenley, *Easter Island, Earth Island* (London, 1992)
Bandy, M. C., 'Geology and Petrology of Easter Island', *Bulletin of the Geological Society of America*,
    XLVIII (1937), pp. 1591–2
Barclay, H. Vere, 'Easter Island and its Colossal Statues', *Proceedings of the Royal Geographical Society of
    Australasia*, South Australian Branch (Adelaide), III (1899), pp. 127–37
Barthel, Thomas S., *Grundlagen zur Entzifferung der Osterinselschrift* (Hamburg, 1958)
—, 'Wer waren die ersten Siedler auf der Osterinsel?', *Ethnologica*, n.s., II (1960), pp. 232–40
—, 'Native Documents from Easter Island', in *Reports of the Norwegian Archaeological Expedition to
    Easter Island and the East Pacific*, vol. II: *Miscellaneous Papers*, ed. Thor Heyerdahl and Edwin N.
    Ferdon, Jr (Stockholm, 1965), pp. 387–9
—, *Das achte Land: Die Entdeckung und Besiedlung der Osterinsel nach Eingeborenentraditionen über-
    setzt und erläutert* (Munich, 1974)
—, *The Eighth Land: The Polynesian Discovery and Settlement of Easter Island*, trans. Anneliese Martin
    (Honolulu, 1978)
Bellwood, Peter, *Prehistory of the Indo-Malaysian Archipelago*, 2nd edn (Honolulu, 1997)
[Benson, N. P.], 'Captain Benson's Own Story', *Rapa Nui Journal*, XV/1 (2001), pp. 31–42
Bierbach, Annette, and Horst Cain, *Religion and Language of Easter Island* (Berlin, 1996)
Blackburn, Mark, *Tattoos from Paradise: Traditional Polynesian Patterns* (Atglen, PA, 1999)
Bork, Hans-Rudolf, and Andreas Mieth, 'The Key Role of *Jubæa* Palm Trees in the History of Rapa
    Nui: A Provocative Interpretation', *Rapa Nui Journal*, XVII/2 (2003), pp. 119–22
Boutelier, James A., 'METEI: A Canadian Medical Expedition to Easter Island, 1964–65', *Rapa Nui
    Journal*, VI/2 (1992), pp. 21–3, 26–33
—, 'METEI: A Canadian Medical Expedition to Easter Island, 1964–65, Part II', *Rapa Nui Journal*, VI/3
    (1992), pp. 45–53
Brown, John Macmillan, *The Riddle of the Pacific* (London, 1924)
—, 'L'île de Pâques et son mystère', *La Géographie*, LX (1933), pp. 335–7
Buschkühl, Matthias, *Missionsgeschichte der Osterinsel, Pater Sebastian Englert OFM Cap (1888–1969)
    zum 100. Geburtstag* (Eichstätt, 1988)
Butler, Kevin, and John Flenley, 'Further Pollen Evidence from Easter Island', in *Pacific 2000*.

Proceedings of the Fifth International Conference on Easter Island and the Pacific: Hawai'i
Preparatory Academy, Kamuela, Hawai'i, 7–12 August 2000, ed. Christopher M. Stevenson,
Georgia Lee and Frank J. Morin, (Los Osos, CA, 2001), pp. 79–81

Caillot, A.-C. Eugène, Histoire de la Polynésie Orientale (Paris, 1910)

Campbell, Ramón, El misterioso mundo de Rapanui (Buenos Aires, 1973)

Casey, R. J., Easter Island: Home of the Scornful Gods (London, 1932)

Castro, Nelson, 'Misioneros y milinaristas: Isla de Pascua, 1864–1914', thesis, Universidad de Valparaíso,
1996

Charola, A. Elena, 'Algunas consideraciones sobra la restauración de un nuevo sitio arqueológico en
Isla de Pascua', Rapa Nui Journal, VI/3 (1992), pp. 59–60

Chauvet, Stephan, L'île de Pâques et ses mystères (Paris, 1935)

—, La Isla de Pascua y sus misterios, Spanish version completed by José María Souvirón (Santiago,
1965)

Clark, Bouverie F., 'Reporting Calling at Sala-y-Gomez and Easter Islands', Proceedings of the Royal
Geographical Society of Australia, South Australian Branch (Adelaide), III (1899), pp. 143–6

Conte Oliveros, Jesús, Isla de Pascua: horizontes sombrios y luminosos (Casilla, Chile, 1995)

Cook, James, A Voyage Towards the South Pole and Round the World (1772–75), 2nd edn (London, 1777)

Cooke, George H., 'Te Pito te Henua, Known as Rapa Nui; Commonly Called Easter Island, South
Pacific Ocean', Annual Report of the Board of Regents of the Smithsonian Institution for the
Year Ending June 30, 1897, Report of the US National Museum, Part I (Washington, DC, 1899),
pp. 689–723

Corney, Bolton Glanvill, ed., The Voyage of Captain Don Felipe Gonzalez . . . , Preceded by an Extract
from Mynheer Jacob Roggeveen's Official Log (Cambridge, 1908)

Cristino, Claudio P., and Patricia Vargas Casanova, 'Ahu Tongariki, Easter Island: Chronological and
Sociopolitical Significance', Rapa Nui Journal, XIII/3 (1999), pp. 67–9

Cristino, C., et al., Isla de Pascua: proceso, alcanses y efectos de la aculturación (Santiago, 1984)

Dederen, François, 'L'évangélisation de l'île de Pâques par les Frères de la Congrégation des Sacrés-
Cœurs de Picpus', in Circumpacifica: Festschrift für Thomas S. Barthel, ed. Bruno Illius and
Matthias Laubscher (Frankfurt am Main, New York and Paris, 1990), vol. II, pp. 103–23

Delsing, Riet, 'Cultural Politics and Globalization on Rapa Nui', Rapa Nui Journal, XII/4 (1998),
pp. 99–108

di Castri, Francesco, 'Tahitian and French Influences in Easter Island; or, The Zoopal Mystery Solved
Thanks to Grant McCall', Rapa Nui Journal, XIII/4 (1999), pp. 100–06

—, 'Toward the Autonomy of Rapa Nui?', Rapa Nui Journal, XVII/2 (2003), pp. 126–30

DiSalvo, Louis H., and John E. Randall, 'The Marine Fauna of Rapanui, Past and Present', in Easter
Island Studies: Contributions to the History of Rapanui in Memory of William T. Mulloy, ed.
Steven Roger Fischer (Oxford, 1993), pp. 16–23

[Dobson, Edward?], 'Journal of the Ship Surry 1820–21', MLA 131, Mitchell Library, State Library of New
South Wales, Sydney, Australia

Dransfield, J., et al., 'A Recently Extinct Palm from Easter Island', Nature, CCCXII (1984), pp. 750–52

Drapkin, Israel, Contribution to the Demographic Study of Easter Island (Honolulu, 1935)

Dunmore, John, The Journal of Jean-François de Galaup de la Pérouse, 1785–1788, vol. I (London, 1994)

Dupetit-Thouars, Aubert, Voyage autour du monde sur la frégate 'La Vénus' (1836–39), 4 vols (Paris,
1841)

Eich, Georges, 'Lettre du R. P. Georges Eich, provincial de la mission de Tahiti . . . 1er avril 1898',
Annales des Sacrés-Cœurs, n.s., V (1898), pp. 416–23

Englert, Sebastian, Tradiciones de la Isla de Pascua en idioma rapanui y castellano (Padre Las Casas,
Chile, 1939)

—, La tierra de Hotu Matu'a: historia, etnología y lengua de la Isla de Pascua (Padre Las Casas, Chile,
1948)

—, Primer siglo cristiano de la Isla de Pascua, 1864–1964 (Villarrica, Chile, 1964)

—, Island at the Centre of the World: New Light on Easter Island, trans. and ed. William T. Mulloy
(London, 1970)

Esen-Baur, Heide-Margaret, Untersuchungen über den Vogelmann-Kult auf der Osterinsel (Wiesbaden,
1983)

Eyraud, Jean, 'Lettre de M. l'abbé Jean Eyraud (Notice biographique sur le frère Joseph-Eugène

Eyraud)', *Annales de la Congrégation des Sacrés-Cœurs*, vi (1880), pp. 804–16

Eyraud, Joseph-Eugène, 'Lettre du F. Eugène Eyraud, au T.R.P. Supérieur général', *Annales de la Propagation de la Foi*, xxxviii (1866), pp. 52–71, 124–38

Ferdon, Edwin N., Jr, 'The Ceremonial Site of Orongo', in *Reports of the Norwegian Archaeological Expedition to Easter Island and the East Pacific*, vol. 1: *Archaeology of Easter Island*, ed. Thor Heyerdahl and Edwin N. Ferdon, Jr (Stockholm, 1961), pp. 221–55

—, *One Man's Log* (London, 1966)

Figueroa, Gonzalo, 'William Mulloy, 1917–1978', in *William Mulloy: A Tribute*, ed. Yosihiko H. Sinoto; special edition of *Asian Perspectives*, xxii/1 (1981), pp. 101–05

—, 'William Mulloy, 1917–1978', in *Estudios sobre la Isla de Pascua*, ed. Claudio Cristino Ferrando et al. (Santiago, 1980), pp. 11–15

Finney, Ben, and Bernard Kilonsky, 'Closing and Opening the Polynesian Triangle: *Hōkūle'a*'s Voyage to Rapa Nui', in *Pacific 2000. Proceedings of the Fifth International Conference on Easter Island and the Pacific: Hawai'i Preparatory Academy, Kamuela, Hawai'i, 7–12 August 2000*, ed. Christopher M. Stevenson, Georgia Lee and Frank J. Morin (Los Osos, CA, 2001), pp. 353–63

Fischer, Steven Roger, 'Rapanui is Rapa Nui is Rapa-nui', *Rapa Nui Journal*, v/3 (1991), p. 42

—, 'Hugh Cuming's Account of an Anchorage at Rapanui (Easter Island), November 27–8, 1827', *Journal of the Polynesian Society*, c/3 (1991), pp. 303–15

—, 'Homogeneity in Old Rapanui', *Oceanic Linguistics*, xxxi/2 (1992), pp. 181–90

—, 'The Calling of hms *Seringapatam* at Rapanui (Easter Island) on March 6, 1830', *Pacific Studies*, xvi/1 (1993), pp. 67–84

—, ed., *Easter Island Studies: Contributions to the History of Rapanui in Memory of William T. Mulloy* (Oxford, 1993)

—, 'The Naming of Rapanui', in *Easter Island Studies: Contributions to the History of Rapanui in Memory of William T. Mulloy*, ed. Steven Roger Fischer (Oxford, 1993), pp. 63–6

—, 'Rapanui's *Tu'u ko Iho* Versus Mangareva's *Atu Motua*: Evidence for Multiple Reanalysis and Replacement in Rapanui Settlement Traditions, Easter Island', *Journal of Pacific History*, xxix (1994), pp. 3–18

—, *Glyphbreaker* (New York, 1997)

—, *Rongorongo: The Easter Island Script. History, Traditions, Texts* (Oxford, 1997)

—, 'Mangarevan Doublets: Preliminary Evidence for Proto-Southeastern Polynesian', *Oceanic Linguistics*, xl (2001), pp. 112–24

—, *A History of the Pacific Islands* (Basingstoke, 2002)

Fischer, Steven Roger, and Charles M. Love, 'Rapanui: The Geological Parameters', in *Easter Island Studies: Contributions to the History of Rapanui in Memory of William T. Mulloy*, ed. Steven Roger Fischer (Oxford, 1993), pp. 1–6

Flenley, John R., 'The Present Flora of Easter Island and its Origins', in *Easter Island Studies: Contributions to the History of Rapanui in Memory of William T. Mulloy*, ed. Steven Roger Fischer (Oxford, 1993), pp. 7–15

—, 'The Palæoecology of Easter Island, and its Ecological Disaster', in *Easter Island Studies: Contributions to the History of Rapanui in Memory of William T. Mulloy*, ed. Steven Roger Fischer (Oxford, 1993), pp. 27–45

—, 'Further Evidence of Vegetational Change on Easter Island', *South Pacific Study*, xvi (1996), pp. 135–41

Flenley, John, and Paul Bahn, *The Enigmas of Easter Island* (Oxford, 2002)

Flores, J., *Te Pito te Henua* (Santiago, 1965)

Forment, Francina, *Les figures moai kavakava de l'Ile de Pâques* (Ghent, 1991)

Forster, George, *A Voyage Round the World in hbm's Sloop 'Resolution' (1772–75)*, 2 vols (London, 1777)

Franceschini, Emile, 'Un animateur et un savant: Mgr Jaussen', *Encyclopédie mensuelle d'Outre-Mer*, iv/52 (1954), pp. 353–4

Geiseler, [Wilhelm], *Die Osterinsel, eine Stätte prähistorischer Kultur in der Südsee: Bericht des Kommandanten S.M. Kbt. 'Hyäne', Kapitänleutnant Geiseler, über die ethnologische Untersuchung der Oster-Insel (Rapanui) an den Chef der Kaiserlichen Admiralität* (Berlin, 1883)

—, *Geiseler's Easter Island Report: An 1880s Anthropological Account*, trans. William S. Ayres and Gabriella S. Ayres (Honolulu, 1995)

Gill, George W., 'William Mulloy and Rapanui', in *Easter Island Studies: Contributions to the History of*

Rapanui in Memory of William T. Mulloy, ed. Steven Roger Fischer (Oxford, 1993), pp. xi–xiii

—, 'Skeletal Remains from Ahu Nau Nau: Land of the Royal Miru', in *Eastern Island Archæology: Research on Early Rapanui Culture*, ed. Christopher M. Stevenson and William S. Ayres (Los Osos, CA, 2000), pp. 109–24

Goldman, Irving, *Ancient Polynesian Society* (Chicago and London, 1970)

Gough, Barry M., *To the Pacific and Arctic with Beechey: The Journal of Lieutenant George Peard of HMS 'Blossom', 1825–1828* (Cambridge, 1973)

Green, Roger C., 'Rapanui Origins Prior to European Contact: The View from Eastern Polynesian', in *Easter Island and East Polynesian Prehistory*, ed. Patricia Vargas Casanova (Santiago, 1998), pp. 87–110

—, 'Origins for the Rapanui of Easter Island Before European Contact: Solutions from Holistic Anthropology to an Issue no Longer Much of a Mystery', *Rapa Nui Journal*, xIV/3 (2000), pp. 71–6

Green, Roger C., and Marshall I. Weisler, 'The Mangarevan Sequence and Dating of the Geographic Expansion into Southeast Polynesia', *Asian Perspectives*, xLI/2 (2002), pp. 213–41

Grifferos A., Alejandra M., 'La otra cara del paraíso: comunidad, tradición y colonialismo en Rapa Nui, 1864–1964', thesis, Universidad de Valparaíso, 1997

—, 'Colonialism and Rapanui Identity', in *Easter Island in Pacific Context. Proceedings of the Fourth International Conference on Easter Island and East Polynesia: University of New Mexico, Albuquerque, 5–10 August 1997*, ed. Christopher M. Stevenson, Georgia Lee and Frank J. Morin (Los Osos, CA, 1998), pp. 365–7

—, 'We Are Merely Asking for Respect: The Reformulation of Ethnicity in Rapa Nui (Easter Island 1966)', in *Easter Island in Pacific Context. Proceedings of the Fourth International Conference on Easter Island and East Polynesia: University of New Mexico, Albuquerque, 5–10 August 1997*, ed. Christopher M. Stevenson, Georgia Lee and Frank J. Morin (Los Osos, CA, 1998), pp. 377–81

Handy, Edward S. Craighill, *The Native Culture in the Marquesas* (Honolulu, 1923)

Hasse, K. M., P. Stoffers and C. D. Garbe-Schonberg, 'The Petrogenetic Evolution of Lavas from Easter Island and Neighbouring Seamounts, Near-ridge Hotspot Volcanoes in the SE Pacific', *Journal of Petrology*, xxxVIII (1997), pp. 785–813

Henry, L. L., 'The Area of Rapa Nui', *Rapa Nui Journal*, VIII (1994), pp. 71–3

Heyerdahl, Thor, *Aku-Aku: The Secret of Easter Island* (Chicago, 1958)

—, 'An Introduction to Easter Island', in *Reports of the Norwegian Archaeological Expedition to Easter Island and the East Pacific*, vol. I: *Archaeology of Easter Island*, ed. Thor Heyerdahl and Edwin N. Ferdon, Jr (Stockholm, 1961), pp. 21–90

—, *The Art of Easter Island* (London, 1976)

Heyerdahl, Thor, and Edwin N. Ferdon, Jr, eds, *Reports of the Norwegian Archaeological Expedition to Easter Island and the East Pacific*, vol. I: *Archaeology of Easter Island* (Stockholm, 1961), and vol. II: *Miscellaneous Papers* (Stockholm, 1965)

Hocker, C., *And Christmas Day on Easter Island* (London, 1968)

Hotus, Alberto, et al., *Te Mau Hatu 'o Rapa Núi: 'Los soberamos de Rapa Nui'. Pasado, presente y futuro* (Santiago, 1988)

Hough, Walter, 'Notes on the Archæology and Ethnology of Easter Island', *American Naturalist*, xxIII (1889), pp. 877–88

Hunt, W., *Heirs of Great Adventure: The History of Balfour, Williamson and Company Limited*, 2 vols (London, 1951–60)

Huppertz, Josefine, *Kulturtraditionen der Osterinsulaner und ihre Christianisierung* (Sankt Augustin, 1994)

Irwin, Geoffrey, *The Prehistoric Exploration and Colonisation of the Pacific* (Cambridge, 1992)

Jaussen, Florentin Etienne ('Tepano'), 'L'île de Pâques: historique et écriture', ed. Ildefonse Alazard, *Bulletin de géographie historique et descriptive*, II (1893), pp. 240–70

Kirch, Patrick V., *The Evolution of the Polynesian Chiefdoms* (Cambridge, 1984)

Klemmer, Konrad, and Georg Zizka, 'The Terrestrial Fauna of Easter Island', in *Easter Island Studies: Contributions to the History of Rapanui in Memory of William T. Mulloy*, ed. Steven Roger Fischer (Oxford, 1993), pp. 24–6

Knoche, Walter, 'De la Isla de Pascua', *Pacífico Magazine*, VI (1913), pp. 347–51

—, *Die Osterinsel: Eine Zusammenfassung der chilenischen Osterinselexpedition des Jahres 1911*

(Concepción, 1925)

Kurze, Joan T. Seaver, *Ingrained Images: Wood Carvings from Easter Island* (Woodland, CA, 1997)

de Lapelin, F. T., 'L'île de Pâques (Rapa-Nui)', *Revue maritime et coloniale*, XXXV (1872), pp. 105–25 and 526–44

Lavachery, Henri, *Ile de Pâques* (Paris, 1935)

—, *Les pétroglyphes de l'île de Pâques*, 2 vols (Antwerp, 1939)

Lee, Georgia, *The Rock Art of Easter Island: Symbols of Power, Prayers to the Gods* (Los Angeles, 1992)

Liller, William, 'Review of Grant McCall, *Rapanui*', *Rapa Nui Journal*, VIII/4 (1994), p. 109

Linnekin, J., and L. Poyer, eds, *Cultural Identity and Ethnicity in the Pacific* (Honolulu, 1990)

López, Carlos, 'How Did Chile Acquire Easter Island?', *Rapa Nui Journal*, XII/4 (1998), pp. 118–22

McCall, Grant, 'Sympathy and Antipathy in Easter Islander and Chilean Relations', *Journal of the Polynesian Society*, LXXXIV (1975), pp. 467–76

—, 'Reaction to Disaster: Continuity and Change in Rapanui Social Organisation', PhD dissertation, Australian National University, Canberra, 1976

—, 'European Impact on Easter Island: Response, Recruitment and the Polynesian Experience in Peru', *Journal of Pacific History*, XI (1976), pp. 90–105

—, *Rapanui: Tradition and Survival on Easter Island* (Honolulu, 1980)

—, *Las fundaciones de Rapanui* (Hanga Roa, 1986)

—, 'Chile's Bitter Pacific Legacy', *Pacific Islands Monthly*, November 1988, pp. 43–5

—, 'Rapanui and Outsiders: The Early Days', in *Circumpacifica: Festschrift für Thomas S. Barthel*, ed. Bruno Illius and Matthias Laubscher (Frankfurt, 1990), vol. II, pp. 165–225

—, 'Nicknames and What They Mean', *Rapa Nui Journal*, V/2 (1991), pp. 17–20

—, '37 Days That Shook the (Rapanui) World: The Angata Cult on Rapanui', in *Proceedings of the Pacific History Association*, ed. D. H. Rubinstein (Mangilao, Guam, 1992), pp. 17–23

—, *Rapanui: Tradition and Survival on Easter Island*, 2nd edn (Honolulu, 1994)

—, 'Rapanui Images', *Pacific Studies*, XVII (1994), pp. 85–102

—, 'Japan, Rapanui and Chile's Uncertain Sovereignty', *Rapa Nui Journal*, IX/1 (1995), pp. 1–7

—, 'French Images of Rapanui (Easter Island)', *Journal of the Polynesian Society*, CIV/2 (1995), pp. 181–94

—, 'Riro, Rapu and Rapanui: Refoundations in Easter Island Colonial History', *Rapa Nui Journal*, XI/3 (1997), pp. 112–22

—, 'Review of Raybaud's *L'île de Pâques de 1862 à 1888*', *Rapa Nui Journal*, XI/4 (1997), pp. 166–7

—, 'Rapanui Wanderings: Diasporas from Easter Island', in *Easter Island in Pacific Context. Proceedings of the Fourth International Conference on Easter Island and East Polynesia: University of New Mexico, Albuquerque, 5–10 August 1997*, ed. Christopher M. Stevenson, Georgia Lee and Frank J. Morin (Los Osos, CA, 1998), pp. 370–8

—, 'A Report from Rapa Nui', *Rapa Nui Journal*, XV/1 (2001), pp. 3–5

—, 'Culture Bursting Out All Over on Rapanui, 2001–2002', *Rapa Nui Journal*, XV/2 (2001), pp. 78–82

McCoy, Patrick C., *Easter Island Settlement Patterns in the Late Prehistoric and Proto-Historic Periods* (New York, 1976)

Makihara, Miki, 'Rapanui-Spanish Bilingual Language Choice and Code Switching', in *Easter Island in Pacific Context. Proceedings of the Fourth International Conference on Easter Island and East Polynesia: University of New Mexico, Albuquerque, 5–10 August 1997*, ed. Christopher M. Stevenson, Georgia Lee and Frank J. Morin (Los Osos, CA, 1998), pp. 33–8

Marin, R., *Pascua: La isla lejana y misteriosa* (Santiago, 1944)

Martínez, Edgardo, *Vocabulario de la lengua Rapa-Nui: Isla de Pascua* (Santiago, 1913)

Martinsson-Wallin, Helene, *Ahu – The Ceremonial Stone Structures of Easter Island: Analyses of Variation and Interpretation of Meanings* (Uppsala, 1994)

Maude, H. E., *Slavers in Paradise: The Peruvian Slave Trade in Polynesia, 1862–1864* (Canberra, 1981)

Maunder, M., 'Conservation of the Extinct Toromiro Tree, *Sophora toromiro*', *Curtiss's Botanical Magazine*, XIV/4 (1997), pp. 226–31

Mazière, Francis, *Fantastique Ile de Pâques* (Paris, 1965)

Mellén Blanco, Francisco, *Manuscritos y documentos españoles para la historia de la Isla de Pascua* (Madrid, 1986)

—, 'Viceroy Amat and the Easter Island Expedition', in *Spanish Pacific from Magellan to Malaspina* (Madrid, 1988), pp. 107–19

Métraux, Alfred, 'The Kings of Easter Island', *Journal of the Polynesian Society*, XLVI (1937), pp. 41–62

—, *Ethnology of Easter Island* (Honolulu, 1940)

—, *L'île de Pâques* (Paris, 1941)

—, *Easter Island: A Stone-Age Civilization of the Pacific*, trans. Michael Bullock (London, 1957)

—, *L'île de Pâques*, 2nd edn (Paris, 1965)

Mieth, Andreas, and Hans-Rudolf Bork, 'Diminution and Degradation of Environmental Resources by Prehistoric Land Use on Poike Peninsula, Easter Island (Rapa Nui)', *Rapa Nui Journal*, XVII/1 (2003), pp. 34–41

Montiton, Albert, 'Lettre du R.P. Albert Montiton . . . à son Supérieur général', *Annales de l'Association pour la Propagation de la Foi*, LXI (1889), pp. 127–36

Moorehead, Alan, *The Fatal Impact: An Account of the Invasion of the South Pacific, 1767–1840* (Harmondsworth, 1966)

Mouly, Dalmas, *L'île de Pâques, île de mystère et d'héroïsme* (Tours, 1948)

Mulloy, Emily Ross, 'Kau Kau Poki: A Tragedy at Anakena', *Rapa Nui Journal*, V/1 (1991), pp. 8–9

—, 'The Destruction of Tongariki', *Rapa Nui Journal*, V/3 (1991), pp. 33–4

—, 'Letter to the Editor', *Rapa Nui Journal*, V/3 (1991), p. 43

—, 'William Mulloy: A Memoir', in *Easter Island Studies: Contributions to the History of Rapanui in Memory of William T. Mulloy*, ed. Steven Roger Fischer (Oxford, 1993), pp. ix–x

Mulloy, William T., 'Foreword', in Sebastian Englert, *Island at the Centre of the World: New Light on Easter Island* (London, 1970), pp. 9–16

—, 'Preliminary Culture-Historical Research Model for Easter Island', in *The Easter Island Bulletins of William Mulloy* (Houston, 1997), pp. 97–111

Mulloy, William T., and Gonzalo Figueroa, *The A Kivi – Vai Teka Complex and its Relationship to Easter Island Architectural History* (Honolulu, 1978)

O'Connor, J. M., P. Stoffers and M. O. McWilliams, 'Time-space Mapping of Easter Chain Volcanism', *Earth and Planetary Science Letters*, CXXXVI (1995), pp. 197–212

Orliac, Catherine, 'The Woody Vegetation of Easter Island between the Early 14th and the Mid-17th Centuries AD', in *Eastern Island Archæology: Research on Early Rapanui Culture*, ed. Christopher M. Stevenson and William S. Ayres (Los Osos, CA, 2000), pp. 211–20

Palmer, John Linton, 'Observations on the Inhabitants and the Antiquities of Easter Island', *Journal of the Ethnological Society*, I (1870), pp. 371–7

Paul, J. Harland, 'The Last Cruise of the Carnegie', *Rapa Nui Journal*, XVI/2 (2002), pp. 105–12

Pavel, Pavel, 'Reconstruction of the Transport of the *moai* Statues and *pukao* Hats', *Rapa Nui Journal*, IX/3 (1995), pp. 69–72

Philippi, Rudolph (Rodulfo) A., 'La isla de Pascua i sus habitantes', *Anales de la Universidad, Santiago de Chile*, XLIII (1873), pp. 365–434

Pike, F. B., *Chile and the United States, 1880–1962: The Emergence of Chile's Social Crisis and the Challenge to United States Diplomacy* (Notre Dame, IN, 1963)

Pinart, Alphonse, 'Exploration de l'île de Pâques', *Bulletin de la Société de Géographie de Paris*, XVI (1878), pp. 193–213

Porteous, J. Douglas, 'The Company State: A Chilean Case Study', *Canadian Geographer*, XVII (1973), pp. 113–26

—, 'Easter Island: The Scottish Connection', *Geographical Review*, LXVIII/2 (1978), pp. 145–56

—, 'The Development of Tourism on Easter Island', *Geography*, LXV/2 (1980), pp. 137–8

—, *The Modernization of Easter Island* (Victoria, 1981)

—, 'METEI: The Canadian Medical Expedition to Easter Island', *Rapa Nui Journal*, III/3 (1989), p. 11

—, 'The Modernization of Rapanui', in *Easter Island Studies: Contributions to the History of Rapanui in Memory of William T. Mulloy*, ed. Steven Roger Fischer (Oxford, 1993), pp. 225–7

Rainbird, Paul, 'A Message for Our Future? The Rapa Nui (Easter Island) Eco-disaster and the Pacific Island Environments', *World Archæology*, XXXIII (2002), pp. 436–51

Ramírez, José Miguel, 'Rapa Nui Land Management: A Personal Chronicle', *Rapa Nui Journal*, XIV/2 (2000), pp. 47–8

—, 'Cultural Resource Management on Easter Island: Utopia and Reality', in *Pacific 2000. Proceedings of the Fifth International Conference on Easter Island and the Pacific: Hawai'i Preparatory Academy, Kamuela, Hawai'i, 7–12 August 2000*, ed. Christopher M. Stevenson, Georgia Lee and Frank J. Morin (Los Osos, CA, 2001), pp. 283–90

Ramírez, J. T., *Navegando a Rapa-Nui* (Padre Las Casas, Chile, 1935)

Ramírez O., Julio T., *El conquistador de Pascua: biografía del Hermano Eugenio Eyraud de los Sdos Corazones*, 2 vols (Santiago, 1944)

Rauch G., Marcos, and María E. Noel B., eds, *Manual de capacitación sobre el patrimonio cultural y natural de Rapa Nui* (Hanga Roa, 1998)

Raybaud, Corinne, 'L'île de Pâques de 1862 à 1888', doctoral thesis, Université Paris x, Nanterre, 1993

—, *L'île de Pâques de 1862 à 1888: 26 années de diaspora pascuane en Océanie Orientale* (Pape'ete, 1996)

Reid, H. E., *A World Away: A Canadian Adventure on Easter Island* (Toronto, 1965)

Rochna, S., *La propiedad de la tierra en Isla de Pascua* (Santiago, 1996)

Rocuant, D. E., *La Isla de Pascua: estudio de los títulos de dominio, de las derechos y de los contratos de Don Enrique Merlet y de la Compañía Explotadora de la Isla de Pascua* (Valparaíso, 1916)

Roggeveen, Jacob, *Extracts from the Official Log of Mynheer J. Roggeveen (1721–22)* (London, 1908)

Roussel, Hippolyte, 'Ile de Pâques' [Valparaíso 1869], *Annales de la Congrégation des Sacrés-Cœurs de Jésus et de Marie*, n.s., xxxii (1926), 305, pp. 355–60; 306, pp. 423–30; 307, pp. 462–6; and 308, pp. 495–9

Routledge, Katherine (Mrs Scoresby Routledge), 'Easter Island', *Geographical Journal*, xlix (1917), pp. 321–49

—, *The Mystery of Easter Island: The Story of an Expedition* (London, 1919)

Saher, Herbert von, 'Some Details of the Journal of Jacob Roggeveen', *Rapa Nui Journal*, iv/3 (1990), pp. 33–5 and 45

—, 'Some Details from the Journal of Captain Bouman on the Discovery of Easter Island', *Rapa Nui Journal*, iv/4 (1990/91), pp. 49–52

—, 'More Journals on Easter Island', *Rapa Nui Journal*, vi/2 (1992), pp. 34–9

—, 'Roggeveen and Bouman: An Inventory of All the Narratives', *Rapa Nui Journal*, vii/4 (1993), pp. 77–82

—, 'The Complete Journal of Captain Cornelis Bouman, Master of the Ship *Thienhoven* Forming Part of the Fleet of Jacob Roggeveen, from 31 March to 13 April 1722 during their Stay around Easter Island', *Rapa Nui Journal*, viii/4 (1994), pp. 95–100

Sainthill, Richard, 'Rapa-Nui, or Easter Island, in November 1868. By an Officer of hms "Topaze"', *Macmillan's Magazine*, xxi (1870), pp. 449–54

Sánchez Manterola, Alberto, 'Cinco años en la Isla de Pascua', unpublished typescript, Viña del Mar, March 1921. Archives of the Institute of Easter Island Studies, Santiago, Chile

Schulze-Maizier, Friedrich, *Die Osterinsel* (Leipzig, 1926)

Seaver (Kurze), Joan T., 'An Ethnography of Wood Carving: Continuity in Cultural Transformations on Rapa Nui', PhD dissertation, University of California at Los Angeles, 1988

Shackley, Myra, 'Cultural Tourism and World Heritage Designation on Easter Island', in *Easter Island in Pacific Context. Proceedings of the Fourth International Conference on Easter Island and East Polynesia: University of New Mexico, Albuquerque, 5–10 August 1997*, ed. Christopher M. Stevenson, Georgia Lee and Frank J. Morin (Los Osos, ca, 1998), pp. 388–92

Sharp, Andrew, ed., *The Journal of Jacob Roggeveen* (Oxford, 1970)

Shaw, Leslie C., 'The Use of Caves as Burial Chambers on Easter Island', *Rapa Nui Journal*, x/4 (1996), pp. 101–3

Shephard-Toomey, Tandy, 'The Development of Rapa Nui (Easter Island), Chile 1967–2001', *Rapa Nui Journal*, xv/2 (2001), pp. 110–13

Skjølsvold, Arne, 'Archeological Investigations at Anakena, Easter Island', *Occasional Papers of the Kon-Tiki Museum*, cxi (1994), pp. 5–121

Skoryna, Stanley C., 'metei: An Epiloque', *Rapa Nui Journal*, vi/4 (1992), pp. 69–72

Smith, Carlyle S., 'The Norwegian Expedition to Easter Island in Retrospect', in *Easter Island Studies: Contributions to the History of Rapanui in Memory of William T. Mulloy*, ed. Steven Roger Fischer (Oxford, 1993), pp. 79–81

Steadman, D. W., P. Vargas and C. Cristino, 'Stratigraphy, Chronology and Cultural Context of an Early Faunal Assemblage from Easter Island', *Asian Perspectives*, xxxiii/1 (1994), pp. 79–96

Stefan, Vincent H., 'Origin and Evolution of the Rapanui of Easter Island', in *Pacific 2000. Proceedings of the Fifth International Conference on Easter Island and the Pacific: Hawai'i Preparatory Academy, Kamuela, Hawai'i, 7–12 August 2000*, ed. Christopher M. Stevenson, Georgia Lee and Frank J. Morin (Los Osos, ca, 2001), pp. 495–522

Stevenson, Christopher M., *Archæological Investigations on Easter Island. Maunga Tari: An Upland Agricultural Complex* (Los Osos, CA, 1997)

Stevenson, Christopher, and Sonia Haoa, 'Diminished Agricultural Productivity and the Collapse of Ranked Society on Easter Island', in *Archæology, Agriculture and Identity: No Barriers Seminar Papers* (Oslo, 1999), vol. II, pp. 4–12

Stevenson, Christopher M., Georgia Lee and Frank J. Morin, eds, *Easter Island in Pacific Context. Proceedings of the Fourth International Conference on Easter Island and East Polynesia: University of New Mexico, Albuquerque, 5–10 August 1997* (Los Osos, CA, 1998)

Te Rangi Hiroa (Peter Buck), *Ethnology of Mangareva* (Honolulu, 1938)

Thomson, William Judah, 'Te Pito te Henua, or Easter Island', Report of the United States National Museum for the Year Ending June 30, 1889, *Annual Reports of the Smithsonian Institution for 1889* (Washington, DC, 1891), pp. 447–552

Toro Hurtado, Pedro Pablo, *Memoria del Ministerio del Culto i Colonización presentada al Congreso Nacional en 1892*, vol. III (Santiago, 1893)

Van Hoorebeeck, Albert, *La vérité sur l'île de Pâques* (Le Havre, 1979)

Van Tilburg, Jo Anne, 'Power and Symbol: The Stylistic Analysis of Easter Island Monolithic Sculpture', PhD dissertation, University of California at Los Angeles, 1986

—, *Easter Island: Archæology, Ecology and Culture* (London, 1994)

—, *Among Stone Giants: The Life of Katherine Routledge and her Remarkable Expedition to Easter Island* (New York, 2003)

Vargas Casanova, Patricia, 'Rapa Nui Settlement Patterns: Types, Function and Spatial Distribution of Households' Structural Components', in *Easter Island and East Polynesian Prehistory*, ed. Patricia Vargas Casanova (Santiago, 1998), pp. 111–30

Vázquez de Acuña, Isidoro, et al., *Primeras jornadas territoriales: Isla de Pascua* (Santiago, 1987)

Vergara, Victor M., *La Isla de Pascua: dominación y dominio* (Santiago, 1939)

Vives Solar, José Ignacio, 'Una revolución en la Isla de Pascua en 1914', *Pacífico Magazine*, x (1917), pp. 655–64

Zumbohm, Gaspard, 'Lettres du R. P. Gaspard Zumbohm au Directeur des *Annales* sur la mission de l'île de Pâques', *Annales de la Congrégation des Sacrés-Cœurs*, series A, v (1879), pp. 660–7; VI (1880), pp. 117–31, 231–42, 377–85, 460–68, 565–70, 633–9, 772–83

Acknowledgements

The past several decades in Pacific studies and linguistics – in particular, my investigation since the 1980s into Easter Island's prehistoric culture, language and especially the *rongorongo* script – have brought me into contact with many remarkable individuals who have dedicated themselves, in one way or another, to the island's unique story. Sadly, many are no longer with us. To them all, present and departed, I owe a profound gratitude. They include: Tricia Allen, Ana María Arredondo, Sir David Attenborough, †Thomas S. Barthel, Annette Bierbach, Olaf Blixen, Nikolai A. Butinov, Horst Cain, †Ramón Campbell, Rosita Cardinali, Patrick Chapman, A. Elena Charola, †Bengt Danielsson, François Dederen, Veronica M. Du Feu, Heide-Margaret Esen-Baur, John R. Flenley, George W. Gill, Juan Grau, Roger Green, †Juan Haoa, †Nicolás Haoa, Niko Haoa Cardinali, Sonia Haoa Cardinali, Toru Hayashi, Enrique Carrasco Henriquez, †Thor Heyerdahl, Alberto Hotus, H.G.A. Hughes, Denise Koenig, Viktor Krupa, †Robert Langdon, William Liller, Charles M. Love, Miki Makihara, Helene Martinsson-Wallin, Francisco S. Mellén Blanco, Brigid Mulloy, †Emily Ross Mulloy, Father Francisco 'Pancho' Nahoe OFM Conv., Josefina Nahoe, Catherine Orliac, Luís 'Kiko' Paté, J. Douglas Porteous, José Miguel Ramírez Aliaga, John E. Randall, W. Wilfried Schuhmacher, Tandy Shephard-Toomey, †Carlyle Smith, Vincent Stefan, Christopher M. Stevenson, Darrell T. Tryon, The Earl and Countess Waldegrave, Rose Marie Wallace, Paul Wallin, and Robert and Nancy Weber.

Archival work was enabled, over many years, by a host of colleagues and friends: Luis F. Capurro Soto, Museo Nacional de Historia Natural, Santiago; David Colquhoun, National Library of New Zealand, Wellington; Richard A. von Doenhoff, National Archives, Washington, DC; Muguette Dumont, Musée de l'Homme, Paris; Irina K. Fedorova, Museum of Anthropology and Ethnology, St Petersburg, Russia; Francina Forment, Musées Royaux, Brussels, Belgium; C. M. Hall, The British Library, London; Warwick Hirst, State Library of New South Wales, Sydney, Australia; Gerd Höpfner, Museum für Völkerkunde, Berlin; Ruth Horie and Janet Short, Bishop Museum Library, Honolulu; C. Kelly, Royal Geographical Society, London; Robert Koenig, Société des Etudes Océaniennes, Pape'ete, Tahiti; Father André Mark, Padri dei Sacri Cuori (SSCC), Rome; Donald S. Marshall, Peabody Museum, Salem, Massachusetts; Gail Millar, School of Oriental and African Studies, London; Véronique Mu-Liepmann, Musée de Tahiti et des Iles, Punaauia, Tahiti; †Hanns Peter, Museum für Völkerkunde, Vienna; Birgit Scheps, Museum für Völkerkunde, Leipzig; Gillian Scott, Pacific Manuscripts Bureau, Australian National University, Canberra; Arne Skjølsvold, Kon-Tiki Museet, Oslo, Norway; Dorota Starzecka, Museum of Mankind, London; David Wigdor, Library of Congress, Washington, DC; and especially the staff of the Interlibrary Loan Department at the Universitätsbibliothek, University of Konstanz, Germany.

A particular debt of gratitude is owed to Francisco Torres, Director of the Museo Antropológico P. Sebastian Englert, Hanga Roa, Easter Island. Very special thanks are owed to Georgia Lee, Joan Seaver Kurze and Paul Bahn. This book could never have been written without the *Rapa Nui Journal*, the official publication of the Easter Island Foundation and the world's leading serial publication in Easter Island scholarship and related Pacific topics. To Michael Leaman of Reaktion Books in London, as ever my heartfelt gratitude.

As always, my love and appreciation to my wife Dagmar ('Taki'), who forever is making the impossible possible.

Photographic Acknowledgements

The author and publishers express their thanks to the following sources of illustrative material and/ or permission to reproduce it:

Collection of Mark and Carolyn Blackburn, Kamuela, Hawai'i: 9; from Stephen Chauvet, *L'Ile de Pâques et ses mystères* (Paris, 1935), Fig. 32, Pl. xv: 5 (sketch by L. Choris); reproduced from Steven Roger Fischer, ed., *Easter Island Studies: Contributions to the History of Rapanui in Memory of William T. Mulloy*, Oxbow Monograph 32 (Oxford, 1993), p. xvi, with the gracious assistance of Georgia Lee and Alan Davis-Drake: map 2; Institute of Polynesian Languages and Literatures, Auckland, New Zealand (Barthel Collection): 13; Museo Antropológico P. Sebastian Englert, Hanga Roa, Easter Island: 6, 10, 11, 12, 14; reproduced from J. Douglas Porteous, *The Modernization of Easter Island*, Western Geographical Series, vol. 19 (Victoria, 1981), p. viii, with kind permission of the author: map 1; from Jacob Roggeveen, *Tweejaarige Reyze rondom de Wereld* (Dordrecht, 1728): 4; sscc, Rome: 7; from Albert van Hoorebeeck, *La vérité sur l'île de Pâques* (Le Havre, 1979), Pl. xxx: 8. All other photographs are by the author, as is the 1995 oil painting reproduced as illus. 1.

Index

Abtao 139, 146, 152
acculturation 124, 163
'Adam Smith' 117
Adios, Brother Modesto de 180
æroplanes *see* aviation
Agassiz, Alexander 160
agente de colonización 140, 143, 144, 150
agitation, political 154, 155, 156, 164, 166–72, 210–18, 232, 236–7, 240, 241, 243, 246, 247, 248, 250
agrarian colonization 140, 143–4, 145, 149, 179
agriculture 26–7, 39–40, 41, 43, 186, 196, 208, 223, 230
ahu 17, 23, 24, 25, 31–33, 35, 69, 80, 83, 97, 124, 176, 182, 185, 190, 200, 203, 208, 222
Air Force, Chilean 217, 219, 220, 224, 229, 232, 248
Air Force, US 219–20, 221, 224
Air France 221
airport, international 196, 201, 224, 232, 236–7
air travel *see* aviation
'A Kapu 38, 83, 107
'A Kivi 35, 207
akuaku 29, 36
Aku-Aku: The Secret of Easter Island 206
alcalde 205, 211, 212, 214, 217, 218, 232, 238, 239, 241, 244, 249
alcoholism 240, 242
Allende, President Salvador 137, 217, 223–4, 225, 226
Allen, Frank 141
Allipén 192
allotments *see* parcelas
Almanzor Hernández, Comandante 170, 171, 179
Americans 123, 131–2, 189, 194–5, 199, 200, 215–16, 217, 219–20, 224, 227, 229, 230, 232, 234, 235, 236, 239
Anacleto Goñi, Commander Don José 107
ancestry 188, 189, 198, 224, 227, 238, 257

Andrade, Dr Guido 213
Angamos 140, 141, 185
Angata 129–30, 143, 147, 167–72
'Angata's Revolt' 166–72, 176, 214
annexation 86, 103, 105, 107, 116, 119, 124, 125, 132, 133, 136, 138, 139, 140, 141, 144
    ceremony 141–2
    proclamation 142
'ao 59, 255, 264
Apolline Emilie 150
Aquila 214
Araki Ti'a, Juan 153, 155, 160
arbitration, naval 146, 152, 155, 170, 214
archæology 127, 131, 154, 165, 166, 175, 177, 188, 200, 203–4, 206, 207, 217, 221, 223, 227, 228, 229, 237–8, 244, 251, 260–61
Arena, Jorge 105, 109, 110, 112
Arena, María 105, 109, 110
'aringa ora 33, 229
aristocracy 21–2, 54
arson 154, 247
art 29–31, 68
asbestos 227–8, 251
Atamu, Florencia 222
Atamu te Kena 128, 132, 142, 143, 147, 248, 251
Atamu te Kena Avenue 248
Atán, Pedro 190, 205
atrocities 73–4
Aukara Tuki, Bene 245
Austronesians 15–16, 17
automobiles 182, 204, 208, 224, 232, 235, 239, 241, 248, 250
autonomy, Rapa Nui 147, 155, 171, 213, 225, 235, 242, 247, 250, 251, 262, 263
Ava Rei Pua 14
aviation 184, 195, 196, 209, 218–21, 232
Aylwin Azocar, President Patricio 236, 237

Baeza Vega, Lorenzo 205–6

Balfour, Williamson *see* Williamson, Balfour and Co.
Balmaceda, President José Manuel 137, 138, 143, 145
banana *see maika*
'banana-stem sledding' *see hakape'i*
Baquedano see *General Baquedano*
Barthel, Thomas S. 208
battles 55, 173
Bayard, E. 121
BBC 235, 236, 250
beautification, village 180, 208, 220, 235, 243
Beck, Monseñor Guido 190, 192, 193
Beechey, Captain Frederick William 79
Behrens, Carl Friederich 30, 48, 50, 52
Beire, Father Domingo de 180
belief system 27–9, 46, 81–2, 84, 98, 126, 127, 134, 143, 148, 162–3, 171, 193
Benson, Captain N. P. 163–4
Berlin Conference 139
Biblioteca William Mulloy 235, 237, 241, 253
bird life 8, 144, 159
Birdman 37–8, 46, 57, 58–60, 63, 64, 80, 82, 84, 94, 99, 119, 123, 126, 166, 255, 264
blackbirding 74, 85, 87–92
archæological 103
Black Eagle 121
Brander, Arthur 157
Brander, John 100, 102, 105, 111–12, 113, 114, 115, 116, 118, 121, 123
Brander Jr, John 128, 129, 130, 132, 141, 142, 143, 145, 146, 149, 157
'Brander's Road' 130
breadfruit 144
British Chilean interests 137, 156, 194, 200
British Museum 103
Brown, Professor John Macmillan 183
'Bryan Report' 181–2, 183
Bryan, William A. 181–2, 185, 260
Butaye, Father Isidore 154
Byrne, Joseph Charles 87

cacique 155, 156, 161, 171
Calderón, Ignacio 161
Calédonien 209
caleta 200, 222, 254
Callao 88, 89, 90, 100, 111
Calligan, Patrick 118–19
Campbell, Dr Ramón 209
Canadians 212–14, 227
canalization 196, 220
cannibalism 55, 80, 89
canning factories 225
cannon 102, 108
carabineros 201, 217, 221
Cardinali, Rafael 150, 154, 160, 188, 232
Cardinali, Samuel 232

caries 43
cars *see* automobiles
carving, wood 29–30, 67, 75, 124, 127, 129, 161, 188, 217, 227, 235
cash economy 144, 152, 160, 164, 184, 197, 252
catechist, Easter Island's 141, 143, 158, 166, 186–7, 208
catechists, Mangarevan 97, 98, 100, 101, 103, 104
Casanova, Monseñor 141
Castán, Father Barnabé 95
Castillo, Comandante L. A. 146, 147, 152
Cater, W. B. 188
Catholic Church 84–5, 90, 92, 96–113, 125, 128, 129–30, 132, 133, 134, 138, 139, 142, 143, 148, 154, 162, 164, 171, 177, 178, 183, 186–7, 192, 193, 229, 233–4, 240
cemetery 108, 133
census 130
Centro de Estudios Rapa Nui 233
Cercle d'Etudes sur l'Ile de Pâques et la Polynésie 231
Chanticleer, HMS 111
chaplain, naval 162, 183, 186, 193, 194
Chavez, Señor 121–2, 123
chiefs 21–2, 27, 46, 54–5, 56, 60, 63–4, 89, 101, 122, 128, 131–2, 147, 155, 156, 158, 162, 168, 171, 210
Chile 136–47, 195–7, 199
Chileanization 215, 216
Chilean Scientific Expedition 161–2
China 15
Chincha Islands 89
Christian Bjelland 203, 205
church, Easter Island's 97, 99, 100, 101, 107, 108, 113, 117, 122–3, 124, 128, 129–30, 133, 134, 143, 146, 147, 148, 151, 154, 158, 162–3, 167, 171, 177, 180, 183, 184–5, 192, 193, 204, 205, 233, 257
cinema 195
citizenship, full Chilean 215, 219
Civil Registry Office 177
civil rights 135, 164, 171, 176–7, 209, 210, 212–14, 215, 217, 225–6, 231
civil territory 215
civil war, Chilean 145, 156
clans 21–4
Clorinda 144, 145, 146
coaling tender, Easter Island as 138, 172, 177
coconut trees 124, 159, 208
Cold War 215–16, 219–20
colonial war 106–13
colonization *see* settlement
commercial development 221, 232, 238
commoners 22, 41–2, 54, 56, 60, 66
'communism' 210, 212, 218
Compañía Explotadora de la Isla de Pascua (*see also* Williamson, Balfour and Co.) 157, 187
'company island' 144, 150, 156, 191, 194, 197, 200

company store 152, 178, 188
confederations *see hānau*
confinement camp 152, 156, 164, 191, 205
Congrégation des Sacrés-Cœurs (sscc) 79, 84,
   90, 92, 95, 96–113, 114, 116, 119, 120, 121, 122,
   125, 126, 128, 129, 132–3, 139, 140, 141, 142, 151,
   154, 184, 248
Consejo de Ancianos *see* 'Te Mau Hatu'
Consejo de Ancianos 2 240, 242, 246, 247, 248,
   254
Constance, hms 128
continentales 218, 220, 222, 226–7, 230, 231, 244,
   257–8
conversion, Catholic 98, 103
Cook, Captain James 30, 33, 39, 53, 56, 60, 64,
   66–70, 72, 73, 80, 86, 182, 220
Cooke, Ship's Surgeon George H. 131
co-operatives 216, 217, 223, 224
Cooper, Horatio 'Horace' 154, 155, 156, 158, 160
copra trade 105, 112, 114
Cora 91
Cormorant, hms 144
Cornejo, Hernán 190
Coronel, Battle of 173
Corporación de Fomento de Producción
   (corfo) 196, 216, 217, 221, 231, 239, 246
Corporación Nacional Forestal (conaf) 224,
   230, 234, 238, 239, 244, 246, 248, 249
Correa, Father Nicolás 183
Costner, Kevin 239
Council of Elders *see* 'Te Mau Hatu'
Council of Elders 2 *see* Consejo de Ancianos 2
coup d'état 225–6
Cousin, Bautista 178
Cousteau, Jacques 230
Cousteau, Phillipe 230
cove *see caleta*
crane, engineering 235, 237
creation legend 13
Crocker, Templeton 189
crops 18–19, 22, 26, 101, 122, 159, 183, 186
Cultural Centre, Hanga Roa 239
culture, material 24–7, 188
Curti, Captain Amaldo 'Gigi' 204
Customs, Office of 238

'Daniel' Ure Va'e Iko 123, 131, 148
Darsie, George 122, 128, 141, 145, 146, 149, 157
Davila, Dr Valenzuela 202
Davis, Edward 46, 60
Dederen, François 234
'deed of cession' 142
deforestation 207
deities, ancestral 27–9, 57, 98
Delabaude, Dr 154, 155
demonstration, airport 237

'Departamento de Isla de Pascua' 215
depopulation 44, 53, 61, 67, 86, 89, 91, 99, 101, 102,
   103, 104, 105, 110, 113–14, 115, 120, 122, 124, 197
Diamante 91
Diamen 118
dictatorship, military 225–36
diet 25, 43–4, 61, 104, 162, 164, 178, 185, 186, 188, 197
discovery, European 47
   Polynesian 16–18, 19
disease 53, 89, 90, 91, 99, 101, 102, 103, 114,
   151, 152, 173, 174, 228
   venereal 75, 83
Dobson, Edward 77–8
dolphin *see* porpoise
Drapkin, Israel 187–9
drought 7
drowning, 'Anakena 205–206
drugs 240
Dutch East Indies Company 45, 53
Dutrou-Bornier, Caroline 110, 119, 120, 121, 130
Dutrou-Bornier, Harriette 118, 119, 120, 122
Dutrou-Bornier, Jean-Baptiste Onésime 100,
   101, 102, 103, 104, 105–20, 121, 122, 125, 126,
   138, 150, 153
Dutrou-Bornier, Marthe Jeanne 102, 105

Easter Island Foundation 233, 236, 237, 241, 253,
   254
ecology 9, 20, 38, 40, 41, 42, 46, 80
Eden, Jacobo 138
edict *see reglamento*
Edmunds, Henry Percy 160–61, 163, 165, 167,
   168–9, 170, 171, 172, 174, 180, 183, 184, 186, 238
Edmunds Paoa, Petero 242, 244, 249, 250, 254,
   262, 263
education 94, 95, 101, 140, 143, 171, 172, 180, 184,
   185, 189, 196, 202, 206, 209, 217, 221–2, 226,
   230, 231, 236, 244, 248, 253
Edwards, Monseñor Rafael 162, 177, 178, 179, 180,
   181, 187, 190, 191, 192
Eich, Father Georges 115, 141, 148, 151
elder *see korohua*
El Dorado 163
elections 135, 147, 212, 214, 217, 218
electrification 196, 216, 224–5, 231, 259
Elizabeth Kimball 118
'Elizabeth' Rangi Taki *see* Pakarati, Elizabeth
   Rangi Taki
Ellen Snow 90
El Mercurio 105, 107, 143, 250
emigration 105, 113–14
employment 150, 152, 155, 184, 188, 191, 195, 197,
   201, 217, 220, 221–2, 226, 242, 252
empremar 220
endogamy 23–4
Englert, Father Sebastian 190, 191, 192, 193, 194,

202, 205, 208, 209, 213, 220, 222, 223, 233
environmental collapse 42–4, 46, 71, 207
erosion 40, 42, 55
escape from Easter Island 76–7, 160, 164, 185, 191, 195, 208
Escolan, Brother Théodule 100–13, 114, 115, 141
esquila, la 160, 184, 195, 202
Estella, Father Bienvenido de 180
ethnic pride 232, 240, 261
ethnicity 238, 241, 244, 254, 257–9
Ethnology of Easter Island 189
eucalyptus 130, 159, 182, 204, 231
Eutimio Rangi Topa 166
exchange systems *see* trade
exile community 114, 130, 184, 234, 247, 250
exodus, the 113–14, 141, 163, 209
expansion, early population 20, 38–42
exploitation, commercial 87, 90, 124, 157–8, 178
   cultural 241
Eyraud, Brother Eugène 29, 92–103, 109, 133, 148, 185, 222

Falcon 175, 182
Falklands, Battle of the 175
Fantastique Ile de Pâques 210
Fati Rongo Pua Tea 166
fauna 8, 227
feasts 27, 160, 202, 214, 222, 237
Ferdon Jr, Edwin N. 203, 204
Festival of Pacific Arts 232
Fife (Scotland) 149, 157
fig trees 130, 159, 208
Figueroa García-Huidobro, Gonzalo 203, 204, 206, 207, 223
Fiji 15
film, Hollywood 239–40
First World War 172–5
fishes 8, 44
fishing 26, 41, 44, 185, 186, 191, 196, 217, 223, 230
flag, Rapa Nui 142, 146, 151, 152, 168, 170, 171, 241, 263
Flenley, John 207, 227
flora 7–9, 43, 227
forest 8, 20, 41, 42, 44, 206, 224, 249
Forster, Georg (*also* George) 30, 62, 66, 67, 68, 69, 70
Forster, Johann Reinhold 66, 68, 69
Fortuna 175
Fournier, Dr A. 117
Franco-Belgian Expedition 187–9, 190, 203
Frederick, George 142
Frei Montalva, President Eduardo 211, 212, 215, 218, 219, 223, 226, 246
frigate bird 59
Fuentes, Francisco 161
Fuenzalida, Humberto 190

Fuller, A.W.F. 161
fundo 184, 201, 208, 216, 231, 234, 261

Gajardo, Dr Roberto 196
Geiseler, Kapitänleutnant Wilhelm 33–4, 126–8, 132
General Baquedano 155, 161, 162, 165, 168, 169, 170, 172, 173, 177, 179, 180, 183, 201
genetic admixture 69
genital enhancement 38
   inspection 38
geology 7, 190
German Pacific Fleet 172–3
Germans 123, 124, 126–8, 132, 150, 161, 170, 172–5, 190, 194, 195, 208
ghosts *see* akuaku
Gironde 143, 144
gods *see* deities, ancestral
González de Haedo, Felipe 60–63
González Videla, President Gabriel 196
Goupil, Auguste 122, 125, 141, 149
gourd, bottle 19, 38
governor 201, 211, 215, 221, 231, 236, 249, 250, 254
Goyenechea Couciño, Isidora 98
Grogan, Lady 165

Ha'apape (Mission) 90, 93, 97, 108, 114, 115, 128, 141
hakape'i 230, 237
hānau 23, 42, 106
hānau 'e'epe 42, 55
hānau momoko 42, 55
Hanga Ho'onu *see* Hanga 'o Honu
Hanga 'o Honu 47, 48, 50, 61, 71, 256
Hanga Piko 67, 94, 95, 103, 116, 141, 174, 182, 184, 195, 197, 213, 216, 217, 219, 220, 238, 253, 256
Haoa Cardinali, Nicolás 251
Haoa, Juan 229
Haoa, Magdalena 183
Haoa, Nicolás 229
Haoa, Rafael 229
Haoa, Sonia 188, 207, 229
harbour 182
Haumaka 14
Hawaiki 13
Hayashi, Toru 235
health 180, 189, 196, 202, 212–14, 226, 228
He Ki'i 47, 48
Henderson Island 16, 17, 18, 39, 41, 46
'Henry Easter' 76
Heyerdahl, Thor 202–6, 208, 223, 233
Hey Paoa, Governor Jacobo 236, 241, 247
Hey Rapu, Sofía 165
Higgins, Charles 146, 147
high school, new 248, 254
'high street' 232
history, traditional 148

Hoa Hakananai'ā, the *mo'ai* 103
Hōkūle'a voyaging canoe 18, 249
HONSA 221, 224
horse–buggy 129
hospital 214, 226
hotels *see residenciales*
Hotu 'Iti confederation *see* 'Otu 'Iti
Hotu Matu'a 13–14, 18, 102, 148, 264
Hotus, Alberto 231, 236, 238, 239, 240, 241, 242, 244, 247, 248
Hotus, Germán 211–12
Hotus, Matías 187
housing 25, 118, 154–5, 182, 186, 220, 223, 227, 251
Huemul 185
Hunneus, Jorge 140
Huntwell 111
huri mo'ai 64–6
Hyäne 127–8

identity, Easter Island 256–62
Ika, Enrique 147, 154, 155
'immigration scheme' 87–92
imperialism 135, 136
improvements, Company 181–2, 186
inbreeding 24
incarceration 152, 156, 159, 162, 164, 191, 205
incorporation, Easter Island's Chilean 215
indentured labour 87–92, 101, 105, 106, 112, 113–14, 116, 118, 123
independence movement 146, 166–72, 199, 210–18, 225, 251
Indiaman 119
industries, local 196
influenza 152
infrastructure, modern 197, 210, 223, 227, 237
infusion, capital 181–2
initiations 37–8, 44, 58, 80
internal colony 199, 262
International Conferences on Easter Island 233
Internet 248
Ionia 105, 116
Island Assembly 248–9
islets 7, 8, 37, 55, 59, 230
isolation 20, 152
Italian 150

Jaffuel, Father Félix 184
Jamet, Father Auguste 116, 118, 132
Japan 163, 192–3, 194, 195, 208, 237, 246–7, 254
Jaussen, Monseigneur Florentin Etienne 'Tepano' 90, 93, 96, 97, 100, 101, 103–8, 110–20, 122–3, 125, 128, 129, 132, 133, 137, 141, 145, 147
Jean 174
jefe 155
Johnson, President Lyndon B. 215, 219
Jotefa Mahe Renga 166

Joyce, Thomas Athol 165
'Juan' Araki Aro Purunga 130
Jubæa sp. 8, 40, 42, 50, 206–7, 248
Junta, the 225–36, 238

Kahukahu o Hera organization 254
Kai Mako'i 'Iti 82, 89
Kamake 106, 108, 110
Kapiera Reva Hiva 166
Kekepu 166
Kennedy, President John F. 215
'Kerekorio' (Grégoire) *see* Manu Rangi
Keremuti Hea, Miguel (Timikore Keremuti) 160, 166
kidnapping 87–92
Kildalton, HMS 174
kindergarten 244
kinship groups 20, 21–4, 228
kio 55–6, 82, 95
Klink, Leutnant 175
Knight of the Garter 163
Knoche, Walter 161–2, 171, 188
kokongo 152, 186, 212
komari 38
'Koreto' *see* Pua 'Aku Renga ko Reto 107
korohua 142, 163, 166, 183, 210, 211, 218, 231, 244
Ko te Riku 207
Kotzebue, Captain Otto von 73
kumara 18, 19, 38–9, 43, 93, 94, 108, 109, 169, 186

labour trade 87–92, 101, 105, 112, 113–14, 116, 118
La Durance 154, 155
La Flore 117
lakes, crater 25
LAN-Chile 221, 225, 229, 237, 238, 242, 252
land dispute 146, 228, 241
Länder, August 128
land purchase 103, 105, 106, 110, 113, 118, 119, 120, 125, 126, 128, 139–40, 141, 145, 149
land registration 227
land restitution 234, 243, 244, 246, 247, 249, 250, 251, 261–2
language, Rapanui 11, 17–18, 41, 44, 49, 54, 63, 67, 75, 88, 91, 94, 96, 99, 114, 123, 148, 160, 161, 163, 175, 180, 183, 184, 190, 210, 218, 239, 257
Lapelin, Admiral T. de 117–18
La Pérouse, Jean-François Galaup, Comte de 33, 41, 70–72
Lapita culture 15
Larenas, Captain Enrique 165
La Suerte 92–3
La tierra de Hotu Matu'a 193
launches 182
La Unión 138, 143, 144, 164, 178
Lavachery, Henri 187–9
Laval, Father Honoré 84, 91, 92, 97, 105, 113–14

Law, Commander C. Anthony 213
leadership, political *see* chiefs
L'Echo de Rapa Nui 234
Lee, Georgia 31, 234
Lejeune, Commander Joseph Laurent 84, 85, 92
leprosery 151, 163, 166, 177, 180, 186, 189, 202, 208, 248
leprosy 151, 163, 177, 179, 196, 212
Letelier, José 247, 251
Ley Indígena 240–41, 249
Ley Pascua 215, 242, 253
library 235, 236
lighters 182, 184
lighthouse project 238
Liller, William 241
Lillian 128
Lima 87, 88, 89, 90, 111
lithic mulch 41, 43
Little Ice Age 41
'living faces' *see* 'aringa ora
'Long Ears' 42
'lost continent' theory 183
Loti, Pierre 118
Luckner, Commander Felix Graf von 175
Lynch, John 235

McCall, Grant 223, 227, 250, 255, 263
McGill University 212
MacKinnon, Lachlan 183, 184, 186, 229
Mahina 111, 118
mahute 19, 43
maika 19, 26, 27, 43
main street 221, 232
Maipo 191
'Maipo' Regiment 153
Maison Brander 100, 102, 105, 106, 111, 114, 116, 117, 119, 120, 121–2, 123, 125, 126, 128, 129, 130, 137, 139, 140, 143, 144, 146, 149
Makemake 13, 56–8, 63, 84, 98, 102
mana 27, 34, 37, 46, 56, 57, 65, 83, 91, 98, 172
'*Mana* Expedition' 164–76
managers, company 150
manavai 43
Mangaia (Cook Islands) 54, 56, 104
Mangareva 13, 14, 16, 17–18, 20, 21, 23, 27, 29, 36, 37, 39, 41, 46, 55, 63, 79, 84, 85, 91, 92, 96, 97, 101, 105, 106, 113–14, 115, 118, 120, 122, 124, 129, 163, 167, 176, 183, 209, 249
Manu Rangi 91, 92, 99, 101, 147
Marama (formerly *Tampico*) 110, 122
Maria i te Aopu 97
Maria Luisa 150
Marion Godeffroy 124
market garden, Easter Island as 137–8, 161–2
market, street 235, 238, 239
Marquesas Islands 13, 16, 17, 20, 29, 39, 84, 86,

90, 91, 100, 115, 119, 206, 249
marriage, mixed 188, 258–9
Martin, Governor José 213–14
Martínez, Edgardo 161, 162
mata'a 55, 59, 93, 108
Mata Ngarahu 30, 37, 64, 82
mata veri 59
Mataveri 60, 82, 94, 102, 103, 104, 106, 108, 109, 110, 111, 117, 119, 121, 122, 123, 126, 127, 129, 141, 150, 152, 154, 155, 159, 160, 165, 167, 182, 184, 201, 204, 215, 219, 224
matato'a 44, 46, 54, 56–7, 59, 63, 80, 117
material culture 24–7
Mati, 'Chief' 122
Mau Rata 82, 89, 91
mayor *see* alcalde
Mazière, Francis 209
Medical Expedition to Easter Island (METEI) 212–14
medical service 154, 177, 188, 189, 196, 201, 202
Melchor, Father 194, 222
'Memoria sobre la Isla de Pascua' 139
Mendaña, Alvaro de 46
Mercator 189
Merlet, Enrique 149–59, 165, 167, 176, 178, 179, 181, 201
mestizos 153, 188, 224, 227, 238
meteorological station 161, 162
Métraux, Alfred 9, 187–9
military, Chilean 144, 160, 191, 194–5, 197, 201, 209, 224, 225–36, 237, 238
millenarian cult 166–72
Mini 108
miro tahiti 130
mission, Catholic 92, 96–113, 116, 126, 132
missionaries 79, 84, 87, 91, 92, 96–113, 126, 132–3, 137, 138, 184, 230
mo'ai 24, 29, 31, 33–7, 40, 41, 54, 61, 64–6, 69, 124, 130, 176, 182, 203, 208, 246
   blackbirding 103, 131, 189
   emblem 200
   erection 36
   eyes 36, 188, 229
   inventory 190
   preservation 222, 254
   re-erection 190, 200, 207, 229, 235, 237, 240, 246
   reproductions 245
   toppling 64–6, 69, 80, 81
   transport 36, 41, 168, 240
mo'ai kavakava 43
modernization 87, 101, 114, 127, 131, 133, 155, 189, 196, 197, 200, 219–20, 223, 225, 251
Mohican, USS 131–2
Montiton, Father Albert 84, 85, 92, 130, 132–3, 148
Montt, Jorge 145

motion pictures 195
mulattos *see mestizos*
Mulloy, Emily Ross 253
Mulloy, William T. 200, 203, 204, 206–7, 220, 222, 223, 227, 229, 240, 246
municipal governance *see municipalidad*
municipalidad 215, 216, 218, 225, 231, 232, 248, 249, 251, 253, 254
murder 50, 51, 52, 74, 77, 79, 80, 89, 92, 96, 108, 120, 135, 153, 154, 156, 178, 198
Mururoa (Tuamotus) 244
Museum, Fonck 237, 239, 241
Museum, Sebastian Englert 234, 235, 237, 241, 253
'mystery of Easter Island' 70, 176, 189, 206, 229, 245

Nahoe, Father Francisco 'Pancho' 240, 250
name, Easter Island's 21, 86, 88, 91, 96
Nancy 73–4
NASA 232
National Park 190–91, 217, 221, 224, 230, 238, 243, 246, 249, 251
nationalization of Easter Island 196–7
Naunau 32, 35, 38, 39, 207, 229
Navarino 217
Navy, Chilean *see* military, Chilean
newsletter 242
nga'ahu reed 8
Nga'ara, *'ariki* 64, 81–3, 209
'Nicolas Pakarati' Ure Pō Tahi *see* Pakarati, Nicolas
Niue 263–4
Nixon, President Richard M. 224
North-West Passage 70
Norwegian Expedition 200, 202–6, 223
nudity 48, 99, 179
nuns 189, 202, 222

O'Higgins 107–8, 119, 138, 144
Olivares, Mario 217
Olivier, Father Pacôme 84, 92, 95, 96, 100, 101
oral traditions 13–14, 148, 164, 166
organization, social 21–4
origins 15–18, 165
'Orongo 25, 30, 32, 37–8, 44, 57, 58, 59, 64, 80, 82, 103, 119, 123, 124, 185, 203, 207, 217, 229, 238, 240, 247, 254
orphans *see pukuranga*
'Otu 'Iti confederation 23, 26, 34, 35, 40, 41, 42, 44, 46, 53, 55, 61, 63, 65, 77, 104, 106, 129
ovens, earth 25

'Padre Sebastian' *see* Englert, Father Sebastian
Pakarati clan 141
Pakarati, Elizabeth Rangi Taki 141, 142, 151
Pakarati, Emilia 229

Pakarati Ika, Governor Enrique 250–51, 254
Pakarati, Leonardo 148, 229
Pakarati, Nicolas 141, 143, 146, 148, 151, 158, 165, 166, 167, 168, 169, 171, 177, 180, 184–5, 193, 208, 250–51
Pakarati, Santiago 186–7
Pakarati, Timoteo 184–5, 186, 208
Pakomio, Andrés 205
Pakomio Mā'ori Ure Kino 91, 124, 129, 143, 148, 166
Palma, President Arturo 192–3
palm trees 8, 40, 42, 208, 235, 240
Paloma 132, 140, 143
Pamata'i (Tahiti) 130, 133, 141, 184
Pane 'a Paohu 92–3, 94
Paoa 'a Hitaki 122
paper mulberry *see mahute*
Papiano Renga Maengo 166
parcelas 152, 177, 183, 197, 204, 226, 234
Paro, the *mo'ai* 80
Parragué Singer, Captain Roberto 196, 209, 219
Paté, Luis ('Papa Kiko') 207, 229
paving project 235, 237, 238, 239, 243, 244, 248, 253
pearl-shell trade 114
penal colony 154, 185
'Peteriko' Vaka Pito 122
'Petero' Toro Veri 105
petroglyphs 31, 38, 57, 59, 63, 188, 189
Philippi, Rudolph 138
photography, earliest 115, 121, 154
'Pierre' Mau 106
Pinart, Alphonse 121
pineapples 183
Pinochet Ugarte, General Augusto 225–36
Pinto 202, 206, 211, 212, 213
pircas 152, 154, 185, 248
Pirivato, José 153, 155, 156
Pitcairn Island 7, 16, 18, 20, 39, 41, 46, 86, 126, 184, 189, 249
platforms, monumental *see ahu*
Plotmer, A. 142
Pōike Ditch 55, 203
Pōike Peninsula 40, 42, 54–5, 61, 159, 231
poisoning 153
pōki manu 37–8, 44, 58, 80
pōki take 37, 38, 44, 80
Policarpo Toro Avenue 221, 222, 224, 231, 235, 238, 239, 243, 248
Pomare v, King 123, 124
Pomare Vahine IV, Queen 111, 123, 125
Pont, Vincent 'Varta' 130, 150, 154, 159, 160, 166, 169, 182, 188
population, bottom 121, 188
peak 45
recovery 124, 127, 128, 135, 154, 188, 204, 222, 226, 230, 231, 234, 250, 253, 256

Porotu (Hongi 'Atua 'a Ure Au Viri) 166
porpoise 20, 44
Porteous, J. Douglas 227, 252
port facilities 182, 242, 253, 256
Portilla, Governor Jorge 212, 213, 214, 217
'poverty' 162, 163, 164, 177, 193
Praga 245–6
priests, Catholic 79, 84–5, 96–113, 117, 122, 132–3,
    143, 162, 180, 183, 184, 190, 191, 192, 233
    Polynesian 22, 25, 48–9, 52, 56, 82, 91, 99
Prinz Eitel Friedrich 173–4
production, material 24–7
pronunciation 11
property title 110, 116, 118, 119, 120, 122, 125, 126,
    128, 130, 133, 139, 140, 144, 149, 151, 176, 181,
    185, 187, 227–8
protectorate 111, 117, 118, 119, 121, 124, 125, 126, 132
Provisional Constitution 179
Ptolemy 45
pua 19, 82
Pua 'Aku Renga ko Reto 107, 110, 118, 119, 120, 121
Pua Ara Hoa 148, 166
pukao 36, 40, 41, 207, 229, 246
pukuranga 101, 102, 109, 112
Puna Pau 35, 42, 68, 261

'race' *see* ancestry
radicalism, political 240, 245
radio *see* wireless communication
radiocarbon dating 17, 203
radio station, local 218, 230, 242, 248, 252, 253
raids 65, 80, 92, 96, 99, 107, 108, 109, 112
Raine, Captain Thomas 77–8
ranch *see* fundo
Ramírez Aliaga, José Miguel 237, 239, 241, 249–50
Rano Raraku 35, 36, 37, 40, 59, 130, 169, 203, 210,
    217, 246
Rapa 39, 91
Rapahango Tepuku, Victoria 165, 229
Rapa Nui Journal 234, 236, 254
'Rapanui manuscripts' 148
Rapa Nui, the name 86, 91, 96, 102
Rapu, Alfonso 'Israel' 210–18, 232
Rapu, Sergio 207, 229, 231, 232, 235, 243, 246, 247
rat, Polynesian 18, 42, 159
Read, Sir Hercules 165
reconstruction projects 200, 207
refuges 55–6
reglamento 155, 171, 191
religion 27–8, 98, 111, 124, 126, 127, 129, 133, 134,
    143, 148, 154, 162–3, 168, 171, 193, 233
remittances 88
Rengifo-Hunneus Report 140
Rengifo, Osvaldo 140
repatriation 91
Republic of Rapa Nui 264

residenciales 224, 226, 228, 243, 250
revolt 154, 155, 166–72, 198, 210–14, 217–18
Rigault de Genouilly 187
'right of cession' 139
rights, Easter Islanders' Chilean 215
Riro, 'King' *see* 'Timeone' Riro
Riroroko clan 147
rites of passage 37–8, 80
roads, kerbed 33, 36, 129
rock art 26, 31, 57, 63, 188, 227, 234
Rodríguez, Alfredo 153
Rogers Sotomayor, Governor Enrique 217, 218
Roggeveen, Jacob 33, 43, 45, 46–53
Rojas, Comandante Basílio 155–6, 171
Rojas, Comandante Guillermo 213–14
Roma 99, 103, 104, 106, 108, 114
rongorongo 63–4, 82, 83, 91, 96, 107–8, 115, 129,
    131, 165, 166, 187–8, 208, 227
'*rongorongo* books' 148
Rotary Club 241
Rouchouze, Monseigneur Etienne 79
Roussel, Father Hippolyte 14, 96–113, 114, 122,
    124, 126, 128, 129, 142, 147, 167
Routledge, Katherine Pease 30, 81, 165–76, 183
Routledge, William Scorseby 165–76, 188
rustling 186

'Sainte-Marie de Rapanui' (Hanga Roa),
    the town 100, 104, 108, 109, 111, 117
Salas, Mercedes 119
Sala-y-Gómez Island 43, 192
Salmon, Alexander 123
Salmon Jr, Alexander 100, 111, 121–2, 123–32, 134,
    138, 140–41, 142, 143, 235
Salmon, Tetuanuireiaiteraiatea (later Mrs
    Brander, then Mrs Darsie) 122, 128, 149
Sánchez Manterola, Alberto 150–54
'Santiago Staff' 108
Sappho, HMS 125–6
Sau-Sau 214
Schmidt, Cecilia 119
Schmidt, Christian 102, 108, 115, 117, 119–20
Schmidt, Mercedes Salas 119
scholarship, international 206, 227, 233
school *see* education
Scottish investment 157–8, 197
sealers' visits 73–4
'Sea of Chile' 226
Seaver, Joan T. 235, 236
Second World War 194–5, 199
sects, religious 233–4
Security Police 201
Seignelay 121
seismic register 161
self-governance 215
'Semana de Rapa Nui' 222, 223, 229

'semi-pyramidal' platforms 65–6, 72
serfs 22, 82, 95, 117
settlement 13–20, 132, 140, 143, 144, 145, 149
sewage system 235
sex 62, 67, 69, 71, 72, 75, 79, 80, 99, 163
shamans 22, 48–9, 52, 56, 82, 91, 99
Shapiro, H. L. 189
shearing see esquila, la
ship, supply 145, 149, 153, 160, 162, 184, 201, 202,
    206, 214, 220, 230–31, 235, 242, 253
shipwreck 102, 111, 118, 121, 145, 150, 155, 182, 245
shooting 50, 51, 52, 68, 71, 73–4, 79, 89, 108, 110, 213
'Short Ears' 42
Sir John Burgoyne 113–14, 116
Skjølsvold, Arne 203, 204, 206
Skoryna, Dr Stanley 212–14
slaves 22, 55–6, 178
smallpox 90, 91, 93, 99
Smith, Carlyle S. 203, 204, 206
Smith, Murdoch 188
Smithsonian Institution 131–2
soap opera 247
social reforms 211
Sociedad Agrícola y de Servicios Isla de Pascua
    (SASIPA) 231, 243, 246, 247, 251, 259
Sociedad de Amigos de Isla de Pascua 195–6,
    209, 236, 237
sooty tern 59, 254
Sophora toromiro 7, 190, 234, 248
South-East Polynesian society 16–17, 18, 19, 39
sovereignty 176, 191
space shuttle programme 232
Special Territory 263
Spee, Admiral Maximilian Reichsgraf von 172–3,
    174–5
sport 230, 254
SSCC see Congrégation des Sacrés-Cœurs
standard of living 181, 202, 204, 205, 212, 221, 240,
    252
statues see mo'ai
statuettes 29–30, 38, 67, 68, 75
statute, Company 158
strike 154, 241, 243
subdelegado marítimo 150, 156, 158, 168–9, 170,
    171, 174, 178, 188, 190, 191, 193, 194, 201
subsidio housing 227–8
suffrage 209, 210, 212, 214, 215
sugar cane see toa
suicide 108
supermarkets 243
surnames, creation of modern Easter Island
    130–31
sweet potato see kumara
Swett, Comandante Arturo 161–2

Tadano Company (Japan) 237–8

Tahai 17, 24, 32, 34, 35, 38, 83, 107, 151, 207, 234, 250
Taiwan 15
Tama Teka 92, 94
Tampico 100, 101, 102
tangata henua 152, 158
tangata manu 58–60
tapa 19
Tāpati 222, 229, 237, 239, 253, 254, 257, 263
tapu 27, 37, 48, 49, 56, 64, 99
Tara Heu 151
taro 18–19, 26, 39, 43, 186
tattooing 30, 37, 48, 81, 99, 229
Tautira 97
Tawera 119, 122
teachers, certified 222
Teao, Anastasia 238
Teao Tori, Carlos 'Charlie' 166–7, 189
Teave Korohua, Daniera 167, 170, 171
Te Haha 166
Te Hatu Tini 107
Te Ingoa 130
telephones 230, 236
television 218, 226, 230, 244, 247, 250, 253
'Te Mau Hatu' 231, 232, 235, 236, 238, 239, 240,
    241, 242, 244, 247, 248, 249
Temperamento Provisorio 176, 185
'Tepano' Rano 'a Veriamo (Juan Tepano) 144,
    153, 155, 156, 160, 161, 162, 166, 169, 171, 173,
    174, 175, 180, 183, 189
'Tepano' Ruti Rangi 151
Te Peu 20, 24, 38, 42, 203, 253
Te Pito 'o te Henua 91, 102
Te Pito te Henua Street 222, 235, 237, 238, 239
Terra Australis Incognita 45, 47, 52, 53, 66, 70
The Mystery of Easter Island 176
The Riddle of the Pacific 183
thievery 49–50, 62, 67, 68, 69, 71, 83, 93, 94, 97
Thomson, Paymaster William J. 131–2
ti 19, 30, 159
'Timeone' Riro, 'King' 147, 150, 151, 152–3, 154, 212
toa 19, 26, 27, 43
Tokerau, rescue-patrol launch 238
'Tomenika' Vaka Tuku Onge 122, 124, 128, 148,
    163, 166
Tongariki 34, 35, 40, 41, 55, 159, 200, 207, 208,
    217, 237–8, 239, 240, 246, 253, 254
Topaze, HMS 86, 89, 103
'topknots' see pukao
Tori 148
Toro Hurtado, Captain Pedro Pablo 140, 143,
    144, 145, 146, 150
Toro Hurtado, Captain Policarpo 107, 132, 133,
    138–47, 148, 149, 179, 221, 226, 251
Torometi 93–5, 99, 102, 103, 104, 106, 107, 108,
    114, 147
toromiro tree 7, 190, 234, 248

Torres, Francisco 253
totora see *nga'ahu* reed
tourism 127, 129, 130, 196, 200, 202, 207, 217, 219,
 220–21, 223, 224, 226, 228, 230, 237, 242, 245,
 250, 251, 252, 259–60
trade 26, 41, 51, 61, 67, 68, 75, 77, 79, 83, 84, 86,
 100, 125, 136, 197
tribal composition 23–4
tsunami 208
tuberculosis 99, 100, 101, 102, 103, 104, 108, 212
Tuki Tepano, Benedicto 245
turmeric *see pua*
Tūpa 'Otu (Tūpahotu) 40, 53, 54, 80, 83, 106, 107,
 141
Tu'u confederation 23, 24, 28, 35, 38, 40, 41, 42,
 55, 65, 67, 77, 84, 104, 106
'Tu'u Hotu 'Iti' performance group 229
Tu'u ko Iho 14, 18, 23, 28, 38, 101–2
Tu'u mā Heke 14, 264

Ugarte, Arturo 204
'uhi 19, 26, 43

Vaihū 68, 95, 104, 105, 107, 109, 111, 112, 117, 129,
 130, 131, 140, 141, 143, 144, 159, 235, 251
Vaitea 18, 43, 159, 184, 195, 197, 201, 204, 216, 231,
 234, 244, 251, 261
Valenta, André 231
Valenzuela, Father Zósimo 162, 177
Vargas, Ruperto 208
vehicles 129, 182, 204, 208, 216, 224, 232, 235, 239,
 241, 248, 250
Verdier, Monseigneur 128, 130, 132, 133, 141, 142
Vergara, Victor M. 139
Veriamo (English 'William', here female) 144,
 155, 166
Veri Tahi 'a Pengo Hare Kohou, María 154, 155, 156
Veriveri, Mateo 13
Viaud, Julien 117–18
Vicuña MacKenna, Benjamin 137
videotape players 230
Vinapū 131, 203, 204, 219
Vityaz 115
Vives Solar, José Ignacio 171, 172, 173, 174, 184
volcanoes 7, 8
voyaging 15–18, 20, 39, 41, 45–6, 249, 259

wages, low 152, 154, 178, 204, 210
Wall, the 152, 154, 159, 160, 162, 163, 168, 183, 191,
 193, 201, 210, 211, 217, 252
walls, drystone *see pircas*
warfare 41, 42, 53–6, 60, 66, 92, 96, 106–13, 114,
 145, 174
'War of the Pacific' 136, 138
warriors *see matato'a*
Watelin, Louis Charles 187

water supply 18, 20, 25, 39, 42–3, 66, 101, 140, 143,
 164, 204, 216, 220, 259
Weber, Nancy 230
Weber, Robert 230
Weisser, Paymaster Candidate J. 127, 132
West Indies Company 46, 53
whaling trade 74–5, 84, 86, 105, 160
 visits 72–80
William and Thomas 118
Williamson, Balfour and Co. 135, 157–9, 164, 165,
 176, 178, 181, 185–6, 194, 195
Williamson, Henry 178–9, 181
Williamson, Stephen Anstruther 157
wine production 126
wireless communication 172, 173, 192, 195, 202
working conditions 152
World Heritage Site 244–5
writing 62, 63–4, 94, 95, 148
Wyoming, University of 207, 229, 233

yam *see 'uhi*
Yelcho 213

Zaca 189
Zumbohm, Father Kaspar (Gaspard) 100–11,
 112, 118, 129, 159